Eroding Empire

ERODING EMPIRE

Western Relations with Eastern Europe

LINCOLN GORDON

with J. F. BROWN
PIERRE HASSNER
JOSEF JOFFE
EDWINA MORETON

A policy study sponsored jointly
by the Brookings Institution
and the Hudson Institute

THE BROOKINGS INSTITUTION
Washington, D.C.

Library of Congress Cataloging-in-Publication Data

Gordon, Lincoln.
  Eroding empire.
  Includes index.
  1. Europe, Eastern—Foreign relations—1945–
  2. Europe—Politics and government—1945–
  3. Europe, Eastern—Foreign relations—United States.
  4. United States—Foreign relations—Europe, Eastern.
  I. Title.
DJK50.G67   1987   327.73047   87-13184
ISBN 0-8157-3214-7
ISBN 0-8157-3213-9 (pbk.)

9 8 7 6 5 4 3 2 1

THE BROOKINGS INSTITUTION is an independent organization devoted to nonpartisan research, education, and publication in economics, government, foreign policy, and the social sciences generally. Its principal purposes are to aid in the development of sound public policies and to promote public understanding of issues of national importance.

The Institution was founded on December 8, 1927, to merge the activities of the Institute for Government Research, founded in 1916, the Institute of Economics, founded in 1922, and the Robert Brookings Graduate School of Economics and Government, founded in 1924.

The Board of Trustees is responsible for the general administration of the Institution, while the immediate direction of the policies, program, and staff is vested in the President, assisted by an advisory committee of the officers and staff. The by-laws of the Institution state: "It is the function of the Trustees to make possible the conduct of scientific research, and publication, under the most favorable conditions, and to safeguard the independence of the research staff in the pursuit of their studies and in the publication of the results of such studies. It is not a part of their function to determine, control, or influence the conduct of particular investigations or the conclusions reached."

The President bears final responsibility for the decision to publish a manuscript as a Brookings book. In reaching his judgment on the competence, accuracy, and objectivity of each study, the President is advised by the director of the appropriate research program and weighs the views of a panel of expert outside readers who report to him in confidence on the quality of the work. Publication of a work signifies that it is deemed a competent treatment worthy of public consideration but does not imply endorsement of conclusions or recommendations.

The Institution maintains its position of neutrality on issues of public policy in order to safeguard the intellectual freedom of the staff. Hence interpretations or conclusions in Brookings publications should be understood to be solely those of the authors and should not be attributed to the Institution, to its trustees, officers, or other staff members, or to the organizations that support its research.

In memory of
Allison Wright Gordon

Foreword

IN THE PAST few decades, Eastern Europe has experienced change internally and the gradual erosion of Soviet imperial control. The evolution, punctuated by dramatic crises, has presented Western nations with subtle policy issues of how to encourage peaceful change in these societies without provoking repression from their own governments or from the Soviet Union. Western influence requires purposive engagement with regimes of questionable legitimacy while also encouraging people-to-people relationships. There are difficult choices between treating the East European nations as consequential in their own right and looking solely to the region's role in East-West relations, between moving only within well-defined bounds of Soviet tolerance and cautiously testing those bounds.

Eroding Empire reviews the attitudes, interests, and policies of the major Western countries toward Eastern Europe since World War II. Western long-term aspirations are broadly parallel, but substantial differences in medium-term objectives and in tactics have caused friction, especially between West Germany and the United States. The study recommends that Western nations seek greater agreement on objectives and more flexible orchestration of methods used to achieve them. They should not miss opportunities for promoting constructive change and should not allow serious discord in this area to weaken a Western alliance already under severe strain.

The study was designed and directed by Lincoln Gordon. J. F. Brown contributed three chapters and also served as general adviser on the project. Josef Joffe, Pierre Hassner, and Edwina Moreton are recognized authorities on German, French, and British foreign policy.

The Brookings Institution especially appreciates the cosponsorship of this study by the Hudson Institute, whose timely encouragement and generous financial support were indispensable to the project's success. The authors gratefully acknowledge the financial support of the late W. Averell Harriman and of the Citibank N.A. and the Equitable Life Assurance Society of the United States. In September 1985 the Defense Intelligence College sponsored a conference at Brookings on the future of Western policies toward Eastern Europe, chaired by Hans Heymann, Jr., which provided critical reviews of drafts of these chapters by specialists from Europe and the United States. The conference report was published by the Hudson Institute.

Lincoln Gordon wishes to thank a large number of present and past ambassadors and officials of the relevant U.S. government departments and of the European Communities, the North Atlantic Treaty Organization, the Organization for Economic Cooperation and Development, the International Monetary Fund, the UN Economic Commission for Europe, and the International Labor Organization, all of whom were promised anonymity. In addition, he is grateful for interviews with or comments on all or parts of the manuscript by Timothy Garton Ash, John A. Baker, Robert R. Bowie, John C. Campbell, Karen Dawisha, Jonathan Dean, Raymond L. Garthoff, John P. Hardt, Ed A. Hewett, Charles Gati, Harry Gelman, Richard Haass, Hans Heymann, Jr., Hanns Dieter Jacobsen, A. Ross Johnson, F. Stephen Larrabee, R. Gerald Livingston, William H. Luers, Jan Nowak, Helmut Sonnenfeldt, Lucja Swiatkowski, and Morris Weisz. He also thanks Elizabeth Klein and William S. Rocco, Jr., for research assistance; James R. Schneider for editing the manuscript; Daniel A. Lindley III and Christine Miller for verifying its factual content; and Virginia Riddell and Christine Miller for retyping various chapters.

The views expressed are those of the authors and should not be ascribed to the persons acknowledged above, to the sources of funding support, or to the trustees, officers, or other staff members of the Hudson Institute or the Brookings Institution.

Bruce K. MacLaury
President

April 1987
Washington, D.C.

Contents

Tables

Figures

Eastern Europe before World War II

Eastern Europe after World War II

ONE

Introduction and Overview

LINCOLN GORDON

THIS STUDY analyzes the attitudes, interests, and policies of the major Western countries toward Eastern Europe, reviews problems of conflict or convergence among those policies, and assesses their influence on broader East-West relationships. It should help to clarify policy choices for governments on both sides of the Atlantic and to enhance public understanding of the issues involved. "Eastern Europe" here refers to the six Warsaw Pact member countries other than the Soviet Union: East Germany (GDR), Poland, Czechoslovakia, Hungary, Romania, and Bulgaria.[1]

Since the close of World War II, Eastern Europe has been a uniquely important region in global geopolitics. The largest revisions of national boundaries took place there. The cold war originated in disputes over East European political regimes. With the consolidation of the North Atlantic Treaty Organization and the Warsaw Pact, this area became the East's front line in the European military standoff. In the 1970s it was the centerpiece of the high détente marked by the Berlin settlement and the Helsinki accords.

Today, more than forty years after the wartime conferences at

1. This usage is simply for convenience, without prejudice to the historical disputes over whether all or part of the region should be called Central Europe. Yugoslavia and Albania are also often considered parts of Eastern Europe, and are occasionally mentioned in the text. Yugoslavia is strategically important to East-West relations and its economic and political difficulties pose serious issues for Western policymakers. Both Yugoslavia and Albania, however, are now independent of the Soviet imperial system. Because their Western relationships are intrinsically different from those of the Warsaw Pact member countries, they have been excluded from this study.

1

Yalta and Potsdam, Eastern Europe is a center of attention only at
moments of crisis. Yet it retains its intrinsic importance. The dramatic
crises of East Germany in 1953, Hungary in 1956, Czechoslovakia in
1968, and Poland in 1980–81 confirmed that the region is under
Soviet imperial hegemony. The six countries constitute the most
valuable parts of the external Soviet empire. There is no viable way
in which that control could be loosened by force, either through
Western efforts to "roll back the Iron Curtain" or through popular
rebellions contrary to Soviet will. Yet their ruling communist parties
enjoy no assured legitimacy; there is chronic popular discontent with
their economic and social performance; and if their peoples were free
to choose, not more than one of these countries would be a voluntary
ally of the Soviet Union. There is continuous pressure from within
their societies to reform their economic systems and sociopolitical
institutions and to adjust their relations with one another and the
USSR in the economic sphere if not the military or overtly political.
There is broad interest among both elites and publics at large in
cultivating—or perhaps exploiting—relations with the West, notably
with Western Europe and the United States. Those relations became
much more dense during the 1970s, a trend that, although temporarily
reversed after 1979 by the worldwide economic recession, has not
been fundamentally altered. There are complex and often obscure
interactions between internal change and external relationships with
both East and West.

Thus the Soviet empire, a seeming anachronism in the late twentieth
century, while showing no signs of collapse or imminent dissolution,
has been gradually eroding. Dramatically by comparison with the
Stalinist period, but also very substantially in relation to the mid-
1960s, there has been growing diversity of internal conditions and
greater emphasis on country-by-country national interests in the
making of East European policies. The word "eroding" in our title is
used in two senses: an adjective describing what has been occurring
over the years and a verb summarizing the thrust of Western policies.

Current scholarly attention to Eastern Europe has focused primarily
on internal developments and on relations with the Soviet Union.
The Western perspective on Eastern Europe, including differences
of interests, attitudes, and policies among the principal Western
nations, has not been carefully examined. The notable exception is
West Germany, where *Ostpolitik* has been a central policy issue. For

the other Western countries, there have been occasional individual studies, but no comprehensive comparative ones. This book is designed to help fill that gap.

Here are some of the critical issues. At a minimum Western countries are presently engaged in parallel efforts to maintain and reinforce the Europeanness or Westernness of Eastern Europe through personal contacts, broadcasting, and other means. Beyond this there is little consistent agreement, either on diagnosis or on prescription. Should we be promoting stability or encouraging liberalizing changes in economic and political arrangements? How should we react to crises? Is it helpful or harmful to promote or to restrain trade, credits, and investment ventures, or are such decisions just as well left to the discretion of individual businesses? What should our attitude be toward proposals for regional arms control or confidence-building measures? Do economic, scientific, and cultural relations with the West, official or transnational (labor union, church, and so forth), have any significant influence on the possibilities of evolutionary change? To what extent can deliberate policymaking by the West enhance such influence?

How substantial is consultation among Western governments on policies toward Eastern Europe? Are those policies truly coordinated, either within the European Communities or the Atlantic alliance? Is disagreement a source of serious tension within the West? Even if not, does such disagreement reduce the effectiveness of Western policies? How serious are the cleavages of recent years on economic policies; are there rational principles that might help to reconcile them? Are differences on the "German Question" a source of potential intra-Western conflict? Does Europeanness imply a qualitatively different kind of relationship between Eastern and Western Europe from that between Eastern Europe and the United States, or merely the difference of degree that flows naturally from geographical proximity? Is there merit in the notion of a division of labor within the West in relations with Eastern Europe?

The design of this study is straightforward. The next two chapters set the stage. Chapter 2 summarizes the current conditions and prospects of Eastern Europe, including the critical role of the USSR. Chapter 3 reviews Eastern Europe's Western connections and the Eastern attitudes and interests in those connections, country-by-country and distinguishing between regimes and the societies they rule. The study then analyzes, in the five chapters that follow, the East European interests and policies of the United States, West Germany, France, the United Kingdom, and Austria, Italy, and the Vatican. For the principal Western countries the authors are specialists in the respective foreign policies. Chapter 9 discusses the extent of convergence and conflict among the positions of these Western nations and concludes with policy suggestions for the West as a whole.

The main findings and conclusions can be summarized in the following propositions:

1. Eastern Europe is a region of continuing cardinal importance to the West—as the locus of an immense military standoff, the restive and uneasy major component of the Soviet external empire, an uncertain weight in the geopolitical balance, and a part of European culture denied its natural heritage.

2. Nevertheless, except for West Germany's prime interest in East Germany, Eastern Europe ranks low in priority among Western foreign policies except at moments of crisis. This low priority results from Eastern Europe's deceptive appearance of stability and the improbability of changes in the formal status quo there.

3. Without formal revisions in status or in types of regime, important evolutionary developments have been taking place in Eastern Europe. With continuing changes in economic and social structures, shifting generational attitudes, and new leaderships, more such developments can be expected. They will not emulate the traditional Soviet model, which has lost such appeal as it may once have had.

4. While the most powerful forces influencing change are internal developments and Soviet policies, the West has shown a substantial capacity for influence, especially since the evolution in the mid-1960s of West German *Ostpolitik* and the American policy of "differentiation," which provides favorable treatment for East European regimes engaged in domestic liberalization or demonstrating a degree of autonomy from Soviet foreign policy.

5. The significant share of Western influence that comes from providing examples of political freedom and economic success requires East European access to those examples. Hence the importance of Western radio and television broadcasting, cultural exchanges, travel, business contacts, and other nonstate relations.

6. Extensive economic relations with the West through trade, finance, and investment are a necessary but not sufficient condition for liberalizing reforms in Eastern Europe. Their positive influence could be fortified by avoiding unilateral subsidies and by making them conditional upon more rational economic processes on the East European side—in the case of government policies, preferably through such multilateral institutions as the International Monetary Fund, World Bank, and General Agreement on Tariffs and Trade (GATT).

7. An environment of overall East-West détente is more conducive to Western influence in Eastern Europe than one of severe tension between the superpowers, but localized détente is not completely out of the question, as shown by relations between East and West Germany since 1983.

8. Taking the past two decades as a whole, change in Eastern Europe has on balance been in the direction sought by the West, notwithstanding the major setbacks in Czechoslovakia in 1968 and Poland in 1981. Thus if Western policymakers can forego expectations of imminent revision in the status quo and settle in for a long haul of evolutionary change, punctuated by periodic crises that may speed change or reverse it for a while, there is no reason to denigrate Western influence.

9. At the level of long-term aims and aspirations, there is general convergence within the West on the objective of lightening the Soviet yoke in Eastern Europe and securing for the peoples more freedoms and better conditions of living. The differences appear in medium-term strategy and the short-term application of policy instruments. If there were any genuine prospect of German reunification, conflicts over the German Question might reemerge, but that is not an operational issue for the foreseeable future.

10. Cohesion within the West has been less threatened in recent years by differences over Eastern Europe than by a variety of non-European issues. Yet there have been substantial frustrations and missed opportunities in Eastern Europe as well. Mishandling of these policy issues could become very costly to the West. A well-managed and deliberate effort at greater convergence on objectives in Eastern Europe would help to limit erosion of the Atlantic alliance while promoting that of the Soviet empire.

11. Western influence could be strengthened by periodic joint assessments at a high political level and by more effective consultation on objectives and strategy. It would be both fruitless and undesirable to seek absolute agreement on the whole range of policy *instruments:* many diplomatic and economic relationships call for no coordination whatever and may well benefit from a diversity of approaches. But it would be highly desirable to secure explicit agreement on medium-term policy *objectives.* They can be analyzed in terms of a spectrum of approaches toward Soviet imperial control, a spectrum running from *accommodation* through *transformation* to *dissolution* and including intermediate positions. Agreement within the West could only be possible in the middle of that spectrum: transformation with less accommodationist tendency on the European side and less dissolutionist tendency on the American side.

12. There are wide differences in the intensity of Western concerns with Eastern Europe. West Germany's are unique, approached in intensity only by Austria. The United States ranks next, followed by France and Italy and at some distance by Britain. The Federal Republic and the United States have the most activist policies and the greatest potential for conflict, as shown in divergent attitudes toward differentiation and sanctions. Enhanced convergence, therefore, should be sought first through discussions between German and American officials, which would then be expanded to include France and Britain, Italy and Canada, NATO as a whole, and finally the broader West, including friendly neutrals.

13. For policy instruments, the aim should be *flexible harmonization*: for example, identical rules on strategic export controls; broad agreement on policies for trade and credits and guidelines for broadcasting; coordination of policies involving conditionality or sanctions; and exchanges of information on high-level visits and on political and economic developments pointing toward systemic reform.

14. Western governments can and should do much more to prepare for fresh crises in Eastern Europe. Consultative machinery for this purpose should be "fixed while the sun is shining."

15. The West must continue to deal with East European

regimes but should also deal directly with peoples, helping through the latter to push the regimes toward liberalizing reforms and greater foreign policy autonomy. That strategy requires positive engagement with East European governments—not indiscriminate but purposive engagement.

16. A pan-European solution to the division of Europe, excluding the United States, is implausible in the visible future, and in some forms its promotion may be counterproductive. East Europeans identify not only with Europe but with the entire West, including America. Unilateral U.S. withdrawal (military or otherwise) from Europe would not be matched by the Soviet Union. Nevertheless, the psychological appeal of the pan-European idea, especially in Eastern Europe, is so strong that it should be maintained as a long-term aspiration.

17. The USSR is not likely to respond directly to Western arguments that Soviet security could be enhanced through relaxing its imperial controls. Yet liberalizing changes in the system—a failed system as matters now stand—are essential to enhance the legitimacy of East European regimes. As changes take place, Moscow may find them increasingly hard to reverse—or find the costs of reversal too high—and with the passage of time come to recognize that Soviet security has not suffered. Parallel changes might strengthen the tendencies toward greater national autonomy within Comecon and the Warsaw Pact, facilitating agreements with the West on regional arms and troop reductions.

18. Formal revision of the postwar European settlement remains an ultimate goal, but it is not on the horizon. Approaches toward it need not be limited to the precedents set by Finland, Austria, or Yugoslavia. Domestic change is more likely to occur first within the structures of the ruling communist parties, while parallel changes could work toward greater national autonomy within a nominally socialist commonwealth. Formal revisionism must be preceded by de facto changes in attitudes and institutions. The challenge for the West is to use its collective influence wisely to accelerate such changes.

TWO

The East European Setting

J. F. BROWN

THE TWO most important factors in the East European situation are the conditions of the countries themselves—their differences and complexities—and Soviet policies toward and relations with them. Obviously these factors can only be considered here in outline, and those aspects that bear on actual or potential Western policy are given more emphasis than those that do not. This bias might cause some imbalance, but what the discussion loses in completeness it may gain in relevance.

The Political Map

With the critical exception of Germany's territorial amputation and partition into two states, the political map of Eastern Europe today is similar to that devised by the Paris peacemakers at the end of World War I. Although its territory has been drastically reduced, Poland and the other East European countries—Czechoslovakia, Hungary, Romania, Yugoslavia, Bulgaria, and Albania—have retained their statehood and most of their territory. What changes have occurred in Eastern Europe have generally benefited the Soviet Union. In addition to the very large territories taken from Poland after 1945, the USSR acquired Ruthenia from Czechoslovakia and Bessarabia and northern Bukovina from Romania. Lithuania, Latvia, and Estonia were recaptured during the war.

Hungary and Bulgaria emerged the two most dissatisfied states, as they had after World War I. Many of their irredentist ambitions had been temporarily satisfied during World War II, only to be thwarted again by their final defeat. In Central Europe Germany became, in territorial terms, even worse off than after the Treaty of Versailles. Not only did it lose much of its historical territory in the east to Poland and the USSR, but what remained was divided. The larger part became a model democracy and economy. The smaller became first a Soviet appendage then an economically powerful satellite. Not only for what it became but even more for what it signified—the emasculation of German power—the German Democratic Republic (GDR) was Russia's historic gain from World War II.[1]

Although the territorial picture in much of Eastern Europe after 1945 remained similar to what it was before, its ethnic composition had changed radically. The Jews and the ethnic Germans, two minorities that had traditionally dominated many areas of its public life, practically disappeared. The Jews were annihilated in the Holocaust, the ethnic Germans driven out through total defeat of the Reich and subsequent mass expulsions. Only in Romania did a sizable German minority remain, but it was half the 700,000 people it had been before the war. In Hungary some 200,000 Germans remained when the expulsions were halted. They are well treated but are gradually being assimilated and their separate ethnic identity erased. In neighboring Romania most Germans now wish to leave. Thus in a short time the German presence in Eastern Europe will have been extinguished. But though the disappearance of the Jews and Germans may have mitigated the problems caused by minorities in Eastern Europe, it by no means eliminated them.[2] Nor for that matter did the Soviet-imposed communist revolution that swept over Eastern Europe after the war, although the revolutionaries believed that with the success of the revolution, elimination of the minorities problem would be axiomatic. Indeed, the minorities problem—for instance, Bulgaria's persecution of its Turkish minority and Romania's discrimination against Hungarians—in itself part of the larger question of nationalism, has emerged once again in recent years to add a new

1. See James F. Brown, *Soviet Relations with the Northern Tier in East Europe*, EAI Papers 9 (Marina del Rey, Calif.: European American Institute for Security Research, 1985), pp. 5–7.
2. See Robert R. King, *Minorities under Communism: Nationalities as a Source of Tension among Balkan Communist States* (Harvard University Press, 1973).

and disturbing dimension to the complexities of contemporary Eastern Europe.

The Revolution and Its Sequel

Had the Red Army not been at the Elbe by the end of World War II, had the Soviet Union not even existed, there would still very likely have been a revolution of sorts in Eastern Europe after 1945. The grim nature of Soviet domination, the egregious errors made by its local satraps, the manifest failure to satisfy popular aspirations and, hence, the widespread rejection of communist rule all tend to distract attention from the inequities, and often the brutalities, of life in most of the East European states between the wars. Hugh Seton-Watson's book on Eastern Europe in the 1920s and 1930s, contemporaneous and fresh, the view not favorably tinted by the knowledge of what happened afterward, demonstrates forcefully that in every country except perhaps the Czech regions of Czechoslovakia, radical change would have been necessary.[3]

The type of radical change these countries came to experience, however, was hardly the most suitable in terms of their histories, predilections, aspirations, or requirements. But the analyst is forced to deal with what was and not with what might have been. Comparisons in this context between such pairs as Czechoslovakia and Austria or Bulgaria and Greece make little more than depressing debating points.

To concentrate therefore on what was, we can consider the history of Eastern Europe since World War II as having completed four phases and as having now entered a fifth.

The first phase, from 1945 to 1948, can be described as pre-Stalinist. Under the shadow of Soviet dominance, all the East European states (East Germany, for obvious reasons, excluded) enjoyed a pretence of democracy. The vicissitudes of this short period, in which communism could claim impressive electoral support only in Czechoslovakia, are irrelevant here. What is relevant is the behavior of most of the communist parties in the region. First, before they achieved

3. Hugh Seton-Watson, *Eastern Europe between the Wars, 1918–1941* (Harper & Row, 1967). The book was first published in 1941. For a much later, more historically balanced view, see Joseph Rothschild, *East Central Europe between the Two World Wars* (Seattle and London: University of Washington Press, 1974).

domination, they erected policy platforms—in agriculture, for example, or relating to nationalization in industry—that barely distinguished them from some of their agrarian or democratic socialist opponents. Much of this reasonableness was spurious, designed to win votes and lay their own bogey. More significant were the early symptoms of what Zbigniew Brzezinski called "domesticism" in the period immediately after the communists had gained overriding control.[4] Without displaying any independent behavior toward Moscow, several of the parties now in power were characterized by a preoccupation with the affairs of their own countries and an apparent readiness to use specific solutions for specific problems.

Domesticism should not be confused with nationalism, but it could easily have become that. This is what disturbed Joseph Stalin, who became less and less satisfied with his satellites' protestations of loyalty and their claims to be operating within an orthodox framework. The climax came when Josip Broz Tito broke with Moscow in 1948. Tito's domesticism was clearly becoming Yugoslavian nationalism. So was Wladyslaw Gomulka's in Poland and Traicho Kostov's in Bulgaria. Even Georgi Dimitrov, who as former secretary-general of the Comintern should have known better, was making unmistakably Bulgarian noises in Sofia and allowing his enthusiasm for Balkan federation to run far ahead of what Stalin had in mind. To check these signs of domesticism, Stalin founded the Communist Information Bureau (Cominform) in 1947 to coordinate activities among communist parties worldwide. But the break with Tito moved him from persuasion to compulsion. Every effort short of invasion was used to try to destroy the Yugoslavian leader, and other East European leaders suspected of independence or even of autonomy of mind were physically or politically liquidated. Gomulka, for instance, paid for his ideas with eight years of disgrace; Kostov with his life. Dimitrov was publicly humiliated in *Pravda*[5] and later summoned to Moscow, where he died under mysterious circumstances. The Stalinist *Gleichschaltung*, the rigid coordination imposed on the Soviet Union itself in the 1930s, was now clamped down on Eastern Europe.

The break with Tito proved to be of incalculable importance. It

4. Zbigniew K. Brzezinski, *The Soviet Bloc: Unity and Conflict* (Harvard University Press, 1960), especially pp. 51–58. See also Hugh Seton-Watson, *The East European Revolution* (Praeger, 1951).

5. *Pravda*, January 28, 1948, cited in Brzezinski, *Soviet Bloc*, note 25, p. 417.

shattered the myth of communist unity almost before the communist bloc had been established. And despite the eventual grave disappointments and failures of Yugoslavia itself, Tito's apostasy remained both a warning to Moscow and an example for others. It could be argued that the break prompted Stalin to impose a regimentation in Eastern Europe more rigid than he otherwise might have felt necessary. What is significant, though, is that these signs of domesticism, crushed in 1948, were subsequently to reappear in more permissive periods throughout the next forty years. They are one of the most important recurring themes in East European communist history.

The imposition of the *Gleichschaltung* from 1948 to Stalin's death in 1953 and its subsequent modification until the dramatic events of 1956 constitute the second postwar historical phase. Despite all the subsequent reform and relaxation, it was this phase that left its indelible mark on Eastern Europe. That mark is not limited to repressive political institutions, cumbersome centralized economic structures, and an inflexibly bureaucratic habit of mind. More profound were the momentous social changes set in train during these years: massive industrialization, huge migrations from rural to urban areas, and agricultural collectivization and the breakup of the old peasant culture. These changes continued and for a while after Stalin's death even accelerated. They are still continuing. They would have occurred without Stalin, but it was he who implemented them with the extremism, massiveness of scale, and terror with which his name is linked.

After Stalin's death the dismantling not so much of the base as of the superstructure of his legacy began. This relaxation led in 1956 to an open disavowal of his methods of rule (though not its substance) by Nikita Khrushchev at the Twentieth Communist Party Congress. In Eastern Europe it began with a "New Course," initiated in 1953 by Georgi Malenkov and Khrushchev himself. Made urgent by the worker riots in East Germany only three months after Stalin died, the New Course involved a reallocation of resources toward producing more food and consumer goods and the demotion of the most tainted Stalinist leaders, such as Mátyás Rákosi in Hungary and Vulko Chervenko in Bulgaria.[6] The partial reversal of this New Course led to the Hungarian Revolution of 1956 and the Polish October in the same year.

6. Brzezinski, *Soviet Bloc*, pp. 153–81.

Communist Eastern Europe's third phase began after the disasters of 1956 with Khrushchev's new policies: essentially a broadening and even more urgent application of the New Course. On the bloc level they involved a strengthening of cohesion, mainly through the new Warsaw Treaty Organization (founded in 1955) and a resuscitated Council for Mutual Economic Assistance (Comecon, founded in 1949), emphasizing cooperation rather than Stalinlike compulsion.

The Warsaw Treaty Organization (often called the Warsaw Pact) was ostensibly established as a counter to the incorporation in 1955 of the armed forces of what had become the sovereign Federal Republic of Germany into the North Atlantic Treaty Organization. Roughly speaking, it is the Eastern bloc's counterpart of NATO. The Pact has a political-consultative committee composed of the party leaders from the member countries that is supposed to meet twice a year but has in fact met only rarely and irregularly. The Pact is both a political and military body and is dominated by the Soviet Union, but, especially since the various reforms announced in 1969, the smaller member countries have at least had some semblance of decisionmaking. The Soviets carry about 80 percent of the Pact's economic burden and supply about 75 percent of its troops (the corresponding American shares in NATO are about 60 percent and 42 percent).[7]

The Council for Mutual Economic Assistance had been founded by Stalin mainly, it seemed, as a response to (or protection against) the American Marshall Plan for Europe.[8] It remained inactive for nearly ten years, however, while the Soviet Union and each of its smaller allies pursued policies of autarkic, all-round industrialization. But after 1956 Khrushchev saw Comecon as the most effective means of recementing the broken alliance and promoting the economic viability of the bloc. In some aspects Comecon is a counterpart of the European Common Market, but it is totally dominated by the Soviet Union, has no formal supranational authority, and has subsequently

7. David Holloway, "The Warsaw Pact in Transition," in David Holloway and Jane M. O. Sharp, eds., *The Warsaw Pact: Alliance in Transition?* (Cornell University Press, 1984), p. 37.

8. See Michael Kaser, *Comecon: Integration Problems of the Planned Economies* (London: Oxford University Press for the Royal Institute of International Affairs, 1965); Jozef M. van Brabant, *Socialist Economic Integration: Aspects of Contemporary Economic Problems in Eastern Europe* (Cambridge University Press, 1980); and Vladimir Sobell, *The Red Market: Industrial Co-operation and Specialisation in Comecon* (Aldershot, England: Gower, 1984).

added to its membership three non-European countries: Cuba, Mongolia, and Vietnam.

On the domestic level, Khrushchev was prepared to concede a degree of autonomy to East European regimes to make necessary local adaptations in policy.[9] This autonomy again led to the kind of domesticism displayed before 1948. Although the framework was now considerably narrower, the instinct was very much the same. In combination with the Great Schism between the Soviet Union and China, the new permisiveness facilitated not only the defection of Albania from loyalty to Moscow in 1961 but also the steadily growing independence carved out by Romania in intrabloc and foreign policy.[10] More important was the impetus that increased autonomy gave to the birth and growth in Czechoslovakia of what became the Prague Spring. Even after Khrushchev was ousted in 1964 the reform movement accelerated, partly because of the momentum it was constantly acquiring, partly because of the relative inexperience of the new Soviet leadership and its preoccupation with shoring up its own domestic position.

The fourth historical phase was ushered in by the Soviet-led invasion of Czechoslovakia in 1968 that crushed the reform movement. This act was perhaps the watershed in Eastern Europe's postwar history so far because it signaled that the Soviet leadership was not prepared to allow domesticism to change the Leninist system in any basic way.[11] To modify, even to repudiate, the methods of Stalin was permissible, but to tamper with the institutions of Lenin, above all the party and its exclusive supremacy in public life, was intolerable. Following August 1968 the Soviet Union attempted to impose closer control over its allies by again strengthening Comecon and the Warsaw Treaty Organization as well as by imposing tighter bilateral ties. These actions were accompanied by a latter-day Counter-Reformation stressing the basic tenets of ideological orthodoxy. The tighter political and ideo-

9. See J. F. Brown, *The New Eastern Europe: The Khrushchev Era and After* (Praeger, 1966).

10. On Albania, see William E. Griffith, *Albania and the Sino-Soviet Rift* (MIT Press, 1963). Much has been written on the Romanian deviation. The most stimulating book is Kenneth Jowitt, *Revolutionary Breakthroughs and National Development: The Case of Romania, 1944–1965* (University of California Press, 1971).

11. The Prague Spring and its destruction have spawned several good books, but on this specific point see Philip Windsor, *Change in Eastern Europe* (London: Royal Institute of International Affairs, 1980).

logical controls were nothing like the *Gleichschaltung* of the Stalinist period: considerable domestic latitude for each country was still allowed. But the inviolability of party supremacy and the unacceptability of political pluralism narrowly circumscribed any freedom of action, even assuming the East European leaderships, most of which had been thoroughly alarmed by the Prague experiments, had wanted it.

In contrast, economic modernization was permitted, even encouraged, under the new dispensation, as well as a policy aimed at raising the standard of living, a policy at least partly designed to keep the masses quiet and to dull their political aspirations. For half a decade this new approach, closely linked with the name of Leonid Brezhnev, seemed to work extraordinarily well, especially in Poland, where Wladyslaw Gomulka, once a popular leader, had been toppled by worker riots at the end of 1970 and the need for rapid increases in the standard of living was particularly acute. The new Polish leader, Edward Gierek, seemed to be achieving just such increases with the aid of massive injections of Western credits and Soviet trade subsidies. Indeed, recourse to Western credits, freely available, became an important part of the economic policy of every East European country except Czechoslovakia, whose regime after 1968 took a paranoid view of any Western intrusion.

The promising situation of the early 1970s was not to last, however. The new relative prosperity was crippled by Western recession and inflation (a sign in itself of the growth of East-West economic relations). Steep increases in the prices of Soviet oil after 1973, occasioned by the rises in the world price imposed by the Organization of Petroleum Exporting Countries (OPEC), affected prosperity even more severely. Impaired by the inflexibility of their economic structures and serious mistakes in economic policy, the East European regimes could not cope with the sudden crisis. The rise of living standards slowed sharply, economic inefficiency increased everywhere, and debts mounted to levels that appeared impossible to repay.[12]

As for the Soviet Union, its grip on Eastern Europe seemed visibly to slacken in the second half of the 1970s, just when new danger signals coming from the region should have prompted closer attention. Perhaps Soviet will and determination to respond were lacking, and

12. See J. F. Brown, "The Future of Political Relations within the Warsaw Pact," in Holloway and Sharp, eds., *Warsaw Pact*, pp. 197–214.

for a long time the danger signals were not unambiguous. Even the Polish riots over food prices in 1976 were apparently considered aberrational rather than alarming. The truth seems to be that after the scare of 1968 Moscow had become satisfied with its work in Eastern Europe. The situation seemed stabilized and normalized; most economies, fed by Western credits, appeared to be working. Though the Soviet leaders were as aware as ever of the crucial geopolitical importance of Eastern Europe, they nevertheless showed signs of taking the region for granted. Their attention seemed dominated by global interests and aspirations and the whole complex of East-West relations. They may well have derived a false sense of security out of the détente in Europe, culminating in the Helsinki Final Act of 1975, a document predicated on the acceptance of the Soviet Union's postwar gains. Furthermore, the perceptiveness of the Soviet leadership may have been impaired by its rapid degeneration from what had once seemed vigor to what by the mid-1970s had become senility.

The situation in Eastern Europe at the end of the 1970s, therefore, hardly fulfilled the promise of the early years of the decade. Even in Hungary the rise in living standards was coming to a halt. In Romania both the economic and the psychological condition of the population had deteriorated steadily under Nicolae Ceauşescu's personal misrule. Czechoslovakia and East Germany, the most comprehensively advanced of the East European states, also saw living standards decline. Czechoslovakia could boast of a low hard-currency debt but of little else; its longer-term economic prospects looked bleak. The GDR was coping with a large Western debt, but it was also making significant economic reorganizations designed to increase economic efficiency. It had, moreover, the strong pillar of West German economic aid to lean on. (Subsequently, its economy was to make a considerable recovery.)

Not surprisingly, the explosion came in Poland. By 1978 the serious deterioration of the Polish economy could not be hidden, and it was only a matter of time before Edward Gierek, who had deceived both Soviet and Western leaders with his air of confident command, fell into the same kind of disgrace that had ended the career of Gomulka. The end came in September 1980, after the third disastrous attempt in ten years to increase the prices of food. The first attempt in 1970 had led to Gomulka's fall and Gierek's rise. The second, in 1976, was the first real indication (largely ignored) that the house Gierek was building was made of cards. The third was one of the reasons for the rise of "Solidarity."[13]

The Solidarity movement was one of the most remarkable developments in twentieth century European history. Although its direct precedent was in the riots of 1970, they were mainly confined to the Baltic coastline and were violent and bloody. Solidarity began in Gdansk, spread to Szczecin and the whole Baltic coast, and quickly enveloped the whole of Poland.[14] It became a national movement but remained a peaceful one, directed—at least initially—not so much at toppling the regime as at extracting far-reaching concessions from it. But the demands became such that no regime could agree to them and remain communist according to the standards prevailing in the Soviet bloc. This is what the moderates in Solidarity realized and why they sought to limit the demands or to obscure their true nature. But the movement, especially when faced by a regime patently insincere in dealings with it, acquired an ever-quickening momentum. Some form of confrontation was inevitable.[15] When confrontation did come, organized Solidarity was smashed with remarkable skill and speed, and with a minimum of casualties. But, as discussed in chapter 3, resistance was not broken easily, and not until the end of 1985 did the regime of Wojciech Jaruzelski begin to acquire and display a real self-confidence.

Solidarity, then, was a distinctly Polish phenomenon. Whereas the Prague Spring twelve years earlier essentially originated, and was led from, within the party and the ruling establishment and only subsequently engulfed large sections of the population, Solidarity originated

13. For an excellent analysis of the causes for the near economic collapse of Poland's economy, see Wlodzimierz Brus, "Economics and Politics: The Fatal Link," in Abraham Brumberg, ed., *Poland: Genesis of a Revolution* (Random House, 1983), pp. 26–41.

14. There are already several books published on Solidarity, none better than that by Timothy Garton Ash, *The Polish Revolution: Solidarity* (Scribner's, 1984).

15. Some experts, like Ash, *Polish Revolution*, pp. 326–27, argue that with a kind of new Marshall Plan to help the Polish economy and with moderate elements of the regime cooperating with the Solidarity leadership, a lasting compromise, tolerated by Moscow, might have been reached in early 1981. This seems doubtful. First, American aid could not have been organized quickly enough. Second, any form of toleration would have meant the abdication of Soviet power and the Soviet Union's perceived retreat from the status of a world power. To begin with, the impact on East Germany would have been disastrous.

as a mass movement of reform, which later spread to the party's basic organizations. The failure of the Czechoslovak reform constituted a serious setback to hopes that a comprehensive regeneration could be initiated within any East European regime in the future. The Soviet-led invasion of August 1968 signaled that the Soviet Union would not allow self-regeneration.[16] The only alternative, therefore, was regeneration from outside the system, from society itself, and against the system if necessary. This point was made strongly by dissident Polish intellectuals toward the end of the 1970s. No one would suggest, of course, that striking Polish workers in the summer of 1980 were consciously drawing on the Czechoslovak experience. For many of them the destroyed hopes of 1970, when they had trusted Gierek, were all the historical background they needed. Some could remember 1956, when reform did originate within the party and spread quickly to society but was subsequently repudiated by Gomulka, not a reformer but a blinkered conservative. Still, the Soviet action against Czechoslovakia in 1968 had relevance for Poland in 1980 because it provided a new dimension in relationships between societies and regimes and their impact on possibilities of change throughout Eastern Europe.

A fifth phase of communist history in Eastern Europe seems now to be approaching, heralded by the accession to Soviet leadership of a man who appears likely to remain at the top for many years and whose influence on the region could be profound. New leaderships are also expected in a number of East European states, and the changes involved will dramatize the new phase. So will the economic situation, which is likely to worsen and to call for important decisions in management, planning, and policy. To all the problems that materialize in the next ten years, Mikhail Gorbachev and the new leaders in Eastern Europe must respond.[17]

Soviet Policy in Eastern Europe

From 1975 to 1985 there appears to have been no coherent Soviet policy toward Eastern Europe. The reasons have already been men-

16. See Windsor, *Change in Eastern Europe.*
17. For a detailed and optimistic assessment of Gorbachev, see Archie Brown, "Gorbachev: New Man in the Kremlin," *Problems of Communism*, vol. 34 (May–June 1985), pp. 1–23.

tioned: the apparent stability of the region, Moscow's involvement in other concerns, and the enfeeblement of the Soviet leadership. To these must be added the briefness of the rule of both Yuri Andropov and Konstantin Chernenko and the attendant introspection and uncertainty in Moscow. There had been periods earlier when Soviet policy in the region also seemed to lack coherence: from Stalin's death until 1956 and from Khrushchev's dismissal in 1964 until the Prague Spring had truly begun. But there have also been periods when Soviet policy was coherent enough. Stalin's policy was all too coherent. Khrushchev had a policy after 1956—a constructive one in the prevailing situation. Beginning in 1969 Brezhnev also had a policy, prompted partly by the determination to make August 1968, and the reasons for it, unnecessary in the future. Now Eastern Europe awaits Gorbachev's considered policy.

The policy will depend considerably on Gorbachev's perception of Eastern Europe's importance. As with his predecessors, this perception must be multidimensional. Some dimensions have been more important than others; some have had more relevance in some periods than in others.[18] Briefly, the Soviets consider Eastern Europe important as a defensive glacis, a base for offensive strategies, a nucleus of international support in world politics, a source of political and ideological legitimization for Moscow, and a source of economic wealth.

The perception of Eastern Europe as a defensive glacis is mainly important to military thinking, but it has recently also acquired an ideological aspect in that the region has been seen—especially by ideological conservatives—as a protection for the Soviet Union against Western liberalism. In the event, of course, Eastern Europe has proved less an ideological moat than a conveyor belt for both Western sedition and its own.

Eastern Europe has also been considered a potential springboard for offensive strategies. Ideologically the Soviets see the region as

18. For a fuller discussion see J. F. Brown, *Relations Between the Soviet Union and its Eastern European Allies: A Survey* (Santa Monica, Calif.: Rand Corporation, 1975); John Van Oudenaren, *The Soviet Union and Eastern Europe: Options for the 1980s and Beyond* (Santa Monica, Calif.: Rand Corporation, 1984); Robert L. Hutchings, *Soviet–East European Relations: Consolidation and Conflict, 1968–1980* (University of Wisconsin Press, 1983); and John C. Campbell, "Soviet Policy in Eastern Europe: An Overview," in Sarah Meiklejohn Terry, ed., *Soviet Policy in Eastern Europe* (Yale University Press for the Council on Foreign Relations, 1984).

both the vanguard and the first fruits of the world communist movement, an example for the rest of the world to follow. Militarily, either for purposes of intimidation or aggression, Eastern Europe is seen as an essential forward base. Politically, the Soviets consider it a suitable base for initiatives designed to manipulate Western Europe, especially the Federal Republic of Germany.

The Soviets also look upon Eastern Europe as the nucleus of an international bloc of states providing political and diplomatic support in world politics. The building and expansion of such a bloc was thought essential if world opinion were to consider the Soviet Union in the same light as the United States. Soviet use of the East European states as proxies—for example, use of the GDR in parts of Africa or use of the Bulgarian government to urge nuclear disarmament in the Balkans—is part of the division of labor within the bloc.[19]

Moscow further considers Eastern Europe a source of Soviet political and ideological legitimization, a view that closely interacts with some of the preceding perceptions. But there is evidently a Soviet conviction that the continuing allegiance of Eastern Europe and the preservation there of a system basically similar to that in the USSR is essential, not only for the Soviet system's domestic legitimacy but also for its overall standing and reputation. Thus the ignominy incurred from periodic repression in Eastern Europe is seen as less damaging than changes in the system that would alter it beyond recognition. It is this factor that, more than anything else, makes hopes for Soviet toleration of any real Finlandization of Eastern Europe—allowing democratic institutions domestically while insisting on a neutralist foreign policy friendly to Moscow—seem unrealistic.

Finally Eastern Europe was once perceived as a source of economic wealth, a consideration, however, that is probably now part of history. The region has long since ceased to be the source of loot it was in Stalin's time, although until about 1954 it did play a considerable role in the postwar recovery of the Soviet Union.

As to Soviet policy, its chief aim in Eastern Europe has been to find a stable balance between cohesion and viability.[20] Cohesion can

---

19. For Soviet use of East Germany as proxy, see Melvin Croan, "A New Afrika Corps?" *Washington Quarterly*, vol. 3 (Winter 1980), pp. 21–37. For use of Bulgaria, see Patrick Moore, "Balkan Sources of International Instability," in Vojtech Mastny, ed., *Soviet/East European Survey, 1983–1984: Selected Research and Analysis from Radio Free Europe/Radio Liberty* (Duke University Press, 1985), pp. 259–65.

20. See Brown, *Relations between the Soviet Union and Its Eastern European Allies*, pp. 2–3.

be defined as a situation in which—allowing for some degree of diversity caused by varying local conditions—there is a general conformity on the part of the Soviet Union and its East European dependencies in both domestic and foreign policies. There is also an essential identity of the institutions implementing these policies. Viability can be defined as a degree of confidence, credibility, and efficiency in the regimes of East European states that would increasingly legitimize communist rule there and consequently reduce the Soviet need for preventive preoccupation with the region.

Moscow has not yet found a stable balance between cohesion and viability. When cohesion has been achieved, viability has suffered; and on the rare occasions when viability has been generated, as in the 1960s, it has tended to acquire a momentum that has undermined cohesion. Because of the basic intractability of Eastern Europe under Soviet domination, it is an emphasis on cohesion, of a kind, that has dominated. Indeed, between 1975 and 1985 the Soviets seem to have been mainly concerned with maintaining control as quietly as possible. That there was no Comecon summit conference for the fifteen years between 1969 and 1984 underscores this lack of engagement. Moscow's toleration of the massive influx of Western credits into Eastern Europe—with all their dangers—also appears to have reflected a lack of commitment. Surface calm alone seems to have satisfied Moscow.

That calm was shattered by Solidarity. But even without such a cataclysm, Gorbachev today would presumably have wanted to undertake a more positive initiative toward Eastern Europe. The Polish disaster only makes such an initiative the more imperative and urgent. But before discussing what his options and likely choice of them might be, it is worth considering in some detail the present East European situation.

The Present and the Prospects

Despite the many differences of detail from country to country, the picture presented by Eastern Europe as a whole in the late 1980s is somber and uneasy. Several factors contribute to that condition: aging and ailing leadership, the continuing failure to establish genuine legitimacy, unpromising economic prospects, unwelcome new economic pressures from the Soviet Union, and growing recognition of

the need for structural reform coupled with fear and uncertainty as
to what reform might portend for the durability of the political system.

AN AGING LEADERSHIP

Few East Europeans can have failed to notice—not without irony—
the striking contrast in age and length of service between the new
Soviet leader and their own leaders. In 1986 Gorbachev was fifty-five
years old and had been in office only a year. In contrast, most East
European leaders were or should have been thinking about their
successors. Todor Zhivkov of Bulgaria, János Kádár of Hungary,
Erich Honecker of East Germany, and Gustav Husák of Czechoslovakia
had all either reached or were nearing seventy-five. Ceauşescu, always
considered the Benjamin of the club but recently believed to be
seriously ailing, was approaching seventy.[21] Only General Jaruzelski,
who owed his position to a bizarre combination of circumstances, was
still in his early sixties. Zhivkov had been party leader for thirty-two
years, Kádár for thirty. The six leaders of the Soviet Union's East
European allies represented a combined total of 120 years in office.

The only certainty emerging from these statistics is that at least
four East European countries will soon be experiencing a leadership
succession. Whether this will involve a crisis is by no means sure.
Although in the past most changes in communist leadership have
either resulted from crises or have caused them, preemptive care
seems to have been taken more recently to avoid the classic upheavals.
The Brezhnev-Andropov-Chernenko-Gorbachev successions, though
marked by serious personal rivalries, took place in a period more of
debilitation than disruption. Much earlier, in 1965, Ceauşescu's
succession after the death of Gheorghe Gheorghiu-Dej was smooth.
So, apparently, was that of Ramiz Alia after Enver Hoxha died in
Albania in April 1985.[22] Now both Kádár and Honecker have appeared
keen to ensure that their departures create no power vacuums in
which factionalism could thrive. But try as they might these leaders
cannot ensure stability from beyond the grave. Chances are that in
one or more of the countries affected power struggles will ensue. In

21. See Anneli Maier, "Press Retouching Photographs of Ceauşescu," *Radio Free
Europe Research*, vol. 10 (September 20, 1985), situation report 13/85.
22. See Viktor Meier, "Im Schatten Enver Hodschas," *Frankfurter Allgemeine Zeitung*,
August 28, 1985.

any case, however smooth the transitions may appear, the new incumbent will need time and skill to familiarize himself with the complexities of the office and to reshape the governing cadres into a form acceptable and loyal to himself.

What could be even more important than the domestic implications of leadership changes is that Mikhail Gorbachev is bound to be involved in them, perhaps at a fairly early stage in his career. He will naturally be interested in seeing that changes proceed with as few disruptions as possible. Even more important, the leaders who emerge will be those with whom Gorbachev will probably work for a long time: it is crucial to him that the "right" men be chosen. Thus he will almost certainly feel it necessary to interfere in East European affairs earlier and to a greater degree than would otherwise be his intention— perhaps before he has fully consolidated his power at home. All East European leaders, of course, have had to go through some form of Soviet vetting. It will be very much in Gorbachev's interest to see that this vetting is more thorough than usual. But even the greatest thoroughness cannot ensure that his choices will be successful.

The picture presented by Eastern Europe to the new Soviet leader can hardly be reassuring. True, no part of the region is in a state of disruption, and such was the numbing effect of crushing Solidarity that disruption need not be feared for some time. But otherwise the picture is one of multiple failures and little success.

TESTS OF LEGITIMACY

None of the regimes in Eastern Europe has gained the degree of legitimacy that could enable it to sustain itself without resorting to the coercive forces at its disposal and ultimately the forces of the Soviet Union. Legitimacy can be defined as popular acceptance of, or even identification with, the political, international, and economic goals of the regime. What it constitutes in practice is a question to which many answers have been given.[23] For any ruling elite in Eastern Europe legitimacy would require conduct of a policy consonant with

23. For an excellent discussion of legitimacy in Eastern Europe, see Sarah M. Terry, "The Implications of Economic Stringency and Political Succession for Stability in Eastern Europe in the Eighties," in *East European Economies: Slow Growth in the 1980's*, vol. 1: *Economic Performance and Policy*, Joint Economic Committee, 99 Cong. 1 sess. (GPO, 1985), pp. 502–40.

the national traditions and aspirations of the bulk of the population; a commonly shared ideology or set of values between rulers and ruled; a minimum and increasing standard of welfare and prosperity; the creation of conditions for social and professional mobility—the provision of a stake in the country; an increasing degree of freedom of expression and association—political, social, economic, and religious; and a general belief that the condition of society will steadily improve.

Obviously these points can be debated, amended, or refined almost endlessly, but they do offer a rough reliable guide to what legitimacy should comprise in the East European context. The relative importance of the elements can vary considerably according to national attitudes and with different historical periods. For example, the Soviet regime enjoys a considerable legitimacy among large sections of its population, although it hardly fulfills all the desiderata mentioned above, something well known to many Soviet citizens. This legitimacy is largely a legacy of World War II, when communism was reinforced by nationalism. Whether the mutual interaction of the two remains strong among members of younger generations is open to question.

In Eastern Europe, with six very different countries, the situation is much more complex. Despite the assiduous efforts of the East German regime to foster a distinct sense of nationality and its success in raising living standards, there is little evidence yet of a new nationalism.[24] As long as a state remains artificial—and the test here is whether the population considers it artificial—then its government hardly begins to be legitimate. In Poland the very mention of the subject would arouse derision, never more so than today. Yet even in Poland the Gomulka regime enjoyed a certain legitimacy in October 1956 and for a short time after. So, perhaps, did Gierek immediately after December 1970. In Czechoslovakia the shortlived regime of Alexander Dubček enjoyed considerable legitimacy, whereas the Husák regime, despite its successful consumer-oriented policy, certainly does not. In Slovakia, though, even if they enjoy only a partial fulfillment of their nationalist aspirations, many people are prepared to grant the Bratislava authority an acceptance that could amount to

24. See, for example, Ronald D. Asmus, "Opening of Luther Celebrations in the GDR," *Radio Free Europe Research*, vol. 8, pt. 2 (May 20, 1983), background report 100/83.

some kind of legitimacy.[25] In Hungary, because of the unique tragedy of the 1956 revolution and the astonishing metamorphosis of János Kádár from traitor to *pater patriae,* the regime has come to acquire some legitimacy, a legitimacy reinforced by its policy of economic reform and a certain atmosphere of relaxation. But such legitimacy is almost entirely centered on Kádár; its true test will come when he departs.

Romania is a case of dissipated legitimacy. With the current deep unpopularity of Ceauşescu, it is easy to forget that for some three years after his accession to power in 1965 he aroused the optimistic expectations of many Romanians.[26] This was not simply because of his defense of Romanian interests against the Soviet Union but also because he set in motion promising domestic reforms and repudiated past crises. In his courageous defiance of the Soviet Union's invasion of Czechoslovakia in August 1968, he undoubtedly had most of his countrymen behind him, nervous though they were. That was Ceauşescu's peak. Everything since has been decline and degeneration. The nationalist-oriented policy has continued, and the years since 1968 have been punctuated by periods of serious tension with Moscow. But the regime's mismanagement has forced Romania back into some degree of economic dependence on the Soviet Union, at least in the energy sector, and often the anti-Soviet stance, though still genuine, has seemed mere posturing. Thus many Romanians, originally enthusiastic about Ceauşescu's nationalism, now weigh this dwindling asset against his mounting liabilities. They have even begun (most reluctantly) to envy the situation in Bulgaria, not to mention that in Hungary.

In Bulgaria popular moods are the most difficult to assess. There have been relatively few signs of discontent. This is not, as many observers would have it, due to widespread love of Russia. Pro-Russian sentiment certainly still exists, although it is less significant among the young and there is often a general embarrassment at the regime's extravagant servility toward Moscow. But many Bulgarians are more concerned with how their regime conducts itself in relations with the

25. Viktor Meier, "Die Slowakei ist selbstbewusster," *Frankfurter Allgemeine Zeitung,* December 13, 1984.

26. See J. F. Brown, "Rumania Today," *Problems of Communism,* vol. 18 (January–February, March–April 1969). Part 1 of the series is titled "Towards Integration," and part 2, "The Strategy of Defiance."

"old enemies," Serbia, Greece, and Turkey. Here there is no servility; sometimes, rather, as with Yugoslavia on territorial disputes over Macedonia, a provocativeness that amounts to surrogate nationalism. Such aggressiveness goes down well with many Bulgarians; so apparently do the recent efforts forcibly to assimilate the large Turkish minority in Bulgaria itself. A more healthy nationalism, however, was shown in the support for the efforts of Todor Zhivkov's daughter, Lyudmila, to publicize in the West the great historical creations of Bulgarian civilization, and to make Bulgarians aware of them too.[27] As for economic prosperity, the Zhivkov regime's record over the past twenty years has generally been good, although since 1985 there have been severe energy and consumer shortages, strong signs of a general downturn, and a widespread national uneasiness. The regime's confidence seems significantly and perhaps indefinitely undermined.

A real and lasting communist legitimacy encompassing all the above-mentioned criteria almost certainly can never be achieved. It is doubtful, indeed, whether any Western democratic system has fully achieved them all. Certainly no East European government in the era between the two world wars did so. But after nearly forty years of communist rule, the most striking aspect of Eastern Europe is that in several countries the legitimacy of the government appears further away than ever. And where legitimacy seems to have increased—in, say, Hungary—it is still not so firmly rooted that it could not be swept away practically overnight.

The quest for legitimacy will be frustrated as long as East European societies are offered no possibilities of influencing or participating in genuine political interaction. Some form of political pluralism, therefore, is essential, either within the party itself, through a multiparty parliamentary system, or through the party's sharing its power with organizations of society such as trade unions or bodies representing other important interest groups. Richard Löwenthal rightly contends that this is a sine qua non for a lasting legitimacy.[28] The Czech reformers of 1968 seemed to realize this, as do radical reformers now

27. Lyudmila Zhivkova died in 1981. The best biographical sketch of her is by Yordan Kerov, "Lyudmila Zhivkova—Fragments of a Portrait," *Radio Free Europe Research* (October 27, 1980), background report 253/80.

28. See "The Ruling Party in a Mature Society," in Mark G. Field, ed., *Social Consequences of Modernization in Communist Societies* (Johns Hopkins University Press, 1976).

in Hungary and Yugoslavia. In Poland, of course, because of the power of the Catholic church, a form of pluralism or duality of power actually exists, though hardly by courtesy of the communist authorities. For it to exist elsewhere would require a break with Leninist ideology, tradition, and practice. The total monopoly of authority by the party is the most important element of substance remaining in communist ideology, largely because it combines practical benefits with doctrinal orthodoxy. The rest of ideology has become a ritual, albeit useful and necessary for the ruling elites, carrying form without substance. A basic change in Eastern Europe, therefore, cannot be looked to with confidence. But it has its proponents who are gathering numbers and arguments. They know they face an uphill task.

ECONOMIC PROSPECTS

What the East European regimes would presumably like to concentrate on is the improvement of economic performance and an attempt to return, at least some part of the way, to the consumerism of the early 1970s. Whether they will succeed is highly questionable.

Between 1982 and 1985 most East European economies seemed to show a resilience in certain fields few would have expected after the disastrous performance of the late 1970s and early 1980s. Eastern Europe as a whole improved its trading position somewhat with the West, largely through the reduction of imports supplemented by export drives. In most countries, industrial production and national income figures improved, as did productivity in those cases where evidence is available. The hard currency debt of all except Poland was reduced, though in Hungary's case not by much. The East German, Hungarian, and Bulgarian governments (as well as the Czechoslovak, if it had had any interest in borrowing) became creditworthy again in Western financial circles. The GDR appeared to be particularly successful and in 1984 claimed its best economic year ever, as usual, however, without acknowledging the extra advantage it enjoys through its special relation with the Federal Republic. This advantage was highlighted in 1983 and 1984 by two separate, unconditional West German credits totaling almost two billion West German marks.[29]

29. "Stabiles Wirtschaftswachstum in der DDR," *Neue Zürcher Zeitung* (Fernausgabe),

But since the middle of 1985 the economic improvement in the region has slowed or reversed. A recession had set in, except apparently in the GDR, and as *The Economist* put it, "the fragile industrial recovery" in the region had been "blown off course."[30] The recession might be only a "hiccup," but that appeared unlikely. Over the longer term, Eastern Europe will have a crucial problem in securing raw materials, especially energy. With the partial exceptions of Poland and Romania the region is poorly endowed by nature, but it has shown a costly profligacy with raw materials. Its level of energy consumption in industry, for example, is much higher than Western Europe's, partly because of bad management and bad habits, and partly also because of antiquated plant and machinery. One of the ostensible objectives in incurring so much hard currency debt in the 1970s was to modernize industry and improve its energy efficiency. While it would be an exaggeration to say that these credits were universally squandered, it cannot be claimed, except perhaps in the GDR, that they have had much impact on energy conservation.[31]

The very high rate of energy consumption, especially of solid fuels, is one reason for the ecological blight that has descended on much of Eastern Europe in the past twenty years. It has become a major issue throughout the region, evoking mounting concern. The areas worst hit include parts of the GDR, southern Poland, and northern Bohemia. The main offender is brown coal, though this hardly affects Poland, which has large supplies of hard coal; but the real culprits are economic planners and officials of successive generations who have often neglected everything except quantity of production, and propagandists who have maintained that pollution was another capitalist monopoly.[32]

July 16, 1985. See also B. V. Flow, "The East German Economy—What is Behind the Success Story?" *Radio Free Europe Research,* vol. 10, pt. 3 (March 22, 1985), background report 23/85; and Henry Tanner, "Germany's Foreign Trade with Germany," *International Herald Tribune* (Paris), May 3, 1985.

30. "A Cold Blast for Comecon," *The Economist,* vol. 269 (August 24–30, 1985), p. 65. Quantitative data on the recent economic performance of the East European countries and on their trade with the West can be found in the appendix to this book.

31. See Sobell, *Red Market,* pp. 38–43.

32. There have been numerous reports on the grave ecological situation in the East European, the West European, and the American press. A very good overall summary is by Scott Sullivan, "A Dying Landscape," *Newsweek* (international edition), January 8, 1985. The most comprehensive study is by Henrik Bischof, *Umweltschutzprobleme in Osteuropa* (Bonn: Friedrich-Ebert Stiftung, 1986).

The ecological and energy problems were dramatically linked in April 1986 by the Chernobyl disaster in the USSR. Poland, Hungary, Czechoslovakia, and Romania were the East European countries most seriously affected, but none went untouched. Politically, the main result was a new dimension added to anti-Soviet feeling. Travelers in both Poland and Hungary attested to the sense of indignation and impotence that gripped society, exacerbated by Moscow's secretiveness about the accident. Economically, considerable damage was done to crops, and the losses were then magnified by Western embargoes on various East European foodstuffs. The disaster may also have shaken the complacency among both officialdom and the public at large about ecological decay; it certainly led to increased vigilance at nuclear power stations. Chernobyl, however, did not result in any turning away from nuclear energy programs in Eastern Europe. Whatever the reservations, the official line was to press ahead. Except in Poland and Romania, nuclear energy was already well established in the region. Some 14.6 percent of Czechoslovakia's total electrical energy, for instance, was supplied by nuclear power in 1985, a percentage projected to double by 1990. In Bulgaria the corresponding figure for 1985 was 31 percent. The propaganda machines were swift to protest that "it couldn't happen here"—or again in the Soviet Union, for that matter.[33]

But however speedy and safe the progress in developing nuclear energy, oil will continue to be decisive well into the future. The Soviet Union's difficulties in maintaining, let alone increasing, its deliveries of oil have thus become a major worry. Exports to the GDR and Czechoslovakia were cut by at least 10 percent in 1982, and though Moscow promised in 1984 to maintain its level of oil supplies until the end of the decade, Eastern Europe's needs were expected to grow.

What will be the situation after 1990? Many experts feel that despite intensive drilling and exploration efforts Soviet oil production has already peaked and may even decrease during the 1990s. And there could be many lean years until the vast deposits in Eastern Siberia and offshore can be worked productively. In the meantime, unless there is a drastic change of policy for political reasons, Eastern Europe may have to take third place on the Soviet oil supply list

33. See "Eastern Europe and Chernobyl: The Initial Response," *Radio Free Europe Research*, vol. 11, pt. 3 (May 23, 1986), background report 72/86.

behind the Soviet Union itself and Western buyers.[34] Eastern Europe
will be compensated with natural gas, supplies of which are expected
to increase appreciably during the 1990s.

It is easy to see why many East Europeans are dismayed at this
prospect. During the 1970s, there was a significant shift away from
coal toward oil in most of the countries. The exceptions were Poland,
where the shift was slight, and Romania, where coal has never supplied
more than one-fifth of energy needs and the use of natural gas and
oil has been predominant. Taking Eastern Europe as a whole, the
proportion of energy supplies represented by coal fell from 68.8
percent in 1970 to 57.7 percent in 1980. During the same period the
proportion represented by oil increased from 18.0 to 24.8 percent.
This shift occurred despite rocketing world oil prices during the 1970s
and, after 1975, the gradual increase of Soviet prices toward the
OPEC level. As a result, while several East European countries had,
at Soviet urging, already begun to get increasing amounts of oil from
the Middle East, they have been forced back to almost total dependence
on Soviet supplies by the huge world price increase and by such
unforeseen political transformations as the revolution in Iran and the
Iran-Iraq war.[35]

With its resources of hard coal, Poland could be best placed to
survive these difficulties. The GDR and Czechoslovakia have already
begun to revert to coal wherever possible. But their coal is mainly
lignite, which is inefficient and adds to the severe ecological hazards
in the two countries. Moreover, even in countries where a considerable
reversion to coal and further switches to nuclear energy are possible,
large supplies of oil will continue to be necessary. This need will be
met in part by the Soviet Union. But if the world price of oil stays
relatively low, some East European countries might buy part of their
supplies in the world market, a move that would bring them more

34. Soviet trade returns for the first quarter of 1985, however, did not confirm
this fear. Compared with the first quarter of 1984, oil exports to the West fell by
40 percent; those to Eastern Europe by much less. See Philip Hanson, "Soviet Oil
Deliveries: Charity Begins at Home," *Radio Liberty Research Bulletin* (September 11, 1985),
RL 293/85.

35. For excellent discussions of the energy problem, see Sobell, *Red Market*, pp.
35–72; John P. Hardt, "Soviet Energy Policy in Eastern Europe," in Terry, ed., *Soviet
Policy in Eastern Europe*, pp. 189–220; John M. Kramer, "Soviet-CEMA Energy Ties,"
Problems of Communism, vol. 34 (July–August 1985), pp. 32–47; and Ed A. Hewett,
Energy, Economics, and Foreign Policy in the Soviet Union (Brookings, 1984).

into the mainstream of international commerce. Otherwise, after 1990 they will have to make do by substituting larger quantities of Soviet natural gas.

SOVIET ECONOMIC PRIORITIES

How cheaply East European countries will get their energy supplies—even how cheaply they are getting current supplies of Soviet oil—is a matter of conjecture.[36] At the 1984 Comecon summit and executive council meetings in Prague and Havana respectively, the Soviet Union made clear to its allies that they were expected to undertake increased investment in various extractive industries in the USSR and to export manufactured goods of the highest quality to the Soviets. East European investment in the Soviet Union had steadily increased during the 1970s, but apparently not quickly enough. And the Soviets had often complained about the quality of imports before. The emphasis and tone of Soviet pronouncements on these subjects in 1984 and 1985 left the impression that a new, more exacting and difficult period for East European–Soviet economic relations was approaching.[37] The Soviets' domestic economic problems would seem to explain this toughening attitude, along with the potential political problem of rising consumer demands from their citizens and exasperation at higher East European living standards.

But it is not only these factors that make the economic future look bleak for the East Europeans. Most countries in the region are unlikely to get Western credits at anything near the levels of the 1970s. They have also been forced, some less unwillingly than others, to agree to Soviet demands for closer economic cooperation bilaterally and multilaterally through Comecon.

Comecon passed through several vicissitudes after Khrushchev recognized its potential in the mid-1950s. Convinced of the need for closer integration and greater specialization, and probably impressed by the rapid progress of the West European Common Market

36. This question is connected with the whole issue of Soviet subsidization and its extent. In terms of methodology and assessment of the question probably the most convincing work has been done by Paul Marer. See his chapters in Terry, ed., *Soviet Policy in Eastern Europe*, pp. 155–88; and in Holloway and Sharp, eds., *Warsaw Pact*, pp. 215–37.

37. See, for example, Robert Gillette, "Soviets Demand More of East Bloc," *Los Angeles Times*, August 25, 1985.

established by the Treaty of Rome in 1957, Khrushchev, with typical impatience, sought to give Comecon certain supranational planning and directive powers. The powers were opposed, openly by Romania and probably with more discretion by other East European countries. After the near disaster of Czechoslovakia in 1968, Brezhnev used both Comecon and the Warsaw Pact as his main instruments in restoring bloc unity. He appears to have considered stringent measures essential to prevent another Prague Spring (both the reform movement itself and the need to crush it); to mitigate any dangers in Eastern Europe that the dawning era of détente might bring; and to strengthen the bloc against what must have been perceived then— the clash on the Ussuri River occurred in March 1969—as a potential threat from China. Though there are indications that Brezhnev might have preferred centralized decisionmaking bodies, he wisely realized after 1968 that such an idea could not be pushed with undue precipitation. He settled, therefore, for second best: a so-called directed consensus in which the reality of Soviet domination was preserved but encouragement and concessions were granted to give East Europeans a greater sense not only of participation, but also of decisionmaking.

Whereas Khrushchev had seemed to want integration from the top down, Brezhnev and his associates chose a slower but surer integration from the bottom up, involving brick-on-brick coordination, joint projects, and mutual specialization.[38] The chief policy document embodying this philosophy and these principles was the Comprehensive Program approved by the Comecon prime ministers in 1971. Much of what it planned has not been implemented, but considerable progress was made during the 1970s and some major undertakings— the second Druzhba pipeline, for example—were completed, for the most part ahead of schedule. The Soyuz (Orenburg) natural gas pipeline was also completed on time by the end of 1978. Multinational electrical power grids were developed and enlarged. Cooperation in both ferrous and nonferrous metallurgy, chemicals production, and nuclear power generation progressed. The number of joint projects, bilateral specialization agreements, and Comecon international economic organizations more than doubled during the decade.

Mikhail Gorbachev evidently intends to extend, intensify, and

38. See Brown, *Relations Between the Soviet Union and Its Eastern European Allies*, pp. 16–26.

accelerate these types of cooperation, and the growing economic weakness of most East European states might make them readier than ever to cooperate. But closer Comecon cooperation means greater Soviet domination. Despite their difficulties, even the most pliant of the East European governments hardly welcomes that. Hence the dilemma all of them recognize. Their domestic economic problems, the looming energy crisis, and growing complexities of technology will push for more, not less, "partnership." On this point even the thoroughly pro-Soviet Czechoslovak leadership and the less than pro-Soviet Romanian leadership are in general agreement.

While multilateral economic ties are being tightened through Comecon, the Soviet Union also seems determined to strengthen its bilateral ties with individual states. Long-term agreements are in force with every East European country. The contents vary: the agreement with Romania is still rather general; the Polish and East German ones are more precise and appear more restrictive of the maneuverability of the smaller cosignatories.

The parallel with the Warsaw Pact here is obvious. Along with the provisions and obligations incorporated in the multilateral Warsaw Treaty of 1955, the Soviet Union has long-term bilateral treaties with each member country, as do all the member countries with one another. Economic relations among the Comecon countries are also still predominantly bilateral: multilateralism is impeded by many factors, including difficulties in currency convertibility and the mosaic of pricing and costing systems. Like the Warsaw Pact, Comecon is dominated by Soviet power, although because of its economic character, the smaller East European countries play a more important role. There is an interaction within Comecon that is absent in the Warsaw Pact in its military role. In political relations within the Pact, the role of the East European countries is more important, but still less than their economic role within Comecon.

THE NEED FOR REFORM

As noted earlier, Comecon has already had some notable successes. It should also be recalled that originally it was not established as an international trading area, such as the European Economic Community. It might better be seen as an international protection area, shielding members from the adverse effects of competition from both inside and outside its confines. "From the beginning, participation in Comecon was associated with the implantation and maintenance . . . of Soviet-type industrialisation to secure growth and maintain the hegemony of the socialised sector."[39] Now, however, as it moves toward its fortieth anniversary, and with the economics of its member countries changed almost beyond recognition, many suggest that basic changes are imperative: reforms in pricing and costing, in convertibility, and in dealing with relative scarcities and comparative advantage. In other words, Comecon should start evolving into a genuine international trading system.

Most calls for such reforms have in recent years come from Hungary, whose New Economic Mechanism, begun in 1968 after careful preparation, has the most market-oriented and sophisticated economic system in the Soviet alliance. Details about the NEM can be obtained elsewhere.[40] In this context four questions arise. Is some degree of political reform now necessary to complement and secure economic progress? Can the NEM survive and disarm the mounting criticism within Hungary itself that it perpetuates rather than removes sectional differences and has brought little prosperity to most workers? Can the NEM survive Kádár? And will the Gorbachev leadership approve of the program?

These questions are interrelated, but the answer to the last could have the greatest ramifications. The Hungarian reform was eventually accepted by the Brezhnev leadership and certain aspects of it, notably in agriculture, won Soviet approval. But between 1972 and 1978 the NEM was almost at a standstill because of the interaction of Soviet suspicions and domestic opposition. Since 1981 the program appears to have acquired new momentum, with the Hungarian authorities courageously responding to the recent economic downturn not by retreating from reform but by advancing into new areas. The Hungarian party congress in March 1985 fully endorsed the reformist course, although several important speakers criticized its adverse social consequences and stressed the need for the less fortunate to be cushioned against them.[41] Such pleas were obviously not wholly

39. Sobell, *Red Market*, p. 6.
40. See William F. Robinson, *The Pattern of Reform in Hungary: A Political, Economic, and Cultural Analysis* (Praeger, 1973).
41. One of the best analyses of the congress was "Ein Stellvertreter für János Kádár," *Neue Zürcher Zeitung* (Fernausgabe), March 30, 1985.

devoid of opportunism, but they had some substance, and unless the regime takes note of them, the reform could be in serious difficulties. That is when Soviet support could be vital. Kádár and his associates must also keep a watchful eye, as they now appear to be doing, on those demanding political pluralism. It was such demands in Prague that led to the Soviet invasion. Although almost twenty years have passed since then, Soviet aversion to political pluralism is probably as strong as ever. Yet the Kádár regime has seen the need for some political concessions. At the national and local elections in June 1985 each constituency had the choice of at least two candidates. It is easy to overestimate the importance of this: great care was taken to see that all the candidates were acceptable. But the meetings to adopt candidates and the preelection discussions were often lively. The June 1985 election could be an important precedent despite its obvious shortcomings.

In its degree of market orientation, progress toward realistic pricing, and encouragement of individual or group entrepreneurship, the NEM is unique, but it is not the only economic reform in Eastern Europe. Since 1978 there have also been efforts worth mentioning in Bulgaria, Poland, and East Germany.

The Bulgarian regime, long known for its massive industrial and agricultural reorganizations, began the first phase—affecting agriculture—of a comprehensive reform in 1978, followed by a second phase affecting industry that began in 1982. The reform surprised many observers by the extent of decentralization involved, its emphasis on profit, and its departure from the long-entrenched Bulgarian principle that big is beautiful.[42] It made its contribution to the improvement of Bulgaria's economic performance in the first part of the 1980s.

In Poland the Jaruzelski regime's reform was comprehensive enough on paper and was formulated by men of undoubted ability. Intended to encourage decentralization, it allowed considerable independence of factory managers and delegated power to local trade unions and works councils. The reform also called for a big cut in government subsidies for consumer goods and services. But most of the proposed changes have been stymied by opposition within the regime that the leadership could not subdue and by a lack of

---

42. See "Bulgariens Vortasten zu neuen Wirtschaftsmechanismen," *Neue Zürcher Zeitung* (Fernausgabe), June 2/3, 1984.

cooperation from the public. The main result of the reforms so far has been inflation.[43]

Measured against the Hungarian reform, the one undertaken in East Germany has been essentially conservative. Instead of the NEM's market-oriented entrepreneurial drive, it has stressed devolution of management, labor saving, and productivity. All the evidence points to its having been successful, as seen in the GDR's relatively stable economic growth rates and effective handling of its foreign indebtedness. The decision in 1979 to organize 90 percent of East German industry into about 130 combines (*Kombinate*) has released much managerial talent. That, coupled with the German workers' discipline, traditional readiness to adapt, and highly developed skills, seems to have been the secret of success. Small wonder that so much favorable Soviet attention has been attracted to the East German reform. Brezhnev found praise for it before he died, and its whole substance and method seemed in keeping with the Andropov style of leadership.

Soviet Choices

At first it seemed that the East German approach to economic reform was similar to Gorbachev's inclinations. This could still turn out to be so. But the radicalism (at least in Soviet terms) of the Soviet leader's pronouncements in the early part of 1987 might necessitate a reappraisal not only of future Soviet policy but also of the impact that policy might have on Eastern Europe.

There is no necessary linkage between the Soviets' domestic policy and the policy they might pursue in Eastern Europe. But from past experience it is difficult to envisage no connection at all. More relaxation and decentralization within the Soviet Union could lead to similar changes in Eastern Europe. Such a policy might also lead to more leeway for the countries concerned in the pursuit of both their internal and external affairs. At work here would be a habit of mind, an attitude of governance that tolerates, even encourages, not so much spontaneity as a certain autonomy, perceived as strengthening rather than weakening the organism as a whole.

There was mounting speculation in early 1987, both in Eastern

43. Jackson Diehl, "Polish Reforms Backfire," *Washington Post*, September 24, 1985.

Europe and the West, about the "Gorbachev impact" on the region. Predictions were so hazardous that a modest discretion rather than self-advertising boldness was advisable. But it would be well to take the following factors into account:

—Gorbachev's reform inclinations were meeting with strong opposition within the Soviet Union itself. A power struggle was still going on that would decide the future of reform and perhaps even of Gorbachev's leadership itself.

—In Eastern Europe Gorbachev's calls for reform also apppeared divisive rather than cohesive. The East German leadership politely but firmly indicated that it was not prepared to be influenced by the clamor for change.[44] In Czechoslovakia the reform issue revealed the latent differences existing for years inside the regime. Politburo member Vasil Bilak, the high priest of dogmatic reaction, was less than polite in his rejection of the new Soviet lead, while Premier Lubomir Štrougal, long known for discreet reformist tendencies, seemed emboldened by Gorbachev's example. In Poland a relationship of confidence seemed to be developing between Gorbachev and Jaruzelski, while in Hungary there was general relief over Moscow's new look. As expected, Ceauşescu rejected any suggestion of being influenced by Soviet reform policy, but the Bulgarian leader, Todor Zhivkov, seemed cautiously inclined to move with the course of events.[45] Gorbachev might well have felt that leaders so long and well entrenched, as most of the East Europeans were, could never adapt or change. He was perhaps taking comfort from the expectation that some were very near the end of the road.

—The wind blowing from Moscow could have more profound and disruptive effects: the divisiveness could lead to serious instability and the setting in motion of forces for change that would be difficult to guide or check. Similarities between Gorbachev's approach and that of Khrushchev after Stalin's death were appearing. Though it was hard to imagine developments in Eastern Europe between 1953 and 1956 ever being repeated, they have remained a warning to any Soviet leader since. So has Czechoslovakia in 1968.

44. See "Distanz der DDR zu Gorbatschew's Reformplänen," *Neue Zürcher Zeitung* (Fernausgabe), February 12, 1987.

45. The various East European reactions are summed up in "Osteuropäische Stimmen zu Gorbatschews Kurs," *Neue Zürcher Zeitung* (Fernausgabe), February 22/23, 1987.

—Though it was too early at the beginning of 1987 to speak of a Gorbachev policy toward Eastern Europe, a dichotomy could be detected in his apparent attitude. On the one hand he seemed to favor some degree of economic and even political reform; on the other hand he was obviously at pains to strengthen "coordination" (read Soviet control) in Comecon, the Warsaw Pact, and the affairs of the alliance generally.[46] He may have considered these two aspects of policy complementary. The experience of the past forty years would indicate that they were contradictory. Moreover, nothing Gorbachev had said so far showed that he was prepared to soften the growing Soviet economic hard line toward the East European states, demanding that they "share" more equally the economic burdens of alliance.

These factors indicate the intractability of the East European problem for the new Soviet leadership. Any policy that is developed, or merely adumbrated, is bound to have inconsistencies that could ruin it. This is because Soviet hegemony, no matter how imaginatively applied, is simply incompatible with East European aspirations. Brezhnev may have dimly realized this after his burst of comprehensive activity in Eastern Europe between 1968 and about 1975. Gorbachev, too, may eventually do the same. Combined with all the domestic and global problems he will face, he may be overtaken by the "Brezhnev progression" in Eastern Europe sooner than many people think.[47] The erstwhile activist may become resigned to trying to keep the region quiet and Soviet policy toward Eastern Europe may become concerned mainly with overall control and maintaining an uneasy calm.

46. See, for example, Vladimir Sobell, "Mikhail Gorbachev Takes Charge of the CMEA," *Radio Free Europe Research,* vol. 10, no. 52 (December 20, 1985), background report 146/85.

47. For a fuller discussion on Soviet choices see Brown, "Future of Political Relations," in Holloway and Sharp, eds., *Warsaw Pact,* pp. 205–07.

THREE

Eastern Europe's Western Connection

J. F. BROWN

THE REALITIES of Soviet domination and of communist rule necessitate that Western policy toward Eastern Europe be conducted on two levels: the state and the societal. The same differentiation is necessary when one considers East European attitudes toward the West. Indeed, on this topic it is essential to recognize not only differentiations but also distinctions, subtleties of perception, and shades of meaning.

East European *regimes* have tended to view links with Western governments mainly in a tactical way: as means of economic support, sources of Western technology, instruments of legitimation vis-à-vis their populations, and sometimes, as Romania has most conspicuously done, as ways to expand their maneuverability in relations with Moscow. But no regime has ever sought a genuine rapprochement with the Western powers, not only because the Soviet Union would not permit it but also because it would be a threat to the very survival of the regime concerned.

For their part, many members of today's East European *societies* would like nothing better than a rapprochement with the West. In fact, they tend to see the West in idealized terms of liberty and prosperity, the antithesis of what they have experienced under communist rule. There are distinctions to be made among the attitudes of East European societies toward the West, however, mostly as a result of their past. The ruling and educated classes of Bohemia, Moravia, Poland, Hungary, Romania, Serbia, and Croatia had an

39

affinity with or sought to imitate their counterparts in Western Europe. (The same, of course, could be said about the ruling class in St. Petersburg.) The artificial creation called the German Democratic Republic is obviously a special case. Central European intellectuals had strong cultural affinities with the West, as Milan Kundera has explained passionately.[1] More comprehensively, the westward gravitational pull of Roman Catholicism gave almost the whole populations of Central and Eastern Europe a sense of common belief and culture with Catholic Western nations. But the religious, cultural, and social affinities of the Balkan states were historically oriented more toward Constantinople, Kiev, or Moscow. Europe was, for most Balkan peoples, a vague concept, a world with which they had little in common. They had little knowledge of and made no distinction among the various countries of Europe. Before World War II, for example, relatively few Bulgarians regarded themselves as being European at all. A young man going to a university in, say, Leipzig or Paris was said to be "going to Europe" for his education.

The question must still be asked: how far down the intellectual and social ladders did Central Europe's feeling of historical mutuality with Western Europe extend? Obviously the mass of nineteenth and early twentieth century Polish, Hungarian, and Czech peasants and workers were hardly animated about European cultural unity. The West for them meant emigration, an escape from the miseries of their existence. And while some Poles found work in the mines and heavy industries of Germany and France, for the vast majority of emigrants the destination was America. Thus for millions of ordinary people in east central Europe, and many parts of southeastern Europe as well, America entered popular mythology and psychology as the land of hope and promise in a way no other Western country could ever do.

Differentiation, therefore, is necessary in this context not only with regard to the East but also to the West. For many years, to a relatively small group of East European intellectuals the West meant the European historical and cultural tradition. For an infinitely greater

---

1. See, for example, Kundera's speech on receiving the Jerusalem Prize for literature, published as "Man Thinks; God Laughs," *New York Review of Books,* vol. 32 (June 13, 1985), pp. 11–12; also his interview with Olga Carlisle, "A Talk with Milan Kundera," *New York Times Magazine,* May 19, 1985, pp. 72–85. For a brilliant review article on this subject, see Timothy Garton Ash, "Does Central Europe Exist?" *New York Review of Books,* vol. 33 (October 9, 1986), pp. 45–52.

number of what are now called East Europeans, the West meant not only the hope of America but also contact with it through relatives and fellow villagers who had gone there.

After nearly forty years of the communist era in Eastern Europe, however, some of these generalizations need to be modified. Soviet domination has undoubtedly made many East Europeans, including those in the Balkan states, more conscious of their Europeanness. The distance in this respect between the northern and southern tiers of Eastern Europe is much narrower than before. To cite perhaps the most extreme example, many Bulgarian intellectuals now set great store by the West European connection. Thus the Bulgarian Academy of Sciences, though still oriented toward the Soviet Union, has developed many fruitful contacts with academic institutions in Western Europe.

Similarly, as the relative political and cultural importance of Western Europe and the United States has undergone a profound change, so the image of the West has become rather different in the eyes of most East Europeans. The distinction between Western Europe and the United States became blurred as America began making a strong impact on the East European mind. Then, as military, political, and even cultural supremacy moved across the Atlantic, the United States displaced Western Europe as the leader and torchbearer of the West. There are many indications of this, one of the most significant being the dramatic rise of English to become the premier foreign language throughout the region. And as international relations became polarized, with the superpower relationship as their determining aspect, the sheer multifaceted power of the United States greatly enhanced its significance. Finally, just as American culture and scholarship began to dominate the attention of East European intellectuals, so American subcultures and countercultures began to prove irresistible to millions of East European young people. This fascination is a matter for some concern among their elders—and not just those in the communist establishment—but the phenomenon shows no sign of fading. For most young people in Eastern Europe, Radio Luxembourg with its incessant American-style rock music remains the most popular Western broadcasting station.

Many Western observers tend to ignore the emergence of American dominance in East European popular attitudes toward the West because of their natural (and justified) excitement about the Euro-

peanness of the whole of Europe, a concept increasingly stressed by
East European intellectuals. The enthusiasm for a united Europe
commonly found in continental Western Europe in the early 1960s
has largely faded. But much of it has passed to Eastern Europe, where
the worsening economic situation has bestowed on the concept the
allure of the impossible dream. Moreover, despite the emergence of
the United States, there remains strong residual Eastern sentiment
for certain West European countries. France is the main beneficiary,
most noticeably in Poland and Romania. Austria evokes nostalgic
memories and current envy. As the citadel of Catholicism, Rome has
remained an inspiration for many, perhaps more than ever with a
Pole on the throne of St. Peter and religion more than holding its
own in Eastern Europe. Many East Europeans also regard Italy with
affection. Conversely, there was originally a strong antipathy in
Poland, the Czech Lands (Bohemia and Moravia), and Yugoslavia,
though not in the rest of Eastern Europe, toward Germany, but this
is now receding. Western Europe, then, remains of great importance
in the minds and imaginations of many East Europeans. And in
physical terms, of course, it is accessible to them in a way the United
States will never be.

Western Europe also retains a fascination for many East Europeans
who form part of the ruling establishments in their countries but are
not part of the leadership. They include the technical and economic
intelligentsia, the managerial strata, and members of the cultural
officialdom. Their opportunities for travel to Western Europe are
greater than to the United States and are considered almost as
perquisites of office. During the détente of the 1970s, technical and
economic officials were unquestionably impressed with achievements
observed in their visits westward and were dismayed at the possibility
of their having to end in the more restrictive economic and political
conditions of the 1980s.

But, without denigrating Western Europe's importance, West
Europeans (and Americans) must recognize that the United States is
no longer the far-off land of hope to which East Europeans emigrated.
The vicissitudes of international power, the cultural and educational
progress of America, and the many-sided revolution in communications have all precipitated the American presence into Eastern Europe,
made America itself less remote, and strengthened popular awareness
of it. That has been the most important development in East European
conceptions of the West in the past half century.

The Evolving Relationship

If the United States has so rapidly gained ground on Western Europe in the popular imagination of Eastern Europe, on the state level East European contacts with Western Europe have been and still are more important than those with the United States. But these contacts have been slow in developing. The Iron Curtain rung down by Stalin shortly after World War II was practically impenetrable and only began to be cautiously raised after his death. Shortly afterwards, the Hungarian Revolution and the Polish October of 1956 impressed on the new Soviet leaders how volatile the situation in Eastern Europe still was and how careful Moscow had to be in allowing contacts with Western Europe.

Intra-European relations were also impeded by the so-called Hallstein Doctrine of the Bonn government, which prevented West Germany from establishing diplomatic relations with any government that recognized the German Democratic Republic. This interdiction was waived by Konrad Adenauer himself in the case of the Soviet Union in 1955, but for the East European socialist states it held for another twelve years. The Hallstein Doctrine was significant because for three decades the Federal Republic of Germany, through its geographic location but mainly through its burgeoning economic power, has been by far the most important West European state in the eyes of East European officialdom.[2]

As early as 1957 two significant developments, the presentation of the Rapacki plan and the signing of the Treaty of Rome, illustrated this importance. The Rapacki plan, put forward by the Polish government through its foreign minister, Adam Rapacki, called for neutralizing a broad belt of Central European territory, including the two Germanys. The West rejected the plan out of hand and it was allowed to die, although recently some West German total pacifists, nuclear pacifists, and neutralists have wistfully resurrected it as an example of Eastern reasonableness, Western intransigence, and "what might have been."[3] Such retroactive yearnings can be dealt with

2. See William E. Griffith, *The Ostpolitik of the Federal Republic of Germany* (MIT Press, 1978).

3. See, for example—although he does not specifically mention the Rapacki plan— Otto Schily's contribution to the published symposium, *Reden über das eigene Land: Deutschland 2* (Munich: C. Bertelsmann Verlag GmbH, 1984), pp. 33–51.

summarily. Although some analysts have argued that the plan was primarily a Polish initiative (few have gone so far as to suggest that it was presented without prior consultation with Moscow),[4] it was actually one in a long list of Soviet and Soviet-inspired efforts to undermine the Western alliance by weakening and manipulating the Federal Republic. The degree of Polish commitment to the proposals is intriguing, however. Certainly Warsaw was acting as a proxy for Moscow, but the Polish regime must have seen the essence of the plan as in the Polish national interest. The plan would neutralize what many felt at the time to be a new German threat looming just after the old one had been defeated at such a high cost.

Within the framework of a Soviet initiative, therefore, the Poles' own interest was being served. There are other examples in Eastern Europe of this syndrome: initiatives under the name of Prime Minister Chivu Stoica of Romania in 1957 and 1959 for an atom-free zone in the Balkans, the Bulgarian initiatives beginning in 1960 for military reductions in the Balkans and for various forms of bilateral (not multilateral) cooperation, and the renewed Bulgarian pressure since 1981 for a nuclear-free zone in the Balkans.[5] The Soviets have used their allies as proxies in many parts of the world—the Cubans and East Germans dramatically in Africa—and a similar East European role in relations with Western Europe should not be ignored.

The second indication of West Germany's importance, the Treaty of Rome establishing the European Economic Community, was to have major repercussions. A protocol to the treaty enshrined the ideal of German unity in a manner that gave the young German Democratic Republic material rewards it could never have expected. In effect, the East German state secured commercial access to the Federal Republic completely free of tariffs and a foothold in the Common Market itself, a fact that partly accounts for (without totally explaining) its subsequent economic successes and that has also aroused the envy of its Comecon associates.

4. For an excellent, balanced discussion of the Rapacki plan, see Helga Haftendorn, *Sicherheit und Entspannung: Zur Aussenpolitik der Bundesrepublik Deutschland* (Baden-Baden: Nomos Verlagsgesellschaft, 1983), pp. 110–16.

5. For Romanian and Bulgarian initiatives in the 1950s and 1960s see J. F. Brown, *Bulgaria Under Communist Rule* (Praeger, 1970), pp. 269–73. For Bulgarian efforts since 1981 see Patrick Moore, "Balkan Sources of International Instability" in Vojtech Mastny, ed., *Soviet/East European Survey, 1983–1984: Selected Research and Analysis from Radio Free Europe/Radio Liberty* (Duke University Press, 1985), pp. 259–65.

In different ways, therefore, the Federal Republic soon was established as the Western state having the greatest importance for the East European governments, and this at a time that its foreign policy was much more passive than active. In the 1960s, when Bonn's *Ostpolitik* slowly developed under Chancellor Ludwig Erhard and Foreign Minister Gerhard Schröder, West Germany's importance and attractiveness increased in Eastern Europe. The divisiveness these qualities could cause was illustrated by the mixed reactions to the so-called peace note of 1966 that Erhard sent to the Soviet Union and its allies, urging a new start in relations between them and the Federal Republic. (The note had been preceded by exchanges of trade missions between Bonn and almost all the East European capitals.) The Soviet Union, Poland, and Czechoslovakia flatly rejected Erhard's overture. Hungary did so less churlishly, while Romania and Bulgaria chose not to reply (at least no reply was ever published). Romania had already established itself as the maverick of the Warsaw Pact and was soon to establish full diplomatic relations with Bonn. But the silence of Bulgaria, considered by many to be Moscow's most subservient satellite, was remarkable. While not daring openly to flout Soviet authority, Sofia unmistakably conveyed to Bonn its wish for better relations when conditions were more propitious.[6]

Later, when the interaction between Willy Brandt's *Ostpolitik* and Leonid Brezhnev's *Westpolitik* became one of the main factors in world diplomacy, Bonn's relations with Eastern Europe were regularized; with East Berlin they became as normalized as that unique situation would allow.[7] The governments in Warsaw and Prague set aside the wartime problems they had inherited in their relations with Bonn, though not without considerable difficulty and a readiness to resurrect the German bogey whenever they were to feel it propagandistically advantageous. With Hungary, Bulgaria, and Romania, the regularization amounted even to a semblance of reconciliation. But whatever the East European governments' motivations, whatever the differences of degree or sincerity in their rapprochement with the Federal Republic, for all of them it was Bonn that came to dominate their relations with the West.

The importance of the West German connection was demonstrated

6. Brown, *Bulgaria Under Communist Rule*, p. 285.
7. See F. Stephen Larrabee, *The Politics of Reconciliation: Soviet Policy towards West Germany, 1964–1972* (Ph.D. dissertation, Columbia University, 1978).

again as recently as the summer of 1984, when differences of interest among members of the Warsaw Pact were made clear. Bonn's decision to begin deploying American Pershing II and cruise missiles in November 1983, after strenuous Warsaw Pact attempts to prevent it, resulted in the Federal Republic's being placed next to the United States as an object of Soviet anger. But it became evident that the GDR, Hungary, Romania, and, in a less demonstrative way, Bulgaria were loath to follow the Soviet lead, while Czechoslovakia and Poland did so enthusiastically. *Pravda* and *Neues Deutschland,* the GDR's official newspaper, even conducted a brief debate in public. Hungary formulated views on bloc cooperation and the role of small states that sounded distinctly Romanian, and a Budapest–East Berlin axis briefly developed. In the end the Soviets restored order. Both Erich Honecker and Todor Zhivkov had to call off planned visits to the Federal Republic, and the public argument stopped, but not before the divisions and the differences had made themselves clear.[8]

West Germany's initial hesitancy and subsequent quiet diplomacy contrasted markedly with the flamboyance of French policy under Charles de Gaulle, whose pan-European vision certainly included Eastern Europe. While accepting the hegemony of the Soviet Union there, de Gaulle argued that the stability of that hegemony would depend on more freedom for the satellites and more responsiveness by the governments to the aspirations of their societies. This was the message he carried on his visits to Poland in 1966 and Romania in 1968. In Poland it was courteously rejected by the Gomulka regime, ostensibly on the grounds that the continuing German menace required East European unity and precluded relaxing controls. In Romania de Gaulle was preaching to the converted, at least insofar as more freedom from Moscow was concerned. His impact on Eastern Europe was considerable, however. He engaged governments directly and aroused expectations among many segments of society. Only after the drama of his interventionism was over and as West German economic supremacy became universally clear did his exaggerated notions of France's role in Eastern Europe lose their credibility. But the gestures were impressive while they lasted. De Gaulle was rapturously received in Poland, recapturing popular affection for France

8. For an excellent narrative, with documentation of the whole dispute, see "East Berlin and Moscow: The Documentation of a Dispute," *Radio Free Europe Research,* vol. 9, pt. 3 (August 31, 1984), background report 158/84.

and restoking the fires of Polish nationalism. The visit gave a new lease of life to French prestige in Eastern Europe, which had been seriously damaged at Munich in 1938, when France acquiesced in giving Czechoslovakia's Sudetenland to Nazi Germany, and even more with the defeat of France in 1940.

Nowhere has the dichotomy between state and society been more evident than in East European responses to American policy. America's initial roll-back policy of the 1950s, associated with the administration of Dwight D. Eisenhower, was enunciated at a time when the communist regimes in Eastern Europe were still new and, despite the backing of the Red Army and their own forces of coercion, were not yet thoroughly confident of their power. Their lack of confidence was not mainly due to the fear of unaided popular rebellions but rather to the possibility—hoped for by many East Europeans—of some kind of deliverance by the West. This made the regimes all the more antagonistic to Washington, which they rightly considered the main source of their danger. The Hungarian tragedy of 1956 disabused noncommunist East Europeans of their illusions. Soviet and local communist domination was there to stay. The Soviets were ready to use force to keep their postwar gains. The West was not ready to use force to reverse them.

American policy after 1956 made manifest that Washington had drawn similar conclusions about realities in Eastern Europe. Since then, as explained in chapter 4, American policy has been generally consistent in content even if its accompanying rhetoric has varied considerably. It has sought a peaceful modification of communist rule, allowing more freedom for both East European states and peoples, with a comprehensive improvement in the conditions of the latter.

The nature of the East European response to this policy is difficult to gauge, and generalizations are dangerous. But it has become clear that the ruling regimes have welcomed Washington's acceptance— however reluctant—of their reality and general stability, and have responded to the American readiness to intensify relations with them. They have done so out of various motives. Romania has sought to use the United States to buttress its policy of semi-independence from Moscow. The GDR, not recognized by Washington until 1972, culti-vates the connection as part of its drive for equality in international affairs with the Federal Republic. Hungary sees the United States as a means of gaining greater diplomatic and economic maneuverability inside the Warsaw Pact. The Polish regime has deepened its relations because of popular pressure. All the East European states, with the possible exception of Czechoslovakia since 1968, have seen the economic value—and still more the economic potential—of better relations with the United States. And, with periodic exceptions, they have tended to see a certain prestige element in cultivating and broadening their relations with the other superpower. During periods of reaction in Eastern Europe, however, as in Czechoslovakia since 1968 and Poland since 1981, after serious confrontation with their own societies the regimes tend to hew closer to the Soviet Union and indulge in strong anti-American rhetoric. This is the natural response of rulers whose lack of legitimacy has recently been so painfully exposed.

As for the responses of East European societies, generalizations are also dangerous. But when the domestic conditions of a country are relatively good and show prospects of improvement, the American policy of aiding peaceful and beneficent evolution seems generally welcomed. This was the case in Czechoslovakia from the beginning of the 1960s until 1968, in Poland during the 1970s, and in Hungary since the mid-1960s. During such periods, most articulate East Europeans have also favored East-West détente, because they consider improved relations, especially between the two superpowers, as safeguarding their own domestic betterment. But when that process of betterment is abruptly terminated, belief in the prospect of gradual improvement is shattered and the resulting bitterness produces a dramatic reversal of opinion. People then demand that the West take a strong anti-Soviet stand and a similarly rigid posture toward the East European government concerned. This was especially evident among most Poles after the declaration of martial law in December 1981. President Ronald Reagan, mainly on the strength of his anti-Soviet and anticommunist rhetoric, became a hero for the Poles in their adversity, while the past or present advocates of détente were considered by many as little short of enemies of the Polish nation.

Such volatility and impressionability must be taken into account by Western policymakers. So should the general European inability to distinguish between the substance of a policy, the different emphases given to different aspects of it at different times, and the rhetoric that can disguise or distort its real character. The rhetoric of John F.

Kennedy's commitment to freedom in his inaugural address in 1961, for instance, and the fiery nature of some of President Reagan's utterances before 1985 were taken as expressions of actual policy. Reagan's sentiments were contrasted with what was considered the weakness of President Jimmy Carter. And yet Carter's initial emphasis on human rights and the generally firm but differentiating approach of his national security adviser, Zbigniew Brzezinski, had been compared favorably with the superpower *Realpolitik* of Richard Nixon and Henry Kissinger that had sought accommodation with Moscow.

Thus what to Americans would seem a consistent policy toward Eastern Europe since 1956 might seem almost the opposite to many East Europeans because they have attached importance to form while ignoring continuity of substance; in fact, for them form is substance. Indeed, no one can blame East Europeans for doubting the American claims of consistency. Their situation, perspective, and perception have been quite different from those of American policymakers. Under their system of government they are used to detecting basic changes from omissions, repetitions, or changes of stress, reading between the lines of official pronouncements. They are often totally unsuited for the task of understanding the openness and, at the same time, the mysteries of Western, and particularly American, public life.

The Economic Dimension

By the end of the 1940s, after the Soviet Union had stamped military and then political control over Eastern Europe, further insistence on economic as well as political and cultural isolation from the West was inevitable. As a result, the structure of East European commerce was almost completely transformed. Between the wars that commerce had been mainly oriented westward—by no means to the total benefit of individual East European countries. Trade with the Soviet Union had been negligible and for some countries nonexistent. Postwar Soviet domination reversed this situation and, in its early years, led to an economic exploitation that made Eastern Europe's misery between the two world wars look mild in comparison. But the transformation was not to remain total for very long. One of the most important aspects of recent East European economic history has been the partial return to relations with the West, especially with Western Europe.[9]

The role of the United States as a commercial partner for Eastern Europe has been relatively small, but it has not been without importance and has often been considered a barometer of Washington's political attitude toward any particular East European state. The granting of most-favored-nation (MFN) status and the provision of surplus grain supplies under Public Law 480 to Poland after October 1956 were the first examples of this policy; these privileges were withdrawn after Wojciech Jaruzelski's coup in December 1981. The granting of MFN status to Romania and later to Hungary also illustrates the point. In purely material terms, privileges such as MFN status may not amount to much, since Eastern Europe exports so little to the United States, but they are eagerly sought by most East European regimes, who resent their withdrawal, as in the case of Poland, or threatened withdrawal, as in the case of Romania. In 1983 Ceauşescu cancelled his proposed calibrated emigration tax, which was based on the estimated amounts of money the Romanian state had spent on a would-be emigrant's education, at least partly for fear of losing Romania's MFN status (and partly also in return for stronger financial inducements from Bonn).

The actual or potential importance of the American connection is also evident in other ways. Poland, whose economic ties were generally closer than those of any other East European country, complained bitterly when the United States imposed sanctions after December 1981. At the end of 1985 the Polish government claimed that they were doing serious damage to the economy.[10] Even allowing for exaggerations made for political reasons to cover up the regime's own economic failings and to discredit the Reagan administration, the damage may have been considerable. The GDR now imports large annual shipments of American feed grain. But it is probably Hungary that in recent years has shown itself, as will be seen later, most anxious to preserve the transatlantic connection.

9. For quantitative data on East European trade with the West, see appendix tables A-3, A-4, and A-5.

10. Jerzy Urban, the Polish government spokesman, claimed that American sanctions had done $15 billion damage to the Polish economy; see *Rzeczpospolita* (Warsaw), October 29, 1985. During 1986, leaders of the church and the Solidarity movement joined in urging the U.S. government to withdraw the remaining sanctions. In response to these views and a general amnesty to political prisoners in October, the United States did so in early 1987.

The role of the United States, therefore, has been small but not negligible. Obviously, Eastern Europe attaches vastly more importance to American trade than does the United States to East European trade. If détente resumes, and as the electronic revolution takes hold firmly in East European countries, they will very much want to strengthen connections with America to acquire the best technology available. This could present the United States with both an economic and political opportunity. If, however, the East Europeans were to encounter a wall of suspicion in Washington and an empty credit well in New York, they would turn to Japan or Western Europe or both. If the obstacles were too great in these markets, there would be no alternative except the introversion of Comecon.

But though there is real potential for the American economic presence to grow in Eastern Europe, it is unlikely ever to rival the West German presence. Indeed, given fairly normal political conditions and international relations, most East European countries will probably press the Soviet Union to permit more freedom to trade with Western Europe in general and the Federal Republic in particular. Moscow would then be faced with the familiar dilemma. It would be difficult to deny the East Europeans. On the one hand, the Soviets would presumably want to expand their own Western economic contacts. Some of Eastern Europe's Western contacts would lessen the need for Soviet support and subsidization, and such contacts would tend to defuse potentially explosive situations sparked by shortages and falling living standards. In addition, some technology could be transferred to the Soviet Union itself through Eastern Europe. On the other hand, the Soviets must be aware by now of the political and ideological dangers of an East European westward drift. Gorbachev's reaction to such a situation will be instructive. He is bent on modernizing his own country, and though one school of Soviet thought insists that this can be done largely alone, he presumably realizes that Western goods could play a key role. It would be difficult then to deny the East Europeans the same access. The problem for Moscow is to mitigate its dangers.

Finally, no discussion of this economic dimension can avoid the question of loans and credits. During the 1970s the GDR, Poland, Hungary, Romania, and Bulgaria, as well as the Soviet Union itself, contracted very big loans, government or commercial or both, on Western money markets. (Outside the alliance Yugoslavia also ran up massive debts.) Industrial modernization, the main purpose of the borrowing, may have been achieved to some extent in the GDR, Hungary, and Bulgaria. But in Poland, Romania, and Yugoslavia it failed disastrously, leaving these countries with serious repayment problems and bad financial reputations.

Western financial circles judged the whole East European credit adventure a calamitous failure, so much so that in 1982 and 1983 there was much talk of possible default. Some of the fears were exaggerated: the Western banking system now has protective mechanisms guarding against widespread financial bankruptcy. In any case the fears soon receded when Western governments and bankers realized that Eastern Europe's debts were far smaller than those of Latin American and other third world countries and that hopes of at least some repayment were not all that dim when measured against the gloomy prospects in those other countries. Indeed, East Germany, Hungary, and Bulgaria, although still heavily in debt, recovered their creditworthiness with surprising speed and began contracting new loans as early as 1984. Romania, too, was exerting every effort— mostly at the expense of the Romanian consumer—to meet its repayment obligations promptly. Yugoslavia and Poland, however, remained in serious difficulty. Yugoslavia, a member of the International Monetary Fund, was trying hard to meet that body's guidelines for sound financial management, although the guidelines had become another divisive issue inside the regime, with the enemies of reform accusing the IMF of flouting Yugoslav sovereignty. For Poland, finally admitted to the IMF in 1986, debt rescheduling became a perennial, difficult, and humiliating round after round of negotiations. For all the countries involved—East and West—the lending and borrowing policies of the late 1960s and 1970s had set in motion a carousel off which neither side could easily jump.[11]

Eastern Europe's *Westpolitik*

Improved economic relations were certainly one crucial reason for Eastern Europe's renewed interest in the West and may have been the impetus that first led to the partial turn westward. But taking

11. For a good review of the progress of East European indebtedness through the 1970s and into the 1980s, see "Günstigere Aussenwirschaftsposition des Ostblock," *Neue Zürcher Zeitung* (December 1/2, 1984), an analysis of *Economic Bulletin for Europe*, vol. 36 (United Nations, 1984).

East European communist history as a whole, there has also been a significant political and diplomatic impetus.

For some East European states, this factor is difficult to define, sometimes difficult to identify; for others it is more simple. Belgrade, for example, cultivated relations with the West because of Tito's break with Stalin in 1948. For five years, when Yugoslavia was beleaguered by Stalin and his minions, the Western security guarantee was vital. Later the siege was slowly lifted and relations with the Soviets improved, but Yugoslavia was also determined to maintain good relations with the Western powers to forward its own independent interests. It became a founder of the nonaligned movement and one of the world's leading neutrals. As such, and as a communist state, no matter how unorthodox, Yugoslavia understandably sought to normalize and improve relations with Moscow, economically and politically. At the same time it has continued to value its relations with the West. It may, indeed, be forced to seek closer relations and more help from the United States, the Federal Republic, and Italy if the Soviets try to take advantage of its growing internal weaknesses.

As a country outside the Warsaw Pact, Yugoslavia does not fall within the purview of this study, but in view of its vital strategic importance it cannot be totally ignored. Its case, too, illustrates a point that Western policymakers tend to ignore at their peril. Yugoslav behavior has often irritated the West. Its foreign policy has seemed less than neutral, often aligning itself with that of the Soviet Union. Its domestic policy throughout the past thirty-five years, and especially recently, has sometimes been contemptuous of human rights. Today it is being governed politically and economically in a manner that often appears little short of disastrous. This situation could lead to calls in the West—more serious than those made hitherto—for a reappraisal of policy toward Belgrade. Yet the facts remain that Yugoslavia was the first communist country to look to the West, its strategic location is vital, and its foreign policy, despite irritating aspects, has on balance been favorable to Western interests for almost four decades. Obviously, the main responsibility for putting their house in order rests with the Yugoslavs themselves. They have so far shown few signs of assuming it; but they would show even fewer without sympathetic Western concern.[12]

12. The best running commentaries in the West on Yugoslav affairs are by the *Neue Zürcher Zeitung, Süddeutsche Zeitung, Frankfurter Allgemeine Zeitung, Le Monde,* and by Slobodan Stankovic in the *Radio Free Europe Research* series.

Albania may also turn to the West for support. Tirana's break with Moscow in 1961 caused it to become a close ally of China rather than the West. Seventeen years later Enver Hoxha formally ended the relationship and set his country on a course of churlish isolation. Yet before his death early in 1985 there were signs that even Albania might be stepping out of its shell in a westerly direction. Under Hoxha's successor, Ramiz Alia, this process might become established and accelerate out of sheer economic necessity. By historical association (though not always the happiest) and geographic proximity, Italy would seem the most likely country toward which Albania would gravitate. But though Italy could presumably give the economic support required, it might not be able or willing to provide the necessary security guarantees. The problem would then become one for the Western alliance as a whole, that is, one mainly for the United States. Again, the arguments for not helping Yugoslavia could apply to Albania. But a glance at the map, rather than any review of the country's human rights record, might be the deciding factor here.[13]

Yugoslavia never was a member of the Warsaw Pact. Albania only formally left it after the Soviet-led invasion of Czechoslovakia in 1968, although it had ceased all active cooperation by 1961. Romania, however, was a founding member of both the Warsaw Pact and Comecon. Today it could hardly be a more passive Pact participant, and it is still Comecon's most difficult member, although economic necessity has recently made it noticeably less obstructive than before.

Romania's long-running quarrel with the Soviet Union is hardly relevant in this context. What is relevant is the means by which it defended and then sustained itself. When the Sino-Soviet dispute was coming to its bursting point in the late 1950s, Bucharest skillfully used the Chinese in its intrabloc sparring with Moscow. Later, after the dispute had become a schism and openly befriending China ran the risk of severe Soviet reprisal, Romania continued its association and was rewarded with considerable Chinese economic aid. But in the 1960s Bucharest also turned to the West, most notably to France and the Federal Republic of Germany, risking Soviet condemnation by establishing diplomatic relations with Bonn in January 1967 when Moscow was opposing such action by the East Europeans. Eighteen months later Romania incurred even more dangerous Soviet wrath by not only refusing to take part in the invasion of Czechoslovakia

13. The best running commentaries on Albanian affairs are by Louis Zanga in the *Radio Free Europe Research* series.

but publicly opposing it. Subsequently, relations with the United States greatly improved, with exchanges of presidential visits and commercial privileges granted by Washington. Romania's trade with the Soviet Union dropped to less than a quarter of its total trade, considerably less than the Western share. Its good relations and reputation with the West appeared assured.

By the early 1980s, however, relations had become shaky. This was evident not in any official action on either side but in a growing Western exasperation with Ceauşescu's domestic mismanagement, abuse of civil rights, personal style of (mis)rule, and what some consider to be an inching back toward the Soviet Union in foreign policy. On the latter score, it has even been argued that because the Soviet Union tolerated the Romanian deviation for so long it must have either discounted its importance or seen advantages in having Bucharest demonstrate the tolerance and liberalism of the Eastern alliance.

While it is difficult to take seriously this interpretation of Romania's external relations, on the domestic side there is no doubt that Ceauşescu's record in the past ten years has led many in the West to question both the wisdom and the morality of supporting him. It has also led many in Romania itself to question the value of a nationalist foreign policy that is accompanied by such oppressive inefficiency at home. And the growing Western antipathy has reinforced arguments about Romania's relative strategic unimportance, certainly when compared with Yugoslavia or even Albania.

But Romania has established itself as a quasi-client state of the West, and as late as the mid-1980s there was little evidence to support complaints that it was reverting to the status of Soviet satellite. If the West were to withdraw its support, moreover, its position in Eastern Europe as a whole might suffer. Withdrawal would be seen as a gesture of weakness vis-à-vis Moscow. Disliked though Romania is throughout the region, abandoning it could lead to a general loss of Western credibility and could discourage other East European regimes wishing to loosen Soviet ties. Abandonment could also lead to the downfall of Ceauşescu. This in itself might be no great loss, but his successor would hardly be encouraged to maintain previous Romanian foreign policy. Perhaps most serious of all, abandonment could shake any self-confidence that might still remain within the inchoate Yugoslav leadership.

Finally, with respect to human rights, it is not quite true that the

West has no influence on Ceauşescu's domestic policy. As previously mentioned, American warnings about potential loss of most-favored-nation status, as well as West German representations and inducements, caused Ceauşescu to shelve his callous emigration tax. The warnings even seemed to persuade him to allow more emigration. Such influence may be relatively weak, and the West has had constantly to endure being manipulated by a Romanian regime still confident that its value permits it the kind of license the West deplores. If the situation calls for patience on the part of Western governments, it also calls for the Ceauşescu regime to take Western public opinion much more seriously than it does domestic opinion.

The Special Case of East Germany

Although Yugoslavia, Albania, and Romania (the last with some reservations) fit into the same broad category of East European states in their relations with the West and in the West's relations with them, the German Democratic Republic is in a category by itself.

Whereas all the other East European members of the Warsaw Pact are dominated only by one country, the Soviet Union, the GDR is dominated by two: the Soviet Union and the Federal Republic. Seldom if ever has a country experienced the invidious distinction of being in such a double shadow, with the countries casting the shadows belonging to adversarial alliances. Of course, the types of domination are very dissimilar. The Soviet Union's is symbolized by the 400,000 troops stationed on East German soil and the oil and gas pipelines that are both the GDR's economic lifelines and symbols of its dependency. The Federal Republic's domination is explained less by material factors, despite the financial and economic advantages the GDR derives from Bonn, than by its very existence as a free, democratic, and prosperous Germany; its attraction for most of the East German population; and the political-psychological compulsion of the GDR's leadership to try to achieve equal and permanent recognition with West Germany on both the European and world stages—and to force such recognition from the Federal Republic itself. By the mid-1980s the attraction may have become somewhat attenuated by the Federal Republic's own economic difficulties, reflected in a high unemployment rate. The GDR, for its part, appeared to have recovered from its own economic difficulties of the late 1970s and was showing greater self-confidence. Many of its citizens also seemed to be losing their inferiority complex vis-à-vis West Germany. But it would take a long time to make any essential change in the character of the established relationship.[14]

Much of East German policy in East-West relations and at the international level generally can be explained by this near obsession with the Federal Republic. To take one example: East Germany's active support for so-called liberation movements in the third world, especially in Africa, is mostly assumed to be a mark of subservience to the Soviet Union, a reflection of true satellite status. While that is undoubtedly true, the support must also result from East Berlin's compelling necessity to show there is another Germany that is powerful and capable of action on the world scale.

The basic policy of the GDR adamantly opposes any eventual German unification or even confederation. Instead, it seeks to achieve full recognition as the third Germanic state (Austria being the second). Outwardly, East Germany has already achieved considerable progress toward this goal. With diplomatic recognition by more than 130 countries, it has come a long way indeed from the pariah status imposed on it by the Hallstein Doctrine. And for fifteen years it has received diplomatic quasi-recognition from the Federal Republic itself. It has built an impressive, well-run economy by communist standards. Even by world standards the GDR is now respected as a substantial economic power. Diplomatically, it derives great advantage from the open opposition in Eastern Europe, and the generally tacit if now perhaps declining opposition in Western Europe, to the very concept of German reunification. Giulio Andreotti, the Italian foreign minister, may have broken the official Western vow of silence on the subject when in 1984 he aired his misgivings about pan-Germanism, but he was simply relaying a widespread West European sentiment.[15] The GDR still does not enjoy much respect as a state, of course—its hallmark is the Berlin Wall and the watchtowers on the border with the Federal Republic. But rarely has a state enjoying so little international respect been regarded as such an international necessity.

14. See Arnulf Baring, "Wieviel Spielraum hat die DDR?" *Frankfurter Allgemeine Zeitung,* October 3, 1985.

15. See James M. Markham: "For Both East and West Two Germanys Is Better," *New York Times,* September 23, 1984.

The diplomacy of Erich Honecker, its president and party leader, should be seen as part of the GDR's quest for national identity rather than a groping toward some form of association with the Federal Republic. Honecker set great store on his proposed visit to West Germany in the summer of 1984, which was scotched, at least for the time being, by a Soviet leadership then in disarray. His purpose in coming closer was to illustrate the distance between the two countries. He would have come as president of the German Democratic Republic, a separate German state, visiting the other German state in his official capacity. Why, then, did Moscow oppose a visit that would have helped symbolize the major Russian international success of the twentieth century, the emasculation of German power? There may be several answers, but perhaps the most important is the basic Soviet mistrust of Germans, West or East, particularly when engaged in something Moscow does not control. Honecker may yet visit the Federal Republic, but Gorbachev will seek to make sure that the visit is coordinated with him and is seen to be so.

There appear to be two main obstacles to the East German aim of a separation accepted as permanent. One is the attitude of most East Germans. There is considerable debate among Western observers and among Germans themselves about just how legitimate the GDR is in the eyes of its own population. The most perspicacious observers agree that, despite the public resignation that started with the building of the Berlin Wall in 1961, the undoubted raising of the standard of living, a residual sense of Prussian discipline in many citizens, and the steady easing of repression over the years—all unquestionably important factors—the only real sense of identification most East Germans have with their state is with its formidable athletes. During the summer of 1984, when Honecker appeared to be pressing for closer ties with the Federal Republic and to be defying or ignoring Moscow in the process, he can hardly have viewed the sharp rise in his popularity at home—precisely the result of what he was doing—with any special enthusiasm. The population also generally greeted with bemusement his efforts to claim historic figures like the once execrated Martin Luther and Frederick the Great as the GDR's very own; even Bismarck has enjoyed a major rehabilitation. Such a campaign should not be dismissed with derision. It is part of a serious East German effort to compete with the Federal Republic in the degree of its Germanness. But many East German citizens will be more impressed by the possibility that Honecker's actions may lead to greater internal relaxation.[16]

What most East Germans appear to have hoped from Honecker's diplomacy in 1984 was the right to visit the Federal Republic, not merely once but on a regular basis, just as Hungarians have been permitted for many years to visit the West. (At present, only GDR pensioners may visit regularly.) The chances are that most would return to the GDR, but the East Berlin regime is still not self-confident enough to take that chance. The most important of the so-called Gera proposals, made by Honecker in 1980, for a full normalization of relations with West Germany, was that Bonn give up its insistence, enshrined in West Germany's Basic Law (its constitution), that East Germans are automatically entitled to citizenship in the Federal Republic.[17] If Bonn were to do this—and some support for such action is growing in the Federal Republic—East Germans would find it much more difficult to become officially absorbed into the Federal Republic. East Berlin might then be prepared to take the risk of easing travel regulations.

The second obstacle to total separation is the GDR's economic dependence on the Federal Republic. Besides the tariff-free access to West German markets permitted by the Treaty of Rome, East Berlin annually receives about DM 2.5 billion from the Federal Republic. This includes more than DM 1 billion from the West German and West Berlin budgets as compensation for various services and for buying out political prisoners in the GDR; private contributions and visa fees make up the balance. The GDR also has access to a steady flow of West German loans: in 1983–84 it received almost DM 2 billion in two spectacular credits that aroused pointed Soviet criticism.[18]

But need this dependence be a real obstacle after all? It would certainly be skillful diplomacy and good business on East Berlin's part if it could get Bonn to finance a part of its pursuit of total separation. But Bonn has maintained its financial generosity year after year,

16. See Baring, "Wieviel Spielraum hat die DDR?" See also "Wandlungen im Geschichtsbild der DDR," *Neue Zürcher Zeitung* (Fernausgabe), October 18, 1985.

17. For a discussion of the Gera proposals, see Ronald D. Asmus, "East and West Germany: Continuity and Change," *World Today*, vol. 40 (April 1984), pp. 142–51.

18. For an excellent review of East German economic relations with the Federal Republic, see John Garland, "FRG-GDR Economic Relations," in *East European Economies: Slow Growth in the 1980's*, vol. 3: *Country Studies on Eastern Europe and Yugoslavia*, Joint Economic Committee, 99 Cong. 2 sess. (GPO, 1986), pp. 169–206.

often in the face of extreme provocation, not only to help alleviate the condition of fellow Germans in the GDR but also to keep open some avenues that might lead to eventual reunification. If the GDR were ever to achieve completely separate status, supported internationally and domestically, this hope would disappear and so, presumably, would much of the financial largesse, although some economic concessions might still continue to flow on humanitarian or strictly economic grounds. The GDR would then be close to getting the best of both worlds.

Developments in the 1980s

Because of the special features of the Western connections of Romania and East Germany, the earlier sections of this chapter have given particular attention to them. It remains to summarize recent developments in the Western relationships of the other four East European countries treated in this study.

POLAND

After December 1981 Poland's special relationship with the West became one of rancor and recrimination. The Jaruzelski regime particularly castigated U.S. economic sanctions, sometimes blaming them for many of Poland's economic ills and sometimes dismissing them as malicious pinpricks that have done no effective damage. As for the popular view of sanctions, most Poles appear to have favored them for a considerable time after December 1981. By the end of 1985, however, this attitude had largely given way. Josef Cardinal Glemp and the episcopate were in favor of their being lifted, as was former Solidarity leader Lech Walesa. When the American government finally withdrew all remaining sanctions in early 1987, Polish opinion generally approved the move as sensible, inevitable, and perhaps overdue.

Poland's relations with the Federal Republic also turned sour during the early 1980s. The Jaruzelski regime revived the image of the German bogeyman after the Soviet Union, having failed to dissuade Bonn from deploying American intermediate-range nuclear missiles, bracketed Chancellor Helmut Kohl with Ronald Reagan as the two main current obstacles to peace. This change came after more than ten years of improving relations between Warsaw and Bonn, which the evident friendship of Edward Gierek and Helmut Schmidt had done much to accelerate. The growing cordiality on the official level had coincided with a diminution of the historical Polish antipathy toward Germans on which Moscow and earlier Polish regimes had successfully played. How much effect the official reversal had on popular opinion is difficult to say. But the propaganda purpose of Jaruzelski's policy toward Bonn was so obvious that the suspicions of many Poles were probably directed more against their own government than against any Western power.

After the 1983 visit of Pope John Paul II to Poland, it seemed to many that the regime was making a genuine effort at reconciliation with the population, an effort reflected in a general amnesty in July 1984. But the murder of Father Jerzy Popieluszko, the pro-Solidarity parish priest, by security officers in October 1984 again widened the gulf between people and regime, even though Jaruzelski was in no way responsible for the crime. The trial of Father Popieluszko's murderers did little to allay public anger. The regime attempted to put the church in the dock along with the four killers and subsequently mounted a campaign against it that did not exclude even the pope. Throughout much of 1985, Polish public life was marked by continuing acrimony. It appeared that Jaruzelski, though his position might be unchallenged, was not able to assert his authority or his will in many areas.

But 1985 also saw renewed Polish efforts to improve relations, and hence to reopen economic possibilities, with the West. Jaruzelski visited New York to attend the special fortieth anniversary meeting of the UN General Assembly. On the way he stopped in Rome, where he had talks with Italian government leaders but failed in his efforts to meet the pope, although John Paul II did receive Foreign Minister Stefan Olszowski in June. In New York Jaruzelski was shunned by senior American officials but nevertheless made it clear that the Polish government wanted more contacts and the normalization of economic relations. In November he achieved a real diplomatic success in being received personally by François Mitterrand in Paris, a gesture for which the French president suffered severe public criticism. A new, more conciliatory approach became evident in relations with West Germany. In December Willy Brandt, chancellor when the Polish–

West German treaty of 1970 was signed, visited Warsaw to mark its fifteenth anniversary. His Social Democratic delegation was courteously received, and it was evident that the Polish friendliness was not meant solely for the Federal Republic's opposition party. The Poles mentioned the desirability of a visit by President Richard von Weizsäcker and, though this seemed hardly likely in the immediate future, the mere suggestion of it reflected a mellowing of the government's attitude.

Finally, early in 1987 came a breakthrough in Polish relations with the West. On a state visit to Italy in January, Jaruzelski was received by the pope as well as the Italian leaders. Almost immediately afterward the U.S. deputy secretary of state, John Whitehead, visited Poland and the way was cleared for lifting the American economic sanctions.

Toward the end of 1985, as Warsaw's Western policy became more active, the Jaruzelski leadership began to show more confidence at home. Active opposition to it was receding, a fact reflected in the inability of Solidarity to organize effective strikes and in the regime's relative success in the parliamentary elections in October 1985, when the underground's call for a boycott went largely unheeded. After the elections Jaruzelski stepped aside from the premiership, which went to an economist, Zbigniew Messner. But he retained the party leadership and became head of state. Most important, he remained commander in chief of the armed forces. The same reshuffle also saw the eclipse of Foreign Minister Stefan Olszowski, believed to be the most prominent and ablest exponent of the hard line.

At the Polish party congress in July 1986, Jaruzelski received a decisive, unequivocal show of support from Mikhail Gorbachev, who attended. It was the clearest indication of Soviet backing since martial law was declared in December 1981. Thus strengthened, Jaruzelski continued his efforts at reconciliation at home and at gaining more respectability in the West. A general political amnesty was declared in September 1986 that released all the Solidarity leaders still incarcerated. But the situation was still fragile. All it needed to collapse was another incident like the Popieluszko murder, or even for several of the Solidarity activists to be thrown back in jail. The regime knew this, as did the Polish people.

In the meantime, one relevant aspect of policy should not be overlooked: the regime's liberality in matters of travel to the West and even emigration. In 1984 the government issued 700,000 passports; in 1985 it was estimated there would be another 1.15 million, almost 4 percent of the total population, a proportion matched in Eastern Europe only by Hungary.[19] The regime's intention was both to provide a safety valve and to rid itself of potential troublemakers. (East German policy in 1984 was similar, but on a much smaller scale.) There was no doubt about the short-term relief this liberality brought, but the hopelessness of the domestic situation was such that many young Poles were deciding to leave permanently. Their departure would be a loss that in the longer term Poland could ill afford.

CZECHOSLOVAKIA

Czechoslovakia's relations with the West have been virtually in cold storage since 1968. Even before that, right from the February coup of 1948, they had fluctuated between the coldly correct and the downright hostile. Czechoslovakia was, except for the special case of the GDR, the slowest East European state to respond positively to Bonn's *Ostpolitik*. During the Prague Spring, anxious though Alexander Dubček was for improved Western relations, the government had to be more circumspect than it might have wished so as to allay Soviet suspicions. In the 1970s, political and cultural relations were kept to the barest minimum; economic relations were reduced as far as possible, and Czechoslovakia took the fewest Western credits of any East European nation. But by the second half of 1985 there were some signs of movement. Proposals were made for joint-venture legislation to bring in Western capital, and though some Czechoslovak leaders evidently disagreed with Gorbachev's policies in Moscow, a receptiveness to reform (type undefined) displayed itself. Czechoslovak economic policy was being reappraised, including trade policy with the West.[20] For many economic officials this reappraisal could not come soon enough. They had long chafed under the conservatism of their superiors.

BULGARIA

Bulgaria did 76 percent of its trade in 1985 with Comecon countries, its dominant partner by far being the Soviet Union, from which it

19. Michael T. Kaufman, "Poles, with Plenty of Passports, Line Up for Visas," *New York Times*, July 22, 1985.
20. "Prag schielt wieder mehr nach Westen," *Neue Zürcher Zeitung* (Fernausgabe), September 25, 1985.

also received important extra economic benefits.[21] But despite this it has used its small margin of commercial maneuver to good advantage. In the détente of the 1970s it began for the first time in its history to become part of Europe. Members of the economic and cultural elites visited Western Europe in greater numbers than ever before. Lyudmila Zhivkova emphasized not only Bulgaria's debt to European civilization but its contribution to it. Young people showed a fascination with the West that, however fantasized, idealized, or selective, became an important political and cultural influence.

Bulgaria remains one of the Soviet Union's most faithful allies, although evidently not immune from Moscow's criticism.[22] But politically, psychologically, culturally, diplomatically, and even economically its dependence is not as great as a generation ago. There is certainly a sub-elite enthusiasm for the Western connection. Leaders may also see the connection as necessary or inevitable, despite such recurring demonstrations of pro-Soviet loyalties as occurred at the party congress in April 1986. Bulgaria's leaders, however, will need to avoid actions that could make the country a pariah among nations. The "bulgarization" of the Turkish minority in 1984–85, for example, and the activities of its secret service that led to the charges of complicity in the alleged plot to kill the pope in 1981 have made it a rogue state among large sections of world opinion.[23] Sofia will need to work hard to remove this stigma.

HUNGARY

Hungary has remained the outstanding example in Eastern Europe of determination on the part of both society and the regime to

21. Bulgaria, for example, was allowed to purchase extra quantities of Soviet oil without using hard currency (as the other East European states were forced to) and then to export the refined products. For Bulgaria's trade percentage share with Comecon countries, see "Economic Plan Not Fulfilled," *Radio Free Europe Research*, February 17, 1956.

22. See, for example, the rambling criticisms by the Soviet ambassador to Bulgaria, Leonid Grekov, in an interview given to *Pogled*, July 1, 1985.

23. In late 1984 and early 1985, all the approximately 800,000 Turks in Bulgaria were forced to adopt Bulgarian names. There was strong resistance, and many Turks were killed in the disturbances that followed.

Apart from the alleged attempt to murder Pope John Paul II, the Bulgarian secret service is widely thought to be involved in huge drug and arms smuggling operations. In March 1986 the main Bulgarian defendant at the Rome trial of those charged for attempting to murder the pope was acquitted for lack of evidence.

maintain Western contacts. For society the opportunities for frequent travel in the West had, by the end of the 1970s, become almost a necessity of life. Any possibility of travel being curtailed through the eclipse of détente was difficult for most Hungarians to contemplate. They therefore enthusiastically supported the Kádár regime in its efforts to carry on *Westpolitik* as if the downturn in East-West relations were a matter entirely for the superpowers to deal with, a matter that had as little application as possible to Hungary and the other smaller states. Budapest's political, economic, and cultural diplomacy in the 1980s has been aimed at continuing, even widening, the progress made in the 1970s. In the course of 1986 there was general relief in Budapest as the Gorbachev leadership made clear its reform intentions. The Soviet leaders, it was now felt, would put few obstacles in the path of further reform in Hungary.

Hungary, therefore, has persisted in cultivating its Western contacts on various levels, and the exchange of high-level visitors has proliferated to a degree never before seen in Eastern Europe. In 1984 alone Hungary received visits from the West German chancellor and the prime ministers of Britain, Italy, Belgium, and Finland.[24] Kádár went to Paris in October of the same year and twelve months later to London. In the summer of 1985, West German Foreign Minister Hans-Dietrich Genscher, Social Democratic party Chairman and former Chancellor Willy Brandt, and SPD Vice-Chairman Hans-Jochen Vogel all visited Hungary within a month.[25] Hungary has maintained contacts with the United States as well. They have been mainly economic, and Hungarian officials traveling to the United States have made clear that they were desperately anxious for them to continue.

In the end, of course, Moscow will be the main arbiter of the extent to which Hungary and the other East European states have contacts with the West. The advantages and hazards of these contacts for the Soviets have been discussed earlier. For the East Europeans there is a special danger that Gorbachev, despite all his reformist inclinations on the domestic front, may try to coordinate foreign relations too closely. His motto might become, "Relations with the West, by all means; but together, not singly!"

24. Alfred Reisch, "Hungary in 1984," *Radio Free Europe Research*, unpublished.
25. Alfred Reisch, "Genscher, Brandt, and Vogel Visit Hungary," *Radio Free Europe Research*, vol. 10, pt. 2 (August 16, 1985), situation report 9/85.

One cannot imagine even the most pliant of the East European leaderships welcoming such a policy. If Gorbachev did try it, he would face severe difficulties. For despite their economic weakness, the East Europeans are not entirely helpless in the face of Soviet dictates. Some have already shown, in various ways, that they have a not inconsiderable bargaining power. Several times over the past forty years, this power has deterred Moscow from a course it preferred. East European relations with the West may be one more issue that Gorbachev decides to leave alone.

FOUR

Interests and Policies in Eastern Europe: The View from Washington

LINCOLN GORDON

THREE BASIC FACTORS have shaped U.S. policy toward Eastern Europe during the four decades since World War II: the critical position of Eastern Europe in the global superpower confrontation, including its direct relationship to the security and political orientation of Western Europe; the influence of organized ethnic groups representing immigrants and their descendants from Eastern Europe; and the idealistic pursuit of the universal desiderata of national self-determination and respect for human rights, it being especially painful to see those principles violated among peoples so akin to Americans. The first is by far the most important, but the second and third have often been decisive on specific issues within a broad line of policy. Although some authorities would add a fourth, the economic interests in trade and investment in Eastern Europe, the scale of these interests is comparatively small and their impact on policymaking only marginal.

The Historical Background

Until the end of the nineteenth century, Eastern Europe was almost terra incognita for the United States. Geographically remote, it had contributed little to America's historical legacy, notwithstanding General Thaddeus Kosciusko's noteworthy role in the American Revolution. In 1900 less than 1 percent of American trade was with this region, in contrast to 26 percent with the United Kingdom, 13 percent with Germany, and 7 percent with France.[1] Events in Eastern Europe posed no evident threat to U.S. security, and the region played no role in America's entry into the First World War.

From the 1890s on, however, immigration from Eastern Europe became increasingly important.[2] After a couple of generations, clusters of East European ethnic groups were taking an active part in urban and national politics. Coupled with Woodrow Wilson's ideal of universal national self-determination, this ethnic element was responsible for the prominence of Eastern Europe in the Fourteen Points, his proposals in 1918 for the postwar settlements. Tomas Masaryk came to the United States that year to win the support of American ethnic groups for a political union of Czechs and Slovaks; in October, the independence of the new Czechoslovakia was declared simultaneously by Masaryk in Washington and Eduard Beneš in Paris. Polish Americans rejoiced in the reconstitution of an independent homeland after 125 years of partition. Organizations of South Slav descendants likewise took a keen interest in the formation of Yugoslavia, the kingdom of Serbs, Croats, and Slovenes. And Wilson played a major part in the negotiations determining the postwar map of Eastern Europe.

Aside from these ethnic connections, however, there was little direct American interest in Eastern Europe after the war. In the 1920s, when U.S. trade worldwide was double prewar levels, Eastern Europe still accounted for much less than 1 percent.[3] The only substantial American investment was the Standard Oil Company of

1. Data calculated from Bureau of Statistics, *Statistical Abstract of the United States, 1901* (Government Printing Office, 1901), pp. 90–125, covering the Austro-Hungarian Empire and Romania.

2. The numbers are striking. In 1882, a peak year in overall immigration not surpassed until 1903, Eastern Europe (comprising Poland, "Other Central Europe," and Eastern Europe other than Russia) was the source of only 35,000 immigrants in a total of almost 800,000. By 1900 Eastern Europe accounted for at least 122,000 out of a total of 450,000, and by 1914, the all-time peak, for at least 300,000 out of 1,200,000; see Bureau of the Census, *Historical Statistics of the United States: Colonial Times to 1970* (GPO, 1975), pp. 105–06.

3. Data calculated from Bureau of Foreign and Domestic Commerce, *Statistical Abstract of the United States, 1927* (GPO, 1929), pp. 462, 488–89, covering Czechoslovakia, Hungary, Poland and Danzig, Bulgaria, and Romania.

New Jersey's in Romanian oil production and refining; by the 1930s this was overshadowed by much larger oil interests in Latin America, the Middle East, and Southeast Asia.[4]

Meanwhile, the fruits of Wilson's war "to make the world safe for democracy" were turning bitter. Pluralist democracy survived in Poland for only a few years. True democracy failed to take root in Hungary, Bulgaria, or Romania. Czechoslovakia was the shining exception in Eastern Europe, its democratic institutions withstanding even the loss of the Sudetenland in the Munich Agreement of 1938. But the region as a whole had forfeited its claim on American political sympathies. There was no basis there to counteract the general turning inward of the American electorate that followed the Senate's rebuff of the Treaty of Versailles and the League of Nations and that was intensified by the Great Depression.

In his first year as president, Franklin D. Roosevelt entered into diplomatic relations with the Soviet Union. But in the main arenas of growing aggression by imperial Japan, Fascist Italy, and Nazi Germany, the United States was only a horrified observer, not an actor. As both economic and security conditions deteriorated in Europe and China, isolationism and neutralism grew in the U.S. Congress. They were manifested in the Johnson Debt Default Act of 1934 forbidding loans to any foreign government in default and in successive Neutrality Acts in 1935, 1936, and 1937. Roosevelt's call in late 1937 for an international "quarantine of aggressors" evoked more domestic opposition than support.

When Eastern Europe came under relentless pressure from Nazi Germany, Americans were deeply worried, but Washington had neither the power nor the political support to create a policy toward the region, even though its map owed so much to Woodrow Wilson. In face of Germany's incorporation of Austria in March 1938, absorption of the Sudetenland in September 1938, and occupation of the remnants of Czechoslovakia in March 1939, Roosevelt could do no more than address vain appeals to Hitler for self-restraint. When the Molotov-Ribbentrop nonaggression pact of August 1939 foreshadowed an imminent invasion of Poland, Roosevelt's calls for arbitration or conciliation were welcomed by the Poles but simply

4. *American Petroleum Interests in Foreign Countries,* Hearings before a Senate Special Committee Investigating Petroleum Resources, 79 Cong. 1 Sess. (GPO, 1945), pp. 339–40.

disregarded by the Russians and Germans. Nor did the Soviets consider American sensitivities when they moved in 1940 to incorporate Estonia, Latvia, and Lithuania into the USSR.

American public sentiment in the early phases of World War II was overwhelmingly anti-Axis but still predominantly anti-interventionist. Without the twin transcendent errors of Japan's December 1941 attack on Pearl Harbor and Germany's immediate declaration of war against the United States, it is not clear when, how, or even if American military force would have become directly engaged on the European continent, earning for Roosevelt a central role in the discussions of Eastern Europe's future at the summit conferences among the Allies. It is appropriate to speak of "discussions" rather than "settlements." Although it is widely believed that the meetings in 1945 of the American, Soviet, and British leaders at Yalta and Potsdam were responsible for Soviet hegemony in Eastern Europe, in fact the geopolitical outcome had already been foreclosed by the military strategy for defeating Germany agreed to at Tehran in late 1943. That strategy led inescapably to a Soviet monopoly of the "liberation" of Eastern Europe and thence to unilateral decisions on both boundaries and political regimes.[5]

Roosevelt's performance at Yalta can well be faulted on other grounds: his overeagerness, strongly backed by the Joint Chiefs of Staff, for Soviet entry into the war against Japan; his misplaced confidence that the embryonic United Nations could correct errors in the postwar settlements; and his tactic of playing Winston Churchill and Joseph Stalin off against one another. With respect to Eastern Europe it is possible that, as Averell Harriman suggests, a more vigorous Roosevelt might have held out for immediate participation of noncommunist Poles in the negotiations and their stronger representation in the future Warsaw government.[6] Judging from subsequent experience in Hungary and Czechoslovakia, however, it is hard to believe that a more representative Polish regime could have effectively resisted full Sovietization, whatever agreements had been

---

5. For a brief but balanced discussion of the interrelation of military and political strategies and their impact on Eastern Europe, see Bennett Kovrig, *The Myth of Liberation: East-Central Europe in U.S. Diplomacy and Politics Since 1941* (Johns Hopkins University Press, 1973), chap. 1.

6. W. Averell Harriman and Elie Abel, *Special Envoy to Churchill and Stalin, 1941–1946* (Random House, 1975), chap. 17, especially pp. 412–13.

subscribed to by Stalin. To do so would have required the help of Allied forces on the ground, and the American public and Congress, including many of the later congressional critics of Yalta, had no taste for that means of enforcing policy. By July 1945, when Harry Truman and Churchill met with Stalin at Potsdam, the outcome was irrevocably foreordained by the withdrawal and demobilization of Western troops and the loss of economic leverage through the termination of Lend-Lease. The preliminaries of cold war between the superpowers were clearly visible.

Before the end of 1947, communist power was consolidated in Hungary, Romania, Bulgaria, and Poland. A Soviet veto prevented Polish and Czech participation in the Marshall Plan. The coup of February 1948 against President Beneš and Foreign Minister Jan Masaryk put an end to hopes for maintaining genuine democracy in Czechoslovakia. The Berlin blockade of June 1948 was the final step in persuading American public opinion that Soviet and American concepts of world order were incompatible and irreconcilable. Washington's policy reaction took the form of "containment." Its main applications were to the defense of Greece and Turkey (the Truman Doctrine of March 1947), the economic rehabilitation of Europe (the Marshall Plan of June 1947), and collective security for Western Europe (the Vandenberg resolution of June 1948, the Berlin airlift of 1948–49, and the North Atlantic Treaty of April 1949). A logical counterpart was support for Yugoslavia after Tito's break with Stalinism in 1948.

These moves were radical innovations in foreign policy for a country with long-held and deeply ingrained attitudes of neutralism and isolationism, but they were strongly supported by both major political parties. The central preoccupation of those years was not with Eastern Europe, but with the fear that Soviet power might be extended to Western Europe, either through Communist party successes in Italy and France or by direct force of Soviet arms.

By December 1949 confidence in West European stabilization had progressed to the point where policymakers in Washington could think in somewhat more daring terms. They wrote then of placing "greater emphasis on the offensive to consider whether we cannot do more to cause the elimination or at least a reduction of predominant Soviet influence in the satellite states of Eastern Europe." The short-term goal was to encourage additional Titoist heresies rather than anticommunist counterrevolutions, but the thrust of the policy clearly went beyond mere containment. The ultimate aim was defined as "non-totalitarian administrations willing to accommodate themselves to, and participate in, the free world community." Military action was explicitly ruled out, except in the event that war in Eastern Europe should be "forced upon us."[7] During the presidential election campaign of 1952, in which the Republican nomination was contested between conservative Robert Taft and moderate Dwight D. Eisenhower, containment was denounced as an inadequate policy that should give way to "liberation" for the "captive peoples."

Bennett Kovrig's classic study of this period, *The Myth of Liberation,* demonstrates that the practical policies of the first Eisenhower administration fell far short of the electoral rhetoric. There were many official warnings against encouraging insurrections. The instrument of liberationist policy was to be moral force, not physical force.[8] The means of policy were mainly negative: avoiding normalization of relations with the "people's democracies" or otherwise legitimizing their regimes. The principal positive means were broadcasts by Radio Free Europe (RFE), established in 1950, and Radio in the American Sector of Berlin (RIAS). Among West Europeans already fearful that the invasion of South Korea might be matched in their region and still in the first phases of rearmament under the umbrella of NATO, the very term "liberation" raised serious concerns. Allied governments remonstrated strongly against any indication that war might be risked in order to "roll back the Iron Curtain."

The short-lived uprising in East Germany in June 1953 was the first demonstration that liberation was not an operational doctrine. The acid test came when Soviet tanks put an end to the Hungarian Revolution of October–November 1956. Partly inspired by the tone, if not the literal wording, of RFE broadcasts and by what they saw as the precedent of U.S. action in Korea in 1950, many of the revolutionaries in Budapest expected American support, either directly or through the United Nations. For them, liberation proved a hollow

7. National Security Council, *Report to the President: United States Policy Toward the Soviet Satellite States in Eastern Europe,* NSC 58/2 (December 8, 1949). At that time the document was classified top secret, but it has been largely declassified and published in U.S. Department of State, Historical Office, *Foreign Relations of the United States 1949* (GPO, 1976), vol. 5, pp. 42–54. The quotations are on pp. 43, 50–51.

8. *Myth of Liberation,* pp. 120–72.

promise. Even without the distractions of the Suez crisis, the presidential election, and the illness of Secretary of State John Foster Dulles, the United States would in fact have been unable to alter the outcome. The Hungarian crisis was a major turning point. Out of that experience evolved the basic lines of policy that still prevail.

THE POLICY PREMISES

In essence policy has sought to find a workable mean between mere containment and unrealizable liberation. Containment alone could easily become endorsement of the postwar East European status quo, which has always been distasteful to American opinion in the short run and unacceptable as a long-run policy objective. Moreover, it has been increasingly evident that impulses toward change within Eastern Europe itself are bound to undermine the stability of the status quo at least to some degree. But with military intervention by the West ruled out, whether in support of popular uprisings or independently, liberation by force is not a viable option. That was the conclusion in the 1950s when the United States held an immense margin of strategic superiority; it has been steadily reinforced over the decades as the Soviets achieved substantial parity globally while maintaining a military lead in the European region.

The remaining possibilities are either passive accommodation, with the hope that spontaneous evolution in both the USSR and Eastern Europe might ultimately lead to more acceptable conditions, or more active encouragement of desired kinds of change through whatever peaceful means are available. The choice has consistently fallen on encouraging change through peaceful means. This line of policy began in 1957 with economic assistance to Poland, where the new leadership of Wladyslaw Gomulka appeared to promise substantial political and economic liberalization. It was carried on and extended to Romania and Czechoslovakia by the Kennedy and Johnson administrations. During the 1960s it came to be called "peaceful engagement" or "bridge-building," terms coined by Zbigniew Brzezinski, whose study on the division of Europe for the Council on Foreign Relations made a lasting impact on American policymakers.[9]

9. *Alternative to Partition: For a Broader Conception of America's Role in Europe* (McGraw-Hill for the Council on Foreign Relations, 1965).

Although hopes for unimpeded change were rudely set back by the Soviet suppression of the Prague Spring in 1968, the central thrust of policy was maintained. Within the broader framework of East-West détente promoted by Richard Nixon and Henry Kissinger, Eastern Europe was to receive separate treatment. The term "differentiation," which dates back at least to 1964, returned to use under Jimmy Carter and remained the hallmark of East European policy under Ronald Reagan. So for three decades, regardless of terminology and notwithstanding wide fluctuations in the tone of overall U.S.-Soviet relations, the content of policy toward Eastern Europe has varied surprisingly little.

Successive administrations have endorsed the essential features of differentiation: that East European countries are not regarded as members of a monolithic Soviet bloc, like component republics of the Soviet Union itself, and that they are to be treated differently from one another. The grounds for more favorable treatment have consistently been two: East European foreign policies at variance with those of the USSR and favorable to Western (or U.S.) interests, and measures of domestic economic, political, and cultural liberalization, including freedom of emigration for dissidents. Romania has been the main exemplar of a foreign policy deviating from that of the Soviet Union, but there have been occasional lesser examples elsewhere. For most of the period, Poland and Hungary (and Czechoslovakia until 1968) have been considered the liberalizers, with Poland falling far behind Hungary after the imposition of martial law in December 1981.

THE ECONOMIC FACTOR

During the 1960s and 1970s, private American relationships with Eastern Europe expanded in parallel with official measures for peaceful engagement. That trend included trade and investment, tourism, journalism, and scholarly exchanges, all requiring positive action on the part of the East European governments. Private relationships flourished during the era of overall East-West détente in the mid-1970s, when most of the region was turning to the West for help in economic modernization. Western supplies of capital goods were normally financed with export credits. In addition, Western commercial banks looked to Eastern Europe as a major new market

Table 1. *U.S. Share of Eastern Europe's Western Trade, Selected Years 1970–85*
Millions of dollars unless otherwise indicated

Area or country	1970	1975	1980	1983	1984	1985
Eastern Europe						
Imports						
From industrial West[a]	4,111	14,834	22,938	14,659	13,974	15,308
From United States	235	950	2,343	884	894	781
U.S. share (percent)	5.7	6.4	10.2	6.0	6.4	5.1
Exports						
To industrial West[a]	3,733	10,216	20,312	16,152	17,992	17,824
To United States	163	519	1,070	1,096	1,749	1,666
U.S. share (percent)	4.4	5.1	5.3	6.8	9.7	9.3
Poland						
Imports						
From industrial West[a]	803	5,461	6,335	2,858	2,932	3,084
From United States	70	583	716	324	318	238
U.S. share (percent)	8.7	10.7	11.3	11.3	10.8	7.7
Exports						
To industrial West[a]	946	3,122	5,535	3,181	3,861	3,889
To United States	104	263	460	209	244	248
U.S. share (percent)	11.0	8.4	8.3	6.6	6.3	6.4
Romania						
Imports						
From industrial West[a]	668	1,953	3,734	1,174	1,287	1,341
From United States	66	191	722	186	249	208
U.S. share	9.9	9.8	19.3	15.8	19.3	15.5
Exports						
To industrial West[a]	505	1,585	3,179	2,583	3,609	3,418
To United States	14	147	341	553	969	951
U.S. share (percent)	2.8	9.3	10.7	21.4	26.8	27.8
Hungary						
Imports						
From industrial West[a]	574	1,819	3,178	2,539	2,475	2,799
From United States	28	76	80	110	88	95
U.S. share (percent)	4.9	4.2	2.5	4.3	3.6	3.4
Exports						
To industrial West[a]	497	1,222	2,698	2,269	2,480	2,549
To United States	7	38	118	172	242	241
U.S. share (percent)	1.4	3.1	4.4	7.6	9.8	9.5

Source: Data from appendix tables A-4 and A-5. Exports from the West to East European countries in those tables are shown here as imports by East European countries from the West.

a. "Industrial West" means the category of "industrial countries" in International Monetary Fund, *Direction of Trade: Annual 1970–76* (Washington, D.C.: IMF, 1977); and *Direction of Trade Statistics Yearbook 1986* (Washington, D.C.: IMF, 1986). Since 1980 the category has comprised the United States, Canada, Japan, Australia, New Zealand, and all of Western Europe except Greece, Portugal, and Turkey. In 1970 and 1975 Australia and New Zealand were not included in the grouping, but their trade with Eastern Europe was negligible.

for relending the vast supplies of petrodollars then pouring into their coffers from the Middle East. Appendix table A-5 shows the dramatic rise in U.S. trade with the region during the 1970s, the peaking of exports to Eastern Europe in 1980, and the sharp falling off as the debt-servicing crisis forced Poland, Romania, Bulgaria, and, to a lesser degree, East Germany to cut imports drastically. U.S. imports from the region also rose substantially during the 1970s and, except for those from Poland, have generally maintained their new magnitudes. Eastern Europe greatly outweighs the USSR as a source of American imports, but the USSR absorbs more U.S. exports because of the grain trade.

These economic developments have created important commercial and financial linkages. Their impact on policymaking, however, remains minor. Despite the large increases in dollar volume, Eastern Europe has never accounted for more than 1.1 percent of U.S. exports or 0.6 percent of U.S. imports. As appendix table A-3 shows, the American trading interest is far smaller proportionately than those of Austria, West Germany, Italy, France, and Britain. As a share of Eastern Europe's total trade with the Western industrial countries, the United States has generally accounted for less than 10 percent of exports or imports (table 1). The largest proportions have been in Poland, Romania, and Hungary, the principal beneficiaries of differentiation policy over the years. On the financial side Western Europe as a whole greatly outweighs the United States as a creditor to Eastern Europe.[10]

The Objectives of Policy

American policies toward Eastern Europe are set within the broader East-West context of relations between the United States and the Soviet Union. Nevertheless, there has been greater continuity over

10. There are no published data showing in comparable terms the amounts of East European debt held by commercial creditors and governments in the West. In early 1982, however, a U.S. Treasury official provided estimated data on Poland's five largest Western creditors, including official and officially guaranteed claims and private claims. The figures were as follows (in billions of dollars): West Germany, 4.4; United States, 3.1; France, 2.8; Austria, 1.9; United Kingdom, 1.7. See *Polish Debt Crisis,* Hearings before a subcommittee of the Senate Committee on Appropriations, 97 Cong. 2 sess. (GPO, 1983), p. 126.

the years in the objectives of America's East European policy than of its policy toward the USSR. In policy toward the USSR important changes have occurred from administration to administration and even within the span of single presidencies. Such changes can be summarized as shifts within a spectrum between confrontation and détente.[11] The extremes of this spectrum are ruled out: deliberate military confrontation would be suicidal in the nuclear age, while the most forthcoming versions of détente have failed to engender the kind of Soviet behavior hoped by their proponents. As a result, the practical objectives of all administrations, if not necessarily their rhetoric, have fallen within the range between selective détente and limited confrontation, with the differences sometimes matters of emphasis or nuance. For Eastern Europe the variation in objectives has been much narrower.

Objectives can usefully be classified as long-term or ultimate, medium-term, and short-term or immediate. Ultimate objectives may be no more than aspirations, without timetables or clearly defined steps for their achievement. But even then they are not entirely lacking in practical meaning, since they point to desired directions of movement and make less likely the adoption of incompatible inter-mediate measures. They tend to be especially unclear in democratic regimes, whose time horizons are for most purposes limited to the three-to-six-year life of elected presidents or parliaments. Such regimes are inherently incapable of executing the long-term strategies of a Bismarck, Stalin, Ho Chi Minh, Mao Zedong, or, perhaps, a Mikhail Gorbachev. In the American experience, declarations of ultimate objectives are as likely to be bids for domestic electoral support as serious definitions of genuine strategic goals. They should conse-quently be read with an appropriate dose of skepticism.

LONG-TERM OBJECTIVES: THE RECORD OF THREE DECADES

With that warning in mind, the analyst will find great similarities in Washington's declared ultimate objectives in Eastern Europe over the three decades since 1956. They focus on national self-determi-nation and respect for human rights and political liberties, amounting

11. For the period 1969–84 this history is analyzed in detail in Raymond L. Garthoff, *Détente and Confrontation: American-Soviet Relations from Nixon to Reagan* (Brookings, 1985).

in effect to a goal of gradual and peaceful detachment from Soviet
political control. They emphasize such themes as "overcoming the
division of Europe" or "giving reality to the Yalta Declaration on
Liberated Europe." Out of respect for West German sensitivities,
American administrations refrained until 1971 from formally endorsing the Oder-Neisse line as the German-Polish border, and
Washington continues to support the doctrine (politically important
for some circles in West Germany) of possible future boundary changes
through negotiation. Nevertheless, the long-term objectives of the
United States have never involved changes in the East European
territorial status quo. Nor have they sought an outright reversal of
alliance by any member of the Warsaw Pact, that is, its shift to
membership in NATO. On the so-called German Question the United
States has generally followed the lead of the Federal Republic:
reaffirming the importance of the goal of reunification in the Adenauer era and soft-pedaling it since the adoption of Willy Brandt's
Ostpolitik. It obviously follows from the basic principle of self-determination, however, that if circumstances were ever to permit a free
expression of popular will on the subject in both Germanys, the
outcome would be respected by the United States.

Viewed in perspective, American aspirations for Eastern Europe
have tended to become less sharply defined, both in content and in
timing. Before 1956 there were high hopes for nationalist breakaways
from the Warsaw Pact on the model of Tito's Yugoslavia. Thereafter
the emphasis shifted to change with the consent—however grudging—
of the Soviet Union rather than against its will. (The Albanian defection
in 1961 was considered sui generis and not a clear gain for the West
in view of Albania's developing ties to China; it did, however, deprive
the Soviets of a valuable submarine base at Vlore.) In the early 1960s
Zbigniew Brzezinski and William Griffith wrote in a seminal article
of "a greater measure of political independence . . . ultimately leading
to the creation of a neutral belt of states which, like the Finnish,
would enjoy genuine popular freedom of choice in internal policy
while not being hostile to the Soviet Union and not belonging to
Western military alliances."[12] In their vision, East Germany would

12. "Peaceful Engagement in Eastern Europe," *Foreign Affairs*, vol. 39 (July 1961),
p. 644. Four years later, Brzezinski speculated on the possibility of a European
settlement based on the Finland model for Eastern Europe as early as "in the course

not remain as a separate state but would be reunited with the Federal Republic, perhaps as a demilitarized zone. But by 1967, speaking now as a member of the State Department's policy planning staff, Brzezinski had tempered his objectives: "an engagement to a process of change, and not a quest for an immediate settlement," with the East European regimes becoming softened to "semidictatorships of increasingly Socialist character (and of less Communist dictatorial kind), including more internal social pluralism. . . . Yugoslavia is a relevant example."[13]

The suppression of the Prague Spring in August 1968 was a major setback to hopes for rapid political liberalization fostered by Western peaceful engagement. Yet it caused only a surprisingly brief pause in Washington's pursuit of a broad détente in East-West relations already being sought by President Lyndon Johnson and amplified in the following years by President Nixon and his national security adviser, Henry Kissinger. With respect to Eastern Europe, while the long-term objectives were now explicitly placed in the framework of superpower détente, their substance reflected more continuity than change. That was even more true of the operational policies. The practice of differentiation was refined and systematized, and in 1973 crystallized in a formal national security decision memorandum.[14] In effect, the trauma of Czechoslovakia extended the already long time horizons without altering the ultimate objectives.

Nixon's intensified dialogue with the Soviet Union was paralleled by an activist approach in direct relations with East European governments, highlighted by presidential visits—the first in Eastern Europe since World War II—to Romania, Yugoslavia, and Poland. The tone was set in Nixon's first annual foreign policy review:

> Our association with Western Europe is fundamental to the resolution of the problems caused by the unnatural division of the continent. We recognize that the reunion of Europe will come about not from one spectacular negotiation, but from an extended historical process. . . .
>
> Ultimately, a workable system of security embracing all of Europe will require a willingness on the part of the Soviet Union to normalize

---

of the next decade or so," implying a target date of the late 1970s. See *Alternative to Partition,* pp. 47–48.

13. "Toward a Community of the Developed Nations," *Department of State Bulletin,* vol. 56 (March 1967), pp. 418–19.

14. See Raymond L. Garthoff, "Eastern Europe in the Context of U.S.-Soviet Relations," in Sarah Meiklejohn Terry, ed., *Soviet Policy in Eastern Europe* (Yale University Press for the Council on Foreign Relations, 1984), p. 322.

its own relations with Eastern Europe—to recover from its anachronistic fear of Germany, and to recognize that its own security and the stability of Central Europe can best be served by a structure of reconciliation.

Later in the review he stated,

It is not the intention of the United States to undermine the legitimate security interests of the Soviet Union. The time is certainly past, with the development of modern technology, when any power would seek to exploit Eastern Europe to obtain strategic advantage against the Soviet Union. . . .

By the same token, the United States views the countries of Eastern Europe as sovereign, not as parts of a monolith. And we can accept no doctrine that abridges their right to seek reciprocal improvement of their relations with us or others.

We are prepared to enter into negotiations with the nations of Eastern Europe, looking to a gradual normalization of relations. We will adjust ourselves to whatever pace and extent of nomalization these countries are willing to sustain.

Progress in this direction has already been achieved in our relations with Romania. . . . A similar relationship is open to any Communist country that wishes to enter it.

Stability and peace in Europe will be enhanced once its division is healed. The United States, and the nations of Western Europe, have historic ties with the peoples and nations of Eastern Europe, which we wish to maintain and renew.[15]

A seeming exception to these consistent statements of objectives was the so-called Sonnenfeldt Doctrine, a journalistic comet that streaked across Washington's policy skies briefly but dramatically in early 1976. Based on both misquotation and misinterpretation of what had been said by State Department Counselor Helmut Sonnenfeldt to a closed meeting in London of American ambassadors in Europe in December 1975, a newspaper column described the doctrine as amounting to "U.S. underwriting of Soviet dominion over Eastern Europe" in order to avoid a third world war.[16] Sonnenfeldt had called for an "organic" relationship, using the term in the common German sense of naturalness, rather than a relationship based on sheer power. The columnists added two words, giving the impression that he had called for a "permanent organic union." Sonnenfeldt had also said

15. "First Annual Report to the Congress on United States Foreign Policy for the 1970's, February 18, 1970," reprinted in *Public Papers of the Presidents of the United States: Richard Nixon, 1970* (GPO, 1971), pp. 130, 132, 181.

16. Rowland Evans and Robert Novak, "A Soviet-East Europe 'Organic Union,'" *Washington Post*, March 22, 1976.

that Eastern Europe is within the Soviet Union's "scope and area of natural interest." At the same time he projected "a policy of responding to the clearly visible aspirations in Eastern Europe for a more autonomous existence within the context of a strong Soviet geopolitical influence." He went on to cite the differentiating characteristics of Poland, Hungary, and Romania.[17]

In subsequent congressional testimony, Sonnenfeldt reiterated the Ford administration's support for "the independence, the national sovereignty and identity, and the autonomy of all the peoples and countries of Central and Eastern Europe." He also stated that the term "sphere of influence" was not to be interpreted as an exclusive preserve or a sphere of domination in which others have no rights or interests.[18]

In fact, no policy departure was involved in recognizing during an off-the-record meeting of ambassadors that Eastern Europe was within a de facto Soviet sphere of military influence. Western inability to oppose Soviet armed intervention in 1953, 1956, and 1968 was sufficient evidence for that conclusion. Nor was there any novelty in recognizing the Soviet security interest in Eastern Europe. But the words "sphere of influence" were (and remain) taboo in public discourse about foreign policy. The term "organic relationship" was new and susceptible of misunderstanding; it also quickly became taboo. Although the newspaper leakage was apparently connected with political maneuverings for the 1976 presidential election campaign, the episode caused strong reactions in both Western and Eastern Europe. Long since repudiated by its purported author, the term "Sonnenfeldt Doctrine" still appears in the literature, meaning acceptance of permanent Soviet control of Eastern Europe's domestic institutions and foreign policies. That was not the position of the Ford administration or any other, before or since.

The Carter administration's initial approach to foreign policy differed substantially from its predecessors'. It was more ambitious concerning arms control and far more demanding with respect to

17. "State Dept. Summary of Remarks by Sonnenfeldt," *New York Times*, April 6, 1976.
18. *United States National Security Policy Vis-à-Vis Eastern Europe (The "Sonnenfeldt Doctrine")*, Hearings before the Subcommittee on International Security and Scientific Affairs of the House Committee on International Relations, 94 Cong. 2 sess. (GPO, 1976), pp. 2, 4.

human rights, yet it also sought to downgrade the relative importance of Soviet-American relations as compared with third world issues and the "trilateral" relationship among the industrialized democratic countries of Europe, Asia, and North America. The priority of Eastern Europe was somewhat raised, partly because of the long-standing interest of Zbigniew Brzezinski, now the president's national security adviser.[19]

Yet the formal review completed during Carter's first year reiterated in essence the policy of differentiation as already long established. Some of the means were intensified, as seen in the emphasis on human rights at the Belgrade review conference on the Helsinki Final Act, the added moral support for Radio Free Europe, and the return to Hungary of the Crown of St. Stephen. There was greater relative emphasis on relations with societies in Eastern Europe rather than regimes. But the long-term objective was not altered. In Brzezinski's words it was "to advance the larger goal of gradually transforming the Soviet bloc into a more pluralistic and diversified entity." In his view, "evolutionary changes . . . are more likely to occur first in Eastern Europe, and the West should persist in its efforts to create ever closer links between Eastern and Western Europe."[20]

Given the confrontational tone that the Reagan administration brought to Soviet relations in its first year, a shift in policies and objectives in Eastern Europe would not have been surprising. It did not occur. Once again a formal policy review was set in motion, but the initial focus of high-level attention was on efforts to discourage Soviet intervention in the crisis in Poland. The formal review was not completed until August 1982; in essence it endorsed the same kinds of differentiation policy that had been developed over the previous quarter century.[21]

Policy toward Eastern Europe was a central theme of a speech by

19. Edmund Muskie, secretary of state during the last nine months of the Carter presidency, was also of Polish ancestry, although he was born in the United States.

20. *Power and Principle: Memoirs of the National Security Adviser, 1977–1981* (Farrar, Straus Giroux, 1983), pp. 300, 541.

21. In interviews with the author, several officials have mentioned that some consideration was given to requiring both internal liberalization and foreign policy autonomy as criteria for favorable treatment, rather than one or the other. In practice, that would have ended differentiation, since Romania would not have qualified on the former criterion nor Poland or Hungary on the latter. Arguments against so radical a change of policy soon prevailed.

Vice President George Bush in Vienna in September 1983 after his return from visits to Yugoslavia, Romania, and Hungary. Its tone was highly polemical, suggesting that Russia had never partaken of nor contributed to European civilization, and its rhetoric sharply attacked the concept that either the Yalta or the Helsinki accords had sanctioned the present division of Europe. To his Austrian hosts it seemed out of keeping with their formal East-West neutrality, while Hungarian officials were fearful that the public praise heaped upon their economic reforms might attract unfriendly Soviet attention. Yet a close reading shows that its substance did not depart from the long-established lines of policy. There was no suggestion of territorial revisionism or support for change through force, the content of differentiation was described accurately (if tactlessly), and the polemics were hedged by a clear disclaimer: "Let me stress here that the United States does not seek to destabilize or undermine any government."[22]

During 1985 Eastern Europe figured in formal statements by the secretary of state and the president. As part of an overall foreign policy review before the Senate Foreign Relations Committee, Secretary George Shultz said,

> The present political division of the [European] continent is wholly artificial; it exists only because it has been imposed by brute Soviet power; the United States has never recognized it as legitimate or permanent. Behind this cruel barrier lie political repression and economic stagnation. In certain countries, there are efforts at liberalization. But *all* the peoples of Eastern Europe are capable of something better, deserve something better, and yearn for something better. We have witnessed in recent years the powerful aspiration for free trade unions, for economic reform, for political and religious freedom, for true peace and security, for human rights as promised by the Helsinki accords. We hope to see the day when the Soviet Union learns to think anew of its own security in terms compatible with the freedom, security, and independence of its neighbors.[23]

The same theme underlay President Reagan's formal statement on the fortieth anniversary of Yalta:

> Why is Yalta important today? Not because we in the West want to

22. "Address at the Hofburg, Vienna, Sept. 21, 1983," *Department of State Bulletin*, vol. 83 (November 1983), pp. 19–23. There had been no systematic interagency review of the text of the speech.

23. "The Future of American Foreign Policy: New Realities and New Ways of Thinking," *Department of State Bulletin*, vol. 85 (March 1985), p. 15. The statement was made before the Senate Foreign Relations Committee, January 31, 1985.

reopen old disputes over boundaries; far from it. The reason Yalta remains important is that the freedom of Europe is unfinished business. Those who claim the issue is boundaries or territory are hoping that the real issues—democracy and independence—will somehow go away. They will not.

There is one boundary which Yalta symbolizes that can never be made legitimate, and that is the dividing line between freedom and repression. I do not hesitate to say that we wish to undo this boundary. In so doing, we seek no military advantage for ourselves or for the Western alliance. We do not deny any nation's legitimate interest in security. But protecting the security of one nation by robbing another of its national independence and national traditions is not legitimate. In the long run, it is not even secure.

Long after Yalta, this much remains clear: The most significant way of making all Europe more secure is to make it more free. Our 40-year pledge is to the goal of a restored community of free European nations. To this work we recommit ourselves today.[24]

At the end of the year, while en route to his first East European visit, Secretary Shultz reiterated America's long-term goal of overcoming the "artificial divisions" of Europe, Germany, and Berlin. At the same time, he was notably cautious with respect to short-term possibilities.

We have all learned a great deal over the postwar period about both the opportunities and the limits of our influence in Eastern Europe. . . . Some day, the Soviet Union under wise leadership may learn that its own security needs can be met without suppressing the freedom of its neighbors. In the meantime, we do what we can to foster greater openness in these countries. We differentiate among them, and between them and the Soviet Union, to encourage more independent foreign policies, greater respect for human rights, and economic and social reforms. Governments that show such positive trends receive our reinforcing acknowledgment.[25]

As pointed out in chapter 3, the actual continuity of U.S. policies has not always been perceived as such by the East Europeans. In the mid-1960s they sensed a phase of more active American interest but they were disillusioned as Vietnam became the overriding concern of

24. "President's Statement, Feb. 5, 1985, 40th Anniversary of the Yalta Conference," *Department of State Bulletin,* vol. 85 (April 1985), p. 46.

25. The reference to artificial divisions was in his speech in Berlin, December 14, 1985. The longer quotation is from a speech in London, December 10, 1985. The full texts, along with those of news conferences in Bucharest, Budapest, and Belgrade, are reprinted in *Department of State Bulletin,* vol. 86 (February 1986), pp. 29–31 with quote on p. 31; pp. 24–28 with quote on p. 27; and pp. 43–49 for the news conferences.

Washington policymakers. Further disillusionment ensued with America's passivity at the invasion of Czechoslovakia. As détente developed in the 1970s, many East Europeans feared a "condominium" arrangement under which Washington would recognize a permanent Soviet sphere of influence, a fear reinforced by the misinterpreted Sonnenfeldt Doctrine. President Carter's emphasis on human rights engendered hopes of more effective U.S. support for internal liberalization. In the early years of the Reagan administration, there were mixed reactions: Polish dissidents welcomed the sanctions against martial law, while both peoples and regimes in neighboring countries, especially Hungary, feared that Washington's confrontational rhetoric might reduce Moscow's tolerance for such degrees of freedom as they had already secured. To a limited extent these perceptions reflected genuine changes in Washington attitudes or shifts of emphasis in short-term policy objectives. But those were minor nuances against a backdrop of basic continuity, both in declaratory terms and especially in actions.[26]

This historical record brings to mind the dolls with rounded and weighted bottoms known in Germany as *Stehaufpuppen*. At one time or another, policy has been pushed by accommodationists from one side or by hard-line confrontationists from the other. It always reverts, and rather rapidly, to a centrist position. The reason lies in objective constraints outside the control of U.S. governments.

MEDIUM-TERM OBJECTIVES

Since long-term aspirations are well beyond the time horizons of operational policies, discussion of them tends to be academic or philosophical. Substantial policy issues more often arise from differences over medium-term objectives. In the mid-1960s, for example, the United States began to press West Germany to relax its rigid Hallstein Doctrine and other efforts to isolate East Germany, but only after prolonged debate in Washington. When Willy Brandt and Egon Bahr initiated their *Ostpolitik* in late 1969, there were similar questions about how much restraint the United States should seek to impose. More generally, economic and social liberalization in Eastern Europe

26. This paragraph summarizes observations of J. F. Brown based on his quarter-century association with the research department of Radio Free Europe.

have been consistent desiderata, but in specific instances it is by no means clear whether particular forms or conditions of support will actually advance those aims. In the early 1970s, for example, the United States and Western Europe were generous with Poland under the leadership of Edward Gierek, but in hindsight the easy and unconditional availability of Western credits, both official and private, appears to have postponed liberalizing economic reforms rather than encouraged them. (This type of uncertainty also applies to many aspects of development support in the third world.) During the 1980s the review of intermediate objectives for U.S. policy has raised central issues of principle, issues that also have the highest potential for creating cleavage between the United States and Western Europe.

Given agreement on the ultimate objective of relaxing Soviet imperial control, the critical question concerns the most effective route to that goal. The possible answers lie along a spectrum running from *accommodation* to Soviet control, through *transformation* of Soviet control, to *dissolution* of Soviet control. These are not three sharply defined options requiring a single choice; they are rather points on a spectrum that permits intermediate positions as well.

The rationale of accommodation is not active sympathy with the Soviet system, which in the United States is infinitesimal. It holds instead that the West cannot exert significant influence anyway, so the only realistic policy is to wait out the development of internal forces for beneficent change within the Soviet Union itself, however long that may take. In addition, accommodationists argue that the Soviets will not permit transformation of their control and that efforts at dissolution will fail or in any case increase the risk of superpower military confrontation. In their view the overriding priority in East-West relations is stability, which should never be jeopardized for lesser objectives.

The argument for stability has at times received limited support in American official circles. It is often attributed to the United States (especially by European writers) as a hidden agenda of "condominium" or "tacit conspiracy" with the USSR for maintaining the European status quo. Military stability has indeed been a consistent objective of U.S. governments, and scarcely a hidden one. But the mainstream of U.S. policy has rejected accommodation to the Soviet system of imperial control, partly on the merits, partly because accommodation could not win public support, and partly because, as suggested earlier, internal forces for change in the region rule out any kind of frozen stability. The accommodationist position, however, does have advocates in the academic world.[27]

Especially during the 1980s, most American policymakers have tended to polarize between advocates of transformation and of dissolution, with some taking intermediate positions. Dissolution of the Soviet empire is a difficult concept in view of Eastern Europe's critical role in the entire Soviet system. Historical analogies to the Ottoman and Austro-Hungarian Empires are scarcely pertinent. The Ottoman Empire took two and a quarter centuries from peak to end and involved a long series of wars with a variety of neighbors. The Austro-Hungarian Empire was much shorter-lived, but its dissolution required World War I. In the nuclear era these are not attractive models. Short of war, however, one school of thought in the United States sees a substantial possibility of Soviet imperial collapse through economic stagnation and decline, accompanied by ideological disillusionment and internal nationalist frictions, not only in Eastern Europe but also within the Soviet Union itself.

The opposing—and thus far dominant—school rejects this prognosis but believes in the possibility of meaningful change in intraimperial relationships without an abrupt discontinuity. Its position in the spectrum favors transformation as the intermediate objective. The course of change it envisions might be likened to the long British road from absolute monarchy to pluralist democracy under a constitutional monarch, while dissolution is more akin to the ending of absolute monarchy by the French Revolution and the guillotine.[28]

What might transformation mean in the Soviet case? The central idea is that the nominal Soviet ground rules for Eastern Europe would be preserved while their practical application is gradually altered. The two basic ground rules inferred by Western analysts (although not explicitly defined by the USSR as the only two for all cases) are continued membership in the Warsaw Pact and maintenance of the leading role of the communist parties. The Romanians have dem-

27. For example, see Roy E. Licklider, "Soviet Control of Eastern Europe: Morality Versus American National Interests," *Political Science Quarterly*, vol. 91 (Winter 1976–77), pp. 619–24.

28. The description of the dissolution and transformation schools of thought is based on extensive interviews by the author with policymakers who have held office in various departments of government under several administrations but who may not be cited individually. The terminology is the author's.

onstrated that the military and political obligations of Warsaw Pact membership can be greatly diluted without following Yugoslavia and Albania out of the Pact, although it must be recognized that Soviet tolerance for their nonconformist behavior is due in part to their relatively unimportant strategic location. Transformationists believe that the nature of communist party leadership might also be gradually modified without contradicting the second basic rule. That was the objective of the Prague Spring ("socialism with a human face"), and its termination by Soviet military force is often cited as evidence that transformation is simply impossible. But it can be argued, with support provided by the Hungarian experience since 1968, that the Czechoslovak pattern is not the only conceivable one. There is also evidence that suppression by the Soviet military was a close call in Moscow, by no means a foregone conclusion.[29]

Transformation is certainly not a goal to be achieved rapidly or easily. To classify it as a medium-term objective does not imply that it could be accomplished within five or ten years. The aim is rather for a process to be set in motion, or encouraged if already in motion, that might in that time span show perceptible movement toward softening the structure and practices of imperial control. Any such movement is unlikely to be all in one direction, since liberalizing initiatives have an innate capacity for getting out of hand and taking on a self-reinforcing momentum that then invites repression.

One skeptical thesis holds that 1968 marked a definitive end to the imperial loosening begun by Khrushchev fifteen years earlier—a sort of restalinization.[30] Those favoring the transformation hypothesis, however, interpret the record as closer to a spiral process that alternates between liberalization and repression but in which each starting point is different from its predecessor. It is obviously a crucial question how much liberalization and autonomy, how much differentiation from Soviet foreign policies and institutional arrangements, will be permitted by the Soviet Union, which holds the ultimate power in the region. But the answers must depend on Moscow's assessment in any situation of the costs and benefits of action to suppress or repress,

29. See Jiri Valenta, *Soviet Intervention in Czechoslovakia, 1968: Anatomy of a Decision* (Johns Hopkins University Press, 1979); and Karen Dawisha, *The Kremlin and the Prague Spring* (University of California Press, 1984).

30. See, for example, Hélène Carrère d'Encausse, *Le Grand Frère: l'Union Soviétique et l'Europe Soviétisée* (Paris: Flammarion, 1983).

as well as on the intensity with which change is pressed by the individual East European polities.

From these differences in objectives there often follow opposed positions on specific policies in Eastern Europe, notably economic policies. The dissolution school seeks to maximize the economic strain on the Soviet Union by depriving its client states of Western trade and finance. If some minimum standard of consumer satisfaction is required to avoid popular outbreaks and possible anti-Soviet sabotage, and if Western credits, investments, technology transfer, or even unsubsidized trade are required to maintain that standard, then, it is argued, the West's refusal to supply these resources will compel the Soviets to come to the rescue. By the same token, any form of Western support for improved economic conditions in Eastern Europe would entail a counterproductive easing of the burdens of Soviet empire as well as a legitimation of unsavory regimes. Thus dissolutionists are sometimes described as favoring a policy of the worse the better. They tend to regard differences between East European countries and the USSR, either in domestic or in foreign matters, as insignificant and are therefore generally opposed to the policy of differentiation.[31]

The transformation school, in contrast, sees no possibility of a Soviet economic collapse and questions the concept of the imperial umbrella. It acknowledges that transfers of military high technology to Eastern Europe would be passed along immediately to the USSR and should therefore be controlled, but it argues that assistance for economic modernization may widen the differences within the Eastern bloc and help to loosen imperial ties. In any event, such assistance should improve conditions of life for the peoples concerned, often a positive interest of their ethnic cousins in the United States.[32] More

31. Strong advocacy of this viewpoint appears periodically in the pages of *Commentary*. For example, see Norman Podhoretz, "The Future Danger," vol. 71 (April 1981), pp. 29–47; and Walter Laqueur, "What Poland Means," vol. 73 (March 1982), pp. 25–30. Advocacy may also be found in the editorial columns of the *Wall Street Journal*. A more restrained variety, which would preserve some aspects of differentiation policy, is presented by Manfred R. Hamm, "Central Europe," in Stuart M. Butler, Michael Sanera, and W. Bruce Weinrod, eds., *Mandate for Leadership II: Continuing the Conservative Revolution* (Washington, D.C.: Heritage Foundation, 1984), pp. 300–07.

32. Conflict along these lines lay behind the controversy about Poland in the earliest days of the Reagan administration, as recounted by Alexander Haig in the memoir of his service as secretary of state; see *Caveat: Realism, Reagan, and Foreign Policy* (Macmillan, 1984), pp. 239–40. In his words, "some of my colleagues in the NSC were prepared to look beyond Poland, as if it were not in itself an issue of war and peace, and regard

generally, this school shows greater concern about human rights and the treatment of dissidents and would-be emigrés. On the strategic front, the transformationist position does not seek to impair the Soviet Union's defensive security, but looks to increased connections between Eastern Europe and the West as a means of fostering doubts in Moscow that Warsaw Pact forces would be reliable partners in any kind of unprovoked aggression.

The polarization of advocates of dissolution and transformation does not apply to all aspects of American policy toward Eastern Europe. At least two types of minimal objectives are very broadly agreed upon in Washington, one directed at the peoples of Eastern Europe and the other at the governing regimes. The goal for peoples is to assist in maintaining their Western orientation, their sense of being part of the great European tradition, and to reassure them that they are not forgotten by the West. The first prerequisite to that end is that they have continuing access to Western culture, both "high" and "pop," and to information and news about the West undistorted by party-line propaganda. Broadcasting and cultural and educational exchanges are the main means, but trade and travel are also relevant.

For regimes the minimal agreed objective can only be stated in negative terms: to avoid forcing them unnecessarily into Soviet arms by depriving them of alternatives. Here the principal means are economic and diplomatic. The implementation of this objective is difficult because it conflicts with the aim of avoiding undue legitimation of objectionable domestic or foreign policies. Moreover, it can be argued that the alternatives involve concessions without a sufficient counterpart in increased national autonomy. Consensus on the principle, therefore, does not rule out sharp dispute over its application to specific cases.

SHORT-TERM OBJECTIVES

Within the broad framework of a policy of differentiation aimed at gradual transformation of Soviet imperial control, the short-term tactical objectives are usually obvious from the nature of the specific policy measures. That is especially the case with economic concessions

---

it as an opportunity to inflict mortal political, economic, and propaganda damage on the U.S.S.R."

and sanctions. The threatened withdrawal of most-favored-nation status from Romania in 1983, for example, was directly linked to Ceauşescu's attempt to impose an education tax on emigrés. Between 1982 and 1987 the step-by-step lifting of economic sanctions against Poland was related to specific measures of domestic liberalization. The detailed programming of visits of high-ranking dignitaries may be designed to send appropriate signals to regimes or peoples or both. Many other examples will be found in the ensuing discussion of policy instruments.

The Instruments of Policy

Policy instruments are best considered in functional classifications: political-diplomatic, informational-cultural (public diplomacy), security, and economic. In Washington all these instruments are employed within a framework of foreign policymaking processes unique to the United States. That framework has been substantially modified in the past two decades and helps to shape all aspects of policy toward Eastern Europe. Along with the nonstate relations that impinge on policymaking, these processes call for a brief review.

POLICYMAKING PROCESSES

The American constitutional separation of powers makes for an ambiguous sharing of responsibility for foreign policy between the executive and legislative branches. Except in times of crisis, Eastern Europe is not a central focus for public or political attention, so that policy toward that region has been less affected by executive-legislative tension than policy toward the Soviet Union. Nevertheless, Congress has always been chary of charges of "softness on communism" and therefore reluctant in its support for the more positive aspects of transformationist differentiation. During the Johnson administration, a proposed bill on East-West trade relations was refused even a congressional committee hearing. That position was partially reversed in 1973 under the impetus of Nixon's policy of détente, but still qualified by the Jackson-Vanik and Stevenson amendments linking most-favored-nation treatment and export credit guarantees to Soviet and East European emigration policies. A year later, Congress blocked a claims settlement agreement with Czechoslovakia because the compensation offered for nationalized property was considered insufficient. In the early 1980s, however, Congress was somewhat more forthcoming than the executive branch on liberalizing export controls and technology transfer to the East in line with the desires of commercial exporters.

Less generally recognized than tension between the legislative and executive branches is the extent to which power has become fractionated and dispersed in the past twenty years within both those branches, a situation complicated by the enhanced role of the press and television.[33] In Congress the power of majority and minority leaders and of committee chairmen has been greatly weakened. Junior members are supported by large staffs, achieve subcommittee chairmanships rapidly, and can often become newsworthy through individualistic maverick initiatives. These factors intensify the historic American tendency to encumber legislation with detailed provisions responsive to special interests. They make for reduced executive discretion and increased formalization and transparency of policymaking. With respect to Eastern Europe, examples can be found in export-control decisions, the granting or withholding of most-favored-nation treatment of imports, broadcasting activities of the Voice of America and Radio Free Europe, and the imposition or withdrawal of sanctions against undesired actions by the East European regimes or the Soviet Union.

Because of their traditional importance in American electoral politics, East European ethnic groups are often assumed to have a major impact on policy. On closer examination, however, that assumption appears questionable. There is a substantial potential base, especially of Polish Americans.[34] There are active organizations, such

33. For a recent exposition of the policymaking process by a group with broad experience in both branches, see Joint Working Group of the United States Association of Former Members of Congress and Atlantic Council of the United States, *The President, the Congress, and Foreign Policy* (Washington, D.C.: Atlantic Council of the United States and United States Association of Former Members of Congress, 1985). The effects of policymaking processes are also extensively discussed in Joseph S. Nye, Jr., ed., *The Making of America's Soviet Policy* (Yale University Press for the Council on Foreign Relations, 1984); and James A. Nathan and James K. Oliver, *Foreign Policy Making in the American Political System* (Little, Brown, 1983).

34. In 1979 the Census Bureau estimated at least partial East European ancestry for the following numbers: Polish, 8.4 million; Czechoslovak, 1.7 million; Hungarian,

as the Polish National Alliance, the Polish-American Congress, the American-Hungarian Federation, and the Assembly of Captive European Nations. Since 1959, pursuant to an act of Congress passed unanimously, Captive Nations Week is solemnly proclaimed each July, accompanied by speeches at cabinet or even presidential level looking forward to ultimate liberation, but those ceremonies are generally recognized to be more ritualistic than substantive. Whichever party is in power, a senior White House staff official is designated to maintain contact with ethnic groups. Their representatives have easy access to members of Congress and to assistant secretaries and office directors in the executive branch, and they are consulted regularly by high officials.

Despite all this, ethnic groups have only limited direct impact on policy. The long-established groups are interested more in maintaining cultural traditions than in influencing current policies. Their general political impact may also be waning as they become geographically dispersed away from the northeastern industrial centers and as successive generations intermarry with outsiders. The main limitation, however, is the absence of clear-cut policy goals. In the late 1950s, Polish-American initiatives were instrumental in securing the agricultural and trade assistance programs that launched the policy of differentiation. Some Polish Americans, however, were reluctant to give any kind of support to a communist regime. Hungarian-American groups, especially those close to the Republican party, succeeded in thwarting the Ford administration's desire to return the Crown of St. Stephen to Budapest, but the Carter administration was able to muster a degree of ethnic group support even though fearing some net political cost. Among Czechoslovak Americans there are often sharp disagreements between the emigrés of 1948 and those who have emigrated since 1968. There are also traditional differences in attitude between those of Czech and those of Slovak ancestry. During the Polish crisis of 1980–81, and in the years since the imposition of martial law, Polish Americans have suffered the same ambivalence as the policymakers themselves: how to bring pressure on Warsaw

1.6 million; Romanian, 335,000 (also Yugoslavian, 467,000). Bulgarians were fewer than 100,000 and East Germans are of course not separately counted within the 52 millions of German ancestry. See U.S. Bureau of the Census, *Current Population Reports,* Series P-23, no. 116, "Ancestry and Language in the United States: November 1979" (GPO, 1982), p. 7.

without needlessly adding to the sufferings of the Polish people. In short, while ethnic group interests are never overlooked, and united opposition on a specific issue can succeed in blocking action, they are not prime factors in the general shaping or implementation of policy.[35]

Within the executive branch, the traditional foreign policy primacy of the Department of State, which was still operative under Truman and Eisenhower, has been abandoned without any coherent replacement short of the president himself. National security advisers have come to regard themselves as coequal formulators of broad policy directions, assisted since the eras of McGeorge Bundy and Henry Kissinger by substantial staffs. The Department of Defense has its own "mini–State Department" under an assistant secretary for international security policy. Foreign economic policy is spread among the Departments of State, Treasury, Commerce, Agriculture, and Energy, together with the Office of Special Trade Representative and the Agency for International Development. International informational and cultural affairs, once formally subordinated to the State Department, have achieved more autonomous status under the United States Information Agency. The result is a combination of bureaucratic inertia and chronic interagency struggle in which issues are forced through a network of committees lacking powers of decision except by consensus and a premium is placed on stubborn advocacy of particularist positions.

Departmental attitudes on specific policies toward Eastern Europe reflect their special responsibilities. The Commerce and Agriculture Departments are export promoters by charter and by virtue of their constant association with the relevant private interest groups. They naturally tend to favor export credits and a liberal position on export controls. They are troubled by evidence that unilateral denial of exports to Eastern Europe will simply result in the displacement of American exporters by others from the West or the third world. The Department of Defense, on the other hand, tends to adopt "worst

35. This conclusion accords with the findings of Stephen A. Garrett, "Eastern European Ethnic Groups and American Foreign Policy," *Political Science Quarterly*, vol. 93 (Summer 1978), pp. 301–23. Interviews conducted in the preparation of this chapter confirm their continuing validity. One leading Polish-American spokesman stated that he would like to raise their lobbying effectiveness at least to the level of the Greek Americans, whom the Polish Americans outnumber eight to one. It should be kept in mind, however, that the most effective Greek-American lobbying in recent years has been on Turkish issues on which Greeks are solidly united.

case" assumptions on the diversion of civilian technology to military use and to argue that any sensitive products made available to Eastern Europe, even in fixed installations, will be passed along to the Soviet Union. Given its primary responsibility for military deterrence and contingency planning for possible hostilities, the department is bound to subordinate bilateral relationships with individual East European countries to a preoccupation with the principal adversary. On such issues as debt rescheduling, the Treasury will always put great weight on the solvency of the larger banks and the integrity of the American financial system. In contrast with the State Department, the U.S. Information Agency is more interested in people-to-people relations than in official dealings state-to-state. Lacking a domestic constituency but in daily communication with its network of embassies, the Department of State is especially sensitive to foreign reactions to proposed policies.

Compared with West European parliamentary systems, Washington undergoes a much more extensive turnover of high-level officials when a new president takes office, especially if there is a change in political party. Until the 1970s, political appointments in the field of foreign affairs were drawn heavily from the "Eastern establishment," most of whom shared in a broad bipartisan consensus. Whatever their nominal party affiliation, they collaborated easily with the permanent officialdom of the foreign service, civil service, and armed forces. (There come to mind such names as Averell Harriman, Robert Lovett, Paul Hoffman, John J. McCloy, and David Bruce.) That has become progressively less the case in the past two decades—the Nixon, Ford, Carter, and Reagan administrations—when many political appointees have come from the more ideologically inclined outer fringes of their parties. The typical four-year cycle therefore now begins with the often unrealistic and highly politicized views of the new appointees in tension with the professional bureaucracy and with unchanging external constraints. During that shakedown period, coherent policymaking is especially unlikely. This was one important source of difficulty in responding to the ongoing crisis in Poland confronting the new Reagan administration in 1981.

In parallel with these intragovernmental changes, the press and television have acquired a more active role in influencing foreign policymaking, partly because public confidence in governmental leadership and candor has been undermined by the experiences of

Vietnam and Watergate. Investigative reporting has grown in volume, assisted by access to official knowledge under the Freedom of Information Act. Policy-oriented columnists and commentators have multiplied. Television interviews are used by officials to advance particular viewpoints as well as established policy. But the most striking change is the growing habit of deliberately leaking inside information to promote policy positions—a direct result of the fractionation of authority within the government and the formation of alliances of like-minded advocates on Capitol Hill, in executive agencies, in the press, and in organized private interest groups. Or leakage can make the press an unwitting ally, motivated by its general commitment to the public's right to know and by the pressures of competition. In these circumstances, confidentiality is inordinately difficult to maintain as policy is being developed, not only with respect to covert action but also in the deliberative processes required by any kind of organization.

Taken together, these matters of process present formidable obstacles to formulating and maintaining a sustained foreign policy, especially when subtlety and nuance are indicated. Formulating policy on Eastern Europe has been less difficult when the region has been out of the political limelight and policy handled mainly by professional diplomats and civil servants. During periods of crisis, however, the institutional complexities outlined here rapidly make themselves felt.

THE INFLUENCE OF NONSTATE RELATIONS

A full appreciation of American relationships with Eastern Europe cannot be limited to governmental policies and actions. Transnational relations among private individuals and organizations also play a considerable part, one that expanded greatly during the 1970s, especially in the countries favored by differentiation. And their role has not reverted to predétente levels despite the shrinkage of trade and financial credits since 1980 and the tension with Poland since the end of 1981. Nonstate relations include tourism, journalism, trade, investment, educational and scientific exchanges, relations between affiliated churches, and labor union activities. The individual U.S. participants are often of East European ethnic origin and command the relevant languages. All these connections provide the American public with sources of information and judgment independent of government channels, with considerable feedback into the formation of official policy. Their relative importance has been enhanced by the general public skepticism of governmental veracity since the experiences of the Vietnam War and Watergate.

Among these groups the trade unions stand out because of the scope of their international activities and the unbending anti-Soviet policy line maintained by the AFL-CIO throughout the postwar period. Originating in the battles of the 1930s against communist control of American unions, this position was fortified during labor's active association with free West European unions in the Marshall Plan years and by the strong personal interest of AFL-CIO Presidents George Meany and Lane Kirkland. The AFL-CIO was instrumental in forming the International Confederation of Free Trade Unions (ICFTU) to combat the communist-dominated World Federation of Trade Unions (WFTU).[36] Labor has used its independent representation in the tripartite system of the International Labor Organization (ILO) to condemn human rights abuses in communist countries and their persistent violation of formal commitments in the ILO charter and conventions. Many labor attachés in American embassies abroad have been drawn from trade union backgrounds, and the AFL-CIO has developed a corps of international specialists almost constituting a foreign service of its own. Although often cooperating with the government, labor puts great value on its independence of judgment, which it defends publicly and vigorously.

The emergence of Poland's Solidarity in 1980 offered a unique opportunity to support a genuinely democratic labor movement in Eastern Europe. The AFL-CIO seized the opportunity so enthusiastically that it was cautioned in turn by Secretaries of State Edmund Muskie and Alexander Haig against the risk of inviting Soviet counteraction. Immediately after the declaration of martial law in December 1981, the AFL-CIO announced that it was supplying office and printing equipment to its fellow unionists in Poland, and Lane Kirkland met with President Reagan to discuss U.S. reactions. The AFL-CIO has continued to maintain extensive direct contacts with leading personalities in the Solidarity movement. It not only com-

36. In the late 1960s the AFL-CIO withdrew from the ICFTU because it opposed the exchange of "fraternal delegations" between Western labor unions and puppet labor organizations in Eastern Europe. In 1982 the AFL-CIO returned to regular membership.

mended the sanctions imposed on both Poland and the USSR but urged that they go much further—that all credits to all Warsaw Pact countries be stopped, that grain to the Soviets be again embargoed, and that the United States withdraw from the Conference on Security and Cooperation in Europe then meeting in Madrid and the arms control talks in Geneva.[37]

In subsequent years the AFL-CIO leadership fought a rearguard action against loosening the sanctions on Poland, even after the Vatican urged their withdrawal. Although the organization's position was never a determining factor, it did delay government decisions on several occasions, and AFL-CIO representatives were consulted in advance in all cases. Paradoxically enough, the AFL-CIO's influence on the foreign policy of an administration it strongly opposes on domestic issues has been greater than that of the less well organized traders and bankers.

POLITICAL-DIPLOMATIC POLICIES

Political-diplomatic policies comprise the most traditional aspects of state-to-state relationships, ranging from the trivial to the fundamental. They provide ample scope for subtle differentiation in treatment: from hostile and confrontational, through cool and correct and varying shades of cordiality, to particularly warm special relationships. In Washington's dealings with Eastern Europe, they reflect the basic paradox of the relationship. Inevitably the policies provide some support for unpopular regimes that American public and official opinion have considered illegitimate for forty years, yet they are essential for maintaining contact with peoples and for any prospect of influencing governmental behavior, external or internal. They consequently cluster toward the cool end of the spectrum, but with considerable variation over time and from country to country.

By 1946 the United States had extended diplomatic recognition to all East European countries except East Germany, where it was withheld pending the evanescent "German settlement." The GDR was finally recognized in late 1974, pursuant to Brandt's *Ostpolitik*, the Four Power Berlin accords, and acceptance of the European

---

37. See Tom Kahn, "Moral Duty," *Society*, vol. 19 (March–April 1982), p. 51; and testimony by Thomas W. Gleason and Thomas Kahn in Senate subcommittee hearings, *Polish Debt Crisis*, pp. 162–74. Thomas Kahn was assistant to Lane Kirkland.

territorial status quo then being formalized at Helsinki. Diplomatic recognition was usually accompanied by settlements of outstanding reciprocal claims, consular conventions, and treaties of friendship, commerce, and navigation. Even these elementary measures are subject to some nuance: level of representation, size of missions and their freedom to travel, numbers of consulates, and the like. Thus they can demonstrate a readiness to reciprocate signs of flexibility on the East European side, permitting mutual interaction toward either improvement or worsening of the overall relationship.[38]

High-level visits are an even more flexible political instrument, providing a variety of potential signals and influencing both governments and peoples. After only six months in office, Richard Nixon became the first president to visit Eastern Europe. He chose Romania, partly to reward President Ceauşescu for a cordial reception when Nixon was still in private life but mainly to "needle the Soviets" by favoring communist regimes that showed independence from Moscow, a sort of preliminary to the opening to China. Later visits to Yugoslavia in 1970 and Poland in 1972 were designed to "encourage sentiments of national independence in Eastern Europe," while also courting domestic political support from the respective ethnic groups.[39] Similar considerations took President Ford to Poland, Romania, and Yugoslavia in 1975 in conjunction with his signing of the Helsinki Final Act. Poland was the only East European country to be visited (in 1977) by President Carter, but in 1978 Secretary of State Cyrus Vance went to Hungary and Treasury Secretary Michael Blumenthal to Romania. President Reagan has not traveled to Eastern Europe, but Vice President Bush visited Yugoslavia, Romania, and Hungary in 1983 and Secretary of State George Shultz visited Hungary in 1985, which demonstrates the high position now occupied by Hungary on the scale of differentiation. In late 1986 and early 1987 Deputy Secretary of State John Whitehead traveled to all the East European countries except East Germany.

At a somewhat lower level, there have been striking innovations in

38. For example, when General Jaruzelski refused to act on *agrément* for a U.S. ambassadorial nominee from 1982 to 1984 (apparently hoping for the retraction of an insulting remark by Secretary of Defense Caspar Weinberger), some consideration was given in Washington to downgrading diplomatic relations with Poland indefinitely as a symbol of displeasure with the military regime.

39. The motivation is discussed in Henry Kissinger, *White House Years* (Little, Brown, 1979), pp. 156–58, 1265–68.

recent years: a visit to Yugoslavia and Romania by the chairman of the Joint Chiefs of Staff and to East Germany by the assistant secretary of state for European and Canadian affairs. Military delegations have also been received in other East European nations. Members of the State Department's policy planning staff engaged in general foreign policy discussions with so-called counterparts in Bucharest and Budapest. And senior American arms control officials gave briefings in Eastern Europe on U.S. positions in bilateral negotiations with the Soviet Union.

In the reverse direction Washington received Romanian President Ceauşescu on three occasions (in 1970, 1973, and 1978), Polish party leader Gierek in 1974, and Polish deputy prime ministers in 1974 and 1981. Gierek's visit epitomized bridge-building during the era of high détente, being marked by formal summit-level joint statements, "Principles of United States–Polish Relations" and "The Development of Economic, Industrial and Technological Cooperation."[40] The foreign ministers of Romania and Hungary came to Washington in 1983. Even Bulgaria, often regarded as the Warsaw Pact member that is most truly a Soviet satellite, was accorded a gentle nod of recognition for its signs of cultural nationalism through a visit in 1977 by Lyudmila Zhivkova, daughter of party leader Todor Zhivkov and at that time chairman of Bulgaria's Committee for Arts and Culture. The common thread in these visits is the demonstration that meaningful bilateral relationships need not pass through Moscow. There have also been a few occasions when a bid by an East European government for a high-level visit has been refused because aspects of its policies have been especially offensive to the United States.

American multilateral diplomacy has also sought to encourage an active and at least partly autonomous role for the East European nations. The main forums to this end have been the Mutual and Balanced Force Reduction negotiations in Vienna since 1973 and the Conference on Security and Cooperation in Europe, which led to the Helsinki Final Act of 1975 and the follow-up conferences in Belgrade in 1977–78, Madrid in 1980–83, and Vienna in 1986–87. Paradoxically, the United States has become progressively disillusioned with

40. For the text of these statements and effusive speeches and toasts by President Ford and First Secretary Gierek, see "First Secretary Gierek of the Polish United Workers Party Visits the United States," *Department of State Bulletin*, vol. 71 (November 1974), pp. 597–606.

the Western-sponsored MBFR but increasingly interested in CSCE, which was initiated by Leonid Brezhnev and the Warsaw Pact. Its unfulfilled "Basket III" commitments to the freer movement of peoples and ideas and to greater respect for human rights are seen as legitimizing international pressures on these issues both in Eastern Europe and in the Soviet Union itself.

These conferences provide opportunities for the expression of separate national positions by East European representatives and for their interaction with West Europeans and, in CSCE, the Neutral and Non-Aligned group. The most spectacular example was Romania's success in securing provisions in the Helsinki Final Act on rights to neutrality, condemning the threat or use of force and military occupation, and forbidding intervention by participating states "regardless of their mutual relations" (an obvious and invidious reference to the Brezhnev Doctrine of 1968, which asserted the legitimacy of Soviet intervention to keep any communist-ruled country within the "socialist camp"). In succeeding conferences there have been occasional indications that East European positions have a tempering influence on the Soviet Union similar in direction, although certainly not in magnitude, to that of Western Europe on the United States.[41] These small straws in the wind are in line with the general objectives of differentiation policy.[42]

PUBLIC DIPLOMACY: GOVERNMENTS TO PEOPLES

In the world's open societies, including most developing countries, government-to-government relations are complemented by a substan-

41. See John J. Maresca, *To Helsinki: The Conference on Security and Cooperation in Europe 1973–1975* (Duke University Press, 1985); Lawrence T. Caldwell, "CSCE, MBFR, and Eastern Europe," in Charles Gati, ed., *The International Politics of Eastern Europe* (Praeger, 1976), pp. 173–91; Nils Andrén and Karl E. Birnbaum, eds., *Belgrade and Beyond: The CSCE Process in Perspective* (Alphen aan den Rijn, Netherlands: Sijthoff & Noordhoff, 1980); and Karl E. Birnbaum, *The Politics of East-West Communication in Europe* (Farnborough, England: Saxon House, 1979).

42. Early in the Madrid review session on CSCE, for example, Judge Griffin Bell, then chairman of the U.S. delegation, complimented Hungary, the GDR, and Poland for "efforts to explore how church and state can better live with each other," and his successor Max Kampelman spoke of "many advances" in Eastern Europe, in contrast to the Soviet Union. See Griffin B. Bell, "Strengthening the CSCE Process," *Department of State Bulletin*, vol. 81 (January 1981), p. 18; and an interview with Max Kampelman, "Russia's Record Since Helsinki: 5 Years of Cheating," *U.S. News and World Report* (February 9, 1981), pp. 37–38.

tial American effort in public diplomacy, which is addressed to publics at large or to especially influential groups such as journalists, teachers, scientists, cultural elites, and political, business, and student leaders. In the closed societies of Eastern Europe, these activities are in constant tension with the regimes, since censorship is a way of life, public information is a state or party monopoly, and the authorities are constantly on guard against "infection" or "subversion" by liberal democratic, pluralist, and capitalist ideas. Those concerns would restrict the activities of any Western government, but they are intensified by the special status of the United States—the superpower adversary of the communists' superpower patron, their nations' traditional golden refuge from oppression, the home of distant cousins, and the source of their youths' most favored films, clothing, and rock music. Today Hungary imposes the fewest limitations, a sign of self-confidence in popular acceptance of the regime and a desire to ingratiate itself with the West. Elsewhere, however, there are continuous negotiations on what may be imported and shown, who may have access, and how closely contacts are monitored. Ambassadors and their staffs have to apply considerable ingenuity in their public appearances, using opportunities the authorities cannot deny, such as World War II commemorations, for communicating official attitudes and even basic information not otherwise available, to say nothing of combating deliberate falsehoods.

In such a context, radio broadcasting has become a very important instrument of American policy. Eastern Europe is one of the major target areas for the Voice of America, which provides global news and official U.S. positions. But it is the full-time and exclusive concern of Radio Free Europe, a unique institution of public diplomacy. RFE was created in 1950 as a nominally private organization, covertly funded through the Central Intelligence Agency and expected to last only a few years. Its early phase of liberationist activism was abruptly terminated by the charges in 1956 that its programs had misled Hungarian freedom fighters to expect military support from the West.[43] Its mission then came to be defined as a "surrogate home

43. Radio Free Europe was exonerated on the more extreme accusations after investigations conducted separately by the West German government and by RFE's own management, but it was undeniable that many Hungarian supporters of the revolution had so interpreted the broadcasts. The episode was followed by major changes in personnel and a sober reassessment of RFE's mission. On the history of

service" informing the East European peoples of what they would learn if they possessed a domestic free press, radio, and television. In the early 1970s RFE went through a major institutional crisis when Congress moved to put government funding on an overt basis, but a minority, led by Chairman William Fulbright of the Senate Foreign Relations Committee, sought its abolition on grounds of incompatibility with the reigning spirit of East-West détente. It is now twinned with Radio Liberty (directed to the USSR) in a nominally private corporation, Radio Free Europe/Radio Liberty, Inc., or RFE/RL, often known simply as the Radios, under the control and supervision of a presidentially appointed Board for International Broadcasting. Since 1983 the members of that board also constitute the directors of RFE/RL, and the chairman is substantially involved in the management as well as the policies of the broadcasting operations.

RFE has alternated between strong presidential support, from Kennedy, Carter, and Reagan, and relative indifference, from Johnson, Nixon, and Ford, but it receives consistent backing from a broad left-to-right spectrum in Congress. It has also survived periods of severe staff tension—not surprising in a group with a large complement of emigré professionals and intellectuals from countries with intense nationalist antipathies. Cynics have sometimes charged that its real purpose is to provide dignified employment opportunities for emigré dissenters, but that objective would scarcely secure the roughly $100 million provided annually through the federal budget. On at least two occasions, chancellors of the Federal Republic are said to have privately urged RFE's termination for fear that its location in Germany might prejudice their *Ostpolitik,* but they withdrew rapidly when the continuing high-level American interest was made clear.[44] As an instrument of policy, RFE is clearly here to stay.

Elaborate program guidelines are designed to avoid some of the errors of earlier times. They emphasize accuracy, objectivity, and balance, and the avoidance of stridency, propagandistic argumenta-

---

RFE generally, see Sig Mickelson, *America's Other Voice: The Story of Radio Free Europe and Radio Liberty* (Praeger, 1983); Paul Lendvai, *The Bureaucracy of Truth: How Communist Governments Manage the News* (London: Burnett Books, 1981); and James L. Tyson, *U.S. International Broadcasting and National Security* (Ramapo Press, 1983).

44. For the instance of Willy Brandt, see John M. Goshko, "RFE Alters Sullied Image," *Washington Post,* November 22, 1970; and "The Essential Business of Radio Free Europe," *Washington Post,* June 26, 1971. For the instance of Helmut Schmidt, see Brzezinski, *Power and Principle,* p. 293.

tion, inflammatory content, or tactical advice to listeners. (Conservative critics in the United States often complain that these guidelines make for excessive blandness.)[45] In contrast with the Voice of America, Radio Free Europe's programs are heavily concentrated on national affairs within Eastern Europe and on East-West relations. As one program director commented in private conversation, the central purpose is to ferret out newsworthy items or aspects of the national history that the authorities are trying "to put down George Orwell's memory hole," and replay them to the listening publics. In practice that includes extensive broadcasts of underground or *samizdat* writings originating in the countries concerned. On as scientific a basis as conditions permit, appraisals of audiences indicate a remarkably high proportion of regular listeners, especially at times of crisis and notwithstanding jamming of the broadcasts in Czechoslovakia and Bulgaria, and in Poland since the declaration of martial law.[46] There is ample testimony to the success of the programs in spreading knowledge of events of intense national interest. In Poland, for example, RFE provided full coverage of the papal visits of 1979 and 1983, the Solidarity movement both before and after the declaration of martial law, the Nobel Prize ceremony for Lech Walesa, and the 1984 trials of the murderers of Father Jerzy Popieluszko.[47]

RFE broadcasting is intensely objectionable to Eastern Europe's governing regimes. In addition to jamming efforts, they make frequent formal and informal diplomatic protests, which are regularly rebuffed. Heavy Soviet and East European pressure has been applied to the international Olympic authorities to prevent accreditation of RFE/RL journalists to the games. The Radios' operations are outside the

45. For the text of the guidelines, see Board for International Broadcasting, *1985 Annual Report* (Washington, D.C.: BIB, 1985), pp. 30–35.

46. Radio Free Europe/Radio Liberty, Inc., "Listening to Western Radio in East Europe, 1983/Early 1984," *Eastern European Area Audience and Opinion Research* (Washington, D.C.: RFE/RL, September 1984), pp. 3, 9, 14, 20, 26, estimates listening by the following percentages of the adult populations: Poland, 66; Romania, 63; Hungary, 59; Bulgaria, 40; Czechoslovakia, 38. RFE is not jammed in Hungary or Romania. It does not broadcast to East Germany, which is completely covered by West German radio broadcasting and 80 percent covered by West German television. In the early postwar years, substantial American resources also were devoted to the station known as R.I.A.S. (Radio in the American Sector of Berlin), which is now operated almost entirely by the West Germans.

47. Typical indications can be found in Timothy Garton Ash, *The Polish Revolution: Solidarity* (Charles Scribner's Sons, 1983), pp. 33–34, 50–51, 120, 131, 137, 265–66.

pattern of normal state-to-state relations, but they are a critical instrument of transformationist policy, helping to maintain the Western orientation of their audiences and to sustain pressure on the regimes for peaceful liberalizing change.

The National Endowment for Democracy is a new and more modest instrument of public diplomacy, established by Congress in 1983 outside the governmental structure "to encourage free and democratic institutions throughout the world through private sector initiatives," a central theme of President Reagan's Westminster address to the Houses of Parliament in 1982. Although the endowment was inspired partly by the government-financed foundations in West Germany affiliated with the main political parties, and analogous institutes have now been created by the Republican and Democratic parties, Congress has preferred to channel the bulk of its funds through trade union, business, and nonprofit organizations. Amounting to $18 million a year in all, the largest share has gone to the Free Trade Union Institute created by the AFL-CIO, which works mainly in the third world but has maintained close contact with labor leaders in Poland since the height of the Solidarity movement. The endowment has also made small grants to support independent cultural, educational, and scholarly activities in Poland and Czechoslovakia and to provide assistance to former political prisoners in Poland.[48]

SECURITY POLICIES

Security policies toward Eastern Europe are obviously only a subordinate component of the military confrontation between NATO and the Warsaw Pact—the subject of an immense literature that can neither be summarized nor supplemented here. The more limited issues pertinent to this study are whether security can be improved through regionally limited measures, negotiated or unilateral, in which the East European nations play an active part, and whether multilateral negotiations are a significant component of Western relations with Eastern Europe. Over the past thirty years, there have been many proposals, private and official, for partial disengagement

---

48. All of the endowment's grants are described in some detail in National Endowment for Democracy, *Annual Report* (Washington, D.C.: NED, 1984, 1985, 1986).

in Europe, nuclear-free zones, and the like, but all so far without concrete results.[49]

In 1973 formal negotiations opened in Vienna—the Mutual Reduction of Forces and Armaments and Associated Measures in Central Europe, better known as the Mutual and Balanced Force Reduction talks, or MBFR. Involving almost all NATO and Warsaw Pact members, the negotiations were initiated by the West mainly to ward off the threat, posed by the Mansfield amendment, of congressionally imposed unilateral withdrawals of American troops from Europe. But given the starting point of the Warsaw Pact's superiority in conventional forces and its inherent geographical advantages, the talks were flawed by the absence of clear conceptions of arrangements that could both add to Western security and offer a real prospect of negotiability. Long periods of stalemate in Vienna have been punctuated periodically by new proposals from one side or the other, with limited convergence on some issues. Neither side has been prepared to break off MBFR negotiations, even when the bilateral strategic arms talks between the superpowers were suspended in 1983. Washington has never given them high priority, and stalemate still seems the order of the day after fourteen years.[50]

A more fruitful path to at least limited improvement in European security appears to lie in so-called confidence-building measures, which are not aimed at force levels or equipment but are designed to reduce the feasibility of surprise attack and the danger of inadvertent war precipitated by misunderstanding or miscalculation.[51] The Hel-

---

49. One of the more noteworthy recent ones emerged in 1982 from the Independent Commission on Disarmament and Security Issues, chaired by the late Olof Palme of Sweden. See *Common Security: A Programme for Disarmament* (London: Pan Books, 1982).

50. On the origins of MBFR, see Kissinger, *White House Years*, pp. 400–01, 947–48. The skepticism of President Carter's national security adviser, if not necessarily of the president himself, is noted in Brzezinski, *Power and Principle*, p. 172. Detailed accounts of the first ten years of negotiation are presented in William B. Prendergast, *Mutual and Balanced Force Reduction: Issues and Prospects* (Washington, D.C.: American Enterprise Institute, 1978); and Lothar Ruehl, *MBFR: Lessons and Problems*, Adelphi Papers 176 (London: International Institute for Strategic Studies, 1982). A more hopeful analysis of their ultimate prospects is Jonathan Dean's, "MBFR: From Apathy to Accord," *International Security*, vol. 7 (Spring 1983), pp. 116–39. Ambassador Dean, however, provides a more ample and less optimistic discussion in *Watershed in Europe: Dismantling the East-West Military Confrontation* (D. C. Heath, 1987), chap. 7. For indications of continuing stalemate in mid-1986, see "MBFR Talks End 39th Round," *Department of State Bulletin*, vol. 86 (November 1986), p. 27.

51. For a balanced discussion with essays from Eastern as well as Western experts, see F. Stephen Larrabee and Dietrich Stobbe, eds., *Confidence-Building Measures in*

sinki Final Act of 1975 provided for twenty-one-day advance notification of military maneuvers involving more than 25,000 troops and
urged that observers be exchanged during such exercises. Most
policymakers see merit in those provisions even though Western
observers have not been invited to Warsaw Pact maneuvers since 1979
and the notification provision was conspicuously avoided by the USSR
in 1981, when major exercises were undertaken near the borders of
Poland.

At the close of the 1983 CSCE review session in Madrid, the thirty-
five participating nations agreed to a proposal long advocated by
France for a security conference to cover all of Europe, including
European Russia. Beginning in early 1984 it met at Stockholm as the
Conference on Confidence- and Security-Building Measures and
Disarmament in Europe (usually referred to as CDE), with a mandate
to work out measures that are "of military significance and politically
binding and will be provided with adequate forms of verification." In
its first eighteen months the contending sides scarcely engaged one
another. The West urged technical steps building on the Helsinki
measures: notification, observation, and verification of out-of-garrison
military activities; improved means of East-West communication; and
exchanges of military information. The East proposed general declarations against the use of force, against first use of nuclear weapons,
and in favor of a European nuclear-free zone. Unlike MBFR, however,
CDE was prodded toward conclusions by the deadline of having to
report to the CSCE review session in Vienna scheduled for November
1986 and the presence of the neutral and nonaligned group with its
demonstrated capacity for promoting common ground between East
and West. Given some impetus by the superpower summit meeting
of 1985, CDE combined aspects of the two initial approaches into a
formal agreement in September 1986. It extended the requirements
for notification and observation down to small-scale maneuvers and
introduced novel provisions for compliance and verification, including
inspection on demand (up to three times a year for each country
inspected) even in European Russia. Although the East rejected a
proposal that inspectors be flown in neutral aircraft rather than planes
belonging to the country under inspection, these arrangements appear

Europe (New York: Institute for East-West Security Studies, 1983). See also Mike
Bowker and Phil Williams, "Helsinki and West European Security," *International Affairs*,
vol. 61 (Autumn 1985), pp. 607–18.

to be a considerable advance on any previous agreements involving the superpowers.[52] During 1986 there was also some movement by both the Warsaw Pact and NATO toward agreement on using a similar thirty-five-nation forum for broadened negotiations on conventional force reduction, but the MBFR experience suggests that early results are not to be expected.

Despite the paucity of formal accomplishments in these multilateral forums, many observers believe that they provide a useful learning process, especially for the smaller participating nations, and contribute to confidence-building by their very existence. They provide additional exposure to the West for important officials from Eastern Europe, and their internal dynamics encourage some degree of national self-assertion even though outward Warsaw Pact discipline is generally well preserved, except by Romania. They offer at least some antidote to Moscow's periodic fear campaigns against "German revanchism" or "NATO plans for aggression."

Seen from the West, the purpose of regional security policies is to improve security by reducing Eastern temptations and capacity for successful aggression against the West, without inviting countermeasures by appearing to increase the vulnerability of the Soviet Union itself. One critical factor in Soviet military calculations must be the reliability—from Moscow's viewpoint—of the East European components of the Warsaw Pact. The Soviets have naturally taken extensive precautions to ensure maximum reliability, but they are bound to harbor continuing doubts arising from the very nature of the imperial relationship, especially if an attack against the West were not to result in a quick and easy victory.[53] If Western policies could intensify those doubts, security would be enhanced.

It is difficult to think of direct policy measures in peacetime to intensify the doubts. Indirectly, some headway toward that objective might be made as a by-product both of policies of active engagement with governments and of public diplomacy addressed to peoples.

---

52. For the text of the documents and formal statements by President Reagan and the U.S. delegation chief, see "CDE Delegations Reach Accord on Military Activities in Europe," *Department of State Bulletin*, vol. 86 (November 1986), pp. 20–26.

53. See Teresa Rakowska-Harmstone and others, *Warsaw Pact: The Question of Cohesion*, ORAE Extra-Mural Papers 29 and 33 (Ottawa: Department of National Defense, Operational Research and Analysis Establishment, 1984); and Edward B. Atkeson, "The 'Fault Line' in the Warsaw Pact: Implications for NATO Strategy," *Orbis*, vol. 30 (Spring 1986), pp. 111–31.

Convincing East European governments that there are no aggressive intentions from the West and increasing their stake in connections with the West should make them less willing partners in any Soviet-inspired aggression. Reinforcing the Western orientation of the peoples might help to make their armed forces less reliable in attacks against the West, especially their conscript troops and reserves, whatever the attitudes of the governments.

On the matter of Warsaw Pact military reliability, the Polish crisis of 1980–81 brought out a significant difference of views in Washington concerning desirable policy. Both the Carter and Reagan administrations went to great lengths to discourage Soviet military intervention, working through bilateral channels and multilaterally through NATO. A minority position, taken by a few advisers within the government and some outside groups, actively preferred a Soviet invasion. It would, they argued, reunite the West at a time of faltering cohesion and for a generation or more would make Poland's armed forces an utterly unreliable instrument of the Warsaw Pact, whether or not there had been active resistance to the intervention. (Presumably such considerations were also weighed by Moscow at the time.) This extreme version of the-worse-the-better school, however, never made serious headway in the higher councils of Washington policymaking.

ECONOMIC POLICIES

Except at times of crisis, economic measures constitute most of the day-in-day-out policy instruments in American relations with Eastern Europe. The practical working out of differentiation lies mainly in more or less favorable economic treatment of a given country. Economic policies have also been a major focus of policy differences within the executive branch and in Congress.

The official elements in bilateral commercial relations are summarized in table 2. The string of yes items on the right shows the favored status of Romania, Hungary, and Poland (before 1982), although there are a few anomalous entries such as the specialized bilateral agreements with Bulgaria. From the East European viewpoint, most-favored-nation status is by far the most important item, because U.S. imports from non-MFN countries are generally subject to the forbidding tariff levels created in 1930 by the Smoot-Hawley Act. Poland secured MFN treatment in 1960, Romania in 1975, and

Table 2. *Status of U.S.-East European Commercial Relations*

Type of relation	Bulgaria	Czechoslovakia	East Germany	Hungary	Poland	Romania
Most-favored-nation tariff treatment	No	No	No	Yes[a]	Yes[b]	Yes[a]
Export-Import Bank facilities	No	No	No	Yes[a]	Yes[b]	Yes[a]
Maritime agreement[c]	Yes	No	No	No	No	Yes
Double taxation treaty[d]	No	No	No	Yes	Yes	Yes
Consular convention[e]	Yes	. . .[f]	Yes	Yes	Yes	Yes
Civil aviation agreement[g]	No	Yes	No	Yes	Yes	Yes
Fisheries agreement[h]	Yes	No	Yes	No	Yes	Yes
Science and technology agreement[i]	Yes	No	No	Yes	Yes	Yes
Long-term economic cooperation agreement[j]	No	No	No	No	No	Yes
Official finanical claims settled	Yes	Yes	No	Yes	Yes	Yes
Foreign business representation offices permitted	Yes	Yes	Yes	Yes	Yes	Yes
Foreign equity investment permitted	Yes	No	No	Yes	Yes	Yes

Source: *Report on Trade Mission to Central and Eastern Europe,* Subcommittee on Trade of Committee on Ways and Means, 98 Cong. 2 sess. (GPO, 1984), p. 96. Original data as of November 15, 1983.
a. Subject to terms of the Trade Act of 1974 (Jackson-Vanik Act).
b. Suspended in 1982 after imposition of martial law and restored in 1987.
c. Provides for decreased notification time for vessels visiting other nations' ports.
d. Avoids double taxation of business, personal service, and investment income.
e. Provides access for embassy personnel to nationals detained in another country.
f. Negotiated; exchange of ratification instruments pending.
g. Permits and establishes civil aviation between countries.
h. Allows for catch allocations within territorial waters.
i. Facilitates scientific cooperation and exchange of information.
j. Facilitates long-term business and economic cooperation.

Hungary in 1978. Romania and Hungary require annual waivers under the terms of the Jackson-Vanik amendment to the Trade Act of 1974. The waivers are based on presidential findings that continued trade benefits will encourage freedom of emigration. The consequences of MFN status are evident in the much larger magnitudes of American imports from the three favored countries. The dramatic fall-off from Poland after 1982, much more severe than the drop in Polish exports to other parts of the West (see appendix tables A-4 through A-11), was at first due mainly to production problems in the items typically exported to the United States, but by the mid-1980s the continued denial of MFN had become a serious obstacle to Polish exports. Partly because of the term "most-favored," East European governments have also come to view MFN treatment as symbolically important. Bulgaria, Czechoslovakia, and East Germany have repeatedly expressed interest in receiving it but have not been willing to meet the Jackson-Vanik conditions. Although the policy of linking trade with emigration adversely affects some U.S. interests and was strongly opposed by the Nixon administration when the Jackson-Vanik amendment was first proposed, the policy has now taken on a political life of its own that could not be easily reversed.

During the détente of the 1970s, Poland and Romania were granted substantial credits from the Export-Import Bank to purchase American industrial goods and from the Commodity Credit Corporation to purchase agricultural supplies. In 1974 the joint statement by President Ford and General Secretary Gierek on Polish-American economic cooperation warmly endorsed these measures as well as private industrial cooperation agreements between American and Polish enterprises. Commercial banks were simultaneously providing very large private credits and some general long-term loans to the three favored countries and also to East Germany and Bulgaria. When the East European balance-of-payments crises came to a head in the early 1980s, U.S. financial agencies became directly involved in negotiations to reschedule the government-held debt, thus providing another opportunity for differential treatment. As to rescheduling private credits, the banking groups exchanged information and assessments with government authorities but made their own decisions, as they did when the credits were first extended.

Unlike purely private transactions, official credits, export guarantees, and insurance all involve some explicit or implicit subsidy.[54] The United States has long sought agreement among the principal industrial countries to regulate the subsidy element by limiting the terms and placing floors under the rates of interest. To this end, "consensus rates" have been negotiated in the Organization for Economic Cooperation and Development, distinguishing among recipients in rich, intermediate, and poor countries. In recent years there has been special concern that export competition might result in free gifts of resources to the Warsaw Pact group, relieving the strain of their choices at the margin among civilian consumption, investment, and military expenditure. At America's urging, the OECD members agreed in 1982 to raise the classification of the Soviet Union, East Germany, and Czechoslovakia from the middle to the highest rate category, and Bulgaria, Hungary, Poland, and Romania from the lowest to the

54. For an effort at quantification, see Daniel F. Kohler and others, *Economic Cost and Benefits of Subsidizing Western Credits to the East,* R-3129-USDP (Santa Monica, Calif.: Rand Corp., 1984).

middle group. Romania, however, is still considered a developing country and is included in the general system of U.S. trade preferences designed to assist third world development.

One group of policy advisers in Washington would go further, eliminating every kind of government credit, guarantee, and insurance on all exports to East European countries. They argue that only completely unsubsidized trade is certain to provide benefits for both sides. Commercial exporters, however, claim that certain types of sales, especially of durable capital goods, are backed by government insurance programs in all the major industrial countries, even when the destinations are stable advanced nations. Withholding such backing, therefore, would amount to positive discrimination against Eastern Europe. As a practical matter, moreover, they state that exporters cannot compete successfully without it. Agricultural exporters also point out that their competitors, notably those from the European Community, are heavily subsidized. As lobbyists with Congress and the executive departments, exporters have not promoted their interests in East European trade as forcefully as they have in Soviet trade, even though many of the same companies are involved. Their East European markets are smaller, as appendix table A-5 shows. But the case for modest government support benefits from the greater public and congressional sympathy enjoyed by Eastern Europe. The opposing position would nullify a significant element of differentiation policy and thus far has not prevailed with respect to Romania and Hungary. The suspension of official credits for Poland from 1982 to 1987 was partly for economic reasons, Poland having become completely non-bankable for new credits, but was mainly a residue of the sanctions imposed in the wake of martial law.

Controls on strategic exports and the transfer of technology have engendered sharp disputes within the executive branch, in Congress, in the powerful high-technology industries, and among the Western allies. The intragovernmental issues are partly substantive and partly bureaucratic rivalries between the Departments of Commerce and Defense, between the technical and policy branches of the Defense Department, and between the Commerce Department and the Customs Service (an agency of the Treasury Department). Industry representatives chafe at the application of unilateral export controls more far-reaching than those agreed in the interallied Paris Coordinating Committee (CoCom). They charge that official determinations of "foreign availability" (a reason for permitting exports, since the East can acquire similar products from other exporters) are too slow and too rigid. They are especially fearful that far-reaching export controls may be applied by the United States to their very large trade with other Western countries in order to prevent indirect diversions to the East. As the most dynamic sector of American industry, exporting successfully in an era of huge U.S. trade deficits, the high-technology industries carry great weight with Congress, which has sought to temper the more extreme positions advocated by the Department of Defense. At the same time, however, spectacular revelations of Soviet industrial espionage and diversion of exports nominally destined to friendly or neutral countries have strengthened the case for tighter controls over truly critical strategic items.

In legislation enacted in mid-1985 to extend and amend the Export Administration Act of 1979, Congress sought to respond to these conflicting pressures. It provided for tighter administration of narrowly defined national security controls and more severe penalties for violations, while also calling for the delisting of obsolescent technology and the speeding up of licensing procedures. On the side of export controls imposed for foreign policy reasons (sanctions), however, it introduced substantial new constraints on presidential action, both in the criteria for imposing such controls and in the requirements for advance congressional consultations. It sharply limited the circumstances in which existing export contracts can be overridden, thus seeking to strengthen the position of U.S. exporters as reliable suppliers. It made easier a showing of foreign availability. The net effect should be moderately favorable to U.S. trade with Eastern Europe, since export limitations to that region beyond those agreed to in CoCom are more likely to be based on grounds of foreign policy than of national security.[55]

Interallied disputes on the scope of strategic controls have been commonplace during CoCom's thirty years of deliberations. But in

55. The legislative text and conference report appear in the *Congressional Record,* daily edition (June 26, 1985), pp. H4905–H4923. Brief Senate comments on final passage are in the *Congressional Record,* daily edition (June 27, 1985), at pp. S8921–S8927 and similar comments in House of Representatives at pp. H5059–H5063. Fuller expositions were made in the Senate on October 10, 1984, and in the House on October 11, 1984. The main issues are summarized in *Transfer of Technology,* S. rept. 98-664, 98 Cong. 2 sess. (GPO, 1984); and U.S. Congress, Office of Technology Assessment, *Technology and East-West Trade: An Update* (GPO, 1983).

the 1980s they were elevated to the highest levels, figuring on the agendas of successive economic summit gatherings and bilateral meetings of heads of government. Tension reached a peak during the 1982 controversy over the export of equipment for the Soviet Urengoi gas pipeline—a crisis perhaps not comparable to the classic alliance crises of Suez and Berlin yet a serious threat to all forms of cooperation within NATO. The issues were both procedural and substantive. The Europeans opposed the extraterritorial application of American controls as an invasion of sovereignty, objected strenuously to the extension of unilateral controls to West-West trade, and maintained their long-held position that exports should be limited only for military reasons, not for broader foreign policy purposes. With respect to re-exports and diversions, there has also been tension between the U.S. government and European neutrals, especially Austria, Switzerland, and Sweden.

Eastern Europe figures in these disputes only peripherally as a potential channel to the Soviet Union. No one contests the principle that whenever military hardware itself and advanced production technologies with major military applications are denied to the USSR, they must be equally denied to the rest of the Warsaw Pact. East European "diplomats" and "businessmen" have served as industrial espionage agents for the USSR. Nevertheless, within the gray area of civilian technology that has only limited military utility, there has been some modest differentiation in the application of export controls to Poland, Romania, and Hungary. For many years, exceptions to restrictions were granted more readily for exports to Poland than to others, one notable example being a catalytic cracker for a Polish oil refinery.

The Export Administration Act of 1979, doubtless mindful more of Yugoslavia and China than of Eastern Europe, provided that

> in administering export controls for national security purposes . . . United States policy toward individual countries shall not be determined exclusively on the basis of a country's Communist or non-Communist status but shall take into account such factors as the country's present and potential relationship to the United States, its present and potential relationship to countries friendly or hostile to the United States, its ability and willingness to control retransfers of United States exports in accordance with United States policy, and such other factors as the President considers appropriate.[56]

56. Export Administration Act of 1979, 96 stat. 72, sec. 5(b). Even greater flexibility was provided in the 1985 amendments.

The severity of export licensing is graduated among formally designated country groups. Bulgaria, Czechoslovakia, and East Germany are assimilated to the Soviet Union, while Poland (until 1982) and Hungary have been treated less restrictively, and Romania marginally still less.[57] One celebrated case entailed approval for the Control Data Corporation's joint investment venture in Romania to produce computer peripherals, followed by supplemental agreements covering newer technology, although always keeping well behind the current state of the art. There have also been cases of dual-use technology licensed for civilian use in fixed installations on condition that periodic inspections be permitted so as to ensure that critical items have not been diverted elsewhere. But under pressure from the Japanese and European governments, CoCom restrictions have been withdrawn entirely from many intermediate-technology products, thereby reducing the scope for differential treatment in Eastern Europe.

The world economy's major multilateral institutions also have an important potential role in a policy of differentiation. The United States has welcomed the participation of the favored East European countries in the General Agreement on Tariffs and Trade (GATT), the International Monetary Fund (IMF), and the World Bank. Czechoslovakia was a founding member of the GATT in 1947 (before the communist seizure of power in Prague), and was later joined by Poland, Romania, and Hungary. Romania joined the IMF and World Bank in 1972; Hungary applied in 1981 and joined in 1982; Poland's application for membership, also filed in 1981, was delayed after the imposition of martial law but finally became effective in 1986. (Yugoslavia has been a member from the start of the institutions.) During its brief liquidity crisis of 1981–82, Hungary was assisted by a bridging loan from the Bank for International Settlements pending the availability of IMF resources, thus avoiding a formal rescheduling of its external debt, a step welcomed by American financial authorities.

The IMF and the World Bank are by charter nonpolitical, and their officers frequently reiterate that they are not to be considered instruments for political change or for altering economic systems. Nevertheless, the conditions typically placed on their lending—rational pricing and efficient management for World Bank projects, and economic "transparency," realistic exchange rates, avoidance of undue subsidies, and improved international competitiveness as elements of

57. See Gerhard Mally, "Technology Transfer Controls," *Department of State Bulletin,* vol. 82 (November 1982), pp. 52–55.

IMF standby agreements—are bound to favor liberalizing reforms and market mechanisms, Hungarian-style or other. The IMF and the World Bank can promote those kinds of economic policies without the political overtones inherent in conditional assistance from individual Western governments or bankers. Their effectiveness, however, is highly dependent on the active interest of the East European governments concerned (or at least of key officials and advisers) in moving in those directions.[58]

SANCTIONS AND CONDITIONALITY

To be effective instruments of policy, economic measures must presumably have some influence on behavior, either implicitly or by virtue of explicit conditions. It is argued, for example, that expanded trade has an implicit Westernizing influence because of wider contacts among businessmen and officials from East and West. But American policymakers (and probably many bankers) look back with regret on the liberality with which both private and official credits were extended to Poland in the 1970s, feeling that they permitted the Gierek regime to set aside its much-heralded reform program instead of making reforms a condition for financial support. The Jackson-Vanik amendment relating most-favored-nation treatment to liberalized Eastern emigration policies is a clear example of explicit conditions.

The history of economic sanctions includes well-known major failures, such as those against fascist Spain in the late 1940s and those against Rhodesia's unilateral declaration of independence in the 1960s. More recently, economic sanctions failed to pursuade the Soviet Union to liberalize its emigration policy or to withdraw from Afghanistan; in the latter case, moreover, sanctions threatened a serious breach in Western unity during the Urengoi pipeline dispute. As a result some observers have concluded that sanctions are useless at best and pernicious at worst. Others have argued that rewards for desired behavior (carrots) are acceptable, but penalties (sticks) are counterproductive. American policymakers concerned with Eastern Europe do not accept those views. The distinction between carrots and sticks is rejected on logical grounds: if behavior ceases to be acceptable and

58. See Paul Marer, "Centrally Planned Economies in the IMF, the World Bank, and GATT," in Josef C. Brada, Ed A. Hewett, and Thomas A. Wolf, eds., *Economic Adjustment and Reform in Eastern Europe and the Soviet Union* (forthcoming).

rewards are withdrawn, the former carrot becomes a stick, as when Poland's MFN status was suspended. By the same token the withdrawal of a stick is itself a carrot. The failure of sanctions to influence Soviet behavior is generally acknowledged, although some policymakers strongly condemned the abandonment of the grain embargo.[59] But the bargaining relationship in Eastern Europe is considered much more favorable to the United States, especially if the desired change in behavior does not affect vital interests and the quid pro quo is of real value. If the West as a whole were to join in sanctions, their effectiveness would become even greater.[60]

Two recent examples are cited. In 1983 Romania withdrew a proposed diploma tax on emigrants under warning of a possible nonrenewal of MFN treatment from the United States. And in 1985 it was reported that the United States had "secured the release of two of Romania's most prominent dissidents, as well as a sharp rise in general emigration, in return for continuing MFN tariff treatment."[61] Less clear-cut is the effect of the sanctions imposed on Poland after the declaration of martial law. At that time, three desired changes in behavior were specified, not only by the United States but by NATO foreign ministers as a body: the termination of martial law; the release of political prisoners; and the renewal of dialogue among government, church, and the Solidarity movement. The third condition remains wholly unmet, but it is believed that Poland's desire for a lifting of the sanctions accelerated the ending of formal martial law in 1982 and contributed in 1984 and 1986 to the breadth of the amnesties for political prisoners. In addition, withdrawal of U.S. opposition to Poland's application for membership in the International Monetary Fund—which had become a kind of supplementary sanction—was bargained against the release of several widely known dissidents (some of whom, however, were subsequently rearrested).

59. See Haig, *Caveat*, pp. 111–16.
60. The recent literature on sanctions generally supports their efficacy under these kinds of clearly specified conditions. See Robin Renwick, *Economic Sanctions,* Harvard Studies in International Affairs 45 (Harvard Center for International Affairs, 1981); Gary Clyde Hufbauer and Jeffrey J. Schott, assisted by Kimberly Ann Elliot, "Economic Sanctions in Support of Foreign Policy Goals," in *Policy in International Economics* (Washington, D.C.: Institute for International Economics, 1983); and David Buchan, *Western Security and Economic Strategy Towards the East,* Adelphi Papers 192 (London: International Institute for Strategic Studies, 1984).
61. *Financial Times* (London), July 26, 1985.

Apart from specific changes in behavior, sanctions are valued as a more tangible demonstration of serious concern than mere words of protest; they are also considered a potential deterrent to undesired behavior in the future. Sometimes a principal motivation for sanctions is to satisfy particular domestic constituencies or a temporarily aroused public opinion. In any event, if differentiation implies more favorable treatment for good behavior, it follows that bad behavior must call for less favorable treatment. Despite their well-known limitations, therefore, sanctions are likely to remain significant instruments of U.S. policy. But it is also recognized that in many cases they can be worthless unless jointly applied by all the target country's main Western sources of trade and finance.

Crisis Management: The Case of Poland

Foreign policies are put to their severest test at times of international crisis. Because conditions then are at their most fluid, crises pose exceptional risks and exceptional opportunities: they attract high-level attention that can overcome normal bureaucratic inertia. Their outcome may influence the course of events long into the future. Poland's crisis in 1980–82 was the deepest in Eastern Europe's postwar history. It involved political, economic, and military factors, each relating to both East and West, and illustrated vividly the problems of process and the dilemmas of substance in American policymaking toward Eastern Europe.[62]

The explosion of the Gdansk shipyard strike into the nationwide free labor organization named Solidarity in August 1980 was as much a surprise to American officials as it apparently was to most Poles. There had been some thoughtful predictions of social unrest following the visit of Pope John Paul II in 1979, but observers did not foresee its depth or breadth and their analyses did not attract the attention of senior policymakers. At the time, Washington's foreign policy preoccupations were the ongoing Iranian hostage crisis, the reshaping

62. In preparing this brief review of policymaking during the Polish crisis, the author consulted a large number of professional diplomats, civil servants, and political appointees from both the Carter and Reagan administrations who were directly involved. It was a condition of the interviews that there would be no quotation of or attribution to named individuals.

of superpower relations following the Soviet invasion of Afghanistan, and the revolution in Nicaragua. The domestic economy was suffering from simultaneous stagnation and inflation. President Carter had just been through a difficult fight for renomination and faced uncertain prospects in his campaign for reelection. Those conditions were not conducive to concentration on Poland.

By a curious coincidence, however, both Secretary of State Muskie and National Security Adviser Brzezinski were of Polish descent and intensely concerned with developments in their ancestral homeland. Brzezinski, moreover, had long been a proponent of peaceful engagement and bridge-building in Eastern Europe. So in late August 1980 an interagency task force on Poland was set up to monitor events as closely as possible and to develop policy options. Notwithstanding the deep fissures on other issues between the National Security Council staff and the Department of State, Poland was not an object of major dispute, either between those agencies or in the other interested departments.

U.S. policy maintained two immediate objectives: to deter a Soviet invasion of Poland and to rescue the Polish economy in a way that would strengthen the new social compact between Solidarity and the government promised by the Gdansk Agreement of August 31. Intelligence collection on Soviet military movements and other preparations was intensified. Believing that in the Prague Spring of 1968 the Johnson administration had gone too far in relieving the Soviet Union of concern about possible Western reactions to military intervention in Czechoslovakia, the U.S. authorities set in motion a concerted campaign to warn the Soviets of dire political and economic (but not military) consequences if Poland were invaded. They also suggested caution and restraint to the leaders of Solidarity, and at one point Secretary Muskie advised the AFL-CIO against too much overt support for fear that it would be provocative. Both diplomatic and public channels were employed, including repeated statements by Muskie and President Carter.

A high priority was put on coordinating public statements and contingency planning with West European governments. Coordination was pursued bilaterally, in quadrilateral meetings with the European Big Three (West Germany, France, and Britain), and in NATO. The United States had already imposed far-reaching unilateral economic sanctions on the USSR, including the grain embargo, in response to the invasion of Afghanistan. If Soviet troops were to move on Poland, trade sanctions would be NATO-wide and would include stopping materiel for the huge Soviet natural gas pipeline project. The possibilities of Soviet intervention short of outright invasion, or of Soviet-inspired repression by the Polish authorities, were also discussed with the allies, but without agreement on contingent responses.

In addition to imposing economic costs, Western policymakers wanted to deprive the Soviets of any possibility of surprise, perhaps thereby creating a further deterrent by making Polish resistance more likely. All these efforts reached a peak in early December, the first of two occasions when intelligence reports foreshadowed an imminent Soviet invasion. At that time the briefings were extended to neutral countries and included a telephone conversation in Polish between Brzezinski and the pope.[63] There were in fact extensive Soviet military movements, intended either as a feint or as preliminaries to an actual invasion. What influence, if any, the Western statements and actions had on the decision not to invade is beyond our knowledge.

Economic rescue was a more complex challenge. Poland's economy was in deep trouble. Per capita output had already been reduced by 2.4 percent in 1979 and was falling a further 3.3 percent in 1980. The hard currency debt-servicing obligations were approaching 100 percent of current export earnings. The country had become totally noncreditworthy for further private international lending, leaving no option beyond default or major debt rescheduling while severely limiting imports.[64] The Western world had rightly become disillusioned with Gierek's economic policies: his failure to implement promised structural reforms and gross misuse of generous Western supplies of capital. By then it was also recognized that Western bankers and governments had been too eager during the 1970s to furnish credits without requiring appropriate conditions or even basic economic information. By 1980 Poland faced a desperate immediate need for foreign exchange to finance imports of agricultural supplies, industrial raw materials, and spare parts.

---

63. See Brzezinski, *Power and Principle,* pp. 463–68.
64. For further discussion of these economic conditions, see Lincoln Gordon, "The Economic Crisis in Eastern Europe," in Jeffrey Simon and Trond Gilberg, eds., *Security Implications of Nationalism in Eastern Europe* (Boulder, Colo.: Westview Press, 1986), pp. 29–48.

During the previous year, the U.S. government had granted Poland agricultural credits and guarantees of $500 million. On September 12, 1980, on the heels of the Gdansk Agreement, President Carter appeared before the television cameras to announce new agricultural credit guarantees through the Commodity Credit Corporation (CCC), amounting to $670 million, the largest such credits ever extended, covering both principal and interest. The form of the announcement was doubtless calculated to appeal to Polish-American voters, but it was also intended to emphasize the U.S. commitment to helping Poland through its economic travail.

In November, immediately after its election defeat, the administration was faced with a Polish government request for far greater assistance: a financial aid package reported to amount to $3 billion.[65] Poland simultaneously sought some $5 billion from other Western governments. American officials held inconclusive discussions with the Germans and other Europeans about joining in a large-scale international aid package. Meanwhile, the Agriculture Department became concerned for the solvency of the CCC, fearing a dangerous precedent of allowing huge new credits for a nearly bankrupt borrower. Others felt that new government credits would be used merely to pay off part of the private debt, postponing the inevitable rescheduling while not really helping the Polish economy. In late November, finally, the president concluded that large-scale new aid was inappropriate for a defeated administration and that the decision must be left to the incoming Reagan team.

This was the period in which some analysts believe that a masssive, coordinated, and carefully conditioned Western aid program (often termed a Marshall Plan for Poland) might have set the Polish economy on the road to productive systemic reforms and stabilized the internal relationship between the ruling party and Solidarity on a basis within the limits of Soviet tolerance. At least, they argue, the West would have lost nothing by trying and the stakes were very high. Party leader Stanislaw Kania and Deputy Prime Minister Mieczyslaw Rakowski were giving signs of possible responsiveness.[66]

65. "White House Studies Poland's Request for $3 Billion in Emergency Assistance," *Wall Street Journal,* November 14, 1980.

66. The case is eloquently stated in Timothy Garton Ash's book under the rubric "A Missed Opportunity: Western Economic Policy":

A carefully co-ordinated western plan of large-scale new credits and economic

Had the Carter administration not been at the end of its tenure and had the U.S. economy been more flourishing, Muskie and Brzezinski together might possibly have won presidential backing for such an effort and carried it through Congress, especially for aid given jointly with Western Europe. But the difficulties either in Washington or in Warsaw should not be underestimated. The Marshall Plan is not a true analog; it required over a year between announcement and the start of implementation, and the Polish economy could not wait more than a few weeks. (A more apt parallel would be the Truman administration's emergency program for Greece and Turkey.) And because the Organization for Economic Cooperation and Development has no operating capacity, some new international organization would have been needed, perhaps along the lines of the aid consortia sponsored by the World Bank for India and other large borrowers. Even with a highly cooperative Polish government, needed reforms in the system would have been difficult to define and enforce, and in the short run might have reduced production even further. Against the obstacle of an entrenched central planning bureaucracy, reforms would have been many times more difficult to secure. And on the critical internal political issue, the working out of Poland's domestic social compact, any serious international consortium would have been drawn into mediating between Party and Solidarity, with Soviet and other Warsaw Pact leaders breathing heavily in the wings.[67]

---

aid, offered without Reaganaut propaganda but with economic strings attached, through an international economic organization like the OECD . . . would have significantly increased the always small chances of a historic compromise between Solidarity and the communist authorities in Poland. This unsung Marshall Plan would not merely have made new credits to the Polish government conditional on a full disclosure of information to the West, and on economic reforms— decentralization, accountability of individual enterprises, controls over managerial competence, etc. It would also have explored more direct possibilities of imposing "conditionality" [aid to private agriculture, food aid through the Church, and direct supplies of the scarcest intermediate goods and spare parts].

See *Polish Revolution: Solidarity*, pp. 326–27.

67. In February 1981 the Royal Institute of International Affairs in London published a diagnosis of the Polish crisis prepared by Professor Richard Portes, a leading scholar of the East European economies. The diagnosis proposed multilateral Western debt rescheduling contingent upon Polish domestic economic reform. The proposal sought to meet some of the difficulties, but it would have required at least tacit cooperation from the USSR, even though maintenance of the social compact with Solidarity was one of its critical elements. In the short run it was unable to enlist support from the newly installed Reagan administration. Even had it done so, hindsight

On a more modest scale, President Carter has been criticized for granting the $670 million of CCC credits without at least some conditions promoting economic reforms. But the obstacle there was institutional. The CCC's task is to facilitate agricultural exports; it had neither the desire nor the competence to negotiate unrelated conditions. As one high official commented, "their main interest was in getting their money back." The proper instrument for a conditioned unilateral aid program would have been the Agency for International Development, but AID could not act without new legislation, both to permit assistance to a communist country and to appropriate the needed funds. In September 1980 there was no practical possibility of that kind of action by Congress.

During the transition of administrations, designees of President-elect Reagan were fully briefed on developments in Poland and allied contingency planning. When the new team came into office in 1981, however, it was hampered by divided counsels from the political appointees. The more conservative element also mistrusted the professionals who had been serving Carter and before him Ford, Nixon, and Henry Kissinger, who was considered the apostle of appeasement in the guise of détente. One substantial group believed that a policy of rigorous economic denial could bring the Soviets to their knees. They opposed any economic concessions to Eastern Europe, including Poland, arguing that the USSR would be forced to replace any resulting losses, thus adding to the costs of empire. There was also a small minority, already mentioned, that positively welcomed the idea of a Soviet invasion. More moderate positions ultimately prevailed on all these issues, but only after the period of intense crisis in Poland had already passed.

Secretary of State Haig quickly secured President Reagan's agreement to a policy of discouraging Soviet military intervention, using public and diplomatic channels and allied consultations in the same pattern as the previous administration. Agreement on economic policy was another matter. The administration's economic priorities were focused on tax reduction and cuts in nonmilitary domestic spending, both inimical to large-scale foreign aid. The-worse-the-better school opposed such aid in any event. Haig himself reveals some ambivalence

suggests that the proposal would have had only the faintest likelihood of succeeding. See Richard Portes, *The Polish Crisis: Western Economic Policy Options* (London: Royal Institute of International Affairs, 1981).

in his memoirs. At one point he writes, "There was never any question that the popular movement in Poland would be crushed by the USSR. The only questions were: when will this happen, and with what degree of brutality?" Yet he describes America's aims as being to "keep Soviet troops out of Poland, and to preserve the reforms achieved by Solidarity." To this end, "in concert with [our European allies, we could] alleviate Poland's desperate economic situation through financial measures and the shipment of food to the Polish people."[68] Some middle-level officials and members of Congress favored a more ambitious Western program but were unable to secure top-level consensus or leadership.[69]

As a result, the spring and summer of 1981 passed with a series of modest economic measures: in February, deferral of $88 million of official debt repayments; in April, $70 million of aid in surplus butter and dried milk to be paid for in zlotys; in August, further deferral of most Polish government loan repayments due in 1981; in October, $29 million more in food aid. Each measure of aid had to be battled through a bureaucratic maze; each time, the issues of principle, which were still under general debate, had to be refought. By autumn, advocates of a larger-scale program coordinated with Western Europe were gaining ground. In their eyes it was a great triumph to secure presidential approval on December 10 for a further $100 million in food aid. Four days later that program was suspended: Warsaw had decreed martial law.[70]

From this record, one must reluctantly conclude that if there were indeed opportunities in 1981 to help preserve the gains of Solidarity, Washington's machinery of crisis management was not prepared to take advantage of them. In Poland in the spring, at least until the beating in Bydgoszcz of rural Solidarity leaders by the police in March

68. Haig, *Caveat*, pp. 239–41.
69. See, for example, Les Aspin, "Bankers' Leverage on Poland," *New York Times*, February 6, 1981, and the opposing hard line views of William Safire, "Reagan's Polish Dilemma," *New York Times*, February 12, 1981.
70. Most of these actions were widely reported in the press, which was also giving extensive coverage to political and economic developments within Poland. See "U.S. Lets Poland Defer Payments," *New York Times*, February 27, 1981; Bernard Gwertzman, "U.S. to Aid Poland with Surplus Food Worth $70 Million," *New York Times*, April 3, 1981; "Polish Debt Delay Signed," *New York Times*, August 29, 1981; Bernard Gwertzman, "U.S. Will Send $29 Million Food Aid to Poland," *New York Times*, October 28, 1981; Hedrick Smith, "Further U.S. Help Is in Abeyance Until Polish Situation Is Clarified," *New York Times*, December 15, 1981.

or even the Polish Communist party congress in July, a political solution might still have been possible.[71] If there were ever a chance of success for a Western program of economic reinforcement, that would have been the last moment for it. But not until autumn was such a program actively discussed, even at middle levels of government. By then the die in Warsaw had been irrevocably cast for martial law. Only thereafter, on December 16, did the administration set in motion its formal crisis management machinery, placing Vice President Bush in charge of a "special situation group" on Poland. This disjunction in phasing may carry lessons for the future.

The astounding success of Poland's repressive military measures caught Washington by surprise.[72] For this contingency, rather than a Soviet invasion, there had been no Western agreement on a response, partly because some European officials suspected possible American ulterior motives. The U.S. government rapidly imposed relatively moderate economic sanctions against Poland, which at that stage did not include suspension of most-favored-nation treatment or resistance

71. While no definitive judgment is possible, this is the opinion of Charles Gati, a well-informed and objective analyst; "Polish Futures, Western Options," *Foreign Affairs*, vol. 61 (Winter 1982/83), p. 296.

72. The surprise was only at the success, not at the attempt to impose martial law. In June 1986 the *Washington Post* reported, and the official Polish government spokesman confirmed, that a general staff officer in Warsaw had provided secret information to the CIA, including detailed plans for the suppression of Solidarity. The Polish government's purpose in confirming the story appeared to be to discredit the Reagan administration in the eyes of Solidarity's sympathizers by indicating that the United States had been in a position to alert the leaders in time to prevent their arrest and frustrate the operation. If fully justified, this claim would appear to represent a clear-cut case of a missed opportunity. Washington officials disputed the account, however, confirming the defection but stating that the information did not include the timing and was only one of many conflicting and confusing reports from Poland as to what steps might be taken. See Bob Woodward and Michael Dobbs, "CIA Had Secret Agent on Polish General Staff," *Washington Post*, June 4, 1985; Jackson Diehl, "Walesa Cites Contradiction," and Reuters, "State Department Criticizes Polish Official's Account," *Washington Post*, June 5, 1986; and T. Kaufman, "Pole Says U.S. Learned of Plans for Martial Law," and Bernard Gwertzman, "U.S. Accuses Poland," *New York Times*, June 5, 1986. The thesis supporting missed opportunities is argued by Eric Chenoweth and Jerzy B. Warman, "Solidarity Abandoned," *New Republic* (July 14 and 21, 1986), pp. 18–20. The interviews for this chapter suggest that those charged at the time with policy toward Poland believed that with its 10 million to 11 million members and sympathizers, Solidarity could not be effectively suppressed without bitter resistance and widespread violence. In particular, Western policymakers, like the Solidarity leaders themselves, did not anticipate the stunning effect of the shutting down of internal telephone communications. Their attention was focused on what seemed to them the more likely possibility of direct Soviet intervention.

to Poland's joining the International Monetary Fund (those measures were added after the formal suspension of Solidarity in October 1982). Washington expressed the hope that similar measures against Poland would be adopted by the Western allies and then turned to sanctions against the Soviet Union as the presumed prime mover. Polish-American groups, hesitant to worsen the plight of their cousins during a bitter winter, endorsed the idea of making the USSR the main target.

Those within the government who advocated economic pressures against the Soviet Union saw martial law in Poland as an ideal instrument to advance their cause through new efforts to block the Soviet gas pipeline. There was also an unsuccessful move in 1982, much debated in Congress and the press as well as within the government, to force Poland into formal default in the hope of imposing further financial strains on the Soviet Union.[73] But Poland was a pretext, not the real reason. As the moderates in Washington look back on it, the cause of the searing 1982 dispute among the allies was the measures against the Soviets. Policy toward Poland itself was less acrimonious, as evidenced by the NATO foreign ministers' agreed declaration of January 1982, even though Bonn's initial complacency in face of martial law was hotly resented in the United States and the European substantive measures generally were far more tepid than Washington would have liked.

Even without allied cooperation, U.S. sanctions had a genuine bite. They added substantial difficulties to the Jaruzelski regime's already formidable balance-of-payments and debt management problems, although they cost nowhere near the $15 billion alleged by the Polish government. The three most important were the termination of CCC credits for agricultural supplies, withdrawal of MFN treatment, and blockage (until 1985) of Poland's admission to the IMF.[74] How much

73. See *Foreign Assistance and Related Programs Appropriations for 1983*, Hearings before the Subcommittee on Foreign Operations and Related Agencies of the House Committee on Appropriations, 97 Cong. 2 sess. (GPO, 1983), pt. 7, "East European Debt and Trade," pp. 39–242; and *Polish Debt Crisis*, Hearings. It is noteworthy that the sponsors of these hearings, both of which were convened to press for a formal default, came from opposite ends of the political spectrum.

74. With respect to withdrawal of MFN treatment, no official estimates have been made within the U.S. government of its quantitative impact. There was a dramatic drop in Poland's dollar earnings from trade with the United States: agricultural exports fell from $119 million in 1981 to $75 million in 1982 and nonagricultural exports

influence these sanctions exerted on government behavior remains a matter of dispute. In subsequent years the sanctions were gradually modified in response to the regime's revocation of martial law, release of some political prisoners, granting of partial amnesties, intermittent dialogue with the Catholic church, and halting half-measures of economic reform. Yet those actions were interspersed with new measures of repression, the rearrest of some of those pardoned, and continuing hostility toward recognizing Solidarity. After a general amnesty for political prisoners in October 1986 and unequivocal advice from church and Solidarity leaders that the measures had outlived their usefulness, the U.S. government withdrew the remaining sanctions in early 1987, but with clear indications that they might be reimposed if there were renewed backsliding in Poland. Thus the balancing act in Polish-American relations—a kind of tacit negotiation—continues, but it no longer qualifies as crisis management.

The Alliance Factor

Over the decades Washington has devoted considerable effort to defining a deliberate policy toward Eastern Europe and using a substantial array of instruments to give it content. Whether the means are even partly sufficient to the ends, whether thirty years of pursuing imperial transformation through peaceful engagement and differentiation have accomplished anything, will be assessed at the end of this study.

Here it is appropriate to note that America's policy toward Eastern Europe has always been made in the context not only of U.S.-Soviet relations but also of U.S.–West European relations. The existence of the Western alliance is constantly present in the minds of the

---

from $276 million in 1981 to $155 million in 1982 and only $95 million in 1983 (data from computer runs by the U.S. Department of Commerce, February 1984 and February 1986). The cessation of CCC credits for exports of feed grains resulted in a major decline in Poland's production and consumption of poultry. The withdrawal of MFN status did not affect U.S. imports of meat and agricultural products. Nor was it mainly responsible for the severe reduction of other imports in 1982, since the policy change did not take effect until October. The main causes at that time were production difficulties within Poland, partly caused by cuts in its imports, and U.S. restrictions on steel imports from all sources. In later years, however, the absence of MFN treatment became a substantial impediment to Polish exports.

policymakers. With rare exceptions, however, such as Konrad Adenauer's cleaving too long to the Hallstein Doctrine, Washington has tended to consider Western Europe overly accommodating to communist hegemony, too ready to engage in normal or even subsidized trade, too soft on strategic controls, and too indifferent to sanctions for unwanted behavior. At the same time, it has seen great value in alliance cohesion and at times has recognized Western Europe's deeper interest in its immediate neighborhood. The interplay of these attitudes and those of the allies themselves is analyzed in chapter 9.

FIVE

The View from Bonn:
The Tacit Alliance

JOSEF JOFFE

GERMANY, as usual, is different. The key factor that sets it (in its ever-shifting political and territorial guise) apart from the other major countries treated in this book is geography. The United States, France, and Britain do not share any borders with Eastern Europe, nor have their involvements in the area achieved even remotely comparable levels of intensity. France has been separated from Eastern Europe by the landmass that is Germany, the two maritime nations by the North Sea and the Atlantic.

Factors Shaping German Policy toward the East

Germany is Central Europe, a part of that ill-defined land between West and East that stretches from the Rhine to the Russian border. In the past forty years one part of Germany, the Federal Republic, has of course been of the West and with the West, but in the flow of history this is a novel development. During the past millennium Germany has been both East and West, perhaps even neither. In the Middle Ages, German colonialism, led eastward by the Teutonic Knights, extended its sway as far as Lithuania. The Habsburg Reich, which would eventually become Austria-Hungary, stretched deep into the Balkans, and it incorporated much of what is today Czechoslovakia, Yugoslavia, and Poland. Modern, post-1871 Germany was essentially the product of Prussian hegemony. Prussia, in turn, had its origins in that part of Europe that is today an integral part of the East—in the Electorate of Brandenburg. Before the Kingdom of Prussia unified the *kleindeutsch* part of the empire, it extended crescentlike almost as far as Krakow in the south and the Niemen River in the north.

Much of modern Germany east of the Elbe was originally settled by Slavic peoples, and this fact underlies the unflattering role Eastern Europe had for centuries occupied in the overall scheme of German foreign policy: as target of opportunity. Given the presence and pressure of such powerful and politically well-established neighbors in the West as France, German energies were bound to seek an outlet in the East. Eastern Europe was thus to Germany what the North American continent west of the Appalachians was to the young American Republic—an object of conquest, expansion, and colonization. Indeed, the rise of Prussia-Germany in the eighteenth century is inextricably tied to conquest in the East. An appropriate symbol is Frederick II's attack on Silesia in 1740, the year of his coronation and the beginning of Prussia's ascent to great-power status. The desire to conquer and colonize continued to dominate Germany's relationship with Eastern Europe until the end of World War II and included several partitions of Poland (1772, 1793, 1795, 1939), the condominial policy against Polish nationalism shared with St. Petersburg by Berlin under Bismarck, the eastward-pushing revisionism of the Weimar Republic, the absorption of Bohemia in 1938, and finally the war of total conquest from 1939 to 1945.

World War II put an end to this militant relationship. One of the war's main historical effects was to stop and then to reverse the process of Germany's expansion into the East. Partition and dismemberment reduced German power, while the intrusion of the United States and the Soviet Union into the heart of Europe, along with their nuclear weapons, emptied any revisionism of its reality. There was certainly plenty to revise, for after World War II Germany had lost much more than the Polish Corridor, which was the main object of revisionism after Versailles. Yet if there was hope for reconquest in the fluid post-Versailles system of the 1920s and 1930s (with the United States withdrawn and the Soviet Union virtually expelled), there was none in a system dominated by two nuclear-armed superpowers. In theory, then, the realities of power and possession should have made for a new relationship between Germany and Eastern Europe, one characterized by separation rather than penetration.

Curiously, though, bipolarity has hardly resolved the problem of expansion versus extrication that underlay so much of Germany's relations with the East in centuries past. Bipolarity has merely posed the issue in a new guise, especially as that system itself began to change some twenty years into its existence.

A key feature of bipolarity in Europe, the partition of Germany, has of course remained unchanged since the end of World War II. One Germany, the Federal Republic (FRG), is unambiguously part of the West, and the other, the German Democratic Republic (GDR), is just as firmly tied to the political-military system the Soviet Union has imposed on its East European glacis. Within that system, both Germanys used to be the most bloc-minded members of the two alliances, acting as the guardians of bloc uniformity and drawing strength and status from an intimate relationship with the United States and the Soviet Union, respectively. As the tight bipolarity of the Cold War gave way to the muted bipolarity of détente in the 1970s, the role of the two Germanys changed pari passu.

Indeed, the 1980s have witnessed a radical transformation of the inter-German relationship. Ideological rivalry and competition for advantage are now supplemented, if not suppressed, by cooperation and the appeal to a common identity. The ritual invocation of the *Verantwortungsgemeinschaft,* the community of responsibility, by which the FRG and the GDR claim a special obligation for the peace of Europe but in fact mean their right to a separate détente for Germany, dimly recalls the older idea of *Mitteleuropa.*[1] That concept represents a vague geographical entity as well as an even vaguer political, economic, and cultural aspiration, but in either case it definitely implies a special role for the European center and an identity that is both East and West. Though they have been the products and pillars of bipolarity in Europe, the two Germanys have emerged in the vanguard of a process that seeks to transcend it. And so there is no end to the "German Problem" that has beset the Continent for centuries, precisely because the German Problem was always a *European* problem.

What does the German Problem mean today? One part of it is

1. For its strong roots in German thinking, see Henry Cord Meyer, *Mitteleuropa in German Thought and Action, 1815–1945* (The Hague: Martinus Nijhoff, 1955); Fritz T. Epstein, *Germany and the East* (Indiana University Press, 1973), especially chap. 3; and Giselher Wirsing, *Zwischeneuropa und die deutsche Zukunft* (Jena: Eugen Diedrichs Verlag, 1932).

familiar, consisting of the age-old tension between state and nation, between political fragmentation and cultural-linguistic unity, now played out by the FRG and the GDR on a diminished stage. A second layer of the problem, state versus state, is also familiar, recalling the secular struggle between Prussian and Habsburg for precedence in Germany. In its postwar guise, the question between the two Germanys has been who shall dominate whom; who is the true and legitimate successor of the Reich; who shall claim leadership of the entire German nation; whose political and economic system shall prevail? A third layer, however, is defined not by rivalry and mutual isolation but by cooperation. Its seeds were planted in the early 1970s when *Ostpolitik* and détente, buttressed by Bonn's contractual acceptance of the postwar status quo, began to mute both containment and bloc cohesion. By the mid-1980s inter-German cooperation had flourished into a tacit, albeit partial, alliance of sorts, dedicated to insulation of the two Germanys from the vagaries of great-power confrontation and to a vague all-German *prise de conscience*.

Finally, there is a fourth aspect, a regional and global one that complicates the other three and that flows from the peculiar role both Germanys play in their respective alliances. On the one hand, each is the brace and pillar of its own bloc and thus the indispensable junior partner of its alliance leader. On the other hand, each is tied to the other by virtue of language, nationality, and an ever-expanding network of human, economic, and financial transactions. (The most vivid manifestation of this unique, though essentially one-way, tie is the sway of West German television, whose electronic images reach almost all of East Germany.) As a result, both Germanys occupy vanguard roles, not only in each other's containment but also in the regional détente process that acts to reassociate the two polities and, willy-nilly, to dilute Europe's bipolar order.

Once more, then, "Germany" has assumed a place in the middle. If each Germany on its own is the brace of its bloc, both together have come to act as a bridge, a role that is a far cry from the relationship of mutual subversion and delegitimation dominant well into the 1960s. Until the great watershed of the New *Ostpolitik* (1969–73), the Federal Republic claimed exclusive succession to the German Reich. It denied formal diplomatic contacts to its counter-state in the East, and it invoked the Hallstein Doctrine to harness its Western allies as well as many third world nations to a global policy of refusing diplomatic recognition to the GDR. Today, however, there is almost a tacit partnership in détente with the East that coexists with the older (and stronger) alliance obligations to the West.

Put differently, the ancient German Problem has acquired a novel dimension. It is no longer just state versus nation, meaning the age-old incongruence between Germany as political entity and Germany as cultural identity. Now the conflict is three-dimensional, encompassing state and nation and system ("system" is used here to denote the ensemble of political, ideological, and economic ties, in addition to the military one, that together define membership in the two European blocs). Where does Eastern Europe fit into this tangled web of interest and allegiance?

From a West German perspective, Eastern Europe is of course no longer the next-door stage of German hegemonial ambitions. Indeed, in the so-called Eastern treaties (with the Soviet Union and Poland in 1970, with Czechoslovakia in 1973), the Federal Republic bound itself explicitly to accept the borders redrawn by World War II and to buttress that recognition with an unqualified pledge to renounce the use of force. (For all its palpable weakness, the Weimar Republic never accepted the territorial verdict of Versailles in the East.) Yet in a more subtle sense, Eastern Europe continues to play a crucial instrumental role in West German foreign policy. To put it in a schematic manner, *Osteuropapolitik* is, first of all, a function of *Deutschlandpolitik,* that is, Bonn's policy toward the GDR. And the demands of both largely determine the nature and thrust of *Ostpolitik,* the ultimate arbiter of which remains the Soviet Union.[2]

To put it more starkly, there was never, nor is there now, such a thing as a neatly compartmentalized policy toward Eastern Europe as a political-geographical entity separate from the GDR and the Soviet Union (though, as we shall see, there are autonomous elements). The driving factor was and remains *Deutschlandpolitik,* as demonstrated by each phase of *Osteuropapolitik* so far. Until the early 1960s (the first phase), Bonn maintained an isolationist policy toward Eastern Europe,

2. None of these terms lends itself to a simple translation. *Osteuropapolitik* denotes policy toward Eastern Europe, including a non-Warsaw Pact country like Yugoslavia but not the GDR. *Deutschlandpolitik* used to mean anything relating to Germany as a whole or to the reunification of Germany; today, it basically designates West Germany's policy toward the GDR. *Ostpolitik* is the most general concept, encompassing policy toward Eastern Europe (*Osteuropapolitik*) and the Soviet Union (formerly *Russlandpolitik*), with the emphasis resting on the latter.

refusing diplomatic relations with Warsaw, Prague, and the others because these regimes had recognized the GDR and thus legitimized the partition of Germany. In the second phase (mid- to late 1960s), Bonn did try a cautious policy of engagement in Eastern Europe, not for its own sake, but to isolate the GDR in its own camp. Though today (the third phase) the FRG seeks to isolate neither itself nor the GDR, while maintaining close relations with the capitals of Eastern Europe, *Deutschlandpolitik* still remains the prime mover of *Osteuropapolitik*. The difference is only that the causal relationship manifests itself in more subtle and indirect ways.

To begin with, the ultimate purpose of *Deutschlandpolitik* is no longer reunification-qua-*Anschluss,* that is, a single, conclusive act whereby the Federal Republic becomes "Germany." The new goal is not a polity but a process, a "dynamic status quo" or a "status quo plus." And the formal objective of reunification, though not officially abandoned, has been replaced by an operative policy of reassociation. The approach is based on the conceptual-legal formula of "two states in one nation," and its "teleology" foresees a gradual evolution that would eventually dispatch the goal of national unity by making its absence tolerable.

To render reunification superfluous would require a maximum measure of interstate permeability: the freedom to travel, trade, and traverse, and to do so not only on the state-to-state but also on a person-to-person level. Partition and separate statehood would no longer grate because they would no longer be a burden. Such a policy, in short, would require an "Austrian situation," where the facts of sovereignty and succession are questioned by none and the fruits of untrammeled movement (as well as a common national identity) are enjoyed by all.

To define the issue thus is to direct attention to the extra-German conditions of *Deutschlandpolitik*. In its ultimate consequences such a policy, though respectful of the territorial status quo, is of course profoundly subversive of both blocs and regimes. The postwar contest over Europe has always been twofold; the stake has not only been territorial possession but also the nature of socioeconomic regimes. Or as Stalin put it in a famous dictum: "This war [World War II] is not as in the past. Whoever occupies a territory also imposes on it his own social system. Everyone imposes his own system as far as his army can reach. It cannot be otherwise."[3] And to create "Austrian" conditions in the GDR cannot but fell the mainstays of a communist system that enjoys neither the consent of the governed nor freedom of diplomatic movement. Too much liberty within and without—above all in the GDR as the very keystone of the Soviet empire in Eastern Europe—would pose a deadly threat to a system built on political as well as pontifical control.

Deutschlandpolitik, in other words, must proceed cautiously or not at all. Given its built-in threat to the status quo (and in particular to the ligaments of Soviet control), the policy must create its own permissive conditions in a wider arena than merely *Mitteleuropa* or Eastern Europe. And thus *Deutschlandpolitik* drives all the rest—West German policy toward Eastern Europe proper and toward the Soviet Union. The crucial intervening variable that links the three levels is détente, the indispensable bridge between aspiration and reality. Détente, as the key assumption of contemporary German *Ostpolitik* has it, will dilute the necessities of empire. A European setting bereft of tension and suffused with cooperation will reassure the communist regimes, allowing the East Germans and East Europeans to relax authoritarian controls while extracting an ever-expanding measure of autonomy from the Soviet Union.[4]

The driving premise of *Ostpolitik,* then, is a benign European climate without differential degrees of détente. In other words, relations between the two Germanys should not be so intimate as to excite the suspicions of the East Europeans, nor must Bonn alienate Moscow by courting the East Europeans more warmly than the Soviets. The East Germans can move no faster and farther than their East European brethren, and both must take care not to rattle their Soviet overlords. Since détente is the ultimate permissive condition

---

3. Quoted by Milovan Djilas, *Conversations with Stalin,* Michael B. Petrovich, trans. (Harcourt, Brace & World, 1962), p. 114.

4. Whether these assumptions will turn out correct remains to be seen. It is by no means clear that the Soviet Union maintains an empire in Eastern Europe because of an ideological and power-political conflict with the West. It is just as plausible—indeed, more plausible—to argue that this empire exists for reasons that have little to do with the rivalry, namely as a *Cordon Stalinaire,* as it were, that protects both the political-economic regime and the territorial entity that is the Soviet Union. Hence it is not at all preordained that the Soviet Union would withdraw from Eastern Europe even if NATO were to disband and American troops were called back across the Atlantic.

of *Ostpolitik*, it must extend all the way to Moscow or come to naught. To complicate the balancing act even more, there is the Western dimension of Bonn's *Ostpolitik*. Unable to face the Soviet Union in Eastern Europe without a reliable counterweight in the West, the Federal Republic must avoid the specter of a separate détente with the East that raises questions about its loyalty and ultimate intentions in the West, particularly in France and the United States. And so the overall climate of East-West relations defines the outer limits of *Ostpolitik*. The rules are defined by the following conditions: German détente requires regional détente, and regional détente requires global détente. Hence the impossibility of separating *Deutschlandpolitik* from *Osteuropapolitik* and either from *Russlandpolitik*. "The division of our people," postulated Herbert Wehner, the long-time parliamentary leader of the Social Democratic party, "can only be overcome to the extent to which the East-West conflict as a whole can be defused."[5]

This has certainly been the historical pattern. When Bonn, in the mid-1960s, tried its hand at a "policy of small steps" that sought to outflank the GDR via economic engagement in Eastern Europe, it provoked an immediate Soviet–East German counterthrust and blocking maneuver that demanded a large price for small steps. If Bonn wanted economic access, it would have to pay in the currency of politics by recognizing the East Berlin regime and the redrawn borders in the East. During the Prague Spring of 1968, when Czechoslovakia threatened to extricate itself from bloc discipline, the response, jointly managed by the Soviet Union and the GDR, was even more brutal: forcible recentralization through invasion.

The more recent past reveals a similar pattern in reverse. For a while, Bonn and East Berlin managed to defy the stringencies of Cold War II (circa 1980–85), cultivating their inter-German garden in the face of mounting clamor between the superpowers. In the end, however, the Soviet Union succeeded in claiming its due. Its veto power over the pace of small-power détente was nicely symbolized by the cancellation of Erich Honecker's long-standing trip to the FRG on the occasion of the thirty-fifth anniversary of the founding of the German Democratic Republic in the fall of 1984. Nor would he go in 1985 and 1986 while the Gorbachev regime was still trying to sort

5. Address in Berlin, December 7, 1966, cited in Bundesministerium für innerdeutsche Beziehungen, *Texte zur Deutschlandpolitik*, vol. 4 (Bonn: Vorwärts-Druck, 1970), p. 92.

out its barely thawed relationship with the United States. In the past a number of high-level inter-German forays had fallen victim to a chill in the East-West climate. The episode in the fall of 1984, however, was the most telling of all. The cancellation was the first to have been preceded by a protracted struggle in the pages of *Neues Deutschland* and *Pravda*. The issue between Moscow and East Berlin was the scope of a separate détente between the lesser powers, and at the end of the day, Honecker chose bloc-minded discretion over all-German valor.

In the final analysis there are two overarching factors shaping West German policy toward Eastern Europe. One is unique, setting Bonn apart from the United States, Britain, and France: the latter-day German Problem, centering on the unresolved tension among state, nation, and domestic regime. The second is the nature of the regional and international arena in which that policy must unfold. Indeed, as the setting changed from Cold War to détente to Cold War II, so did Bonn's objectives and methods. It is the bipolar system that limits the FRG's aspirations; to realize the latter, the West Germans must change the former. To reassociate the two Germanys requires reassociating the two halves of Europe by breaking down the barriers of bipolarity and weakening its hold over the Continent. And thus *Osteuropapolitik* is not so much about Eastern Europe as it is an integral part of East-West relations in all of Europe.

Objectives of Policy: The Many Guises of Continuity

No other Western nation's purposes in Eastern Europe have remained as constant as those of the Federal Republic, yet none has changed its policy as thoroughly as has Bonn during the past four decades. This is the central paradox of West German *Ostpolitik* in need of explanation. Constancy has surely informed the country's key national aspirations as laid down in the Basic Law (the FRG's ersatz constitution), in countless international treaties, and in myriad official utterances: to overcome the division of the nation. Yet this aspiration has been compatible with stark variations in the operative objectives of West German policy. They have ranged from the sheer refusal of an autonomous *Ostpolitik* in the 1950s to a German vanguard role in the East during the 1970s, from a stance of confrontation during the Adenauer era to détente as permanent imperative in the 1980s.

To unravel this paradox is to focus on the single most important factor in all of West German foreign policy: the nexus between national diplomacy and its regional setting (the international system). As the setting changed, so did the policy, and such a causal pattern should hardly come as a surprise. For a half-nation that is both the product and prime victim of the Cold War, the system, to paraphrase Freud, is destiny. For a state that is so tightly chained to bipolarity as the Federal Republic, the setting provides both the decisive constraints and the opportunities. Hence the system must be either obeyed (in the short run) or changed (in the long run). That rule, as we shall see, explains much of the variation in Bonn's policy toward the East.

REVISIONISM WITHOUT POWER, 1949–63

When the Federal Republic was born in 1949 as direct progeny of the now dominant conflict between the United States and the Soviet Union, its officially proclaimed identity was that of an incomplete nation. Or, as the preamble of the Basic Law puts it until this day, "The entire German Nation remains summoned to consummate the unity and freedom of Germany by free self-determination." Though the Basic Law speaks wisely of the vague goal of *Einheit* (unity) rather than the specific quest for *Wiedervereinigung* (reunification), it was the latter that informed both public policy and public rhetoric for the first twenty years of West German history. Reunification was portrayed as a kind of *Anschluss,* and *Germania Redenta* as a Federal Republic writ large: of the West and with a liberal-democratic constitution.

It followed, therefore, that there was no such thing as a second German state east of the Elbe. What there was bore the name of Soviet Occupation Zone, *Unrechtsstaat* (outlaw state), or "the so-called GDR." It followed further that the Federal Republic, and only the Federal Republic, was the legitimate successor to the defunct German Reich; that there could be no official contacts with an East Berlin regime whose only legitimate function was to prepare for its speedy self-liquidation.

These assumptions and claims informed a policy toward the East that boiled down to the refusal to have one. For to have an *Ostpolitik* would require dealing with a hateful counter-state, hence legitimizing an entity whose very existence posed a grievous challenge to the mission and raison d'être of the Federal Republic. Nor could Bonn extend diplomatic contacts to nations that, like those in Eastern Europe, had trampled the banner of national unity by recognizing Moscow's satrapy in East Germany.

Ostpolitik and *Deutschlandpolitik* did not exist save as subspecies of *Westpolitik.* Their main function was to deny legitimacy and permanence to the Federal Republic's counter-state across the Elbe and to postpone (if not to evade) the day of reckoning that the verdict of World War II demanded. Hence the "policy of the open status quo" (also known as the "policy of strength"), as laid down in the grand bargain with the United States, France, and Britain in 1954 that defined the terms for the dismantling of the occupation regime and West Germany's admission to NATO.[6] In exchange for accepting stringent limits on its sovereignty and contributing an army of 500,000 men to the Atlantic coalition, the Federal Republic, previously a pariah in the community of nations, gained a remarkable position in the overall scheme of East-West relations in Europe.

By dint of contractually sanctified agreement with its former occupiers, the Federal Republic acquired a kind of derivative great-power status vis-à-vis the East. This status rested on a triple pledge of the three Western powers. First, they agreed that the Federal Republic, and only the Federal Republic, was "entitled to speak for Germany as representative of the German people in international affairs," thus underwriting Bonn's *Alleinvertretungsanspruch* (claim to sole representation) and precluding, by implication, Western recognition of the GDR. Second, by agreeing that the "final determination of the boundaries of Germany" must await a freely negotiated settlement, the West not only denied the legitimacy of the postwar demarcation lines (the inter-German and Oder-Neisse borders) but also reassured the FRG against a Potsdam-like peace treaty imposed by fiat of the Four Powers. Third, the United States, Britain, and France vowed "to achieve, by peaceful means, their common aim of

6. For the relevant documents see "The London Conference (September 28–October 3, 1954)" and "The Paris Conference (October 20–23, 1954)" in Peter V. Curl, ed., *Documents on American Foreign Relations, 1954* (Harper for the Council on Foreign Relations, 1955). For an analysis, see Josef Joffe, "Germany and the Atlantic Alliance: The Politics of Dependence, 1961–1968," in William C. Cromwell, ed., with Nigel Forman and Josef Joffe, *Political Problems of Atlantic Partnership: National Perspectives* (Bruges: College of Europe, 1969), pp. 345 ff.

a reunified Germany enjoying a liberal-democratic constitution, like that of the Federal Republic, and integrated within the European Community."[7] This pledge was the capstone of the entire bargain. In a formal way it committed the West to reunification. Yet its real function was to insure Bonn against the central nightmare of Chancellor Konrad Adenauer's (1949–63) foreign policy: it dispelled the specter of a collusive Four Power arrangement with the Soviet Union that might lead to a reunified but neutral and closely controlled German entity.

These commitments, the hard-won fruit of Adenauer's tenacious bargaining with the three Western powers, crystallized a revisionist posture toward the East that was even more demanding than the territorial claims of the Weimar Republic. The commitments were designed virtually to guarantee the abiding hostility of the Soviet Union, Poland, and Czechoslovakia, not to speak of the GDR as target of negotiated extinction, and to preclude any autonomous West German *Ostpolitik*. Nonetheless, such a posture was hardly irrational at that point. It was in fact the key prize of Adenauer's postwar policy.

That prize was not reunification here and now but a German veto power over Western *Ostpolitik*. The crux, according to Adenauer, was to obtain an iron-clad insurance policy against yet another *cauchemar des coalitions* (nightmare of coalitions), the abiding obsession of German foreign policy since Frederick the Great's Prussia was almost crushed by an all-Continental alliance during the Seven Years' War (1756–63). Nothing can elucidate the mainsprings of German foreign (and hence of its Eastern) policy during the 1950s and 1960s (and beyond) better than the following interview the chancellor gave in 1953. If Bismarck's historical trauma was encirclement by an all-European coalition, Adenauer's horror vision was Potsdam:

> It is no coincidence that the Soviets keep referring to this agreement over and over again. To them it represents an eternal Morgenthau Plan imposed by the Four Powers. . . . Every Soviet reference to this agreement constitutes a Soviet invitation to the West to conclude such a bargain on our backs. . . . Potsdam signifies nothing but: Let us strike a bargain at Germany's expense. . . . Bismarck spoke about his nightmare of coalitions against Germany. I have my own nightmare: Its name is Potsdam. The danger of a collusive great power policy at Germany's

7. Curl, ed., *Documents on American Foreign Relations, 1954*, pp. 116–17, 139. "European Community" at that point was a general concept rather than the specific set of European institutions the term denotes today.

peril has existed since 1945, and it has continued to exist even after the Federal Republic was founded. The foreign policy of the Federal Government has always been geared to an escape from this danger zone. For Germany must not fall between the grindstones. If it does, it will be lost.[8]

Though the grand settlement of 1954 precluded an autonomous German *Ostpolitik*, it also denied the West a free hand in Eastern Europe and Moscow. By underwriting Bonn's maximal objectives, the West had minimized its freedom of maneuver in the East. Or as Franz Josef Strauss (minister of defense from 1956 to 1962) put it: the basic point of the 1954 trade-off was to create a "situation which makes a Four Power bargain at our expense impossible."[9] It was a brilliant antidote for West Germany's impotence, endowing Bonn with a veto power over Western *Ostpolitik* and hence with a hefty measure of derivative power. Though destined to remain unsolved, the German Problem was now the decisive barrier in the overall East-West relationship, and the Federal Republic was the guardian at the gate.

With its *Westpolitik* the FRG had denied itself any access to the East, but it had gained precisely the *Ostpolitik* it wanted. Whenever East encountered West in the 1950s and beyond, the twain could not meet. The three Western powers were treaty-bound to honor West German claims, hence unable to deliver to the Soviets and their allies what they craved most: the consecration of the postwar territorial and political status quo. Since a revisionist solution of the German problem had become the sine qua non of everything else, détente, arms control, and other cooperative ventures were now hostage to West German preconditions. The open status quo in the East was thoroughly locked, and the keys lay in West German hands.

Yet the FRG's veto power was derivative; it was strength on lease. Bonn's role as arbiter of East-West affairs depended on the willingness of the West (and especially the United States) to subordinate its search for a modus vivendi with Moscow and its allies to the FRG's orthodoxy, whose main dogma proclaimed "No détente without national unity"— hence, in effect, no détente. Bonn's derivative strength also depended on the Soviet Union's meekly submitting to such a Western agenda. That it did not was amply demonstrated by the protracted Berlin

8. Radio interview with Ernst Friedländer, June 11, 1953; see Presse- und Informationsamt der Bundesregierung, *Mitteilungen an die Presse*, 561/53, pp. 3–4.
9. *Verhandlungen des Deutschen Bundestages*, July 16, 1952, p. 9853.

crisis that began in earnest with Khrushchev's notorious ultimatum of November 1958, climaxed with the building of the Berlin Wall in August 1961, and subsided only after the Cuban missile crisis in October 1962.

ORTHODOXY REFINED: THE POLICY OF MOVEMENT, 1963–66

The Soviet Union's basic message was the obverse of Adenauer's: no stabilization without ratification, meaning the formalization of the postwar faits accomplis—partition, possessions, and borders. After the construction of the Berlin Wall, which literally sealed the status quo in concrete, President Kennedy made the obvious explicit when he admitted, "Germany has been divided for sixteen years and will continue to stay divided."[10] While he refused to associate the United States "legally with that division and thus weaken our ties to West Germany and their ties to Western Europe," Kennedy drew an increasingly rigid distinction between America's and West Germany's conflict with the Soviet Union.

After the duel at the nuclear brink in Cuba, the military milieu had to be stabilized through arms control and negotiations, regardless of other outstanding issues. Because "the reunification of Germany seemed [to Kennedy] an unrealistic negotiating objective,"[11] Bonn was, in effect, politely put on notice that its leased veto power was being withdrawn. The FRG had to go along or go it alone, facing a specter only slightly less oppressive than the *cauchemar des coalitions*: the nightmare of diplomatic isolation.

Yet how could the FRG join the détente trek in the name of raison d'Etat without betraying its raison de nation? The answer was a "pure" *Osteuropapolitik* that tried to circumvent the dilemma by circumventing both the GDR and the Soviet Union. Gerhard Schröder's (foreign minister from 1961 to 1966) vaunted "policy of movement" was dedicated to economic engagement in Eastern Europe, which was presumably eager to partake of Western economic plenty and to lighten the burden of Soviet dominance. Since his policy sought to bypass the hard-core problems of the inter-German and German-

10. Conversation with Finnish President Urho Kekkonen in October 1961, quoted in Arthur M. Schlesinger, Jr., *A Thousand Days: John F. Kennedy in the White House* (Houghton Mifflin, 1965), p. 399.
    11. Ibid.

Soviet conflict, it was bound to assume an anti-GDR and anti-Soviet thrust—and fail.[12]

The premise of that policy (shared and propounded, by the way, by the Johnson administration) was based on an exaggerated view of East European stirrings of independence. It assumed:

—that East European polycentrism (much touted in those days) was necessarily anti-Soviet and liberalizing;

—that the thresholds of Soviet and East German sensitivities were high enough to ignore West German probings in Eastern Europe; and

—that such an outflanking maneuver would isolate the GDR and then soften the target to the point that Bonn could define the terms of the relationship with the GDR and the measure of liberalization within the GDR.

Events were to bear out none of these assumptions, plausible as they may have seemed during the period of relaxation and retraction of Soviet power that followed Khrushchev's failed missile gamble in Cuba. The development of trade relations with Eastern Europe did not spill over into the political realm. For the first time since the end of World War II, Bonn managed to establish an economic presence in Eastern Europe by opening trade missions in Poland, Romania, and Hungary in 1963 and Bulgaria in 1964. Yet its failure to reach an agreement with Czechoslovakia demonstrated the stringent limits of deutschemark diplomacy. Prague refused to discuss trade without a political down payment toward the resolution of the Munich legacy, a resolution Schröder studiously sought to avoid.[13] Moreover, as Romania's behavior showed, advocating polycentrism abroad and supporting Stalinism at home made for quite comfortable bedfellows.

12. For an excellent analysis of Schröder's policy, see Philip Windsor, *Germany and the Management of Détente* (Praeger for the Institute for Strategic Studies, 1971), especially chap. 3.

13. The Munich Agreement by which Czechoslovakia was forced to cede the Sudeten territory to Hitler's Germany in 1938 remained a persistent source of contention between Bonn and Prague until 1973. After the war the Sudetenland had reverted to Czechoslovakia, which proceeded to expel about 3 million Germans. While the Erhard government (1963–66) fell short of conceding the invalidity of the agreement, it did renounce all claims to the Sudetenland. Thereafter, the remaining issue was whether the agreement was invalid from the beginning or only rendered void by the German occupation of Czechoslovakia in March 1939 and who could lodge material compensation claims against whom. On December 11, 1973, Bonn and Prague finally signed a treaty establishing diplomatic relations and renouncing mutual compensation claims.

There was no necessary connection between a maverick foreign policy and domestic liberalization; hence the GDR looked no more reactionary than its more venturesome brethren in Eastern Europe.

Nor did East Germany have to worry about stigmatization in the face of a foray that sought to combine a cautious opening to the East with the retention of maximalist claims. If there was spillover from the economic into the political realm, it came in the most counterproductive of manners—by strengthening rather than weakening the East German opposition. West Germany's refusal to concede the finality of the Oder-Neisse line and to dispense with the Hallstein Doctrine allowed Moscow and East Berlin to cast Bonn in the role of the ultimate cold warrior.[14] It was not the last time that the Soviet Union and its junior partner would wield the specter of West German revanchism as an effective tool of bloc discipline.

Chancellor Erhard and Foreign Minister Schröder had evidently failed to appreciate the GDR's central role in the Soviet scheme of things. True, East Berlin was probably more beholden to Soviet succor than any other Warsaw Pact regime. Yet it did not follow that the tender blossom of East European autonomy, as nourished by Bonn's capitalist cornucopia, would somehow weaken the position of the GDR. In fact, the opposite was true. East Germany was not the predestined victim of polycentrism but the Soviet Union's best card against its uncontrolled spread. Because the presence of a huge Soviet army in the GDR "enabled the Soviet Union . . . to encircle and contain the more independent regimes, East Germany *buttressed* the framework of polycentrism. . . ."[15] Rather than isolating East Berlin, the policy of movement accomplished the opposite: it made the GDR all the more important to the Soviet Union. The much-advertised Treaty of Friendship and Mutual Assistance concluded between Moscow and East Berlin in June 1964 clearly demonstrated the point.

14. After the establishment of diplomatic relations between the Soviet Union and the FRG in 1955, the so-called Hallstein Doctrine was formulated. It branded the recognition of the GDR as an "unfriendly act . . . tending to deepen the division of Germany." (Adenauer before the Bundestag, *Verhandlungen des Deutschen Bundestages,* September 22, 1955), p. 5647. The intent of the doctrine was to prevent the international recognition of the GDR by threatening third countries with the rupture of relations, but it was also a self-denying ordinance for the FRG itself. Under the doctrine, Bonn could not exchange ambassadors with the nations of Eastern Europe that had already established diplomatic ties with East Berlin.

15. Windsor, *Germany and the Management of Détente,* p. 63. Emphasis added.

It was the end of an *Osteuropapolitik* that sought to act without, if not against, the Soviet Union and the GDR.

HALF-HEARTED REFORMATION: THE GRAND COALITION, 1966–69

Not only did Bonn fail to outflank its hostile brother; the ultimate irony was that in the end the isolator himself became isolated. While the GDR and the Soviets succeeded in blocking Bonn's eastward foray, the FRG, once the guardian at the gate, was progressively overtaken by its own key allies. France and the United States, both for their own reasons, now rendered explicit what John F. Kennedy had signaled to Konrad Adenauer at the time of the Berlin Wall: the great powers would underwrite Bonn's security but not its ambitions. By the mid-1960s the United States and France called in the "power loan" they had granted to the FRG by withdrawing Bonn's derivative veto power over East-West affairs. Moving toward détente with Moscow regardless of the unresolved German Problem, both Washington and Paris drove home the point that they were no longer willing to allow the Federal Republic to impose its conditions on détente in Europe.

Charles de Gaulle, having exhausted his two previous strategems on the road to dominance in Europe (first the idea of a NATO directorate with Britain and the United States, then an axis with Bonn), in the mid-1960s fell back on the oldest strategy in the French repertoire. Approaching Russia, France's traditional ally, De Gaulle offered himself as a partner in détente against the American "hegemon" and his West German "Continental sword." In early 1965 a German editorial noted correctly that there was now "nothing left of the Gaullist concept that no concessions ought to be made to the Soviets as long as there is no sign of Soviet acccommodation on the German problem."[16] Instead, the new French shibboleths were "détente, entente, coopération" and "Europe from the Atlantic to the Urals."

Nor did Bonn find any solace in the American connection. If de Gaulle moved from axis (with the FRG) toward entente (with the Soviet Union), the United States of the Johnson era turned from Europe to Vietnam. As Washington tried to globalize containment in

16. *Die Welt,* April 29, 1965.

Southeast Asia, it could hardly afford to antagonize its Soviet rival in Europe, let alone allow Bonn to harness the United States to its "separate conflict" (as Richard Löwenthal has put it) with Moscow. The most dramatic manifestations of that shift were the abandonment of the multilateral force that Bonn had coveted so much as a token of ersatz nuclear status and the attempt at a quasi-condominial policy in matters nuclear, as exemplified in the Nuclear Non-Proliferation Treaty jointly sponsored by the United States and the Soviet Union.

It is these drastic shifts in a seemingly frozen postwar constellation in Europe that explain equally weighty changes in West German *Ostpolitik*. The impact of the "system" was duly noted by Herbert Wehner, the Social Democratic architect of the Grand Coalition of the Christian Democratic Union/Christian Social Union (CDU/CSU) and the Social Democratic party (SPD) in 1966–69: "we have until now lived beyond our means, as if we had been a victor power by adoption."[17]

The Grand Coalition, though a fleeting phenomenon of German electoral history, prepared the way for what would soon gestate into a veritable diplomatic revolution in West German foreign policy: the New *Ostpolitik*. Its centerpiece was a total reversal in the orthodox order of things: reunification was no longer the price but the long-term prize of evolution in Europe. Shifting premises, the Kurt Kiesinger–Willy Brandt government would no longer "burden the policy of détente in Europe with any preconditions" because the "problems of Europe, like those of Germany, cannot be settled in a cold war atmosphere."[18]

Gingerly, the Federal Republic set out to rejoin the mainstream of allied policy, yet all the while clinging to the legal positions staked out in the 1950s. If the Grand Coalition assured Eastern Europe that it had no territorial claims,[19] it continued to insist that the definitive status of Germany's borders had to await a comprehensive peace settlement. While assuring Poland that "we now understand far better than before [its] desire to live at last in a territory with secure

17. Quoted in "Die Wirtschaft warnt vor den Folgen des Atom-Sperrvertrags," *Die Welt*, February 20, 1967.

18. Foreign Minister Willy Brandt before the Consultative Assembly of the Council of Europe, January 24, 1967, *Bulletin*, no. 8 (January 26, 1967). (Published by the Presse- und Informationsamt der Bundesregierung, Bonn.)

19. Willy Brandt on June 10, 1968, *Bulletin*, no. 73 (June 12, 1968).

borders,"[20] the Federal Republic did not concede the finality of the Oder-Neisse line. And while it dismantled the Hallstein Doctrine that had stood in the way of diplomatic relations with Eastern Europe, the FRG was careful not to discard all the pieces—the doctrine would still be invoked against third world countries. The only major success of the New *Ostpolitik* was the exchange of ambassadors with Romania in early 1967.

Yet again Bonn failed to breach the core of the Warsaw Pact. It still drew a rigorous distinction between the GDR, to which no form of recognition was to be granted, and the rest of Eastern Europe, and it offered conciliation without codification of the status quo.[21] Yet given the inroads West Germany had made in Romania, the GDR was now effectively threatened in its own hinterland. It is a nice testimony to the symmetrical roles both Germanys play in their respective blocs that the GDR now succeeded in acquiring a position as guardian at the gate. Indeed, Walter Ulbricht (Adenauer's ancient antagonist and the general secretary of the East German Communist party) managed to impose a Hallstein Doctrine in reverse on his Warsaw Pact allies: no recognition of the FRG without the latter's recognition of the GDR. It was flanked by twenty-year treaties of friendship with Poland and Czechoslovakia. The Ulbricht-forged Iron Triangle manifestly raised the price of Bonn's access to Eastern Europe: recognition of the GDR, ratification of the Oder-Neisse border, unequivocal renunciation of the Munich Agreement, and a vow of abstinence from any nuclear-weapons-sharing arrangements in NATO. Like Adenauer in the 1950s, his East German hostile twin Ulbricht had acquired a veto over his bloc's policy toward the other side.

THE NEW *OSTPOLITIK*

The crucial triggering factor of the New *Ostpolitik* was the election on September 28, 1969, when the Social Democrats captured the West German government for the first time since the late days of the

20. Chancellor Kurt Georg Kiesinger in his inaugural address before the Bundestag, December 13, 1966, *Bulletin*, no. 157 (December 14, 1966).

21. The largest concession was formulated thus by Willy Brandt: "Détente . . . in Europe must include détente in Germany," and hence "we aspire to an 'organized coexistence' (*geregeltes Nebeneinander*) in Germany." *Bulletin*, no. 8 (January 26, 1967).

Weimar Republic. Because the contest had been dominated by *Deutschlandpolitik* and *Ostpolitik* issues, the outcome suggested a new consensus as well as a new mandate.

The Brandt government quickly signaled its resolution to do what all previous Bonn administrations had sought to resist: to accept the postwar status quo for what it was. The word "reunification" was not even mentioned in Brandt's inaugural address. Dispensing with the FRG's claim to "sole representation," Brandt spoke of "two states in one Germany." While the last step of formal recognition would not be taken, there would be "contractually regulated cooperation" with the GDR. An agreement to renounce the use of force would respect the "territorial integrity" of each signatory state.[22]

The stage was now set for a multidimensional diplomatic exercise that, a generation after Germany's surrender, would add up to a virtual settlement of World War II. The vehicles of reconciliation with the East were renunciation-of-force agreements with Moscow and Warsaw (based on the affirmation of the territorial status quo), the basic treaty with the GDR (regulating state-to-state contacts minus formal recognition), and a treaty with Prague that declared the Munich Agreement null and void.

It was no surprise that the GDR proved to be the prime obstacle. Like the FRG earlier, it mounted an all-out effort to retain its role as guardian at the gate between the two blocs. Both had gained their identity and derivative power through their vanguard role in the East-West rivalry. Monopolizing the national heritage, each had drawn legitimacy from denying it to the other. Both Bonn and East Berlin had succeeded in harnessing their alliances to a hard-line approach against each other by cultivating intimate links with their bloc leaders. However, as with the United States in the early 1960s, the Soviet Union was now no longer willing to subordinate its own interests to the claims of its junior partner. Indeed, Ulbricht's quiet ouster in May 1971 (no doubt with Soviet prompting) evoked comparison with the fate of Adenauer, whose political decline began in earnest in the wake of the Berlin Wall and the U.S. turn toward détente after the Cuban missile crisis in 1962.

For the Soviet Union the New *Ostpolitik*, the all-European Conference on Security and Cooperation in Europe (CSCE), and the

---

22. Bundesministerium für innerdeutsche Beziehungen, *Texte zur Deutschlandpolitik*, vol. 4, pp. 11–13, 38–39.

American offer of détente cum parity represented the fruits of a quarter-century struggle to gain Western recognition for its postwar possessions in Europe. With that prize about to be delivered, it withdrew from East Berlin what the West had already taken from Bonn: its derivative veto power over East-West relations on the Continent. And thus the GDR had to content itself with the second prize: it did not obtain de jure recognition from the FRG, nor did it gain an explicit shift in the status of West Berlin to a "third" German entity. The fine distinction between de facto and de jure was drawn by the fact that both German states now maintain "permanent missions" rather than embassies in each other's capitals.

BEYOND THE NEW *OSTPOLITIK*: WHICH GERMANY, WHICH EUROPE?

Before the great watershed of 1972–73 when the treaty network with the GDR, the Soviet Union, and Eastern Europe was ratified, the key official objective of Bonn's *Ostpolitik*—and the sine qua non of evolution in Europe—was reunification as *Anschluss*. The resolution of the postwar German Problem was to lead evolution in Europe, and it was predicated on a fundamental transformation of the European balance in favor of the West. By contrast the New *Ostpolitik* represented a triple change. It put paid to the official revisionism of the Second German Republic; it changed the objective from *Anschluss* to two states in one nation; and it reversed the underlying premise of policy by defining evolution as cause and resolution as its long-term effect.

To put the issue thus is to underline a transformation in Bonn's Eastern policy that amounts virtually to a diplomatic revolution: self-denial in Eastern Europe gave way to massive engagement, the isolation of the GDR to accelerating cooperation, and Bonn as brakeman to Bonn as driver of détente in Europe. Yet in a more profound sense there is solid continuity. Nor has Bonn's basic purpose changed as power passed from Willy Brandt to Helmut Schmidt in 1974 and from the Social Democrats to Helmut Kohl's Christian Democrats in 1982. The old *Ostpolitik* and *Deutschlandpolitik* were inseparably tied to a fundamental rearrangement of the European system, with both Germanys becoming one and added to the Western side of the ledger. Significantly, the new crux is not that much different. Though it is "reassociation" and not "reunification" under Western auspices, though it is evolution first and resolution after, the crucial permissive condition is again a thorough change in the nature of the postwar European order.

Since bipolarity is the underlying cause of Germany's unnatural condition, since it is the presence of two antagonistic political-military blocs in the heart of Europe that divides Germans from Germans, relief can only flow from a reformed European order. The basic game has changed from Adenauer's "open status quo" (and waiting for a better day) to a "moveable status quo" (that will bring that day nearer day by day), but in either case the nature of the European system remains the penultimate permissive variable of German policy.

This is the underlying logic of West German *Ostpolitik*.[23] How then must the system change to accommodate German national aspirations? At first sight this is a paradoxical way of phrasing the issue, since the very leitmotiv of *Ostpolitik* from Brandt to Kohl is the scrupulous refusal to challenge the political and territorial status quo in Eastern Europe. Yet it is stability with a dialectical twist. Precisely by paying relentless homage to the realities of power and control, *Ostpolitik* from 1969 onward hopes to loosen their harsh grip to the point where the falling barriers of separation turn reunification into an irrelevant, because unnecessary, objective. The task of system transformation, previously envisioned as a kind of "rollback," has shifted from the external to the domestic level, on the premise that *reassured* regimes will also be *relaxed* regimes. (Whether that premise actually conforms to the realities will be analyzed further in the concluding section.) Secure in their rule, the East European regimes might relinquish the worst of authoritarian controls and deliver unto their citizens that measure of liberty that pulls the sting of the partition of Germany and Europe. This is surely the underlying aspiration of Egon Bahr's fabled 1963 formula, *Wandel durch Annäherung* (change through rapprochement), which was in essence an appeal to forsake the Cold

---

23. What follows is a description of the underlying thrust and structure of *Ostpolitik*, as the author sees it. It should not be confused with three issues that are analytically distinct. First, to describe a set of assumptions is not to pass judgment on their solidity or realism. Second, to elucidate the logic of a policy is different from compiling the utterances of politicians and officials. Leaders do not necessarily say what they mean or mean what they say; nor are they always conscious of what they do. And thus the task of analysis is to distill the determinants of policy from pronouncements, events, and consequences that are merely the raw data of analysis. Finally, to analyze is not to advocate; the basic assumptions that inform West German *Ostpolitik* are critically examined in later discussion, especially in the section, "The Problems of Policy."

War, mute the ideological rivalry, and accept communist regimes as partners in cooperation—and which would serve as the central premise of Willy Brandt's New *Ostpolitik* launched six years later.

Reassurance plus growth-enhancing economic benefits from abroad must serve as the functional equivalent of consent at home, of which there is no surfeit in polities beholden to the "dictatorship of the proletariat" and ultimately to Soviet arms. And so we return inexorably to the systemic conditions and targets of *Ostpolitik*. It postulates that a substantial part of regime insecurity in the East derives from the ideological and military confrontation in Europe. Muting the latter will diminish the former, and confident regimes from East Berlin to Moscow will in turn act to undo, at least in part, what bipolarity has wrought. Seeing its glacis secure and unchallenged, the Soviet Union will relax imperial controls in Eastern Europe. Its cohorts will then enjoy a larger margin of maneuver, in terms of both domestic liberalization and diplomatic movement. Presumably, such a dynamic will set in motion a "virtuous circle"—with reforms enhancing domestic consent and the latter allowing for ever more reforms. Thus though still divided by different alliance obligations, Europe will inexorably grow together again, linked by a flourishing network of trade, travel, and all manner of communication and cooperation.

It follows that confrontation is the deadly bane of this benign vision. (This is why the Schmidt government fought tooth and nail to defend regional détente in Europe against the encroaching chill of superpower conflict in the wake of the invasion of Afghanistan.) Confrontation and Cold War lead to regime insecurity, allowing Moscow to brandish the external threat as a tool of alliance discipline, forcing the regimes to tighten the reins on their populations. At a minimum, confrontation will always redound to the profit of the hard-liners in the Soviet bloc, enhancing their power against their reform-minded comrades. To soften the realities of power, its claims must be devalued by policies that emphasize conciliation and cooperation. Détente, in short, becomes a permanent imperative, to be sacrificed only for the most cataclysmic of reasons.

Nor is it only détente with the GDR and Eastern Europe. From historical experience, beginning with the Erhard government's policy of movement, the Federal Republic has learned that *Deutschlandpolitik* must begin in Moscow or it will swiftly end there. Eastern Europe cannot move faster and farther than East Berlin and Moscow will allow—that is the lesson of *Ostpolitik* in the 1960s, culminating in the invasion of Czechoslovakia and reconfirmed by the self-invasion of Poland in the 1980s. Neither can East Germany (though it has managed to go a long way) pursue a wholly separate *Mitteleuropa* détente with Bonn, as exemplified by Moscow's nonviolent intervention in the fall of 1984 when the FRG and the GDR appeared too zealous in plowing their inter-German garden.

It is the Soviet Union, first and foremost, that must be reassured and doubly so. Moscow's empire in Eastern Europe must be protected not only against a replay of the Cold War but also against the challenge of too much détente. If yesterday's strategy posed a direct, manifest threat to Soviet possessions in Eastern Europe, today's does so in a more subtle and perhaps more subversive manner. Hence there must not be too much of a good thing lest it degenerate into its opposite: uncontrolled eruption followed by forcible *Gleichschaltung* as in Czechoslovakia in 1968 or by a more indirect kind of recentralization as in Poland in 1981.

Nor can there be too little détente; that corollary, too, flows from the Moscow-first rule. It was nicely exemplified during Cold War II. As the United States and the Soviet Union reverted to overt confrontation in the 1980s—with much of it acted out in and over Europe, the traditional locus of the Soviet-American rivalry—the lesser nations' margin of maneuver was compressed accordingly. First, power, and especially its military wherewithals, once more returned to center stage, devaluing both diplomacy and economics, the classic currencies of small-power influence. Second, the renewal of the contest between the great strengthened their hold over the small. Since the stake was again the balance between East and West, alliance obligations were dramatized, forcing the weak to set aside their particular interests and rally—though resentfully—to the purposes of the strong.

The bane of *Ostpolitik*, which must maneuver in the interstices of bipolarity, is too much or too little détente since both are the fathers of bloc recentralization. The golden mean is stability cum movement, hence the term *Berechenbarkeit* (literally "calculability," more appropriately translated as "consistency of expectations") that has become the standard invocation of *Ostpolitiker* from Willy Brandt via Helmut Schmidt to Helmut Kohl and Hans-Dietrich Genscher. Implicit in this concept is the priority of the Soviet connection as Bonn faces the GDR and Eastern Europe. Since Moscow holds the key to managed change in Eastern Europe, the Federal Republic and the Soviet Union have, willy-nilly, become partners in stability (not for the first time, if one recalls Russo-German cooperation under Bismarck against Polish nationalism). Unless Moscow can count on *Berechenbarkeit*, hence on controlled change, it will turn against any change as a threat to its political and pontifical domain. This fear explains Bonn's excruciating reserve, indeed its unspoken resentment of Solidarity, which threatened to overturn all calculations and even to provoke Soviet military intervention during the Polish upheavals following the summer of 1980.

In the last analysis then, *Deutschlandpolitik* and *Ostpolitik* remain subcategories of *Russlandpolitik*. Yet there is an even more profound continuity, one that links Adenauer and Brandt, Helmut Schmidt and Helmut Kohl. Since global détente is the permissive condition of regional détente, and regional détente that of inter-German détente, Bonn must protect the first in order to shelter the second so as to safeguard the third. And thus *Ostpolitik* is, at heart, *Westpolitik* once more. Bonn's purposes in Eastern Europe can only flourish if it succeeds in holding the United States and the West to the détente bargain struck in the early 1970s, hence in reenacting what Adenauer achieved in the 1950s: the Germanization of the global détente process. Or as Willy Brandt once put it, "progress toward German unity can occur only to the extent to which overall East-West relations are improved."[24]

The Means of Policy: Many Carrots, Few Sticks

Given the premises of the New *Ostpolitik*, it follows that conciliation must take precedence over confrontation, and hence that incentives are more important than penalties. To reassure Moscow and its East European cohorts, the FRG has all but dispatched the legal-rhetorical revisionism of the 1950s. The Eastern treaties with Moscow and Warsaw (signed on August 12 and December 7, 1970) certified the "inviolability" of the postwar territorial status quo and enveloped that

24. Before the Bundestag on February 23, 1972, *Verhandlungen des Deutschen Bundestages*, p. 9791.

guarantee in a comprehensive pledge to renounce the use of force.[25] To reward the Soviet Union and the East Europeans for taking the risk of partial devolution (which reassurance was to engender), the Federal Republic has primarily focused on economic down payments: credits, technology transfers, and trade.

DEUTSCHEMARK DIPLOMACY AND ITS LIMITS

Even in the worst days of Cold War I, inter-German trade enjoyed a privileged position in the overall scheme of West German economic policy. Inter-German trade was classified as intra-German trade and thus exempted from tariffs. Since 1957, when the European Economic Community was founded, the GDR has thus been a silent semimember because East German goods can enter West Germany duty-free. Another special dispensation that has remained substantially immune to the ups and downs in the political relationship is the so-called swing, a no-interest overdraft privilege to be drawn upon by the GDR in settling its trade deficits with the Federal Republic.

During the decade of détente (1971–81), both intra-German and Eastern trade grew by about a factor of four (more in dollars but less in deutsche mark; see figures 1 and 2 and appendix table A-6). For the Federal Republic, trade with the GDR and Eastern Europe turned out to be quite profitable during that decade. By 1984 the FRG had accumulated an aggregate excess of exports over imports of DM 3 billion in its trade with the GDR; vis-à-vis Eastern Europe that excess amounted to DM 34 billion.[26]

Trade with socialist countries, however, does not loom large in the West German account. Including China, Vietnam, Albania, and

25. Nonetheless, elements of the open status quo, as laid down in the "Western treaties" of 1954, still remain. While Article 3 of the Moscow Treaty declares the postwar borders as "inviolable," a postratification Bundestag resolution of May 17, 1972, affirms that the Eastern treaties "do not establish a legal foundation for currently existing borders." Article 1 of the Warsaw Treaty states that the Oder-Neisse line "constitutes the western State frontier of the Polish People's Republic." Yet Article 4 of the same compact affirms the continued validity of earlier international agreements pertaining to Poland and Germany, hence of the Western treaties of 1954, which reserve the final determination of Germany's boundaries to a comprehensive peace settlement.

26. Deutsches Institut für Wirtschaftsforschung, *Wochenberichte*, March 7, 1985, p. 124, table I; and "Im Handel mit dem Westen gewinnt Osteuropa Bedeutung," *Süddeutsche Zeitung*, March 28, 1985.

Figure 1. *Merchandise Trade between West and East Germany, 1975–86*

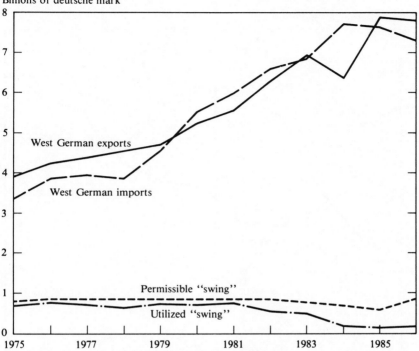

Billions of deutsche mark

Sources: Deutsches Institut für Wirtschaftsforschung, *Wochenbericht* (DIW: October 1986), p. 120; and *Süddeutsche Zeitung,* March 7, 1987.

Mongolia, West Germany's exports to socialist countries in 1983 amounted to less than 5 percent of its world total; if about DM 7 billion worth of exports to the GDR are added, the proportion rises to slightly more than 6 percent.[27] Still, though profitable on its own terms and fairly unimpressive in its proportions, trade with the Soviet bloc has always been endowed with a special political significance. Eastern trade, as the former West German economics minister, Otto Count Lambsdorff, has put it (and before him any number of other German leaders) is "a foundation of . . . peaceful coexistence between East and West." It is "an element of a policy of peace."[28]

27. Statistiches Bundesamt, *Statistisches Jahrbuch für die Bundesrepublik Deutschland, 1984* (Stuttgart: Kohlhammer, 1984), pp. 257, 277.
28. "Osthandel ist Ostpolitik," *Quick* (January 17, 1985), p. 17.

Figure 2. *West German Trade with Eastern Europe (Excluding the GDR)
and the USSR during the Decade of Detente, 1971–81*

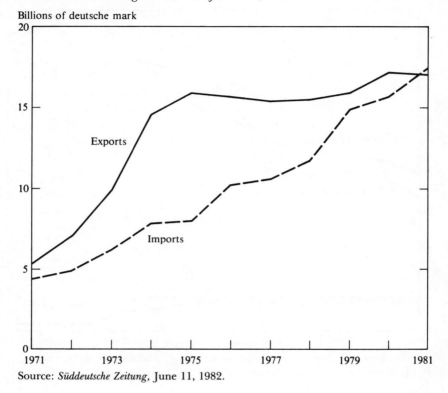

Billions of deutsche mark

Source: *Süddeutsche Zeitung,* June 11, 1982.

And it is more—a tool of political influence in Eastern Europe.
Toward the GDR it is often literally money for political payoffs. In
July 1985, for instance, the Federal Republic raised the swing from
DM 600 million to DM 850 million. On the same day, the GDR
announced that it would close its international airport in East Berlin
to asylum seekers from Asia (unless they had valid West German
visas) who previously had passed unhampered through the Wall into
West Berlin. (During the first half of 1985 about 17,000 foreigners
had used the East Berlin conduit to gain illegal entry into West
Berlin.)[29]

In the past, West German money has regularly bought political

29. See "Bonn erhöht 'Swing' im Handel mit Ostberlin," *Süddeutsche Zeitung,* July
6–7, 1985.

concessions from the GDR, and in a fairly obvious manner. In December 1981, for instance, the FRG-GDR swing agreement was about to run out. Before year's end, it was extended by another six months. In February 1982, East Berlin suddenly announced a series of *menschliche Erleichterungen* (humanitarian improvements) that increased opportunities for East Germans to travel westward on urgent family business. In June the GDR announced more *Erleichterungen*, and in the same month a new five-year swing agreement was signed, followed in September by additional minor liberalization gestures.[30] Altogether, the GDR is estimated to receive DM 2.5 billion in cash annually from the Federal Republic (apart from trade), including straight ransom (estimated to vary from DM 20,000 to DM 100,000 a head) for political prisoners. According to figures published at the end of 1986, the FRG "bought" 2,500 political prisoners from the GDR in 1985—the largest number ever.[31]

Other political-monetary trade-offs are less direct. In June 1983, during a harsh Western credit squeeze on Eastern Europe, a West German bank consortium extended a DM 1 billion government-guaranteed loan to the GDR. The deal was largely brokered by Franz Josef Strauss, the leader of the Christian Socialist Union element of the Kohl coalition. There was no obvious quid pro quo this time, but in a more long-term sense, the credit was cash for good conduct. And that return favor was badly needed in a period that would soon (November 1983) see Pershing II missiles installed on West German soil, with the threat of Soviet retribution not far behind. In August the Soviets warned that, after deployment, the West Germans would have to look at their East German brethren "across a dense palisade of missiles."[32] Yet while Soviet-American relations plummeted, the pace of inter-German contacts quickened. Erich Honecker received a string of high-level West German visitors throughout the summer. In late September two more minor humanitarian improvements were announced. And as the date of deployment drew nearer, East Berlin and Bonn either resumed or continued a series of negotiations on

---

30. For the documents, see *Deutschland-Archiv*, no. 8 (1982), p. 889–92.

31. As released by the minister for inter-German affairs, Heinrich Windelen, on December 9, 1986. See "Der Freikauf politischer Häftlinge aus der DDR," *Süddeutsche Zeitung*, December 10, 1986.

32. Thus a *Pravda* editorial, "Peace—for Europe and the Entire World," August 1, 1985.

subjects as diverse as cultural exchanges and postal communications.[33] Money, in this case, seemed to have bought a precious political asset: the insulation of the inter-German détente from the sharpening quarrels of the superpowers.

Cash bought so much insulation, in fact, that the Soviet Union began to suspect deviation. In an extraordinary editorial in August 1984, *Pravda* attacked East Berlin under the guise of attacking Bonn. "On the Rhine," it admonished the wayward East German comrades, "revanchist designs toward the German Democratic Republic are currently being reactivated. In many respects, these designs grow on calculations that would use economic relations with the GDR as a means of interference in the sovereign affairs of the Republic and for the purpose of slowly subverting the foundations of the socialist order in the GDR." *Pravda* continued by reminding the East Germans of the true aim behind intensified trade and lavish West German credits. "All of this is not to serve humanitarian improvements . . . but the search for new channels of political and ideological influence [over the GDR]."[34]

In Eastern Europe proper, the quid of money and trade has in the past bought a similar quo, that is, freedom of emigration for ethnic Germans. But in general the sought-after relationship between economic emoluments and political returns has been less direct and more conceptual. Vis-à-vis Eastern Europe (and its Soviet guardian, the looming background variable in all *Osteuropapolitik*), Bonn has usually followed the "Kissinger theorem," also known as "linkage politics."

On the most general level, linkage bade the West to cast a net of interdependence around the Soviets and their allies, enmeshing them in trade and technology transfers, credit lines, and sundry cooperative ventures. Having acquired a stake in profitable relations with the West, the Soviet Union would behave according to Western standards, like any reasonable power that ought to value peace and prosperity more highly than the costly pleasures of aggrandizement. The Kremlin, according to the tenets of linkage, would not risk the horn of capitalist plenty for an opportunistic geopolitical foray. Moreover, to lighten the burden of empire, Moscow would look kindly on Western economic engagement in Eastern Europe. The West Germans were,

33. For a review of these events, see Ronald D. Asmus, "East and West Germany: Continuity and Change," *World Today*, vol. 40 (April 1984), pp. 142–51.

34. "On the Wrong Path," *Pravda*, August 2, 1984.

and continue to be, particularly interested in such an exchange rate between economic largess and political access. The East European regimes, hungry for Western capital and knowhow, would presumably open their societies to the West, grant an ever-increasing dose of domestic liberties to their citizens, and, at a minimum, act as a restraining influence on the Soviets should Moscow ever be tempted by retrograde imperial instincts.

In theory, Soviet retrogressions should have been met with the denial of cooperation and the severing of links. Yet in practice, Western responses did not follow the logic of linkage but rather a differentiation among the allies themselves in the degree of détente. When, after the invasion of Afghanistan, the United States sounded the clarion call to arms and imposed economic sanctions on the Soviet Union, former Chancellor Willy Brandt denounced what he saw as "venomous stammerings" and "sterile agitation" of the superpowers, appealing to Germans and Europeans alike to stand ready to save what could be saved of détente.[35] And Helmut Schmidt limned one of the key reasons for such détente-minded discretion: "Increasing global tensions will indubitably compress the margin of maneuver of East European states and their governments."[36]

CRISIS MANAGEMENT AND THE CASE OF POLAND

Events in Poland, though much closer to home and inexorably moving toward military repression, did not make much of a difference. Indeed, since forcible intervention by the Soviet Union would have dealt a death blow to the premise of *Osteuropapolitik*—"relaxation through reassurance"—West German leaders were quick to decry the bipolar dimension of the Polish crisis and to avoid rattling the Soviet Union. Castigating Washington for "indulging in an orgy of impotence," Willy Brandt, chairman of the Social Democratic party, turned aside the U.S. claim that Poland was a problem for the alliance. "Poland has a great deal more to do with Poland than with the

35. As quoted in "Mit den Amerikanern nicht in den Tod," *Der Spiegel*, vol. 18 (April 28, 1980); and "Die Zweifler üben sich in Solidarität," *Süddeutsche Zeitung*, January 18, 1980.

36. Interview with Werner Halzer and Eghart Märbif, "Es sind auch noch grössere Dummheiten im Wahlkampf denkbare," *Frankfurter Rundschau*, August 12, 1980.

relationship between East and West."[37] Before Poland's occupation by its own troops, Chancellor Schmidt and Foreign Minister Hans-Dietrich Genscher did join the United States, Britain, and France in warning Moscow not to intervene. Afterward, however, Schmidt denied for several weeks that the Soviets shared any responsibility for the coup so as to avoid having to blame Moscow and to join Washington's renewed call for sanctions against the Soviet Union. Willy Brandt, speaking for the Socialist International, thought that "unsolicited opinion or remarks formulated in a hard way" would do nothing to "aid the people of Poland," a declaration that was harshly rejected by the socialist parties of Italy and France.[38]

West German management of the Polish crisis was essentially dedicated to downplaying it. To be sure, the Bundestag was the first Western parliament to condemn General Jaruzelski's coup of December 13, 1981. Two weeks later, Foreign Minister Genscher told visiting Deputy Prime Minister Mieczyslaw Rakowski that the government expected the speedy lifting of martial law, the release of all prisoners, and the resumption of the regime's dialogue with the church and Solidarity. But Bonn would "continue to adhere to the principle that Poland must solve its problems by itself and without interference from abroad."[39] That was a subtle way of driving home the essential point about Bonn's future policy: if given some cooperation, say in form of a softened martial law, the Federal Republic would hold the line for the Jaruzelski regime against any harsh countermeasures by the Reagan administration and thus against anything that might provoke the Soviet Union to intervene directly in Poland.

As early as January 1982 Chancellor Schmidt practically precluded German sanctions against Poland. "We do not like the news coming out of Poland," he said just before meeting with President Reagan to hammer out a joint Western policy, "but we would find it extremely difficult to impose sanctions against Poland."[40] Why was the Schmidt government (and especially the Social Democratic party) so "blind to

37. Interview with Harry Schleicher, "Nicht mit Wörten tapfer sein . . . ," *Frankfurter Rundschau* (Paris), December 19, 1980.

38. Quoted by John Vinocur, "West Germany Uneasy over Poland," *International Herald Tribune* (Paris), December 23, 1981.

39. Quoted in "Bonn erwartet von Polens Militärregime 'schnellstens' Aufhebung des Kriegsrechts," *Süddeutsche Zeitung*, December 31, 1981.

40. Interview with the *New York Times* as quoted in "Schmidt: Sanktionen problematisch," *Süddeutsche Zeitung*, January 4, 1982.

the moral indignation in the Western world," all the more so since "a stronger condemnation of the putsch would not have endangered world peace"?[41] The answer does not grow out of Bonn's presumed moral obtuseness but out of the very logic of *Ostpolitik.* An anonymous adviser of Chancellor Schmidt put it thus: "If the Russians invade, everything is *kaputt.*"[42]

Heinz Rapp, a member of the SPD Grundwerte-Kommission (the SPD Executive's Commission on Basic Values), put the same message in terms of three axioms. First, "freedom of maneuver for reform movements requires détente." Second, "détente and noninterference [in the domestic affairs of other countries] are equally conditioned on one another." By way of elucidation, Rapp added as a third axiom, "The status quo [in Eastern Europe] must be consolidated so that it may change." And as far as Poland was concerned, "punishment would merely hinder the return to normality" that would permit a "change for the better."[43] Egon Bahr, the architect of Willy Brandt's *Ostpolitik,* expressed the basic point more brutally: "The maintenance of world peace," meaning stability in Eastern Europe and a confident Soviet Union, was "more important than Poland."[44]

That Western pressure would endanger the peace was of course a calculated exaggeration. But to provoke the Soviets into intervention would clearly have endangered, if not destroyed, the prospects of *Ostpolitik* for years to come. Since Moscow is the ultimate arbiter of evolution in Eastern Europe, the Soviet Union must be reassured even to the point where *Ostpolitik* becomes a silent—and above all, discreet—partner in the maintenance of regime stability and Soviet authority in Eastern Europe. This is why the Schmidt government was not enthusiastic about Solidarity, why Schmidt initially denied any Soviet responsibility for the Jaruzelski coup, why his government helped to launch a massive food support campaign to stave off

41. Dieter Schröder, "Polen spaltet den Westen," *Süddeutsche Zeitung,* December 31, 1981. He continues: "This is particularly true for [Social Democrats like Egon] Bahr, [Erhard] Eppler, and Brandt. Even the most recent statements by Brandt show that he no longer understands what is happening in Poland. One might almost conclude that he views the signing of the Final Act of Helsinki as the establishment of a kind of Holy Alliance and himself as a second Metternich."

42. Quoted in "Wir wandeln auf dünnem Eis," *Der Spiegel,* January 4, 1982.

43. Heinz Rapp, "Das Kriegsrecht in Polen und die Seele der SPD," *Vorwärts,* February 4, 1982.

44. "Bahr: Weltfriede wichtiger als Polen," *Süddeutsche Zeitung,* December 22, 1981.

eruptions that might trigger a Soviet intervention after all (the federal post office charged no postage for food parcels sent to Poland), and why Bonn worked hard to hold off Western sanctions.

As in the aftermath of the invasion of Afghanistan, Bonn (along with its European allies) refused to take part in economic sanctions against either Soviets or Poles. (The FRG, however, did join the Olympic boycott against Moscow.) Together with Britain, France, and Italy, the Federal Republic strenuously resisted the American embargo against the Urengoi gas pipeline, imposed in direct response to the Polish putsch in December 1981 and extended in the summer of 1982. To have followed the American lead would have sinned against every commandment of *Ostpolitik*, which is to reassure rather than rattle the Soviets, to protect regional and German détente against the fallout from a renewed Cold War, and to treat the East Europeans not as enemies worthy of punishment but as hapless victims, even as tacit allies in the quest for a *Mitteleuropa* zone of peace.

Linkage politics requires not only links but also the freedom to cut them. That freedom the West Germans do not think they have—not because some 200,000 jobs depend on exports to the East, but because to cut means to confront and hence to refreeze what the decade of détente had so painstakingly thawed. From 1980 to 1983, the height of Cold War II, West German exports to Eastern Europe and the Soviet Union stagnated only briefly, resuming their growth in 1982 and continuing to grow in 1983.[45] Nor was the steady rise of exports to the GDR interrupted in these years. It only dropped off in 1984, not for political reasons but because the GDR drastically reduced Western imports to improve its position as a debtor nation (see figure 1). By 1985 Eastern trade showed a dramatic rise again. Exports to the GDR rose by 23.3 percent, and exports to Eastern Europe and the Soviet Union (including Albania but excluding the GDR and Yugoslavia) grew by 5.3 percent.[46]

DIPLOMACY AND DIFFERENTIATION

Contrary to an old tendency of American policy toward Eastern Europe, West German diplomacy does not emphasize—or at least, no

---

45. *Statistisches Jahrbuch, 1984*, p. 277.

46. Calculated from data in deutschemarks in Statistisches Bundesamt, *Statistisches Jahrbuch 1986* (Stuttgart: Kohlhammer, 1986), pp. 247, 268–69. Calculations from the data in dollars shown in appendix table A-6 would be somewhat different because of changes in the dollar-deutschemark exchange rate from year to year.

longer emphasizes—differentiation. Differentiation, as practiced from Nixon to Reagan, was to "encourage sentiments of national independence in Eastern Europe," wrote Henry Kissinger in his memoirs.[47] The idea is, and continues to be, to reward with high-level visits, diplomatic attention, and economic benefits those Eastern bloc nations who show independence from Moscow in terms of domestic liberalization or diplomatic movement and to compensate for Soviet influence and penetration strategies in Western Europe. The classic target of differentiation has always been Romania, especially in the heyday of Ceauşescu's "Gaullist" policy toward the Soviet Union. Later favorites were Poland and Yugoslavia, followed in the 1980s by economically reform-minded Hungary.

Bonn, of course, did once try its hand at differentiation. Indeed, its first timid steps into an autonomous *Ostpolitik*, as launched by the Erhard government in the mid-1960s, constituted differentiation par excellence. Unwilling to extend even the most modest form of recognition to its hostile counter-state, Bonn tried to circumvent and isolate the GDR with a strategy of economic engagement in Eastern Europe. The failure of that strategy, which actually increased the GDR's political weight in the Warsaw Pact, became most evident in the wake of its first and only success: the establishment of diplomatic relations with Bucharest in 1967. That breakthrough, willy-nilly anti-Soviet and anti-East German, drove Moscow and East Berlin into each other's arms, mobilized the fierce resistance of both, and allowed the GDR to become the policeman and taskmaster of bloc orthodoxy.

The New *Ostpolitik* (1969–72) and all of *Ostpolitik* thereafter were essentially dedicated to the proposition that differentiation between the GDR, Eastern Europe, and the Soviet Union militates against the attempt to gain access in Eastern Europe because Moscow and East Berlin, above all, see it (correctly) as a strategy to drive a wedge between them. Hence all of subsequent *Ostpolitik* has followed a policy that is the opposite of differentiation, namely "synchronization." Since the GDR, the foremost target of *Ostpolitik,* cannot move faster and farther than its brethren, and since none of Moscow's allies can venture faster and farther (in terms of domestic liberalization, economic reform, or diplomatic deviation) than the Soviet Union can tolerate, all must move more or less in synchronization.

In particular, to avoid even the slightest taint of anti-Sovietism,

47. *White House Years* (Little, Brown, 1979), p. 1265.

Bonn has taken pains not to emulate American policy by favoring one East European country over another. Of course, *Deutschlandpolitik* favors the GDR by definition, involving a unique intensity of economic and political interaction. Yet even at the height of Cold War II, when the FRG and the GDR successfully cultivated their inter-German garden, Bonn took care not to traverse the threshold of Soviet sensitivity.

Nor has the Federal Republic rewarded individual countries for reformism or deviationism. If there is a high-level visit to Hungary (economically the most progressive Warsaw Pact member in the 1980s), similar such visits to the most retrograde members, such as Czechoslovakia, are sure to follow. If Romania, the diplomatic maverick, is favored with West German attention, Bulgaria, the most pro-Soviet member of the bloc, is guaranteed to receive similar favors either before or after. In short, since Bonn must not offer itself as a target of Soviet suspicions, which are quick to unleash campaigns against West German "revanchism" and "subversion," the New *Ostpolitik* has always respected the rule of synchronization.[48] That was the lesson all successive governments have drawn from the Erhard administration's hapless attempt in the 1960s to isolate the GDR via economic engagement in Eastern Europe. Regardless of the *Mitteleuropa* détente pursued in the 1980s, the rule of synchronization ultimately implies a certain Soviet *droit de regard* over the tempo and thrust of Bonn's diplomacy toward East Germany and Eastern Europe.

SECURITY POLICY: THE PRIORITY OF ALLIANCE

West German security is not so much an objective of *Ostpolitik* as its *condition*. A strong Western alliance and, even more important, a strong American connection define the sine qua non of any policy toward the East that combines great political ambitions such as the progressive transformation of the status quo with great vulnerability and military weakness. (The Federal Republic shares a thousand-mile border with the Warsaw Pact, and it would be the prime venue and victim of any East-West war in Europe.) Since the military balance in

48. See for instance the anti–West German campaign (which was actually a barely concealed attack on East Germany's attempt at self-differentiation) in the summer of 1984, especially the two *Pravda* pieces on July 27 and August 2 titled, respectively, "In the Shadow of American Rockets" and "On the Wrong Path."

Europe is so vital for Bonn's political purposes in Eastern Europe and since the European balance depends ultimately on the global nuclear one, there is little temptation in the government (although there is in the SPD left and among the Greens) to venture outside the bipolar framework.

While the Federal Republic took a vanguard role in the convocation of Mutual and Balanced Force Reduction (MBFR) negotiations in 1973, it did so primarily for security and not for political purposes. If there was a political purpose, it did not focus on the East but on the United States, where Senator Mike Mansfield had been leading an annual assault on the American military presence in Western Europe. Since the mid-1960s the then majority leader had introduced successive Senate resolutions calling for substantial cuts in the American contribution to NATO's defenses on the ground. MBFR was an anti-Mansfield weapon designed not to diminish forces in Central Europe but to blunt the senator's ardor for unilateral cuts.

Acting in close cooperation with the Nixon administration, the West German government urged the establishment of the MBFR forum on the assumption that Senate unilateralists would hold their fire as long as the Vienna negotiations continued. That assumption proved correct. In 1987, fourteen years later, without a single force reduction agreement to its credit, the MBFR forum was still operating. Neither was there any reduction of the U.S. military presence in Western Europe (there was, temporarily, during the Vietnam War), though by 1986 Mansfield seemed to have found an heir in Senator Gary Hart, who had begun to comment in public that the United States was not like Rome and hence not likely to stay in Europe for 300 years. Similarly, widespread American resentment of Western Europe's "near-unanimous disapproval" of the U.S. bombing raid on Libya prompted Henry Kissinger to demand the "redeployment" of U.S. troops into a "strategic reserve."[49]

Bonn remains active in MBFR negotiations but not avid. The most recent Western proposal, on the table since December 1985, was jointly prepared by Britain and the Federal Republic. It circumvents the old data base issue (NATO has been counting 150,000 more Warsaw Pact troops in the relevant area than the Pact has been willing to admit) by focusing on a first-stage withdrawal of Soviet and

49. "Alliance Cure: Redeployment," *Washington Post,* May 13, 1986.

American troops and on on-site inspections (which would solve the data issue on the spot, as it were).[50]

Bonn has also been among the promoters of the Stockholm Conference on Confidence- and Security-Building Measures and Disarmament in Europe, better known under the more parsimonious acronym CDE. Unlike the sterile MBFR exercise, the CDE boasts the additional membership of the European neutral and nonaligned countries, which were originally seen as a force for agreement that might transcend the two blocs. Ironically, they turned out to be more of an obstacle during the two and a half years of discussions. Particularly, the Swiss objected to confidence-building measures that they regarded as too intrusive, such as the inspection of their mobilization exercises.

NATO and the Warsaw Pact pursued their familiar diverging strategies in Stockholm. The West, with the Federal Republic in the vanguard, was mainly interested in measures to reduce the opportunities for an unreinforced surprise attack, hence in the close supervision of Warsaw Pact deployments and in restraints on the mobility of the Pact's forces. The East chose to use the CDE as a forum for public diplomacy, issuing and reissuing calls for nuclear-free zones, no-first-use pledges, and general declarations of peace-mindedness.

Last-minute agreement in September 1986, however, did result in a measure of improvement over the Helsinki Final Act of 1975. While the Final Act enjoined the signatories to announce maneuvers with more than 25,000 troops, the CDE dropped that number to 13,000. More importantly, CDE members did at last agree on modest inspection procedures, though the Warsaw Pact successfully turned aside a key demand of the West that "on-challenge" inspections should be more numerous and be carried out with the aircraft of the state making the challenge.[51]

While Bonn has pursued the diplomatic game in Stockholm as a cherished symbol of détente restored, it has harbored few hopes that the conference would in fact tangibly enhance security in Europe by

50. For a detailed analysis of the Western proposal, see Günther Gillessen, "Westlicher Interimsvorschlag bei den Wiener MBFR-Gesprächen," *Frankfurter Allgemeine Zeitung,* December 21, 1985.

51. For the key elements of the agreement, see "Schwierige Frage der Inspektionsflugzeuge," *Frankfurter Allgemeine Zeitung,* September 23, 1986.

compressing the Soviet Union's options for surprise attack. West Germany's security rests on the alliance and on the American deterrent, and thus the CDE remains a subsidiary theater of Bonn's security policy, as opposed to its détente policy.

PUBLIC AND ELECTRONIC DIPLOMACY

While the American public diplomacy effort is worldwide and buttressed by federal bureaucracies like the U.S. Information Agency and government-controlled radios like the Voice of America, the Federal Republic has to resort to more modest means. Its around-the-world radio, the Deutsche Welle, is dwarfed by both the British Broadcasting Corporation and VOA, and its foreign cultural policy is handled not by a USIA-type operation but by the Goethe Gesellschaft, at least nominally independent from the Foreign Office, which maintains Goethe Houses in key foreign cities.

In Eastern Europe, and of course in the GDR, however, the Federal Republic has some powerful comparative advantages. Almost any West German radio station can be heard in almost any part of the GDR. Similarly, West German television penetrates virtually all of East Germany and a goodly part of Czechoslovakia. There is also the Deutschlandfunk (DLF), which is specifically targeted on East Germany and the three key East European countries—Poland, Hungary, and Czechoslovakia (with programs in their languages). Like all West German radio stations, the DLF is not formally run by the state. It is subject to a board (*Rundfunkrat*) whose members are drawn from the political parties, the churches, and the unions. However, the DLF receives two-thirds of its operating funds from the Ministry of the Interior, it is constituted under a federal law, and the board accurately reflects the distribution of electoral power in Bonn. In other words, while not like the VOA, the DLF comes as close to a government voice as is possible in the federalist and neocorporatist setting that is typical for West Germany's electronic media.

Since DLF cannot conduct any listener polls in the GDR and Eastern Europe, its influence is hard to measure, and like other Western radios broadcasting into Eastern Europe, it has to fall back on indirect polling techniques. A recent one was conducted by Infratest (a Munich polling firm) among East Germans who had legally emigrated to the Federal Republic. Although this was not a representative sample because it encompasses a group that is presumably less than friendly to the regime, the figures still deliver a striking political message. No more than 5 percent of the sample admitted to having listened regularly to any of the East German radio stations while still residing in the GDR, but one-third had listened regularly to the Deutschlandfunk. Nonetheless, this quasi–"Voice of West Germany" did not rank as number one in the listener attention of East Germans. Forty percent turned regularly to RIAS, an American-sponsored station in West Berlin. Radio Bavaria was in third place, followed by Radio Luxembourg.[52]

Another study revealed that in Eastern Europe proper the DLF is clearly outclassed by Radio Free Europe, VOA, and BBC. In 1982–83, about 57 percent of Poles, Czechs, and Hungarians listened to RFE, 33 percent to VOA, and 21 percent to BBC, while only about 11 percent tuned in on DLF.[53] These 11 percent, however, seem to make for an important political effect. In official GDR publications, the DLF has recently been attacked more frequently—as "Subversionsfunk," even as "Feindsender" (this appellation, "enemy radio," is a remnant of Nazi terminology). The East German journal *Theorie und Praxis des sozialistischen Journalismus* claimed that "the FRG's electronic mass media which broadcast into foreign countries are used as political instruments serving a counterrevolutionary campaign against the GDR."[54]

While the data of the Infratest sample are hardly representative for 17 million East Germans, they do deliver a clear moral: in the realm of the electronic media, East Germany is virtually part of the Federal Republic. For television the figures are even more dramatic than for radio. Only 25 to 28 percent of the sample watched the two East German TV channels regularly, while up to 42 percent tuned in regularly to the two West German channels, ARD and ZDF. To get the full flavor of West German TV penetration, these macrodata must be broken down to distinguish among East German areas that do and do not receive West German TV signals. In the part of the

52. Anne Köhler and Volker Ronge, *Die Übersiedlerwelle aus der DDR im Frühjahr 1984* (Munich: Infratest, 1984), pp. 63–67.

53. "Die Hörerschaft des Deutschlandfunks in Ost-Europa," unpublished paper of the Deutschlandfunk (October 24, 1983), p. 1.

54. Quoted in Karl Wilhelm Fricke, "Der DLF im Spiegel der DDR-Publizistik," *DLF-Jahrbuch 1983–1985,* (Cologne: Deutschlandfunk, 1986), p. 21.

GDR under the sway of West German transmitters only 7 percent watched GDR I regularly, while 80 percent watched ARD, its West German counterpart.

In practical political terms, this means that the GDR is in a class by itself within the Warsaw Pact. West German radio and in particular West German TV are impressive means of influence merely by virtue of propinquity. In Eastern Europe, RFE and VOA at best are only able to compete against the domestic information monopoly of the governments. Bonn, however, has effectively broken the party's information monopoly in the GDR because it can extend across the Elbe River contemporary society's most powerful medium. In effect, there is a state of electronic reunification that must surely keep alive a common culture and language in spite of political separation. It must just as surely blunt a key tool at the disposal of totalitarian regimes: the ability to manipulate information freely.

PARTIES AND FOREIGN POLICY

The Social Democrats, inventors and executors of the New *Ostpolitik*, were forced out of government in the fall of 1982 when the Free Democratic (Liberal) party (FDP) joined hands with Helmut Kohl's Christian Democratic Union (CDU) and their Bavarian affiliate, the Christian Social Union (CSU). Since then the SPD has followed a course strongly accentuated by its new-found role as the opposition after thirteen years at the helm. Less trammeled by the responsibilities of power and the exigencies of diplomacy, the SPD began to explore the outer limits of those premises that informed the *Deutschlandpolitik* and *Ostpolitik* of Helmut Schmidt and his successor Helmut Kohl.

The key premise is the so-called open German Question, meaning West Germany's unwillingness formally to ratify the finality of the postwar status quo, in particular Germany's division into separate, sovereign states. Hence the peculiar construction by which the FRG and the GDR are viewed as two states in one nation; hence the nonrecognition of a separate East German citizenship; hence the existence of "permanent missions" rather than embassies in Bonn and East Berlin. Nor has the FRG formally consecrated the post-1945 borders. According to the "Eastern treaties" of the early 1970s, these borders are "inviolable," the implication being that legalization under international law must await a peace treaty between Germany and the wartime coalition.

In opposition, individual members and regional organizations of the SPD have sought to accord finality to that which is officially open. Some would like to renounce the idea of reunification and to change the preamble of West Germany's Basic Law.[55] Others have proposed the recognition of a separate East German citizenship.[56] On the fringe of the party, there are those who argue for a fundamental rethinking of West German priorities, meaning a loosening of the tie that binds the FRG to NATO and the United States. In 1986 the party executive (*Landesvorstand*) of the West Berlin SPD formulated a resolution stating inter alia that for the sake of "Europe's self-assertion," the Federal Republic should, if necessary, "defend the policy of détente to the point of conflict within the alliance" as long as "the United States persists in its policy of strength and superiority."[57]

The underlying logic of such slogans is of course implicit in the New *Ostpolitik* launched by Willy Brandt and his chief strategist Egon Bahr. Pushed to its extreme, *Ostpolitik* must perforce subvert the structures of the postwar order, since it is bipolarity that compresses the margins of *Mitteleuropa* détente and Germany's room for maneuver. Conversely, anything that strengthens bipolarity and alliance cohesion is perforce the bane of *Ostpolitik*. Erhard Eppler, a leading ideologue of the SPD left, has gone farther than many of his comrades in making that logic brutally explicit: "Only the loosening of the Western alliance can open a way" for what the SPD left likes to call the "self-assertion of Europe," that is, the retraction of the blocs from Central Europe and, ultimately, the withdrawal of American and Soviet troops. In opposition the SPD has been willing to pursue a

55. See for instance Peter Philips, "SPD-Linke gegen Wiedervereinigung," *Die Welt*, February 25, 1986.

56. For instance Egon Bahr and the current prime minister of the Saarland, Oscar Lafontaine. See "Bahr: Drei von vier Geraer Forderungen annehmbar," *Frankfurter Allgemeine Zeitung*, September 17, 1984; and Albrecht Hinze, "Bundesregierung über Lafontaine verärgert," *Süddeutsche Zeitung*, November 15, 1985. See also Axel Vornbäumen, "Jusos wollen neue Ostpolitik," *Frankfurter Rundschau*, June 24, 1985, reporting on the congress of the SPD youth wing, the *Jungsozialisten*, which conceded to the GDR all of its key extant demands, among them the recognition of a GDR citizenship.

57. "Antrag zur Sicherheits-, Deutschland- und Berlin-Politik" (unpublished paper, Berlin, May 1986). For an analysis, see Manfred Wilke, *Die SPD vor der zweiten Phase der Entspannungspolitik* (Bonn: Institut für Gesellschaftswissenschaften Walberberg, 1986).

rhetoric that is necessarily directed against the United States as alliance leader, although SPD spokesmen take care to evade the charge of anti-Americanism by targeting Reagan's America as culprit. According to Peter Glotz, secretary-general of the SPD, U.S. foreign policy of the "Reagan/Weinberger type" is "anti-European, because it robs the East European states in the Soviet corral of all freedom of movement."[58]

On the level of policy, the SPD in opposition began to conduct what the critics call *Nebenaussenpolitik,* a separate foreign policy that tends to outflank and put pressure on Bonn's official diplomacy. The best example is a draft treaty on a chemical weapons free zone in Central Europe, written jointly by high-level working groups of the SPD and the SED (the Communist party of the GDR) in 1985. There are also discussions about a nuclear weapons free zone in Central Europe. Similar joint ventures have been organized with the Hungarian, Czech, and Polish parties concerning economic cooperation, environmental policy, and confidence-building measures, respectively.[59]

The logic of these initiatives is also rooted in the logic of the New *Ostpolitik,* which at heart seeks to push back the barriers of bipolarity in Europe, to enlarge West Germany's scope for maneuver in Eastern Europe, and to lighten the country's security dependence on the West. Hence also the ultimate goal, which is the demise of bipolarity: "a European order of peace that will overarch and finally overcome the [two] power blocs."[60]

For the time being, the Social Democrats are, metaphorically speaking, trying to rearrange the interior architecture of bipolarity so as to gain maximum freedom of movement without jeopardizing its pillars, notably the American security guarantee. The willingness to test the structure is clearly greater on the left than on the right of

58. Eppler and Glotz as quoted in Jürgen Engert, "Frühlingserwachen in der Baracke," *Rheinischer Merkur,* November 30, 1985.

59. For reports, see "Die SPD will die Entspannungspolitik in ein 'Netzwerk' einbinden," *Frankfurter Allgemeine Zeitung,* July 17, 1985; "SPD verlangt von Kohl Gespräche mit der DDR," *Süddeutsche Zeitung,* July 17, 1985; "Umstrittene Ostkontakte der SPD," *Neue Zürcher Zeitung,* November 27, 1985; and "Deutsch-deutsche Verlockungen," *Neue Zürcher Zeitung,* November 30–December 1, 1985.

60. *Regierungsprogramm 1987–1990 der Sozialdemokratischen Partei Deutschlands* (Bonn: Vorstand der SPD, October 1986), p. 40. This pamphlet served as the party's platform for the federal election on January 25, 1987.

the party. In government the SPD might once more be subject to the restraint of tenure. Yet even in opposition, it scored an indirect success in 1986 when the Kohl government, responding to the SPD and public pressure, all but negotiated away U.S. chemical weapons in West Germany. The substance of the agreement foresees the withdrawal of the current stockpile once the U.S. starts producing binary weapons, as planned for 1987. These will be stationed outside Germany, to be moved forward in times of military need, which, given the political realities in Germany, will not happen and thus amounts to the effective dechemicalization of the Federal Republic.

Unlike the SPD, the Greens, with their anarchic structure, have as many *Ostpolitiks* as there are factions and ideological splinters. There was a time during the height of the anti-Euromissile campaign in the early 1980s when the Greens sought to link up with peace groups in the GDR and elsewhere in the Soviet bloc. Those contacts were suppressed once the GDR authorities decided that the contagion effect at home might outweigh the destabilizing effect abroad. Since then the Greens have not been able to develop a single party line that would lay down an alternative *Deutschlandpolitik*. There are those who wish a plague on both houses, meaning the regimes in East and West, and instead would mobilize "social forces" on either side of the divide. There are those who would essentially pursue the course of the SPD left—toward formal recognition of the GDR, radical arms control, and territorial defense (which would dispense with nuclear weapons and, ultimately, NATO). And there are those who would simply destroy the framework of bipolarity through withdrawal from the alliance and neutralization. The third tendency scored a notable victory in 1986 when the national congress of the Greens demanded the dissolution of NATO.[61]

The coalition parties, the CDU/CSU and FDP, have a more complex attitude toward foreign policy. With the exception of the 1957–61 period, no party has ever ruled with an absolute majority, and even then Chancellor Adenauer rounded out his battalions by keeping his old allies, the Free Democrats, in the cabinet. The enduring pattern of governance in West Germany has been by coalition, with the CDU/CSU ruling in tandem with the FDP until 1966, a Grand Coalition of Christian Democrats and Social Democrats presiding over the country

61. For an analysis of the foreign policy of the Greens, see Wilfried von Bredow and Rudolf H. Brocke, "Dreimal Deutschlandpolitik: Deutschlandpolitische Ansätze der Partei der Grünen," *Deutschland-Archiv*, vol. 19 (January 1986), pp. 52–61.

until 1969, the SPD holding power with the FDP until 1982, and a CDU/CSU–FDP coalition governing since then. The coalition nature of West German government has always implied a certain degree of intramural tension that, if acute enough, has periodically led to the breakup of the coalition and the subsequent shift of the balance of domestic power from the CDU/CSU to the SPD and vice versa.

A key role has been played by the Liberals (the FDP), who have drawn electoral strength from their role as balancer, tilting either left, when in coalition with the CDU/CSU, or right, when joining forces with the SPD. In the final years of the Schmidt government (1974–82), Hans-Dietrich Genscher's FDP emphasized alliance obligations over détente, *Ostpolitik*, and arms control. In coalition with a right-of-center senior partner after 1982, Genscher predictably shifted gears, presenting himself as guardian of *Ostpolitik* and détente, opposing American demands for a close identification on the Strategic Defense Initiative, and generally stressing the Federal Republic's mission in Eastern Europe.[62]

The other wing of the coalition, the Christian Social Union, the Bavarian sister party of the Christian Democratic Union, has played a mirror-image role, generally moving right as the FDP moved left. If the FDP has tried to siphon off votes on the left of the CDU by posing as trusted guarantor of détente-minded continuity, Franz Josef Strauss's CSU has tried to do the same on the right by harping on the revisionist themes of *Ostpolitik*: Germany's right to reunification, the unfinished business of borders, the claims of the refugees from the East. It is difficult, however, to extract real diplomatic intent from the domestic purpose of such rhetorical flourishes, and hence to imbue them with a significance that would transcend the electoral campaigns of the day.

THE POLICY PROCESS: CHANCELLOR'S OFFICE VERSUS FOREIGN OFFICE

Given the coalition nature of German government, which since 1966 has juxtaposed the chancellor of one party with a foreign

62. An instructive example of Genscher's finely tuned balancing strategy was his reflex reaction to a speech in Munich by U.S. Undersecretary of Defense Fred Iklé that had postulated a "grim, enduring, and dangerous competition," especially in the military field. Promptly, Genscher retorted that the exclusive search for security through military strength would "endanger stability, block disarmament, and dissolve a vital consensus within the Alliance." Quoted in "Genscher lehnt Härte gegen den Ostblock ab," *Süddeutsche Zeitung*, March 4, 1986.

minister of another,[63] tension has been preordained between the two centers of foreign policymaking, the Chancellor's Office and the Foreign Office. A second structural cause of tension results from another peculiarity of the West German foreign policy process: the familiar and unresolved German Problem.

According to the orthodoxy laid down at the birth of the Federal Republic, the GDR was originally not even a real state, but only the Soviet Occupation Zone. And though Bonn did extend formalized relations to the GDR after 1973, it did not grant diplomatic recognition under international law. Legally, the Federal Republic treats the GDR not as a foreign country but as an ambiguous entity that is neither a separate state nor, as in the 1950s and 1960s, a part of the German Reich (which, according to official legal lore, remains one, pending a formal peace treaty with the Four Powers). As the contemporary legal formula has it, there are two states in one nation, and the FRG and GDR are not *Ausland* (foreign countries) to each other. Though these subtle distinctions rest more on legal fiction than political reality, they continue to leave their mark on the institutional processes of West German foreign policy.

On a symbolic level, for instance, names tell part of the story. Though in 1969 the Ministry for All-German Affairs was renamed to take account of the new relationship, the label was merely changed to "Ministry for Inter-German Affairs." To have called it the "Ministry for GDR Affairs," as the realities might have suggested, would have conceded too much separate statehood to the East Germans. For precisely that reason, the GDR does not fall under the authority of the Foreign Office. Instead, the West German–East German relationship is managed (at the under-secretary level) by the Chancellor's Office. This means that the Foreign Office deals with every other member state of the Warsaw Pact but not with the GDR because, by definition, East Germany is not a foreign country.

Under the West German constitution, the chancellor is the ultimate authority, both in domestic and foreign policy. As Article 65 of the Basic Law stipulates, the chancellor "determines the guidelines of

63. During the Grand Coalition the CDU's Kurt-Georg Kiesinger was chancellor while Willy Brandt (SPD) served as foreign minister. From 1969 to 1982 the Social Democratic Chancellors Willy Brandt and Helmut Schmidt had to contend with the FDP's Hans-Dietrich Genscher in the Foreign Office. Thereafter Genscher remained foreign minister while Christian Democrat Helmut Kohl took over as chancellor.

policy." In practice, this has tilted the balance of power in favor of the Chancellor's Office in matters of "high politics." During Willy Brandt's tenure as chancellor (1969–74), the New *Ostpolitik* was essentially enacted by the Chancellor's Office and not by the Foreign Office (in FDP hands from 1969 until the present). Key negotiations in Moscow were conducted by Brandt or his confidant, Egon Bahr. A similar pattern obtained under Chancellors Schmidt and Kohl, who have taken the lead in the East-West arena by dint of executive privilege while dominating *Deutschlandpolitik* automatically because it falls under the institutional purview of the Chancellor's Office.

Yet to some extent, the foreign minister represents a separate power center as leader of the junior coalition partner on whom the chancellor must depend for his majority. As foreign minister and SPD chairman during the Grand Coalition, Willy Brandt used the Foreign Office's planning staff (directed by Egon Bahr) to map out the New *Ostpolitik* he would later execute as chancellor, while his superior, Chancellor Kiesinger, was largely left in the dark. Depending on the electoral fortunes of the FDP, Foreign Minister Genscher has regularly maintained a carefully calculated distance from either Helmut Schmidt's or Helmut Kohl's foreign policy: to the right of Schmidt as the SPD began its long slide into antinuclearism and "equidistance between the superpowers," and to the left of Kohl where, in the mid-1980s, he hoped to garner electoral strength as purveyor of a more pliant *Ostpolitik*.

Such maneuvers of differentiation normally multiply in years before national elections, as they did in 1986 when the FDP and Foreign Minister Genscher began to stake out positions on arms control, East-West affairs, and *Ostpolitik* that appeared closer to those of the SPD than to the policies enunciated by the CDU/CSU. Nonetheless, the overall weight of the Foreign Office is bound to be limited as long as it is in the hands of the junior coalition partner. The foreign minister has a relatively free hand where standard diplomatic practice dominates the agenda, such as routine visits to the capitals of Eastern Europe. Yet economic affairs—Eastern trade and credits— fall under the sway of the Finance and Economics Ministries. And where high politics are at stake—Bonn's position between Washington and Moscow or the inter-German relationship—it is the chancellor and his office (run by a cabinet-level director) that retain supreme authority.

FOREIGN POLICY AND THE ROLE
OF NONGOVERNMENTAL INSTITUTIONS

Churches, trade unions, and other domestic pressure groups (like the organizations of Germans expelled from Eastern Europe) have not played any consistent roles in West German relations with Eastern Europe. Their activity and influence has waxed and waned. The refugee organizations wielded a lot of domestic power in the 1950s, when they could claim to represent the interests of some 9 million Germans who had been expelled, or who had moved, from Eastern Europe at the end of World War II. For a while they even had their own party to represent them, the Bund für Heimatvertriebene und Entrechtete (BHE), literally "League of Expellees and Disenfranchised." In the 1950s Chancellor Adenauer, who followed a deliberate policy of integration so as to mop up any reservoirs of revisionism, took care to have BHE members in his cabinets. Eventually, the BHE was absorbed by the Christian Democrats, Social Democrats, and Free Democrats.

The influence of the refugees on foreign policy, however, is hard to measure. Their rhetorical revisionism in the 1950s and early 1960s paralleled precisely the *Ostpolitik* Adenauer presumably would have conducted even without a large refugee population. Thus correlation must not be taken to prove causation, meaning an *Ostpolitik* held hostage by the refugees from the East. In any case, at the threshold of the 1970s their organizations were not strong enough to veto Willy Brandt's New *Ostpolitik* (which all but laid to rest German claims to formerly German regions that are now Polish and Russian).

The domestication of millions of refugees may well reflect the success of Adenauer's policy of integration, which made sure that the newcomers would be quickly resettled and compensated for property losses sustained in formerly German areas. As a result, the 9 million immigrants from the East plus some 3 million from the GDR never settled into breeding grounds of revanchism like the Palestinian refugee camps that were deliberately created around Israel's periphery after the independence war of 1948–49.

After a long period of quiescence, refugee politics returned briefly to the fore in 1985 when the Silesians chose "Silesia Remains Ours" as the motto for their upcoming annual congress, at which Chancellor Kohl was slated to speak. Such a slogan was not exactly beholden to the status quo that *Ostpolitik* had consecrated; yet Kohl did go to the congress after a compromise was struck. In its final version, the motto read, "Forty Years of Exile—Silesia Remains Our Future—In a Europe of Free Peoples."[64] But the leaders of the German refugees, Herbert Hupka and Herbert Czaja, who kept making revisionist noises throughout 1985 and 1986, were born in 1915 and 1914, respectively. Their birthdates and those of the rank and file suggest some biological limits to the politics of refugee "revanchism." Some hundred billion deutsche mark in compensation moneys and a prudent resettlement policy (which tried to avoid geographic concentrations of refugees) have created powerful ligaments of integration. And since the Conservative-Liberal Kohl government has carefully avoided any real encouragement of refugee revisionism, a forty-year-old pattern of Germanization of millions of expellees and refugees has continued to hold.

Unlike the American labor movement that took an active role in the making of postwar American foreign policy (in particular, by encouraging the growth of noncommunist unions throughout the Western world), its counterpart, the Deutsche Gewerkschaftsbund (DGB), has traditionally concentrated its political energies at home— with the exception of the 1950s when communists beholden to Moscow and East Berlin were purged. By the 1980s, limited communist influence was again visible in the West German labor movement, but though there was sporadic cooperation with the diminutive West German Communist party, which follows the Moscow and East German line, the DGB has remained true to its postwar tradition. Unlike the SPD, which has moved from its passionate anticommunism of the 1950s and 1960s to intensifying cooperation with the East German Communist party in the 1970s and 1980s, the DGB continues to eschew all collaboration with the party-run trade unions of the GDR and Eastern Europe.

The churches have also played a limited role in the making of *Ostpolitik*—with one extremely important exception. The high point of church activism came in the mid-1960s when the Evangelische Kirche Deutschlands, the national organization of the German Protestant Church, took a widely heralded step that many today regard as the very foundation of the New *Ostpolitik* consummated by Willy

64. For the details, see Dietrich Strothmann, "Das letzte Aufgebot," *Die Zeit,* January 25, 1985.

Brandt. In October 1965 the EKD issued a much-publicized memorandum that stated: "The striving for a new international order must not be judged solely from the point of view of whether it will realize a unilaterally claimed German legal right."[65]

Though laborious and equivocal, that sentence foreshadowed the quasi-ratification of the Oder-Neisse line in 1970, which made possible a reconciliation with Poland. And though by now reduced to a mere footnote in the annals of *Ostpolitik*, the 1965 EKD memorandum was a true watershed because it either reflected or accelerated the transformation in West German public opinion that would allow for the passage from the de jure revisionism of the Adenauer years to the de facto acceptance of the postwar status quo that has underlain all of *Ostpolitik* from Brandt to Kohl.

In the 1980s the activism of the Protestant church has been mainly concentrated on the GDR. Taking a vanguard role in the West German peace movement of the early 1980s, a considerable part of the Protestant clergy tried to build links to their counterparts in the GDR. For a while—that is, as long as the Honecker regime thought it useful to strengthen the West German peace movement—cooperation across borders looked like a promising transnational strategy. By 1984, however, East Berlin began clamping down on its own diminutive peace movement; since then political contacts have been reduced to isolated joint statements on rather abstract issues of peace and war.[66]

The Problems of Policy:
How to Change the Status Quo through Its Acceptance

Basically, all of *Ostpolitik* (the inseparable ensemble of approaches toward East Germany, Eastern Europe, and the Soviet Union) narrows

65. Excerpts in Heinrich von Siegler, ed., *Dokumentation zur Deutschlandfrage*, vol. 3 (Bonn: Siegler, 1966), pp. 713–28. On the occasion of the twentieth anniversary of the memorandum, Hans-Jürgen Wischnewski, a leading Social Democrat, said that it "helped to prepare the way for concrete steps toward reconciliation." Quoted in Manfred Barchtenbreiter, "Versöhnung nicht nur Ziel der 'grossen Politik,'" *Süddeutsche Zeitung*, October 7, 1985.

66. See for instance the "Wort zum Frieden," published jointly by the Protestant churches in East and West Germany on the occasion of the fortieth anniversary of Germany's surrender. For the text, see "Das Kriegsende als Erfahrung von Zusammenbruch und Befreiung zu neuen Zeugnis," *Frankfurter Allgemeine Zeitung*, March 19, 1985.

down to a bold, if not breathtaking, gamble: that a consistent policy of political reassurance and economic rewards can trigger (and, more crucially, maintain) an evolution that will liberalize regimes and encourage Moscow to relax its imperial grip over its vassals. Nor is this all; it is but the beginning of West Germany's excruciating tightrope act in Eastern Europe.

Change, once engendered, must proceed at a safe rate of speed. Unless it stays just below the threshold of Soviet imperial and ideological sensibilities, as well as below the threshold at which East European regimes are destabilized, change will end in renewed repression. In decades past, this point of crisis was reached four times, and in each case the solution was Soviet intervention: directly and bloodily in East Germany in 1953 and Hungary in 1956, directly and without bloodshed in Czechoslovakia in 1968, and indirectly and nonviolently in Poland in 1981.[67] And then there is the Western dimension of *Ostpolitik*. West German policy in the East must achieve all of the above without alienating the West and without weakening an alliance that was, is, and remains the indispensable condition of any *Ostpolitik*.

THE GAMBLE

On the level of reassurance and rewards for Eastern Europe the key problem was well described by Pierre Hassner some years ago. It is not clear, he wrote, "whether this increased self-confidence [on the part of Eastern regimes] is supposed to bring the elites to lower their guard and to promote an unwitting . . . structural change, thereby working against their own real interests, or whether [the goal is] real stabilization which would allow them to keep their domination but

---

67. It is possible to conclude from the declining rate of violence that, with the passage of time, the Soviet Union has been deterred, or become self-deterred, from the use of force and to credit détente with that benign outcome. It seems closer to the truth, however, to argue the exact opposite, that force, both real and potential, is increasingly productive. Accordingly, each successful intervention has made the next one easier, either by discouraging would-be imitators completely or by deterring the insurgents from pushing the rebellion too far. Having demonstrated its resolve and capacity to suppress national revolt in the previous case, the Soviet Union could proceed to undo the subsequent one with an ever-improving exchange rate between force and influence. Rather than self-deterrence, the thirty years since the Hungarian Revolution demonstrate the increasing economy of violence in the relationship between the Soviet Union and its East European vassals.

dispense with the more pathological measures born out of insecurity."[68]

If lowered guards are the objective, what will prevent the regimes between East Berlin and Moscow from seeing through the game and pocketing the gains without paying in the currency of structural reform? If, however, the real goal is not some kind of benign subversion but a latter-day Holy Alliance that will ensure regime authority minus the authoritarianism, the underlying assumption might even be more sanguine than in the first case. What if communist regimes are *constitutionally* unable to accept conciliation from the West and to extend it to their populaces without triggering the next cycle of revolt and repression? Polities that do not rest on the consent of the governed and are held on a short imperial leash are not ideal candidates for thorough domestic reform.

THE RATE OF CHANGE

This problem was well illustrated by events in Poland from 1980 onward. (The suppression of Poland's Solidarity is so instructive because it took place after a decade of détente and not, like those of the GDR and Hungary, in the heyday of the Cold War.) The imposition of martial law on Poland during the final days of 1981 demonstrated that the détente process has had a built-in tendency to turn upon itself. Like the aftermath of the two previous détentes—de-Stalinization in the mid-1950s and the minithaw of the mid-1960s—the Polish putsch showed that neither the regimes nor the Soviets could really respect the verdict of détente once it threatened the party's monopoly and the Kremlin's political and pontifical empire in Eastern Europe. While the Soviet Union has consistently sought to encourage the loosening of bipolarity in Western Europe, it was not prepared to countenance such an outcome in its own glacis. As compared to the past, the difference in 1981 was that *Polish* troops moved to occupy Poland in order to forestall a replay of the 1968 invasion of Czechoslovakia.

68. "Western European Perceptions of the USSR," *Daedalus* (Winter 1979), p. 145.

THE RATIONALE

Yet no West European, and certainly no West German, government is ready to accept these brutal consequences of détente as a final verdict. French President Valéry Giscard d'Estaing put the abiding rationale as well as any West European leader: "This policy of détente has allowed a modification of relations between the European countries. Thus, relations between France and certain [East European countries] . . . have been transformed. . . . I tell you, for the benefit of those who talk so willingly about giving up détente, that this would plunge some European countries' peoples into despair, those who are our partners in the quest for détente."[69]

This rationale is shared by a vast majority of West Germans, from the far left to the moderate right. It reflects, first, a new basic attitude that regards the East Europeans not as enemies but as hapless victims and even tacit allies. It also reflects the emergence of a shadowy parallel system in Europe that transcends the mainstays of bipolarity and that is defined by all manner of economic, political, and, above all, psychological ties among the European members of the two blocs.

In the past the East European regimes were seen as creatures and cohorts of the Kremlin, indistinguishable from their Soviet masters who had installed them as overlords to rule their disenfranchised populations. A Walter Ulbricht, who governed the GDR until 1971, or a János Kádár, who was imposed on Hungary after the 1956 revolution, was in the past no more deserving of friendly treatment than his Soviet patrons, regardless of the deprivation suffered by his captive subjects.

Yet today, neither Kádár nor Ulbricht's successor, Erich Honecker, is seen as a mere satrap of Moscow. Instead, the leaders of Hungary, East Germany, and, indeed, even post-putsch Poland appear as prudent patriots who must strike a precarious balance between the realities of power and their countries' national aspirations. Or, as Helmut Schmidt said, "Jaruzelski . . . was not a man whom Moscow had installed. They didn't like him; they didn't trust him; and deep in his heart he utterly disliked the Russians. He thought it was his

69. Interview on Paris radio program, "1 Hour with the President," Foreign Broadcast Information Service, *Western Europe Daily Report*, February 28, 1980, p. K5.

national duty to prevent open intervention [by the Soviets] and to act as he did."[70]

THE DILEMMA

Though chained to empire and beholden to an inimical ideology, the regimes of the East are regarded as silent partners in an all-European enterprise that must lighten the dead weight of bipolarity and pierce the barriers of partition. The East Europeans, hostages rather than hostile, must not be punished for Soviet transgressions. Instead, their freedom of maneuver must be carefully enlarged through conciliation and cooperation.

And this tacit alliance poses the insoluble dilemma of differentiation between the Soviet Union and the rest of the bloc. Differentiation regularly collides with a basic rule of Soviet bloc diplomacy in times of East-West tensions: "Clients must not enjoy significantly better relations with the West than patrons." (The long-term exception to this rule has been Romania, undoubtedly because that country does not share a common border with the West.) Hence, West Germany must extend its benevolence all the way to Moscow or suffer Soviet retribution. Since the Erhard government's policy of movement, the Soviet Union has reacted to the perils of differentiation with heavy-handed recentralization, including the overt use of force against Prague in 1968 and the oblique use of it against Solidarity in 1981.

Nor has the passage of time really weakened the Soviet grip. Having threatened a new ice age in the aftermath of the Euromissile deployment, the Soviet Union emplaced its new generation of short-range missiles in the GDR and Czechoslovakia—against the preferences of Honecker, as he intimated publicly on various occasions.[71] And even

70. Craig R. Whitney, "A Talk With Helmut Schmidt," *New York Times Magazine*, September 16, 1984.

71. In an interview with *Die Zeit* (January 31, 1986), Honecker said with respect to the "removal of operative tactical missiles, which were stationed in the GDR as a countermeasure to the USA medium-range missiles in Western Europe: It is agreed that these shall be withdrawn, once the reasons for their deployment have disappeared. In other words, if the Federal Republic can prompt the USA to withdraw [its] medium-range weapons, then their counterparts would also be removed from the GDR." This reflects East German unhappiness about the deployment by implication, since the Gorbachev proposal of January 15, 1986, to which the statement refers, had nothing to say about the removal of short-range rocketry from the GDR and Czechoslovakia.

though Moscow had on its hands a subdued rebellion by a regime in East Berlin in 1984, it managed to show at the end of the day that its writ over the *Westpolitik* of its allies ran as strong as ever. With the familiar exception of Romania, all members of the Warsaw Pact had boycotted the Olympic Games in Los Angeles. Thereafter, Bulgaria and the GDR were brought face to face with the niggardly limits of Soviet tolerance when their leaders were forced to cancel long-standing travel plans to the Federal Republic. Nor did Erich Honecker travel to West Germany in 1985 and 1986 while Moscow was groping for a new relationship with Washington and holding the Kohl government at arms's length.

In short, as holders of the key, the Soviets must be the ultimate beneficiaries of the quest for bloc-transcending collaboration with Eastern Europe, a quest that is virtually irreversible. West Germany's scope for a policy of denial and counterpressure is inexorably limited, first by its raison de nation, hence a sense of obligation to the GDR, and second by its raison d'Etat, which bids all medium and small powers to resist tight bipolarity as inimical to their freedom of movement and to assert their common interests against the superpowers. Since the Soviets have repeatedly demonstrated that they can set the terms of interaction (and veto those contacts they do not like altogether), détente ultimately defies differentiation. Détente in Central Europe, unlike elsewhere, is either indivisible or impossible. It must either encompass the Soviet Union or dwindle into a futile ambition.

THE PROBLEM

And this is where *Ostpolitik* collides with *Westpolitik*. Since the Federal Republic must protect détente in order to protect everything else, conflict, though not foreordained, is destined to erupt under conditions of dissynchronization among the processes of global,

---

At the end of 1986, Honecker repeated the same point more forcefully: "Once the issue of the medium-range missiles is solved, there is no longer any need to keep tactical missiles (with a range of less than 1,000 kilometers) in the GDR. That would present the opportunity to remove that Satan's brood [*Teufelszeug,* which is also a favorite term of SPD leaders] from the territory of the GDR." Speech to the Central Committee of the SED as printed in "Mit Initiative Schöpfertum und Tatkraft verwirklichen wir die Beschlüsse unseres XI. Parteitages," *Neues Deutschland,* November 22/23, 1986.

regional, and German détente. The Federal Republic resisted adamantly in the 1950s and early 1960s, when the global and regional
process threatened to outpace Bonn's capacity for détente on the
inter-German level. It did the same during Cold War II of the 1980s,
when the United States, moving in the opposite direction, shifted
toward militant neocontainment and threatened to foreclose the
options détente had brought.

The Schmidt government's first, and instinctive, response was
insulation. Or as Willy Brandt, the architect of *Ostpolitik*, put it:
"Today, we and other Europeans face the problem . . . of how to
prevent the deteriorating relations between Washington and Moscow
from having a negative effect on Europe."[72] And so Helmut Schmidt
tried to straddle the conflict, trying to render unto the United States
(by participating in the Olympic boycott) without taking from the
Soviet Union (by applying real economic sanctions). Yet mere insulation was not enough to weather the advancing frost.

Trying to harness its allies to the cause of neocontainment, the
United States demanded loyalty, not benign neutrality. As a result,
the West Germans were confronted with the deadliest challenge of
their foreign policy: a choice between their Western obligations and
their Eastern mission. To deny allegiance to the United States was
impossible for a nation that depends for its security on its overseas
patron. Nor could Schmidt allow the United States to drag Bonn into
its global quarrels with Moscow short of sinning against every commandment of *Ostpolitik* and provoking Soviet retribution where it
mattered most: in terms of access to the GDR and Eastern Europe.

To avoid either horn of that dilemma, Schmidt tried to execute
from a position of underlying weakness what Bismarck had only been
able to play out (and then without enduring success) from a position
of underlying strength: the role of intermediary and mediator. To
save *Ostpolitik*, he had to defend détente in Europe, and to achieve
both, he tried his utmost to hold Moscow and Washington to the
global bargain struck in the 1970s. Schmidt thus sought to mute the
conflict between the strong that, if unchecked, would inevitably impose
the most fearful choices on the weak. Putting himself forward as an
"honest interpreter of Western policy," he proclaimed, "We have an
important role to play in [preserving the dialogue between the

72. Interview with Norddeutscher Rundfunk (North German Radio), November
4, 1981, as quoted from stenographic record, Bundespresse- und Informationsamt,
Nachrichtenabteilung, Bonn, file number 827065.

superpowers], both toward our friends in the United States and toward the Soviet Union."[73]

That Schmidt tried to "Germanize" European détente and to "Europeanize" global détente is powerful testimony to the Federal Republic's (indeed Germany's) enduring dilemmas. That he failed (and fell in part as a result of his inability to hold the superpowers to the détente bargain, especially with regard to the Soviet buildup of the SS-20 arsenal) is an equally powerful testimony to Germany's enduring weaknesses as a country of the middle. While Bonn tried to act as a bridge and a brace, it was in fact the premier stake of the renewed Soviet-American contest. Though acted out on the chessboard of strategy, with Euromissiles as the pawns, the real issue was the balance of power in Europe, and that issue has always boiled down to the age-old question: Who controls Germany? It is at this point that *Ostpolitik* is bound to collide mercilessly with *Westpolitik*, raising the great question of détente: How much dissolution in the West for how much evolution in the East?

The Conservative-Liberal Kohl coalition has presented more modest answers than Schmidt to this question and accompanied them with a determined effort to restrengthen Bonn's American and alliance connections. The best and most comprehensive statement on contemporary *Deutschlandpolitik* and *Ostpolitik* is a speech by Wolfgang Schäuble, director of the Chancellor's Office, with cabinet rank, who is also charged with relations with the GDR. On the one hand there are several changes in nuance that distinguish Kohl's approach from that of his Social Democratic predecessors and that reflect the oldest tradition of West German *Ostpolitik* and a sober assessment of Germany's strength and autonomy at the dividing line of bipolarity in Europe. The Kohl government stresses the "opposition of freedom and bondage" that separates the two German states. The "profound clash of values between East and West is not a matter for compromise." There is also the explicit recognition of the indispensable Western dimension of the Federal Republic's role in world politics: "Any estrangement from the Atlantic Alliance would render the Federal Republic incapable of conducting a *Deutschlandpolitik* and *Ostpolitik* deserving of the name."[74]

---

73. Speech before the Federal Association of German Newspaper Publishers on November 10, 1981, as quoted in *Süddeutsche Zeitung*, November 11, 1981.

74. "Die deutsche Frage im europäischen Rahmen," address before the Swedish

At the same time Schäuble stressed a more recent tradition, the legacy bequeathed by Brandt and Schmidt. The "consequences of partition for [our] people" must be "rendered more tolerable." The emphasis on conflict of values between East and West must neither "sound arrogant nor provoke the GDR." There has to be "dialogue and cooperation." All of Europe "shares a vital interest in secure borders." Finally, he paid homage to the key principle of *Ostpolitik* in language that could have been Brandt's or Schmidt's: "Overcoming the partition of Germany means to overcome the partition of Europe." And then there is that critical quantum of obeisance to Soviet sensitivities and interests: the government knows only too well "that a *Deutschlandpolitik* that would try to circumvent Moscow could not be successful."

Simultaneously, the Kohl government has continued to cultivate precisely that tacit partnership with the GDR that has informed the separate *Mitteleuropa* détente between the two German states since the beginning of the 1980s. And significantly, the East German regime has affirmed that partnership in spite of the pressures and isolation tactics against Bonn that the Soviet Union launched just before the missile deployment and that, following a classic Soviet pattern of attempted interference in the domestic politics of the Federal Republic, reached new heights on the eve of the 1987 national election. If Moscow claimed that relations with Bonn were "poisoned," East German Prime Minister Willi Stoph pledged simultaneously that his country would "take particular care to secure the peace and good-neighborly relations at the dividing line between the two social systems and great military blocs in the heart of Europe."[75] In the midst of Moscow's anti-Kohl campaign, the GDR thus sent an audible signal to Bonn by once more promising to stop the infiltration of illegal immigrants from Asia and Africa into West Berlin via East Berlin. (In the first eight and one-half months of 1986, some 40,000 applicants for political asylum arrived in West Germany or West Berlin via East Berlin's international airport.)[76]

Institute for International Relations, Stockholm, May 15, 1986, as published in *Europa-Archiv*, vol. 41 (June 1986), pp. 341–48.

75. Quoted in "Moskau: Beziehungen zu Bonn vergiftet" and "Stoph: Um gute Nachbarschaft bemüht," *Süddeutsche Zeitung*, November 28, 1986.

76. "Ostberlin lenkt in der Asylantenfrage ein," *Süddeutsche Zeitung*, September 19, 1986.

There is perhaps no better summary of the new nuances and the abiding continuities than an interview Helmut Kohl gave at the end of 1984. "In my view," he said, "it is a hoary illusion to believe that the relationship between . . . the GDR and the Federal Republic of Germany can really improve while the global political climate remains at subzero temperatures." And then Kohl cited an old peasants' saying from his home state: "A big stream carries the small river with it," which is another way of saying that, in the end, the systemic conditions have to be right for *Deutschlandpolitik* to flourish.[77]

This was, of course, precisely the premise of all his predecessors, and though more pliant and alliance-oriented than Schmidt, Kohl has not abandoned the course. He has been just as careful not to provoke Moscow (beyond allowing emplacement of Pershing IIs) and only slightly less adamant in pressing the United States toward a new détente with the Soviet Union. What has disappeared is the sound and fury of the early 1980s, and for a good reason. *Ostpolitik* and *Westpolitik* no longer clash as noisily as in the aftermath of the invasion of Afghanistan because neocontainment has lost its strident edge. American *Ostpolitik*, turning toward summitry and at least partial détente in 1985–86, had, as it were, become Germanized.

77. Interview with Süddeutscher Rundfunk (South German Radio), December 18, 1984, as cited from mimeographed record of the Bundespresse- und Informationsamt, December 19, 1984, no. II/1218-5.

SIX

The View from Paris

PIERRE HASSNER

DOES ANY Western power have an East European policy? Or are all *Osteuropapolitiken* both more and less than policies toward Eastern Europe in the sense that they usually involve more than Eastern Europe and amount to less than policies? This question is legitimate for all the Western countries considered in this book, but for none more than France.

In a sense France is the positive exception to a generally negative answer. While the Federal Republic's interests and policies are directed above all to the German Democratic Republic and those of the United States to the Soviet Union or the Soviet bloc as a whole, France has paid special attention to the division of Europe symbolized by the Yalta Conference, in particular to East Central Europe as such. This was especially the case under de Gaulle, but has been shown more recently by the attention, greater than in any other Western country, given in France to the Polish events of 1980–81.

Once upon a time, this attention could even have been called a policy. Not only was France present at the creation of the East Central European states out of the Ottoman and Austro-Hungarian empires, but the post–World War I system of alliances in the region could rightly be called "the French system."[1] World War II started as a direct consequence of that system, when France and Britain, having abandoned Czechoslovakia, went to war to honor their guarantees to Poland.

1. See Bertrand de Jouvenel, *D'une guerre à l'autre*, vol. 1: *De Versailles à Locarno* (Paris: Calmann-Lévy, 1940), pp. 111–27.

In another and more important sense, however, the French case illustrates even better than the others that Western interests in Eastern Europe are more indirect than direct and more declaratory than effective. Unlike the Federal Republic, France has no bilateral problems with Eastern Europe, whether in terms of a broken national unity, common borders, or special pressures from minorities. Unlike the United States, it has no built-in East European lobbies in the guise of important ethnic minorities. If, unlike Britain or other West European countries, it has nevertheless always, with the relative exception of the Fourth Republic (1946–58), proclaimed an active interest in Eastern Europe, this interest was not, to use Arnold Wolfers's classical distinction, in the nature of "possession goals" but rather of "milieu goals."[2] It was part of a strategy aimed at Germany, Russia, or the United States; or of a vision of the future of Europe; or of a conception or presentation of itself as the champion or the spokesman for small nations or human rights.

Most of the time France has needed Eastern Europe for this strategy, this vision, or this self-presentation. But almost never has it been able either to count on Eastern Europe's playing the part expected of it or to affect its fate decisively. The years between the world wars, when the alliance of France and Eastern Europe was central to the fate of Europe and did affect expectations and behavior in the most momentous way, ended precisely in mutual disappointment and disaster. After the war, as Eastern Europe lost its autonomy and France its status as a great power, their mutual links could affect their diplomatic and strategic situations only marginally. Just as Charles de Gaulle has been called "a man of the day-before-yesterday and the day-after-tomorrow," so the relations between the two Europes had to do with nostalgia and prophecy.[3] From de Gaulle to Francois Mitterrand, French leaders were cast more than ever as specialists in vision rather than policy, in words rather than deeds.

This description should not be taken as necessarily derogatory. A prophetic vision may be more important historically than a short-term—let alone a short-sighted—military or economic policy; standing

2. Arnold Wolfers, *Discord and Collaboration* (Johns Hopkins University Press, 1962), pp. 73–77.

3. François Gorand, one of the most eloquent advocates of an active French policy toward Eastern Europe, characteristically titles his article "L'Europe de la nostalgie"; see *Politique étrangère* (Spring 1984), pp. 127–35.

up for the truth may, morally, be the most important of deeds. Yet for a middle power constrained by its geographical situation and by limited resources and engaged in a complex struggle for influence and security, such a claim to moral and historical leadership has a certain odd character about it. Its origins call for a complex historical explanation, and its future raises difficult political questions.

Factors Shaping the French Viewpoint

The traditional French aspiration was best captured in a remarkable text written in 1910 by the royalist writer Charles Maurras, which President Georges Pompidou was to quote sixty years later:

That France may maneuver and grow: It would be a great mistake to assume that any newly constituted nation must necessarily succumb as a satellite to the gravitational pull of the nearest big neighbor. Each empire will find it increasingly difficult to maintain undiluted its influence and protection over its clientele of subject nationalities. For a long time to come, then, the world will appear not as a checkerboard of medium-sized and small states, but rather as a composite of these two systems: several empires, with a certain number of small and medium-sized buffer state nationalities between them.

Such a world will be far from tranquil; its weak members will be too weak, its strong ones too strong, and international peace will be based on nothing more than the terror the giant powers inspire in one another. An appallingly interdependent order, a company of mutual intimidation, organized cannibalism! . . .

In this state of affairs, between the two elements defined above, this general fear and competition would provide just the right terrain on which France could maneuver, freely and frankly, if only because it would find itself very fortunately placed, by size and structure, midway between the giant empires and the cloud of small nations jealous of their independence. Circumstances are propitious for the interposition of a state of medium magnitude with a robust and firm makeup like our own. This fortunate constitution of ours would keep us from falling into any ill-advised abuse of imperialist and colonialist policy and would open the way to the best, most active, and most fruitful policy of influence. For our king, as absolute master of his army, navy, and diplomatic corps, would enjoy the necessary independence to be watching abroad for the inevitable excesses of arrogant policy which the Germans, the Russians, the British, and the Americans could not thereafter avoid making.

We would need neither to seek friends nor to invite them; the secondary states would be driven in our direction by the force of circumstances; we would see them flee toward us. It is up to us, then, to be wise enough and show ourselves vigorous enough to inspire confidence, to appear as effective protectors and not as tyrants. . . . The policy which the Kings of France always followed, of blocking the creation of any worldwide monarchy or the excessive growth of this or that coalition, would again triumphantly shine from Paris. As in times past, by reason of the numerical inferiority which sometimes stranded us without putting us at a real disadvantage, we may not take as much space on the map as the biggest powers; we shall, however, enjoy moral authority thereon, based on a much better kind of strength. More skillfully than Prussia or Piedmont before the unifications of Germany and Italy, we shall multiply our assets by an adroit use of friends, protégés, and newly liberated peoples trained and strengthened by our help. This policy of generosity will bring other results besides its beauty, for our chivalry will elevate us to empire.[4]

Of course there were times when it was France itself, under Louis XIV and Napoleon I, that represented the threat of empire over Europe. Some of the connections with Eastern Europe, particularly with Poland, as well as the claim to a special authority over Europe, may go back to these experiences. From Napoleon III to Mitterrand via de Gaulle, French policy can be interpreted as an attempt to resurrect past grandeur in the absence of the means that had once made it possible. Yet it is true that the most fundamental French self-perception is not of strength but of physical limitations in men, territory, or wealth, limitations that have to be made up by superior diplomatic skill, historical lucidity, institutional privileges, or moral authority.

The most basic device is the *alliance de revers,* the alliance with the neighbors and potential rivals of one's potential enemy. "It is the oldest and firmest principle of French diplomacy that against a power one fears, one must seek help through an *alliance de revers.*"[5] A more multilateral or structural extension of the same principle of finding additional strength through diplomacy or alliances is the search for a new European order. That order either would give France greater freedom of action than its stronger rivals (this was the revisionist strategy of Napoleon III against the system created by the Congress of Vienna and of de Gaulle against the results of Yalta) or would

4. Charles Maurras, *Kiel et Tanger: La République Française devant l'Europe* (Versailles: Bibliothèque des oeuvres politiques, 1895, 1905, 1913, 1921, rprt. 1928), pp. 136–41.
5. Bertrand de Jouvenel, *D'une guerre à l'autre,* vol. 2: *La décomposition de l'Europe libérale,* (Paris: Plon, 1941), p. 50.

encircle the main potential enemy through a rigid system of alliances and legal constraints (this was France's anti-German status quo strategy after the Treaty of Versailles, and potentially de Gaulle's solution of the German Problem in 1945 and again in the February 1965 press conference that envisaged a special status for Germany guaranteed by its neighbors). Finally, the most universalistic direction for policy, inspired by the message of the French Revolution, is the support of self-determination, of national independence, and of individual freedom everywhere, particularly in Europe.

All three formulas have been combined, with varying emphases, in French policies toward Eastern Europe. Napoleon III's policy was best characterized by Ludwig Dehio: "He had decided to play the role of protector of the nationalist movements in Central and Eastern Europe even before these people had acquired the freedom to develop. Borne along by the very currents that had carried Napoleon I to his doom, he claimed to gain for France, by skillful maneuvering and with no great effort, a camouflaged version of the supremacy that his powerful uncle, fighting the current, had been unable to obtain. His policy of low risks, craftily stage-managed, sufficed to achieve surprising initial successes; but it lacked the force to consolidate them. In the decisive field of foreign affairs, Napoleon III could not, in the long run, master the problems raised in 1848, of how to weave the forces of popular nationalist movements into the calculations of power politics."[6]

These same problems, in a different form, have plagued France, but not only France, ever since. During the Franco-Russian alliance before World War I, sympathy for oppressed nations, in particular Poland, or minorities like the Jews clashed against the constraints of the *alliance de revers* with the Russian empire. Of course, the latter won. Secret agreements between the Entente powers (Britain, France, and Russia) would have given Russia a free hand in Eastern Europe if it had won the First World War.[7]

THE SYSTEM OF ALLIANCES BETWEEN THE WARS

The outcome of World War I, with the simultaneous defeat or disintegration of Germany, Austria, and Russia, gave both France

6. Ludwig Dehio, *The Precarious Balance: The Politics of Power in Europe 1494–1945* (London: Chatto and Windus, 1963), pp. 205–06.

7. Henry L. Roberts, *Eastern Europe: Politics, Revolution, and Diplomacy* (Knopf, 1970), p. 72.

and Eastern Europe their great opportunity. France remained the only major Continental power. Hence the worry of its leaders, particularly Marshal Ferdinand Foch, at the disappearance of Russia as a partner of an *alliance de revers* against the danger of German resurgence. And hence the urge to replace it with the Polish and Czech alliances. Together, Poland and Czechoslovakia had the same population as France. With the sponsoring of the Little Entente among Czechoslovakia, Romania, and Yugoslavia, and the attempts at a Balkan confederation and an Eastern version of the 1925 Locarno Pact, in which Germany guaranteed the inviolability of the boundaries of its neighbors to the West, it would seem that France had reconciled four requirements: a system based on an *alliance de revers* against potential revisionist powers; aspiration to the leadership of small and middle-sized European powers; commitment to the principle of national self-determination; and commitment to democracy. Yet the whole construction was soon to show its fragility. At bottom, as Henry Roberts put it, "France was the one great power really committed to support the status quo in Eastern Europe, and France, as it proved, was not enough."[8]

Beyond this structural factor, however, a number of more avoidable social, economic, political, and military developments had a decisive role still worth pondering today.

First, France's Eastern allies themselves were less than united (the quarrels between Poland and Czechoslovakia were particularly harmful) and more preoccupied with the dangers from Hungary than from Germany and the Soviet Union. Their commitment both to democracy and to the French alliance seemed less than stable.

More important, however, was the insufficient priority given by France to maintaining this stability. Diplomatically, it tended more and more to deal directly with Germany and the USSR, which encouraged its nervous allies to do the same. Economically, in the early 1930s when the East European agricultural countries were badly hit by the world depression and desperately needed to sell their products, Western Europe, including France, refused to grant them the preferential access (as against overseas competition) and the credits that might have given them a chance.[9] Militarily, the adoption of a purely defensive strategy based on the Maginot Line, aimed solely at protecting French territory, was incompatible with the political

8. Ibid., p. 62.
9. De Jouvenel, *D'une guerre à l'autre*, vol. 2, pp. 294–96.

commitments implied by the *alliance de revers* and the East European system.

Finally, France's hesitation in the triangular game with Germany and Russia combined with its hesitation between honoring the sanctity of commitments and preserving peace to ensure the worst outcome for all.

Parallels with current dilemmas over the support of the Polish economy during the Solidarity period, over neutralism, and over extended deterrence deserve to be noted, although in the postwar world the essential triangle that determines the structure of European politics is the one formed by the Soviet Union, the United States, and Germany. But the relations within this triangle may, in certain circumstances, occupy the whole scene or, on the contrary, leave a certain space for the maneuvers of yesterday's actors, such as the middle powers of Western and Eastern Europe, beginning with France itself.

GAULLIST DESIGNS

A certain room for maneuver existed in de Gaulle's judgment, in 1945 when "the collapse of Germany, the tearing apart of Europe, and Russo-American antagonism offer[ed] France, saved by a miracle, exceptional opportunities for action,"[10] and again twenty years later, when he thought America's preoccupation with the Vietnam War, Russia's preoccupation with China, and Germany's mixture of dissatisfaction with its division and inability to overcome it could give the grand design of "Europe from the Atlantic to the Urals" a second chance.

Certainly, respect for the national aspirations of East European countries and recognition of the incompleteness of Europe without them was an essential part of de Gaulle's criticism of the Yalta agreement, which was instantly and gratefully recognized by the peoples of the region. But it is no less certain that such concerns were firmly subordinated to the politics of France's two triangular relations: with Russia and Germany on the one hand, Russia and the United States on the other. In both, Russia was essential in the *alliance de*

---

10. Charles de Gaulle, *Mémoires de guerre*, vol. 3: *Le Salut* (Paris: Plon, 1959), p. 210.

revers function. De Gaulle had opposed Churchill's plan for an Allied landing in the Balkans, which would have had a chance of preventing, at least in part, the Sovietization of Eastern Europe, because a landing in France would give France a better chance of asserting its independence. He justified his acceptance of the Oder-Neisse line, the provisional boundary between Poland and East Germany, by telling Stalin it would prevent any future reconciliation between Germany and Poland. He went further and earlier than his Western allies in establishing links with the Lublin Committee, the Soviet-controlled and communist-dominated bidders for power in Poland. He insisted on preventing Britain from joining the Franco-Russian alliance on the ground that France had no disputes with the Soviet Union but had conflicting interests with Britain. In his declarations Eastern Europe appeared only as an argument for dividing Germany because, as he told Truman, in the absence of a German threat the national interests of East European states would keep them from remaining satellites of the Soviet Union. It was clear that the primary consideration was to enlist Soviet support for France's anti-German policy and to increase French bargaining power with the Anglo-Saxons.

The effect on Soviet policy, however, was negligible. Even de Gaulle's France was considered just another member of the Western bloc, and a contemptible one at that. After 1947, whatever room for maneuver had seemed to exist either for France or for Central European countries like Czechoslovakia clearly disappeared. The Fourth Republic coincided with the cold war, when, as Raymond Aron put it, there was no diplomacy except between allies. French relations with Eastern Europe were indistinguishable, for all practical purposes, from East-West relations in general. Perhaps the only specific feature was a hostility (greater, for instance, than Britain's and present to this day) toward proposals like the Rapacki plan for nuclear-free zones out of fear that they might lead to a neutralized Germany and prevent its integration into Western Europe.

With de Gaulle's return in 1958, an early gesture (denying the legitimacy of the GDR, but coupling the denial with a call for the recognition of the Oder-Neisse line and for détente) indicated the direction of his new *Ostpolitik:* no longer an alliance with the East against Germany but an attempt to act as a mediator between Germany and the East.

The active phase of this policy was delayed on the one hand by the Algerian war and the Berlin crisis and on the other by emphasis on the alliance with Konrad Adenauer's Germany and criticism of the Kennedy détente. But from 1964 to 1968 a new phase took place, when for the only time since World War I France was leading the way in East-West relations. Its dialogue with Eastern Europe seemed one promising avenue to overcome the division of the Continent. With de Gaulle in the West and Mao Zedong in the East, the breakdown of bipolarity seemed the order of the day. In Eastern Europe itself, Romania and Albania were resisting Moscow. The postulate of French all-European policy (another version of which can be found in the disengagement proposals of the 1950s and the slogans of the neutralist wing of the peace movement and of socialist parties today) was that to encourage the independence of Eastern Europe from the Soviet Union one had to begin by making Western Europe independent from the United States. De Gaulle's hope in abandoning the integrated structure of NATO was to encourage a similar movement in Eastern as well as Western Europe and to reach a situation in which the Soviet Union would loosen its grip over Eastern Europe and accept a certain French influence in exchange for a lessening of American influence in Western Europe and for a more forthcoming German attitude brought about by French prodding and example.

De Gaulle knew that he could get nowhere in Eastern Europe without Soviet acquiescence, but he could not get this acquiescence if there were no pressure from Eastern Europe and no promise from Germany. The order of his visits shows a carefully calibrated strategy. He went first to the Soviet Union in 1966, then in 1967 to a faithful ally—Poland—that he was nevertheless recalling to its Central European cultural tradition, then to heretic Romania in 1968, while avoiding the GDR. He showed no interest in the Prague Spring, because it was led by communists and intellectuals, focused on domestic reform rather than national independence, and looked more to Germany than to France.[11] Yet the failure of this strategy appeared more and more clearly with Wladyslaw Gomulka's cool reception of his visit, with Romania's remaining the only parallel maverick, and

11. See the recollections of the then ambassador of France to Moscow, Olivier Wormser, who remembers de Gaulle's startling formula: "Vous comprenez, monsieur l'Ambassadeur, dans ces conditions, la Tchécoslovaquie, je m'en bats l'oeil!" See "Le Coup de Prague (II): L'occupation de la Tchécoslovaquie vue de Moscou," *Revue des Deux Mondes* (July 1978), p. 45.

above all with the Soviet invasion of Prague. Although he refused to admit it, and his was the first Western government to reestablish contacts with the Soviets after what his prime minister, Michel Debré, had called "a traffic accident on the road to détente," de Gaulle knew that his attempt for "another order, another equilibrium" had failed. Soviet actions and French dependence on the Common Market and the United States (increased by the domestic turmoil of May 1968) forced him, in the short run at least, to look more in the direction of his Western allies.

OSTPOLITIK AND DÉTENTE

De Gaulle's successors, in particular Georges Pompidou, were also forced to look to the West. To the limited extent that Pompidou's presidency had any grand design at all in foreign policy, it had to do with West European unity and British entry into the Common Market as a way of balancing Germany and the United States, rather than with "Europe from the Atlantic to the Urals." But this does not mean that East-West relations and détente were given short shrift. On the contrary, Pompidou met Leonid Brezhnev five times. But this preoccupation with Moscow was, more than ever, based on preoccupation with Bonn and Washington.

The reason lies in the paradox that, while the invasion of Czechoslovakia killed the revisionist or Franco–East European version of détente, it created the conditions for launching, in 1969–70, a more effective one. This time, détente was based on the recognition of the status quo and, in particular, on the role of the superpowers. It was focused on the dialogue between the Soviet Union and the two Western powers from whom Moscow had something to fear and to whom it had something substantial to offer: the Federal Republic and the United States.

After 1969, East-West relations in Europe were dominated by Germany's treaties with its Eastern neighbors and by the superpower dialogue on arms control. Pompidou and Michel Jobert viewed both with the greatest distrust.[12] They insisted, of course, on France's

12. See the unpublished paper by Andreas Wilkens, "La politique française à l'égard de l'Union soviétique pendant la présidence de Georges Pompidou," Cycle supérieure d'Etudes politiques (Paris, September 1984), in particular Michel Jobert's interview.

indispensable role, in particular as an occupying power, for the Berlin settlement. But beyond that, Pompidou encouraged the notion of a special Franco-Soviet relationship. That led him to accept not only a common declaration and an institutionalization of summit meetings but also the Conference on Security and Cooperation in Europe, which de Gaulle had been reluctant to support, in order to prevent a German-Soviet tête-à-tête. Conversely, when in 1973 Jobert, in his Helsinki speech, denounced the illusions connected with the conference and with the notion of European security, he was primarily reacting to the American-Soviet dialogue and, in particular, to the agreement on the prevention of nuclear war in which he read the danger of a superpower condominium.

In both cases Eastern Europe as such hardly played a role in French preoccupations at the highest level. In the actual handling of the preparatory talks, however, French diplomacy was very active and took a leading part in bringing the nine members of the European Communities together, in encouraging an autonomous role for East European states (for instance, in rejecting bloc-to-bloc discussions and reacting favorably to Romanian or Yugoslav proposals for confidence-building measures), and in originating the so-called Third Basket of provisions to safeguard human rights and cultural contacts. At the same time, the classical dilemma of helping to protect the rights of East European nations and peoples without jeopardizing the special relationship with Moscow was never absent.

With Valéry Giscard d'Estaing, too, Eastern Europe was not a specific object of policy, let alone a primary one. But it was less absent from his more general vision. Rather than being focused on diplomatic rivalries within the great-power triangle, that vision was predicated more on interdependence and disarmament, cooperation, and convergence. From all these points of view East European countries, particularly Gierek's Poland, were involved and could even be seen as precursors or models in the détente process. They also could help facilitate contacts with the Soviet Union in a time of crisis. Basically, however, the policy was directed at the Soviet Union and aimed at maintaining the military balance, including the balance in Africa; at improving economic relations, which were beginning to deteriorate; and at moderating the style of the East-West confrontation. Germany was still important, but more as an associate than a rival, since Giscard's close relationship with Helmut Schmidt had replaced Pompidou's

distrust of Willy Brandt. But there was also still present an element
of competition with the Federal Republic, which played a role in
Giscard's ill-fated Warsaw meeting with Brezhnev in the spring of
1980. In the hope of convincing Moscow to withdraw, Giscard was
the first Western statesman to meet the Soviet leader after the invasion
of Afghanistan and was criticized by François Mitterrand for "playing
the messenger boy."

The most decisive influence upon Giscard d'Estaing's policies came
from factors beyond his control, both external and internal, particularly at the end of his administration. It coincided with the crisis of
détente, the invasion of Afghanistan, and the emergence of Solidarity
in Poland. Domestically, he was faced with the growing unpopularity
of the Soviet Union, the growing interest in human rights and in
Soviet and East European dissent among the intellectual elite, and
the conversion of the new generation of Gaullists to an anti-Soviet
line. But his electoral interest in having the Soviet Union exercise its
influence on the Communist party against the Union of the Left,[13]
the interests of the French economy, and his own belief in dialogue
were pushing him to stick with past policies. The result was a changing
and ambiguous attitude, expressed in declarations on Afghanistan
and Poland that his aides busily tried to minimize or interpret away.[14]

THE MITTERRAND ERA

In ways partly identical with and partly opposite to those of Giscard
d'Estaing, Mitterrand's policies too are the result of the interplay
among his personal views, the permanent constraints of the French
situation, and the new domestic and international context. He shares
the traditional perception of common security interests with Moscow
because of the German Problem (the sentence in the Socialist program
that "the road to French security goes through Moscow" was suggested
by him), but he has also been influenced by the League of Nations
ideology of collective security. For both reasons a certain openness to
the all-European idea relates him to de Gaulle more than to Pompidou

13. Michel Tatu has insisted on this aspect in his contribution to Sammy Cohen
and Marie-Claude Smouts, eds., *La politique extérieure de Giscard d'Estaing* (Paris: Presses
de la Fondation Nationale des Sciences Politiques, 1985), pp. 196–218; and in his *Eux
et Nous: Les relations Est-Ouest entre deux détentes* (Paris: Fayard, 1985).
14. See Cohen and Smouts, eds., *La politique extérieure*, pp. 246–60.

and Giscard d'Estaing and helps explain his reviving the "beyond Yalta" theme.

A very hard and realistic (some would say cynical) view of power relations, however, inspires his utter skepticism as to the possibilities of the evolution of the Soviet system and, even more, the chances for individual East European countries to escape from the Leninist straitjacket. Hence on Solidarity and the Jaruzelski coup he showed a passivity based on pessimism that was to culminate in December 1985 with Jaruzelski's visit to Paris and Undersecretary of State Jean-Michel Baylet's visit to Warsaw in defiance of both Polish and French public opinion.

Before acceding to power, however, the domestic needs of left-wing politics, in particular the building of the Union of the Left, had led Mitterrand and the Socialist party to a policy of contacts and visits with ruling communist parties, ranging from a particularly ill-timed meeting with Antonín Novotný on the eve of the Prague Spring to a visit to Hungary in 1975, when a joint communiqué praised the achievements of "the Hungarian working class under the leadership of its party." Those contacts showed both a great indifference to ideology and a great insensitivity to East European social and political realities. One may also mention the caution shown about condemning the repression in Czechoslovakia after the signing of the Programme Commun, the electoral pact between the French Communist and Socialist parties.[15]

Times change, and by the late 1970s the shifts in the military balance of power, the Soviet invasion of Afghanistan, the threat of the Soviet SS-20s, and the danger of German tendencies toward neutralism and pacifism combined with the French change of mood in prompting Mitterrand to harden his tone and criticize Giscard d'Estaing's weakness and illusion in face of the Soviet Union. Once Mitterrand was in power, with communist participation, domestic and international considerations (the need to show independence from his communist allies, the need for German and American financial good will, the dangers to the deployment of Euromissiles in Germany, the state of emergency in Poland) strengthened even more the incentives to break with the tradition of Franco-Soviet intimacy and to go, as one of his advisers put it, into a "cure de désintoxication."

15. See Pierre Grémion, *Paris-Prague: La gauche face au renouveau et la régression tchécoslovaques (1968–1978)* (Paris: Julliard, 1985)

Hence the declarations (significantly made by his foreign minister, Claude Cheysson, rather than by Mitterrand himself), according to which Franco-Soviet relations could not be normal as long as the situations in Afghanistan and Poland persisted. Hence, too, the firmness shown in condemning repression in Eastern Europe, particularly in Poland, and the chiding (for instance, within the Socialist International) of Germany's Social Democratic party for its softness.

But other elements in the international and domestic context militated against turning the hard words into action. The needs of the French economy in a time of crisis and the desire not to let the Reagan administration use the crisis with the East to limit French independence weighed decisively against any real policy of sanctions and even against any real coordination within the West of policies to restrict terms of credits (with the partial exception of Poland) and technology transfer (with the partial exception of CoCom).

Moreover, the sections of the French political and cultural elite that identified most strongly with Solidarity, and were the prime movers in the extraordinary mobilization of French public opinion after General Jaruzelski's declaration of martial law on December 13, 1981, were precisely those (the so-called second left: the independent union Confederation Française du Travail, the left-wing Catholics, the supporters of socialist candidate Michel Rocard, the "new philosophers") whom Mitterrand and his team distrusted most. After a month of paying lip service to their concerns, the government, by signing the Urengoi gas pipeline agreement on January 22, decided against their main recommendation to cancel the agreement or at least postpone signing it as a way of exercising leverage on Soviet behavior toward Poland.[16] The decision was criticized by the whole opposition, which by now had jumped on the bandwagon of human rights and economic sanctions. The sole exception was former prime minister Raymond Barre, who for both diplomatic and economic reasons remained favorable to Franco-Soviet cooperation and hostile to the political or ideological use of the economic weapon.

Since 1984 both domestic and international considerations have

16. According to the most precise account published, the actual timing was not the result of a deliberate decision but rather of the bureaucracy following its course. Mitterrand did not, however, reverse it in spite of misgivings that did not touch the decision itself. See Samy Cohen, *La Monarchie nucléaire* (Paris: Hachette, 1985), pp. 228–32.

pushed Mitterrand toward a course of normalization with the Soviet Union and Eastern Europe, in spite of the lack of progress in Afghanistan and Poland. On the domestic side the departure of the communists from the government liberates him from having to show that he is not their prisoner and creates an incentive to placate their electorate. Internationally, the deployment of the Euromissiles re-establishes the balance in Europe; the peace movement is on the decline; and the American strategic defense initiative (SDI) is seen as hurting French interests as well as Soviet ones. This new course is symbolized by the numerous presidential or ministerial visits to the Soviet Union and Eastern Europe, and by Mikhail Gorbachev's visit to France.

In this groping for a new détente, two specifically Franco–East European dimensions remain visible. First, in the new dialogue between the French Socialist party and the German SPD, in which the two parties are trying to overcome their differences of 1981–82 and to move toward a common European policy, the French insist on the idea that German *Ostpolitik* has to be Europeanized and enriched by the French theme of going beyond Yalta. They argue that the real source of insecurity in Europe is the lack of autonomy and human rights in Eastern Europe and that European arms control can only be meaningful if it is part of a broader political strategy for overcoming the division of Europe through the progress of democracy and communication.[17]

Second, more sectors of the French bureaucracy, particularly in the Foreign Ministry, have adopted the theme of the importance of reaching beyond Eastern Europe's governments and ruling elites in order to establish contact with the respective societies, in particular the dissident counter-elites, and help them in their struggle to maintain their democratic, national, and European identities. (That theme is propagated by what French political jargon calls the "second left" or "antitotalitarian left," grouped around the Confederation Française du Travail (CFDT), periodicals like *Esprit,* and supporters of Michel Rocard.) They have had some success in pushing for contacts with

17. See Jacques Huntzinger (secretary for international relations), "L'alliance et le développement d'une position européenne," speech presented at the Lisbon conference of Socialist parties from Atlantic alliance countries, March 20–22, 1984; and the declaration on European security adopted by the executive bureau of the French Socialist party on June 26, 1985.

the church and with dissidents by embassy representatives and during official visits, for maintaining the theme of human rights in official speeches, and most importantly for taking practical steps to improve France's cultural presence in Eastern Europe and its own openness to Eastern Europe's culture. Hence what Karl Birnbaum had called the French indirect road to European security through political, social, and cultural dialogue and change, rather than disarmament and arms control, and the French belief in the political importance of ideas and culture continued to have a certain impact on French policy, at least as long as Claude Cheysson was foreign minister, even though this policy was dominated by the perceived constraints of the strategic and economic situation.

It must be said, however, that Mitterrand's actions in December 1985 made both this part of the French bureaucracy and French public opinion in general (not to speak of those in Eastern Europe who were putting some hope into French policy) wonder whether this impact was not an illusion. He chose to be the first Western head of state to receive General Jaruzelski, thereby causing a domestic uproar, including "troubles of conscience" for his prime minister. Even more importantly, he forbade Foreign Undersecretary Jean-Michel Baylet, on a visit to Warsaw, to make symbolic gestures in the direction of Polish society (a visit to Father Popieluszko's grave or a meeting with leaders of the opposition), which had become traditional for the visits of Western ministers such as Hans-Dietrich Genscher, Sir Geoffrey Howe, and Bettino Craxi; even Willy Brandt, while refusing to meet Lech Walesa, did see one of Solidarity's Catholic advisers, Tadeusz Mazowiecki. The reasons for this self-inflicted "diplomatic Dien Bien Phu," which Jaruzelzki had predicted for French policy toward Poland, and for so completely abandoning France's self-appointed role as defender of East European freedom remain mysterious. But whether they are to be sought in the president's irritation with the French second left, or in a desire not to lose French economic and diplomatic positions in Eastern Europe in a new age of competitive détente, or in the illusion of a deal with Gorbachev that would give France a special mediating role, one thing is certain: the idea of providing an example of an East European policy carefully balanced between constraints of the present and hopes for the future—and balanced among East European societies, their governments, and the Soviet Union—cannot have ranked high. It seems to rank even lower in the mind of the new Prime Minister Jacques Chirac. While by the end of 1986 there had been no direct innovations in French policy toward Eastern Europe, there was an indirect and ominous one: the reduction of credits for Radio France Internationale and its transfer to direct management by the Foreign Ministry. These measures would considerably reduce its ability to reach East European societies and limit the freedom of its message.

DETERMINANTS AND OBJECTIVES

Perhaps this long, yet highly simplified, narrative will illustrate why, in spite of France's being the country of "raison d'Etat," an analysis going from a list of determining factors through a list of objectives to a list of instruments would be too rational and elegant to do justice to the inextricable combinations of the objective and the subjective, the structural and the conjunctural, the domestic and the international.

By way of summary, however, let us indicate the main factors that have emerged from this historical analysis and the objectives that would seem to derive from them.

The most important factor is the geopolitical one: France's position as a middle power, part of the West but located between two actually or potentially more powerful Continental powers, Germany and Russia, and an actually or potentially dominating maritime power—formerly Britain and today the United States. Hence France is interested in a more multipolar Europe and a more autonomous Eastern Europe to increase its margin of maneuver, but its primary interests are in Franco-German, Franco-Soviet, and Franco-American relations.

The second factor is France's historical self-perception as a country with a mission, a country that is not itself if it does not defend a goal beyond itself—whether a principle or a vision of European or world order. Hence a sympathetic attitude toward national independence and human rights in Eastern Europe.

The third, growing factor, is the economic one. In de Gaulle's time economic considerations were more a consequence of French policy than an influence upon it. Montesquieu's dictum applied perfectly: "The English have the politics of their commerce; the French have the commerce of their politics." Between 1966 and 1970 France seems to have derived a certain economic advantage from its political opening to the East because the Soviet Union and Eastern Europe tended to favor it over the Federal Republic.[18] But after West Germany embraced détente, it rapidly overtook France.

During the 1970s France's trade with the East was in line with the average of the European Common Market countries. Unlike the Federal Republic and even Italy, its share of East-West economic exchanges was not larger than its share in world trade.[19] An amount (including the USSR) of around 4.5 percent of French exports and 3 percent of its imports certainly does not constitute overall dependence.[20] However, the picture is different if one looks at the importance of Soviet and East European markets for specific industrial sectors. Those markets seem to have played an important cushioning role against the effects of the world recession. For instance, in 1975 the expansion of sales to the East enabled France to counterbalance the effects of the stagnation of demand in Western economies: that year trade with the Soviet bloc accounted for one-fifth of the growth of French exports. Without East-West trade, the French commercial deficit would have been twice as large.[21] Since these exports would be impossible without state credits, it is not hard to explain France's reluctance to limit them through "consensus" negotiations in the Organization for Economic Cooperation and Development.

This interest also explains the relative disarray produced by the general decline of East-West trade. France has been particularly hit; apart from the Soviet Union, its main relations were (partly for political reasons) with the two countries, Poland and Romania, that were themselves most severely affected by the economic crisis in Eastern Europe. France was also disadvantaged by the structure of its industrial exports, which took the form of large contracts whose number declined rapidly. The other major source of French exports to the East—food and agriculture—also started to decline, and by 1980 France had a commercial deficit with the Eastern bloc. This

18. See Georges Sokoloff and Gérard Wild, "Les relations économiques de la France avec l'Est," in Cohen and Smouts, eds., *La politique extérieure,* pp. 218–31.

19. Gérard Wild, "Les dépendances de la France dans ses relations économiques avec L'Europe de l'Est," *Courrier des Pays de l'Est* (October 1981).

20. See "Annex: Les échanges commerciaux de la France avec les pays de l'Est," in Thomas Schreiber, *Les relations de la France avec les Pays de L'Est (1944–1980),* Notes et Etudes Documentaires (Paris: Documentation Française, 1980), p. 97.

21. Ibid., p. 94.

deficit was spectacularly increased by the deal for buying Soviet natural gas, but it is due just as clearly to the decline in exports to the Soviet Union. While this decline has its economic reasons, it is clear that at the margin the Soviet Union has been showing its displeasure with the Mitterrand government just as, in the late 1960s, it showed its pleasure with de Gaulle.

In general terms, then, while the Eastern bloc is more dependent upon the West than vice versa, in the case of French relations with the Soviet Union and some of its satellites like the GDR, it is rather Paris that is in a position of "demandeur," and it is Moscow or East Berlin that, implicitly or explicitly, asks for political concessions in exchange for an increase in economic relations. This was clear during Mitterrand's visit to Moscow in 1984 and Laurent Fabius's visit to East Berlin in 1985. Nor is this dependence due to the gas deal and the ability of the Soviet Union to turn off the tap. As Philip Hanson points out, in that particular case it is France that has exerted a certain customer leverage.[22] The point is rather France's desperate need for exports and jobs.

This does not necessarily create a greater interest in Eastern Europe as such. As with all other West European countries, France's economic relations have been spectacularly reoriented in recent years toward the Soviet Union to the detriment of the smaller East European countries (see appendix tables A-4 and A-7). The trend is slightly slower in relations with Poland and Romania but is nevertheless unmistakable. Whatever the favorable intentions toward trade with Hungary for economic reasons, or whatever the desirability of exercising political leverage toward Poland, the structure of the situation seems to be particularly unfavorable for Franco–East European relations. Eastern Europe needs the West, and hence France; but France needs the Soviet Union and cannot be expected to go very far in risking its economic relations with Moscow in order to influence the political evolution of Eastern Europe.

Other domestic factors influencing French policy are the existence of a comparatively strong, although declining, Communist party (which can influence policy toward the East in several paradoxical ways) and a strong shift in public opinion since 1974–76, especially in the media and among intellectual elites, toward a negative attitude

22. Philip Hanson, "The Franco-Soviet Trade Talks and Soviet Trade with the West," *Radio Liberty Research Bulletin* (April 17, 1985), RL 117/85.

to the Soviet Union. Combined with the traditional sympathy toward Poland and with the search by the second left, which felt uneasy with communist participation in government, for an identification with a noncommunist or anticommunist social movement, this has produced a particularly strong pro-Solidarity and anti-Jaruzelski reaction.

That reaction has been particularly noticeable among left-wing or former left-wing intellectuals, such as André Glucksmann, and their friends like Yves Montand. After their disappointments with the evolution of China, Vietnam, and Cuba, they were particularly shaken in 1974–75 by Alexander Solzhenitsyn's description of the "Gulag Archipelago." In their basically Manichaean view of the world, Soviet totalitarianism took the place of American imperialism, Solzhenitsyn himself or Lech Walesa took the place of revolutionary heroes like Ché Guevara, and the sufferings and struggles of the Polish people replaced those of the Algerians or Vietnamese. For once, then, former Maoists, Christian trade unionists, and bourgeois conservatives were united, just as Jean-Paul Sartre, Raymond Aron, and André Glucksmann had shared a platform a few years earlier to ask greater French assistance to the Asian boat people.

To list these factors is to explain why a statement of objectives of French policy cannot go very far. In terms of the traditional alternatives of Western policy, de Gaulle stressed the encouragement of national autonomy and cultural identity in Eastern Europe (the so-called desatellization or Romanian road) while under Mitterrand more attention was given to human rights and hence to liberalization (the Hungarian road). It is not by chance that the first state visit to Eastern Europe after the Jaruzelski coup was to Hungary, while a presidential visit to Romania was cancelled in 1982 because of an obscure affair involving the attempted assassination of a Romanian emigré writer. As for democratization in Poland, it has been supported somewhat more actively than under Giscard d'Estaing (who in 1981 publicly expressed his doubts about anything more than economic reform being compatible with Poland's geopolitical situation), but with almost as much skepticism and almost as few means. Democracy and cultural identity in Eastern Europe can really be called objectives only for certain individuals or segments of the French Socialist party or the Foreign Ministry. This is reflected in government policy, but only for a time and even then only in a relatively marginal or diluted way.

The real objectives of French policy concern relations with the great powers. Criticism of the Yalta agreements was, for de Gaulle, primarily a stick with which to beat the United States in order to attribute the responsibility for the division of Europe to a deal between the superpowers. Policy toward the GDR has been largely determined by relations with the Federal Republic; policy toward Poland, until recent years, by relations with Germany and the Soviet Union. The encouragement of national autonomy in Eastern Europe has often been a convenient argument for refusing France's own supranational integration into NATO or the European Communities, or for attracting Soviet attention with a view toward a general European settlement.

Such a settlement was an operational objective of French policy during three or four years (1965–68) under de Gaulle. Since then its status has been very precisely defined by François Mitterrand in his 1982 New Year's speech: "Anything that goes against Yalta is good, but let us not forget history's slowness." This statement was both the expression of a genuine dream for the long term and a reaction to the Polish events and the protests aroused by the declaration he had instructed his foreign minister, Claude Cheysson, to make on December 13, 1981: "Of course, we shall do nothing."

French policy toward Eastern Europe is, like most policies, a combination of long-range aspirations for a different European economic and political order and short-run reactions to international and domestic pressures. What is less easy to discern, and perhaps less present, is a middle-range strategy putting deliberately chosen instruments at the service of conscious and operational objectives.

The Instruments of Policy

For reasons already mentioned, the instruments of France's policy, at least the material, military, and economic ones, are limited by the constraints on it as a middle power, particularly at a time of economic crisis. In a more general way, all instruments are limited by the lack of priority and continuity at the top.

The main assets, then, are the traditional French ones of imagination and diplomatic skill, the art of doing something with nothing or at least of making the best out of a not very strong hand. To understand the French successes and failures in putting them into practice, one must look at the peculiarities of the French system, particularly under the Fifth Republic.

POLICYMAKING PROCESSES

One characteristic of France is the extended role of the state. Both in economic and cultural policies its organizational and financial direction and support are much greater than in other Western democracies. In the diplomatic and security fields that, by definition, are the state's preserve everywhere, it is much more protected from the pressures and reactions of society.

This protection in great part stems from the internal structure of government under the Fifth Republic, with its great primacy of the executive over the legislative branch. Parliament has no role to speak of in foreign policy, certainly not in relations with Eastern Europe. One could define the system as an absolute monarchy tempered by a rigid bureaucracy. Decisions about foreign affairs are at the ultimate discretion of the president (a reality given theoretical status by Jacques Chaban-Delmas with the unofficial but so far widely accepted and practiced formula of "domaine réservé"). In most foreign policy matters the president does actually decide alone.

While de Gaulle was of course the master of the lonely strategy, he tended to consult and inform his ministers and officials rather more than Giscard d'Estaing, let alone Mitterrand. Mitterrand shares with the founder of the Fifth Republic a taste for mystery, so that his own ministers and their subordinates are left guessing about his real intentions and are liable to be brusquely overruled. (This happened to Cheysson and the Quai d'Orsay in the course of negotiations with the United States about credits to the East in 1982.)

On some matters, particularly under Giscard d'Estaing, the preparation of decisions and coordination of their implementation were very carefully handled by interministerial committees or meetings, such as the Comité interministerial pour les questions de coordination économique européenne (SGCI) for European Communities matters, the Conseil de défense (with the relevant ministers and military officials), the newly created Conseil de politique nucléaire extérieure for controlling exports of nuclear technology, and ad hoc conseils restreints that can be convened on any subject considered important enough. Only once under Giscard d'Estaing did such a conseil restreint meet on a subject related to Eastern Europe—January 15, 1981—and it discussed economic relations with Moscow and the likely effects on them in case of an invasion of Poland.[23] But such major decisions as the trip to Warsaw in April 1980 were prepared and made in complete secrecy (with the help of Giscard d'Estaing's political confidant and associate Michel Poniatowski).[24] Neither general foreign policy nor the daily management of foreign affairs was covered by the interministerial committees.

Even on matters that traditionally were handled by these institutions, President Mitterrand has preferred to rely on informal channels. The SGCI has been dismantled and the conseils restreints are no longer called. But while decisions and authority are more personal and centralized than in the United States, there is no equivalent of the National Security Council, let alone of its bureaucratic expansion since the 1960s. The president relies on a handful of people (essentially the diplomatic adviser, who is a junior foreign service officer, and his deputy; the secretary general and his deputy; and one or two personal advisers) of whom only two specialize in foreign affairs. Hence normally at the other end of the spectrum there is great latitude for the permanent factor of the French state, the bureaucracy. As a practitioner writing under a pseudonym has recently put it: "Two major and paradoxically opposite tendencies characterize today the conduct of France's external activity. The first is an increased presidentialization of this activity; the second a trend toward the dismemberment and atomization of foreign policy."[25]

Basically, military policy is made by the military, the Treasury has a decisive influence on financial policy, including the handling of East European debt, and semiautonomous state bureaucracies like those of nationalized industries follow their own policies (Gaz de France in the case of the gas deal with the Soviet Union). The attempts of the Centre d'analyse et de prévision (the French version of the Policy Planning Council, created by Michel Jobert in 1973) to impose a strategic purpose or coherence on the several dimensions of foreign policy have foundered, particularly on economic issues, in the face

23. Sammy Cohen, "La Politique extérieure de 1974 à 1981: Un seul homme? Un homme seul?" in Cohen and Smouts, eds., *La politique extérieure*, p. 23.

24. For a detailed account, see Cohen, *La Monarchie nucléaire*, pp. 126–35.

25. Bernard Adrien, "Un problème majeur: Le démembrement de la politique étrangère," *Politique étrangère* (Winter 1985), p. 975.

of resistance from entrenched bureaucracies. Its recent attempt to inject a new political dynamism into French cultural policy in Eastern Europe has met the classical obstacles of insufficient resources and bureaucratic rigidity.

Occasionally, when the policy of one bureaucracy clashes with that of another, Elysean thunderbolts may strike one of the aides. According to some press reports, for example, the head of the Direction de la surveillance du territoire, one of those secret services well known for their anticommunist orientation, was fired in August 1985 for having leaked documents about Soviet industrial spying to the press and television on the eve of the meeting of the Franco-Soviet Commission on Trade, causing an irate public protest from the minister for foreign trade, Edith Cresson.[26] Unpredictability at the top makes it hard for France to have a policy; inertia at the level of the different bureaucracies makes it hard to use them as instruments. The signing of the gas deal with the Soviet Union on January 22, 1982, is a nice illustration. According to one account, the timing was decided by Gaz de France without the knowledge of the president, who reprimanded the bureaucracy vehemently when he learned about it. But he had given no indication earlier that he wanted the timing changed—let alone to have the decision reversed—because of the Polish events.[27]

French policymakers do, however, enjoy one advantage that their counterparts in most democratic countries do not: their great freedom from outside interference. On issues touching Eastern Europe, interference comes only from business pressures (which are much weaker than, for instance, in Germany and concentrate mainly on relations with the Soviet Union) and the political calculations of the president about the likely reactions of public opinion, the media, or the Communist party. As already mentioned, such calculations played a part mainly during the Polish crisis, and they affected the president's declarations more than his actions.

Are things different after the elections of 1986? Of course, the "cohabitation" between a left-wing president and a right-wing parliamentary majority produces a built-in struggle over the control of foreign policy. So far, Mitterrand has sought (not unsuccessfully) to

26. *Le Monde*, August 2, 1985; and Sean Schmitt, "Notre agent à Quimper," *Le Point* (August 5, 1985), p. 43.

27. Cohen, *La Monarchie nucléaire*, p. 232.

assert his special responsibility for defense matters and to veto certain appointments. But policy toward the East has provoked no particular conflict, if only because no real policy has emerged, and certainly no new one. When this episode has passed, it seems likely that the French system will remain centered on the president but that, in personal terms, no successor will have either the authority of de Gaulle or the secretiveness of Mitterrand, and in institutional terms the evolution of the Fifth Republic will be more in the direction of the Fourth, that is, toward a greater role for political parties.

It is hard to imagine, though, policy toward Eastern Europe becoming a bone of contention in French political debate. The broader issues of détente, human rights, and relations with the Soviet Union may do so, as happened to some extent in the presidential elections of 1981. The hardening of French majority opinion, particularly among the political elite, from socialists to Gaullists, is likely to last. There is a certain half-hidden cleavage between this majority line and a minority surviving from the past. The former is symbolized by a declaration of François Léotard, the coming young man of the conservatives, according to which the three grand old men of the right, Giscard, Chirac, and Barre, having been raised politically under de Gaulle, were still affected by a positive attitude toward détente and by the notion that good relations with the Soviet Union were desirable, whereas Léotard's generation has no such leftovers from the past. The minority line, running from Raymond Barre to the communists via Jean-Pierre Chevènement and Mitterrand's adviser, Régis Debray, sticks to the old Gaullist theme of the primacy of national interests over human rights and ideology and the need to keep contact with the Soviet Union in order to balance Germany and the United States.[28] Giscard d'Estaing and Chirac (influenced both by the mood in favor of dissidents and human rights and the popularity of the Reagan administration in the French right) have moved with the times, going so far as to make statements against the gas deal or even (in the case of Chirac) for cutting off economic relations with the Soviet Union.

It is highly unlikely, however, that they really mean it. Once in power, economic and diplomatic constraints have seemed to make

28. See Debray's book *Les empires contre l'Europe* (Paris: Gallimard, 1985); and my review, "Sur la balançoire des mythes," *Le Monde,* June 25, 1985, and *Intervention* (Fall 1985).

the Chirac government return, quite predictably, to traditional French positions (as was the case for the Socialists on the issue of arms sales). Indeed, the new foreign minister, Jean Bernard Raimond, a former ambassador to Warsaw and Moscow, combines a pessimistic view of communist regimes with an equally pessimistic view of the scope for working with their oppositions or influencing their societies. The only exception is the upgrading of contacts with the Afghan resistance, one of whose leaders was received by Chirac. Nor is the government subjected to strong political pressures for a radical change of course. If only because of its relative lack of both domestic salience and ability to influence external events, French policy toward Eastern Europe is likely to stay under the sign of continuity and to remain in the hands of the bureaucracy until the next spectacular crisis between the Soviet Union and one of its satellites.

POLITICAL-DIPLOMATIC POLICIES

Continuity is particularly the rule in the field of diplomacy, where certain officials of the Foreign Ministry have had almost a free hand in constructing French policy. The role of France in the Conference on Security and Cooperation in Europe (CSCE) was in great part created by Jacques Andréani, who headed the European desk during the preparatory and early phases. He was the inventor of the concept of the "Third Basket" and the moving force behind the coordination of the nine EC members. Similarly, the Conference on Confidence- and Security-Building Measures and Disarmament in Europe (CDE), which was born out of Giscard d'Estaing's general desire for France to make some positive suggestions on disarmament, was the brainchild of the Centre d'analyse et de prévision and has ever since been "the baby" of Benoit d'Aboville, for many years the Foreign Ministry's leading expert on disarmament and now its deputy director for political affairs.

But before speaking of these multilateral undertakings, we must examine bilateral diplomatic relations. In the French conception, they are the ones that have pride of place. Under the Fifth Republic, France has always had a preference for multiple bilateralism over multilateralism, partly because of the Gaullist art of manipulating triangular situations and partly because, in general, bilateral relations are more conducive to flexibility while multilateral ones tend to reinforce bloc solidarity. Even when he was preaching and practicing "détente, entente, et coopération," de Gaulle resisted the Soviet campaign for the European Security Conference, which he feared would freeze the status quo rather than change it. His successors have moved away from this intransigent opposition to multilateralism. Pompidou did so by accepting the conference and participating in the preparatory talks; Giscard d'Estaing signed the Helsinki Final Act (which Michel Jobert claims, probably wrongly, that Pompidou would never have done), continued the process through Belgrade and Madrid, and promoted the Conference on Disarmament in Europe. But both CDE and CSCE are described as the opposite of the Mutually Balanced Force Reductions talks (MBFR), which were branded as bloc to bloc.

Whether in a multilateral or bilateral setting, the center of French policy is, to use the formula of one of Claude Cheysson's collaborators, to "encourage anti-Yalta behavior," behavior that transcends the division of Europe into two blocs, even if it cannot do away with the division or with the two alliances themselves.[29] Translated into concrete terms and applied to Eastern Europe, this means encouraging East European states to be as independent and to have as many contacts with the West (particularly France) as possible without going so far as to provoke the Soviet Union.

For France it means both acting independently itself and paying particular attention to those East European states that adopt a similar behavior. Three countries have been singled out in this spirit: Romania, Poland, and more recently and to a lesser extent Hungary. For the first two, the only East European countries visited by de Gaulle, there are solid historical and cultural foundations for a special relationship, and they have led to a special economic relationship as well. For Hungary, however, there are no historical and cultural ties and economic relations are scarce; the new attention is purely political and symbolic.

In a very exaggerated and simplified form, one might almost say that Romania was the favorite under de Gaulle, Poland under Giscard d'Estaing, and Hungary under Mitterrand. But of course there is much overlap: Romania has remained the prime interlocutor on

29. Denis Delbourg, "Est-Ouest: Contre vents et marées," *Politique étrangère* (Summer 1985), p. 328.

security matters; Hungary has become so on cultural ones; Poland remains, in a way, the most important in all respects.

As "the Gaullists of Eastern Europe," the Romanians have remained France's favorite East European interlocutors for such matters as CSCE, CDE, and confidence-building measures. Regular consultations on security matters are institutionalized. President Pompidou received President Ceausescu in Paris in 1970; Prime Minister Chirac visited Romania in 1975; President Giscard d'Estaing did so in 1979. President Mitterrand's visit, scheduled for 1982, was postponed because of the emigré writer affair already mentioned. This was symptomatic of Romania's loss of prestige because of its dismal record on both human rights and economic matters.

Poland is the most complex and exceptional case. De Gaulle tried to encourage a sense of Central European identity among the Poles, but despite, or partly because of, an enthusiastic popular reception, was politely brushed off by Gomulka. For all his good will toward France (due, in particular, to its recognition of the Oder-Neisse line), Gomulka stressed Poland's geographical situation and its unwillingness to rely on "moon alliances" with distant Western powers. Pompidou went to Poland in 1970 and received Gierek in Paris in 1972, noting the convergence of views between the two countries. But the great acceleration and intensification of relations occurred under Giscard d'Estaing.

His first visit to the East, in 1975, was to Warsaw. In 1977 Gierek came to Paris; in 1978, the second meeting in two years, Giscard returned to Poland, and the joint communiqué they issued used the exceptional formula of "personal friendship and great trust." The following year, Foreign Minister Jean François-Poncet went to Warsaw for what was described as an "institutional visit" in the framework of annual consultations that had been agreed on in 1975. Both in their bilateral aspects and in coordinating the preparation of CSCE, Franco-Polish relations had been declared "exceptional" by Giscard d'Estaing as early as his first visit in 1975, and so indeed they were. The cultural agreement and the charter on the principles of cooperation signed on this occasion went beyond the Helsinki Act's provisions for the freer exchange of people and ideas.

It is not surprising, then, that when the storm broke in 1980, first, after Afghanistan, the special relationship between Gierek and Giscard d'Estaing played a role in the latter's attempt to build a bridge between the West and the Soviet Union in his famous Warsaw meeting with Brezhnev. Then, in the Polish crisis, the main preoccupation of the French president (as well as of Helmut Schmidt) was to help Gierek, which he did both by financial support and by public counsels of moderation to the Solidarity movement.

It was left to the Mitterrand administration to live through the height of the crisis. Its attitude was generally sympathetic to Solidarity but fairly passive. It is well symbolized by Foreign Minister Cheysson's two formulas: "Good luck to the Polish people!" in the spring of 1981, and "Of course we'll do nothing" on December 13. In condemning the various violations of human rights, above all the state of emergency and the dissolution of Solidarity, and in asking for a return to a dialogue with society, Mitterrand and Cheysson were second to none except the Reagan administration. But except for stopping credits to Poland, they refused to follow the United States on the road of sanctions, particularly against the Soviet Union. Hence this writer's often repeated formulation that the French talk like the Americans but act like the Germans, or that the Americans believe in sticks, the Germans in carrots, and the French in words.

Since 1982–83 the French have joined (although more slowly than the Germans) in the slow trend toward normalization of relations with the Jaruzelski regime. Pierre Joxe, then head of the socialist group in the National Assembly and subsequently minister of the interior, visited Warsaw in 1982. The Polish minister for foreign trade was received at the Quay d'Orsay in June 1985. This trend culminated in December 1985 with the Jaruzelski and Baylet visits mentioned earlier. Since the elections of March 1986, the trend has been confirmed by the appointment of Jean-Bernard Raimond as foreign minister. Raimond, who had previously spent a few months as ambassador to Moscow, was ambassador to Warsaw from 1982 to 1985 and was known to favor normalizing relations with the Polish regime. The Polish press greeted his new role, as well as a speech by Prime Minister Chirac on the occasion of Josef Cardinal Glemp's visit to Paris in April 1986, as indicating of a return to the old, friendly Gaullist line.

With Hungary, which had first been ostracized after 1956 and then more or less ignored, relations started to warm up when the country appeared as the only survivor of the Khrushchevian era of reform, after the killing of the Prague Spring. Still, Hungary was coupled with Bulgaria for the visits of Foreign Minister Maurice Schumann in 1971 and Prime Minister Pierre Messmer in 1973. It was interesting, though, that Foreign Minister Jobert chose Budapest, on June 4, 1973, to correct the impression he had given in his speech at Helsinki of challenging the legitimacy of the East European regimes.

But it was not until the end of the 1970s and in the 1980s that relations with Hungary came into the limelight. János Kádár visited Paris in 1978; Mitterrand, who had visited Kádár in 1975 as head of the Socialist party, chose Budapest for his first presidential visit to the East; and in 1984 Kádár's visit to Paris, just at the time when the Honecker and Zhivkov visits to Bonn were cancelled, served to symbolize what was left of intra-European détente.

With Bulgaria, the other East European country without any traditional ties with France, relations remain good and uneventful. But in 1982 Foreign Minister Cheysson announced in Sofia a forthcoming visit of President Mitterrand that has yet to take place. During the time of her attempt to revive a sense of national pride in Bulgarian culture, President Zhivkov's late daughter seems to have shown an interest in a cultural opening to Paris.

It remains to deal with Czechoslovakia and East Germany, two countries in which, for different reasons, relations have failed to reach, or have been late in reaching, the general level of cordiality. Czechoslovakia's continuing repression since 1968 has kept its relations with France in a distinctly colder climate than those of its neighbors. Although Prime Minister Lubomir Strougal and Foreign Minister Bohuslav Chňoupek visited Paris in 1975, Foreign Minister Jobert's visit to Prague in 1982 was the first on that level in six years. In 1979 a scheduled visit by Foreign Minister François-Poncet was the only one under Giscard d'Estaing to be cancelled for a human rights motive—the trial of the Charter 77 signatories, who had sought to defend human rights in Czechoslovakia. In 1985 Foreign Minister Roland Dumas visited Prague as part of a general trend toward normalization with Eastern Europe. His aides made a point of meeting with well-known dissidents.

Finally, in the GDR another dimension of French policy appears— that of relations with the Federal Republic. Until the development of West Germany's *Ostpolitik,* France scrupulously avoided recognition of the GDR in order not to alienate the Federal Republic. At the time of Willy Brandt's initiatives, Pompidou pointedly remarked that France would have to make its own moves, but he delayed formal recognition until 1973 and waited until 1974 to exchange ambassadors. Since then, however, relations have been developing actively, with the signing of a cultural agreement (including the opening of reading rooms in each other's capitals) and, in 1985, Prime Minister Fabius's visit to East Berlin. However, an incident that occurred during the visit (the presence of GDR Defense Minister General Heinz Hoffmann in uniform, which from the French point of view was a deliberate violation of the demilitarized status of Berlin), shows how relations with East Germany cannot be divorced from the German and Berlin problems as such.

Yugoslavia is not within the scope of this book, but our picture of French policy toward Eastern Europe would not be complete without some mention of the symbolic role of relations with Belgrade. They had been cool under de Gaulle, apparently because of his personal antipathy toward Tito, linked to the execution of General Draža Mihajlović.[30] They warmed up under Pompidou, who received Tito in 1970. In 1976 Giscard d'Estaing and Tito proclaimed the "six principles of Belgrade," stressing the independence and equality of nations. And in 1983, in his second (and so far only) visit to Eastern Europe after Hungary, Mitterrand chose Belgrade as the place from which to make an opening to the Soviet Union, indicating that a harmonious cooperation with Moscow was indispensable to the peace of Europe.

In all these dealings, one is struck—as always in the French case— by the great role of declaratory policy, in particular of declarations of principles. But if one acknowledges this propensity for words instead of more tangible actions, one must also recognize the coherent and balanced character of the French discourse: the independence of states and the opening up of societies are the two themes and the two criteria that, modified by certain personal or traditional factors, offer the key to France's bilateral relations. While state-to-state relations, independently of political regimes, have never been put into question, the emphasis on cultural relations and the open denunciation of human rights violations have kept French policy from the extremes either of strident propaganda or of hypocritical silence.

30. Mihajlović was the leader of the noncommunist Serbian resistance movement against Nazi occupation during World War II who was tried and executed by Tito's government for alleged collaboration.

By and large, this has been the French attitude on CSCE. Of course, the traditional contradiction or balancing act among favoring a coherent West European foreign policy, favoring the national affirmation of East European states, and maintaining a special relationship with Moscow was particularly delicate in this multilateral context. Yet on balance, French diplomacy has not been unsuccessful in satisfying the three requirements, just as it has not been unsuccessful in reconciling its concern for social communication and human rights. France has been the driving force, particularly during the preliminary phase, behind the West European caucus and the handling of the CSCE by the European Communities' political cooperation mechanism (first called the Davignon Committee), yet it has sought to maintain the CSCE as a conference of states and has fought to reduce the presence of the European Communities as such. It has also been the driving force behind the Third Basket, particularly in promoting cultural exchanges (for instance, in the preparation, in collaboration with Hungary, of the Budapest cultural forum) but has also favored compromise by avoiding formulations too unacceptable to the East (such as "the free flow of people and ideas"). France has been helped in this by its own structure and tradition concerning the control of information and culture, which are almost midway between those of liberal and communist states. On human rights it has, along with the other Western powers, fought victoriously for proclamation of the principles of the Helsinki Charter and for periodic review of their implementation, but it has also participated in the collective capitulation of the West concerning the freedom of the Helsinki watch committees in the East. It has tended to take up a position halfway between the vigorous American denunciation of human rights violations and the German discretion in the name of détente.

France did for a time break with the Western front and provide some ammunition to Soviet tactics in promoting the Conference on Disarmament in Europe. In the debates in Belgrade and Madrid the West had been insisting on human rights and the East on military détente. The French proposal, in the name of not leaving the theme of disarmament to the other side, went in the direction of the Soviet agenda and deflected from the priority of human rights—all the more so since, after some hesitation, it was not withdrawn after the coups in Kabul and Warsaw. However, France did insist, in agreement with its Western partners, that the conference should be institutionally linked to the CSCE and that its meeting and continuation should be made conditional upon the continued discussion of the implementation of the Helsinki human rights provisions. The French doctrine is that all the provisions of the Helsinki Final Act should be considered equally urgent and that each basket should be balanced by itself.

CULTURAL POLICIES

The category of cultural policies has no real equivalent in the other Western countries studied in this book. But the role of the state in cultural exchanges, and the importance given to such exchanges by French diplomacy, make it imperative to see them as an instrument of political-diplomatic policies as much as an aspect of contacts between societies.

Since 1945 the Foreign Ministry has had a general Directorate of Cultural Affairs (on the same level as Political and Economic Affairs), which absorbs almost 45 percent of the budget of the ministry (it administers the French *lycées* and institutes abroad). It has negotiated state-to-state agreements on cultural exchanges administered by bilateral commissions. Its network of cultural institutes and centers, which had been very important in prewar Eastern Europe and were forcibly closed under Stalin, is being reconstituted. In terms of physical presence, it is the most important of Western presences in Eastern Europe. Yet in spite of all this personnel and all these buildings, as well as the special priority given by France to this dimension of its external role, French cultural influence, particularly in Eastern Europe, is declining, especially as compared with the American.

The organization of French cultural policy abroad is subject to fierce competition between the Foreign Ministry and the Ministry of Cultural Affairs. More importantly, its philosophy is uncertain. It is torn between giving priority to teaching the French language and giving priority to spreading French values, culture, and society and making those of the host countries known in France. In Eastern Europe, French institutes, centers, and reading rooms seem to be very traditional and passive and to shy away, much more than their American and German counterparts, from anything controversial or political, such as illustrating France's democratic regime or maintaining contacts with the dissident culture.

When it tries to go beyond, it runs into predictable difficulties. For instance, the agreement with East Berlin has led to mutual dissatis-faction. The GDR complains because of the lack of interest of the French public; France complains because, contrary to the agreement, East German citizens have been discouraged from visiting the French reading room. Some of these difficulties have been overcome, however, and in 1986 the French Institute in East Berlin looked like a success.

At any rate, as already mentioned, this is the area where those sections of the Foreign Ministry most interested in Eastern Europe are trying—with limited success so far—to inject a new vitality both to encourage contacts between societies and to keep alive the notion of a single European culture transcending the division of the Continent.

GOVERNMENTS TO PEOPLES: BROADCASTING

French broadcasting toward Eastern Europe illustrates some of these same shortcomings, needs, and efforts for revitalization very nicely, but in a more directly political way. It is provided by one branch of the French public radio, Radio France Internationale.

In 1975 on the eve of the Helsinki meeting, two important decisions about Radio France Internationale were made by Giscard d'Estaing: discontinuing foreign language broadcasts to Eastern Europe and setting up a program of modernization and new transmitters to Africa. Understood in the light of Giscard d'Estaing's belief in European détente and his activist stand in Africa (illustrated by France's inter-vention in Zaire to help suppress an uprising in Shaba Province), these decisions clearly indicate his sense of priorities.

But under Mitterrand, in March 1982, another decision concerning French language broadcasts for foreign audiences went in the same direction: merger of the Southern program, directed toward Africa, and the Eastern program. The broadcasting of a common program for Africa and Eastern Europe meant in fact, as Jacques Rupnik points out, the absorption of the East by the South.[31]

Since the Polish events of 1981–82, however, a movement in the other direction has begun. Broadcasts have been resumed in Polish (at first ten minutes a day, growing to seventy-five minutes in 1985),

31. This section relies almost exclusively on Rupnik's unpublished paper "La Présence Radiophonique Française dans les Pays du Centre-Est Européen: Un Bilan et Quelques Suggestions" (June 1985).

in Russian, and in Romanian (one-half hour, to be doubled under a decision of August 1985).

The broadcasts in French are centered on Africa and are apolitical. They arouse no interest in Eastern Europe. Broadcasts in Russian are dedicated essentially to presenting French realities. But broadcasts in Romanian and, above all, in Polish are focused on the problems of the receiving country. They are very successful in Poland where, without being able to compete quantitatively with Radio Free Europe, the Voice of America, or the British Broadcasting Corporation, they are apparently very lively and intellectually stimulating and have an audience of more than 10 percent of the more educated strata of the population.

Efforts are being made to resurrect broadcasts in the other East European languages and to give them the same dynamic spirit, especially since the buying of French programs by the official radios of the East European countries has proven very disappointing. But as mentioned earlier, there are many indications that the Chirac government does not appreciate the importance of this role of French broadcasting and contemplates clipping its wings, both financially and politically. In general, the much lower budgetary priority given to cultural activities is bound to affect France's role in Eastern Europe adversely.

SECURITY POLICIES

In the French case more than in others, a sharp distinction should be made among three meanings of security: security in the narrow sense of defense; security in the broader sense of negotiations on arms control and disarmament; and security in an even broader sense, that of CSCE, of the political and, indirectly, economic, social, psychological, and cultural conditions of security, that is of the European political order.

In the first sense, Eastern Europe plays almost no direct role in French policy, which is entirely focused on preserving French independence and the East-West balance. Toward security in the second sense, regional arms control and disarmament, France has been, at least until the CDE (and perhaps even in this case if one interprets the CDE as an exercise in damage limitation), essentially negative. Above all, it is preoccupied with preventing possible adverse military or political consequences on the East-West balance, the French nuclear force, or the future of Germany or European unity. But it is mainly in the third sense, which involves primarily conference diplomacy and symbolic projections of Europe's future security, that Eastern Europe occupies an important role in French security policies.

One of the basic tenets of the traditional French position holds that process is as important as substance and that it is as important to know who is negotiating about a given arms control measure or who would be affected by it as to know the content of that measure itself.[32] French opposition to MBFR negotiations was based partly on their bloc-to-bloc character but also on the fact that they were carving out a special zone in Central Europe. In the French view, that posed the risk of a special status for Germany (which might be first denuclearized, then neutralized), a division between West European countries, and a subordinate status for all the participants in the zone: they would be subjected to superpower controls that would not apply to the superpowers themselves.

Similar objections are raised against the various proposals for nuclear-free zones, from the Rapacki plan to those of the Palme Commission. Besides their pronuclear bias and concern for the military balance, the French argue that such zones would involve less sovereignty for their participants rather than more and would tend to insulate them or marginalize them from European security as a whole, which must involve the entire continent, including the European part of the Soviet Union.

France's own brainchild, the CDE, first proposed in 1980 and meeting in Stockholm until the fall of 1986, has had all the opposite features. It involves negotiations among the thirty-five CSCE members and is firmly placed within the CSCE framework. The area covered goes from the Atlantic to the Urals; hence it includes Soviet territory for the first time and constitutes the only concrete incarnation of the Gaullist concept. It concerns only conventional disarmament: the French argue that there is such a thing as a conventional European balance but not a nuclear one—a bit of special pleading obviously inspired by the desire of avoiding limitations and controls over their own nuclear deterrent, but not entirely devoid of objective validity.

32. See Benoit D'Aboville, "CBMs and the Future of European Security," in F. Stephen Larrabee and Dietrich Stobbe, eds., *Confidence-Building Measures in Europe* (New York: Institute for East-West Security Studies, 1983), p. 203.

Moreover, the first, and so far only, phase of the conference involves confidence-building measures. Here the interests of France and the East European states coincide the most. The French argue that these measures give the smaller members of the alliances as well as the nonaligned countries an opportunity for constructive involvement. The whole concept of confidence-building measures has been inspired in great part by the desire to make another intervention on the model of Prague 1968 more difficult, and it has been particularly advocated by Romania and Yugoslavia. But the French insist on measures that should be both binding and militarily significant. To some extent they are worried that their creation may take on a life of its own at Stockholm and run counter to French interests and conceptions by falling prey to the double temptation, encouraged by the Soviets and the pacifist mood of public opinion, of drifting toward vague declarations of principle and becoming concerned with nuclear matters.

This illustrates a more general problem with French security policy. Its orthodoxy in terms of the strategic balance and nuclear independence clashes with the general antinuclear mood in Europe and also with the attitudes and aspirations of many East Europeans. Ever since the Rapacki plan, the governments of Eastern Europe have hoped that proposals for nuclear disengagement or arms control, while serving Soviet policy, will also increase their own margin of autonomy. They fear that the missile deployments in Western Europe so strongly favored by France will increase the Soviet presence on their soil and the military integration of the Warsaw Pact. In addition, many of the dissidents, particularly in Czechoslovakia and Hungary, hope that a denuclearized Central Europe might be one of the few possible paths toward Soviet political disengagement. They find more easily a common language with many West European pacifists, particularly European Nuclear Disarmament (END), than with the French, in spite of the latter's political good will.

The French Socialist party has been trying to reestablish contact in this respect with the mainstream of the European left. In its 1985 declaration on security it reacted positively to the proposal of the Palme Commission for a zone free of battlefield nuclear weapons and to the idea of including tactical nuclear weapons in the CDE discussions. This evolution seems to originate in the bilateral talks between the French Parti Socialiste and the German SPD. But there are no signs of French official positions moving in the same direction, and there are precedents for the continuity of French diplomatic and military policy winning out over socialist commitments and suggestions.

ECONOMIC POLICIES

On economic no less than on security policies, raison d'Etat reigns supreme. In this case it concerns the interests of the French economy rather than any idea of linkage or political influence in Eastern Europe. There are, to be sure, instances when political considerations have influenced the terms of economic agreements. This was especially the case with Poland: the influence was positive with Giscard d'Estaing and Gierek; it was negative, at least in the collective Western presentation of the refusal to reschedule the Polish debt, after December 1981. There have also been occasional statements of belief in the political significance or use of economic relations. Giscard was the foremost French believer in the virtues of peace through trade, in convergence between East and West, and in starting détente with economic relations, going from there to human and cultural ones, and leading to a transideological unified world.[33] Conversely, in 1981–82 many intellectuals and some bureaucrats advocated a policy of conditionality designed first to help Solidarity and then to push Jaruzelski away from repression and toward reform. But none of this ever really influenced French policy. Under Giscard, as before and after him, the basic purpose of the French government was to help French industry rather than either détente or human rights. Economic conditions have provided a constraint or a priority rather than an instrument.

This is certainly not due to a doctrinal unwillingness or a practical incapacity for state interference in economic transactions. On the contrary, French foreign trade is as heavily organized as any in the Western world, and France's dealings with state economies have led to an orgy of institutionalization through all kinds of long-term economic agreements and bilateral commissions, on the model of the

33. See his extraordinary preface, written in 1972, to the book of his friend Samuel Pisar, the ideologue of coexistence through commerce and the lawyer of Armand Hammer and Occidental Petroleum: *Transactions entre l'Est et l'Ouest: Le cadre commercial et juridique* (Paris: Dunod, 1972).

Franco-Soviet Grande Commission and Petite Commission. These are
run, in effect, by a powerful but complex bureaucracy in close touch
with business interests but relatively free from political instructions
or control. That bureaucracy includes the Treasury, which has the
last word on anything involving financial affairs (for example, for the
Polish debt, the negotiations on which over a long period were led
by a single man, Jean-Yves Haberer, director of the Treasury under
Giscard d'Estaing); the Direction des relations économiques exté-
rieures, a branch of the Ministry of Foreign Trade, which sees its role
mainly in promoting French exports and has close links with French
exporting firms; and the Foreign Ministry, whose Direction des affaires
économiques has a much smaller role, limited in practice to the
negotiation of trade agreements, but which also seems to adopt a
commercial perspective. That perspective is centered mainly on the
big importers, such as Gaz de France with the Soviet gas deal, who
practically do their own negotiating. Gaz de France also had excellent
access to the Elysée through its former executive, Pierre Bérégovoy,
who was then the secretary-general of the presidency and subsequently
finance minister.

     To the extent that there is a common philosophy to all these
bureaucracies, it lies in the inability of the French economy, because
of its structural weaknesses, to dispense with the protected markets
of communist countries. To defend its declining share of these markets,
it needs to use the resources of the state: financial credits and to some
extent political credit or friendliness. Where there are divergences,
they tend to be between financial and commercial considerations. For
instance, since 1982 the Treasury has prevailed in having French
credits paid in hard currency, which helps France's own monetary
needs but, according to other segments of the French bureaucracy,
puts it at a disadvantage compared with other Western competitors.
But there was apparent unanimity in the long fight to keep French
prerogatives in entering agreements with Eastern bloc countries
against the European Community's Common Trade Policy, and in
extending subsidized credits at a more favorable rate than available
in the market or from its Western partners. On this last issue, after
a long battle (mainly with the United States but also with West
Germany) over the role of the state in their respective export credits,
France has had since 1982 to accept the OECD consensus and to live
with it. This has recently become easier because of the fall of interest

rates to less than the 12 to 12.5 percent internationally agreed minimum levels, which frees the French state from the need to make up the difference.[34] But as far as political restrictions are concerned, France has remained one of the countries most opposed to the philosophy of recent American administrations. There is continuity between the official statement of August 1978 that it "is not French practice to subordinate the sale of industrial civilian equipment to political considerations"[35] and the declarations of President Mitterrand, according to whom an embargo is an act of war and is only meaningful if it is total and indicates a first step toward overt hostilities.[36]

Even in the case of Poland, France has refused to avail itself of the modest means of conditionality that the United States has put to some relatively effective use in relations with that country and with Romania. France has maintained most-favored-nation status for all East European countries regardless of their political behavior, and it supported Polish accession to the IMF unconditionally. It participated in the rescheduling of the Polish debt in July 1985 and subsequently has applied financial, not political, criteria in the granting of new credits.

In general the French bureaucracy is preoccupied with the fact that France now has a commercial deficit, not only with the Soviet Union but with all East European countries except Bulgaria (and sometimes Hungary). It tries above all to maintain an economic presence in each of these countries, including Poland, so as not to lose the opportunities that may arise with an improvement in their growth and investments.

Crisis Management: The Case of Poland

Much of the little to be added on the crisis in Poland has already been mentioned or implied. All through the crisis, three levels of French response are to be distinguished and can be seen as interacting:

34. See *Financial Times* (London), August 19, 1985.

35. Quoted by Gary K. Bertsch and John R. McIntyre, "The Western Alliance and East-West Trade: In Pursuit of an Integrated Strategy," in Gordon B. Smith, ed., *The Politics of East-West Trade* (Boulder, Colo.: Westview Press, 1984), p. 227.

36. See Jim Hoagland, "Mitterrand Rejects U.S. Campaign for Economic War against Russia," *International Herald Tribune* (Paris), June 12, 1982.

a strong concern and pressure for action coming from certain sectors of the public; an effort from a small group in the bureaucracy to respond to this concern and devise appropriate measures to influence events; and great discretion and ultimately great passivity at the top.

During the whole of 1981 the Centre d'analyse et de prévision brought together a group of independent experts, specialists on Eastern Europe or those connected with Solidarity, and officials from the Foreign Ministry and the various economic departments involved in relations with Poland. This group discussed various scenarios for potential developments within Poland but also possible measures or strategies to help Poland, to prevent a Soviet invasion, and to react if it happened. After December 13, 1981, it met twice a week for two months. Several higher members of the Foreign Ministry participated occasionally. It became clear toward the end of January 1982, however, that the group had no real impact on policy; it was becoming a discussion group in which information and views were exchanged but no real planning or advice was involved. After a few months it stopped meeting. Meanwhile, the government had been doing its share of contingency planning at the level of the European Communities and NATO, where it seems to have adopted a middle position between American hawks and German doves. It participated positively in the EC decision to grant special food aid to Poland in the fall of 1981. However, it opposed a German proposal for the EC to send a mission to Poland in early January 1982. The French aversion to common planning was asserting itself even though verbal condemnations were louder in France than anywhere else.

But the moment of truth came with the signing of the Urengoi gas pipeline agreement. Many voices called for its cancellation or at least its postponement; it was signed hurriedly (to the great satisfaction of the Germans, who were quick to point out that they, who were branded as soft on Poland, at least had signed it before December 13) in conditions that have not been entirely clarified. One version, noted above, claims that neither Mitterrand nor Mauroy were aware that the time for signing was so close. What is certain is that there was no presidential decision to use the occasion as a signal connected to the Polish crisis. The speech of Prime Minister Mauroy, defending the agreement in Parliament, was symbolic: "France is mourning the freedoms of the Polish people," he said, but added in a formulation that may remain his truest claim to immortality, "Let us not, on top of the suffering of the Polish people, add the suffering of the French people who would be deprived of heating this winter."

Nonstate Relations

Nonstate relations are not terribly important in a traditional structural sense—or rather they have traditionally been much more important for the East European societies who were looking to France for education and inspiration than for the people of France. But they are very important politically, in a positive or negative sense, for the Communist party, the trade unions, and the second or antitotalitarian left. The Communist party and many front or associated organizations long entertained a permanent network of visits, political tourism, and even personal ties, some dating from the resistance, some from youth festivals or peace gatherings. Often, intellectuals who had met on these occasions as communists were to meet again as East European dissidents and French anticommunist writers.

The Communist party itself, after defending (or extolling as an example) everything that happened east of the Iron Curtain, had its moment of provisional break when it condemned the invasion of Prague in 1968. But it soon returned to its old positions by approving the normalization in Czechoslovakia. For a number of years the strategy of the Union of the Left produced a certain timidity in the Socialist party on speaking out about Eastern Europe while, on the contrary, Czechoslovakia in 1968, after Hungary in 1956, was the occasion for many intellectuals to break with the Communist party.[37] Interest in East European culture has tended to follow these political events. The Prague Spring and its repression produced a great fashion for Czechoslovak cinema and literature. Today this interest is revived by nostalgia for turn-of-the-century Central Europe.

The presence in Paris of many refugees and dissidents, East European and Russian, has contributed to the evolution of much of the French left (for instance the milieu around the periodical *Esprit*) and to the love affair between the French intelligentsia and Eastern dissidence, which was to reach its peak during the Solidarity period when even personnel of the French state-owned television were appearing with Solidarity buttons.

37. See Pierre Grémion, *Paris-Prague* (Paris: Julliard, 1984).

Some academic institutions have translated this interest into permanent policies by combining exchanges with the official learning institutions of the East European countries and direct support, financial and moral, for their respective dissidents in the form of fellowships, invitations, and visits. The Ecole des Hautes Etudes en Sciences Sociales is probably the best example.

Another institution that has permanent links with the East and has been politically active, especially in support of Solidarity, is the noncommunist trade union movement, in particular the Confédération Française du Travail and, to a lesser extent, the Force Ouvrière. The CFDT has identified with the cause of Solidarity to a degree unrivaled by any other West European movement by collecting funds, organizing demonstrations, making demands on the government, and so forth. Some intellectuals have tried to imitate with it the relationship of Solidarity with its experts.

In a less spectacular way, the Catholic church is also a link with the various East European countries, particularly Poland.

Conclusion: The Alliance Factor

This chapter has pointed out that France's Eastern policies as such are directed to Germany and the United States as much as to the Soviet Union and, in a sense, more than to Eastern Europe itself. Hence the tendency, even when preaching (and to some extent practicing) Atlantic solidarity in military matters, for France to avoid a bloc approach in policies toward Eastern Europe and to encourage the East European states to do the same on their side. The priority for France's national interests and the stress on its independent role have often been rationalized as being in the best interests of Eastern Europe. Such an approach reaches its limit, however, with the realization that, as far as independent policies go, the American and German ones carry more weight. Hence in some quarters of the French political or bureaucratic scene, the call for a common European *Ostpolitik,* which would be more effective not only in the East-West context but also for the permanent goals of preventing West Germany's drift into neutralism and giving a positive, nonmilitary purpose to Franco-German and European cooperation.

Of course, once more, interest in Eastern Europe appears as

deriving from a preoccupation with the German problem rather than being an end in itself. But in this view that interest should lead to a more genuinely European conception, both on the Western side, where the temptations of German and also of French nationalism should be overcome, and on the choice of Eastern interlocutors, since the fixation on a single country (the Federal Republic's on the GDR and to some extent France's on Poland) should give way to a broader concept encompassing the whole region.

At the level of public opinion, the startled reaction to Mitterrand's reception of Jaruzelski and the strongly negative verdict of opinion polls show that as of December 1985 the spirit of "Solidarity with *Solidarnosc*" was not dead. At the same time, the effervescence did not last more than a few days, and the issue did not figure significantly in the electoral campaign. By the spring of 1986 the French public's interest in Eastern Europe was mostly visible indirectly through the fashion and nostalgia for Central Europe, for the Habsburg Empire, and for turn-of-the-century Vienna, which served as a reminder that, to use Milan Kundera's widely quoted expression, Prague, Warsaw, and Budapest, at least, are "kidnapped parts of the West."

This scattered, partial, and sporadic attention to Eastern Europe, always reviving in a different sector of the French public and on a different occasion, seems to confirm the starting point of this chapter: France does not have a policy toward Eastern Europe. The French have no built-in interests in the region based on ethnic ties or border problems; yet more than any of the many countries that share this geopolitical distance, France does have a potential concern for the region, if only as a consequence of broader preoccupations with Germany or with Europe, with the Soviet Union, and with human rights. This concern is never solid or salient enough to lead to a long-range policy, but it is too lively and resilient to be dismissed as purely superficial or hypocritical. Two characterizations of France and its politics by Alexis de Tocqueville come to mind: "immuable et changeante" (permanent and changing) and "agitation immobile" (immobile agitation). Which one can best be applied to French attitudes toward Eastern Europe remains for the reader to judge.

SEVEN

The View from London

EDWINA MORETON

IN 1984 Sir Geoffrey Howe, Britain's foreign secretary, began a series of visits that was to take him to all the capitals of the Warsaw Pact states within two years. Previous foreign secretaries had made the occasional foray into Eastern Europe, but never had so much British attention been focused for so long on these few Soviet allies. Prime Minister Margaret Thatcher herself had opened the program of visits with a hurried trip to Hungary early in 1984, which surprised even the Hungarians. She also demonstrated her interest in better relations with the Soviet Union by attending the funerals of both Yuri Andropov and Konstantin Chernenko in Moscow and by welcoming to London the soon-to-be Soviet leader, Mikhail Gorbachev, in December 1984. East European foreign offices from Warsaw to Sofia could be forgiven for thinking Britain had launched its first major diplomatic initiative in the region since World War II.

The reasons for this sudden shift from neutral to drive in Britain's *Ostpolitik* are explored here against the backdrop of Britain's interests and objectives in Eastern Europe. The burst of activity in Eastern Europe and the Soviet Union by a prime minister who had shown herself to be staunchly anticommunist was really not so surprising. There had in truth been far more continuity than change in Britain's policy toward both Eastern Europe and the Soviet Union since the 1960s, and such variation as occurred over the years reflected differences in tactics and style rather than strategy and long-term objectives.

Forces Shaping British Policy

The roots of Britain's policy toward Eastern Europe are traceable from factors that shaped policy toward Europe as a whole before the war. The first of these is political geography. Although Britain was and is geographically a part of Europe, as an island it has no common land frontiers (although plenty of maritime disputes) with its European neighbors. Unlike France, which borders on strategically important Germany, and unlike Germany itself, which has traditionally looked to both East and West, Britain has traditionally regarded Europe as literally a continent apart. In many respects this island mentality survived both the First and Second World Wars. Only in the past ten years has it begun a decisive political change, focused on Europe's western half, under the impact of Britain's membership in the European Communities (EC). Thus it is scarcely to be wondered that a country which has found it difficult to cooperate closely with its immediate West European neighbors should feel even less affinity with a more distant Eastern Europe.

Geographical separateness has not, of course, translated directly into an equivalent political isolation. As a major power before 1939 Britain was directly involved with the continental European powers, especially France and Germany, both in Europe and in the competition for colonies and trade. Within a quarter century, British armies twice fought long and exhausting wars to try to settle the political future of the Continent and defend Britain's security interests there. But with the exception of relations with Russia before the 1917 revolution, Britain's political and military engagement was primarily in what is now known as Western Europe.

This geographical and political remoteness is also responsible for Britain's lack of interest in economic relations with Eastern Europe. Unlike mainland Western Europe, Eastern Europe, with the partial exception of the Soviet Union, was never an important trading hinterland for Britain, whose trade patterns, both before and for a time after World War II, were directed more to other continents by interests of empire and Commonwealth. (However, in the 1960s, before East-West trade expanded on a broad front, Britain's trade with Poland compared favorably with that of other Western countries.)

In its general lack of economic interest, Britain contrasts sharply with Germany and France, whose industries have traditionally relied for their markets on Poland, Czechoslovakia, and the Soviet Union as well as on their Western neighbors. Since the war, British industry has been easily outstripped in the race for East European and Soviet contracts by French, West German, and Italian competitors.

Nor did Britain's involvement in Europe as a major power before the war leave much residue in the way of cultural connections or affinity. Although France and Britain, as European rivals, have had over the centuries more cultural and linguistic impact on one another than either likes to admit, in this century, at least, British society and politics have been shaped more by the residue of empire than by the politics of Europe. Its largest ethnic groups and therefore the ones with the greatest potential political clout are Indian, West Indian, and Pakistani. The postwar upheavals in Europe that have helped to swell the Polish community in the United States and that result in one out of every three families in West Germany having either come originally from East Germany or else still having close family ties there have had little impact in Britain. Although there are small Polish, Ukrainian, Russian, and other East European emigré communities (if that is not stretching the meaning of the word) in a number of British cities, these together amount to less than 1 percent of the population and have had little impact on the conduct of British foreign policy. The intellectuals exiled voluntarily or otherwise after the upheavals in Czechoslovakia in 1968 and Poland in 1981 have gravitated to France and Germany and sometimes the smaller West European countries, but rarely to Britain. At the same time, few Britons choose to travel to Warsaw Pact countries, so that they have little understanding of or affinity for life in Eastern Europe.

If policy aims derive from interests, then Britain's overriding interests in Europe before and after the Second World War were its own physical security and that of its trading routes. To that limited extent Britain was bound to have at least some concern with the fate of Eastern Europe. Yet Winston Churchill had evinced an unusually hard-nosed attitude toward postwar arrangements in Eastern Europe in the controversial "percentages" discussion with Joseph Stalin in Moscow in October 1944. To try to reach some sort of understanding on spheres of influence in Europe after the war, Churchill proposed and Stalin accepted that in Greece, Britain (in agreement with the

United States) would have 90 percent predominance, Russia 10 percent; in Romania the positions would be reversed. Influence in Yugoslavia and Hungary would be split fifty-fifty, and in Bulgaria the Russians would get 75 percent to Britain's 25 percent.[1] But as was clear at the time, Churchill's rather crude logic was designed more to protect British national interests, above all in Greece and along the trade routes, than to weigh up and settle the political fate of all of Europe. In fact, Britain lacked political interest in or even sympathy for those smaller East European states such as Romania and Hungary that had fought against the Allies in the war. It has been argued that at no time after 1944 did Britain make more than half-hearted efforts to keep Hungary, Romania, and Bulgaria from falling into what was rapidly emerging as the Soviet sphere of influence in Eastern Europe.[2] Only Albania attracted some British and American attention when in 1949 the two plotted—unsuccessfully—to overthrow the communist regime of Enver Hoxha.

After 1945 the Labour government could do very little anyway to alter the course of events behind the Iron Curtain. Neither could the Labour party, whose interest in and sympathy for Eastern Europe steadily diminished. Such contacts as the party's international committee tried to foster became attenuated under pressure from various national communist parties backed by the Soviet Union.[3] All but the extreme left of the Labour party began to view Soviet actions in Eastern Europe with growing concern. By ending whatever illusions might have remained after the purges in the 1930s that Soviet socialism was compatible with democratic institutions, the Soviet Union itself forced the major left-wing party in the United Kingdom into opposition to its policy in Europe. The British Trades Union Congress had a similar disillusioning experience. Although it had joined the World Federation of Trade Unions in 1945, it left in early 1949 to help organize a Western-backed trade union body, the International Confederation of Free Trade Unions.[4]

1. Herbert Feis, *Churchill, Roosevelt, Stalin: The War They Waged and the Peace They Sought* (Princeton University Press, 1957), p. 448.
2. Elisabeth Barker, "British Policy towards Romania, Bulgaria and Hungary, 1944–1946," in Martin McCauley, ed., *Communist Power in Europe, 1944–1949* (London: Macmillan, 1977), p. 216.
3. Elisabeth Barker, *The British Between the Superpowers, 1945–50* (London: Macmillan, 1983), pp. 41–43.
4. Ibid., pp. 91–95, 180–81.

The only country to benefit directly from official British government assistance was Yugoslavia. In late 1948 Ernest Bevin, the foreign secretary, decided to help Tito discreetly. Britain also helped persuade the United States not to use exiled anti-Tito nationalists to replace Tito with a noncommunist pro-Western regime, even though he was in a precarious position. Such a policy would have further antagonized the Soviet Union.

The one country in Eastern Europe that ought to have deserved special British attention was Poland. Britain had declared war on Germany in 1939 because the government of Neville Chamberlain had undertaken with France to guarantee Polish independence (though not, it has since been pointed out, its territorial integrity), a guarantee quickly tested by the German and Soviet invasion of Poland in September of that year. The year before, however, when Czechoslovakia had been swallowed by Hitler, Britain had played its ignominious part in sealing the country's fate at the Munich conference in the hope of appeasing the Germans and ensuring security without resort to war. Although the underlying motive—security—was similar in both instances, in terms of its own security, at least, Poland was Britain's sticking point.

As the war drew to its close, therefore, it was a source of considerable political embarrassment and regret to the Churchill government that Poland should now find itself under the thumb of a different, this time Soviet, dictator. At Yalta in 1945 Churchill tried to impress upon Stalin that the fate of Poland was a matter of honor for Britain.[5] But the ground had already been cut out from under him by Roosevelt's statement, made two years earlier at Tehran and repeated again at Yalta, that American troops would be withdrawn from Europe within eighteen months of the war's end. Whether Churchill really tried hard enough to help the Poles out of their predicament becomes irrelevant. First, the Red Army was occupying Poland and was not about to back off. Second, Britain itself faced an entirely new international situation by the end of the war—impoverished, deprived of great-power status, and soon to be bereft of empire. Whatever the sense of moral obligation to Poland, these facts conspired to ensure that Poland's fate would come too low on Britain's new list of priorities. The lingering sense of moral obligation combined with the practical

5. Michael Charlton, *The Eagle and the Small Birds: Crisis in the Soviet Empire from Yalta to Solidarity* (University of Chicago Press, 1984), p. 16.

realities of a cold war that limited opportunities for intervention meant that for some years Britain pursued what might best be described as an attitude toward Eastern Europe rather than a policy.

Britain's Postwar Choices

Leaving aside the details of the settlements to be hammered out between the wartime Allies, the biggest question facing Britain's new Labour party leaders in 1945 was what part they would play in the peace following a war of which it has been said, "However misguided it may appear now, they thought they had won."[6] Britain had earned its place at the victors' conference table. It was still a colonial power with interests to defend around the globe and was concerned to protect them. As Ernest Bevin put it memorably at Potsdam, "I'm not going to have Britain barged about."[7]

That was easier said than done. Britain had ended this war, unlike the previous one, with no territorial claims on anyone. Yet suffering the ravages of the war and with American Lend-Lease assistance abruptly terminated, Britain found itself stuck with its global interests, with an empire to run and support, under much straitened circumstances. What is more, it now found itself dependent for influence on the support of one or other of the bigger and stronger powers, the United States and the Soviet Union. To cap it all, the military basis of Britain's global reach and its prewar supremacy, its sea power, was rapidly being eroded by the new bomber (and later missile) power and the development of the atomic bomb.[8]

In Europe, with Germany defeated, France badly weakened by the war, and the prospect of American forces being withdrawn from the Continent within two years, even a war-weakened Soviet Union posed an increasing military and political threat. The wartime strategy of containing Germany was to become the postwar strategy of containing the Soviet Union. Eastern Europe was a direct concern to British security policy only to the extent that it represented the long arm of

6. Allan Bullock, *Ernest Bevin, Foreign Secretary, 1945–1951* (W. W. Norton, 1983), p. 844.

7. David Dilks, ed., *Retreat from Power*, vol. 2: *After 1939* (London: Macmillan, 1981) p. 13.

8. Bullock, *Ernest Bevin*, pp. 112–18.

Stalin in the affairs of Europe and constituted an irritant in wider East-West relations. It was a reflection of the Soviet threat rather than a target of policy.

In this new postwar world only the United States now had the power to stop the Soviet Union from encroaching on British interests in the Middle East and Asia as well as in Europe. (Britain did not pull back from "east of Suez" until 1968.) The cold war confirmed that realism. Henceforth Western Europe, to the extent that it managed to hang together, would in the eyes of successive British governments be a weight within this broader Western alliance. In more practical terms, then, Britain's attitude toward Eastern Europe, the Soviet Union, and the division of Europe into two halves was shaped by three main factors: Britain's special relationship with the United States, its determination to remain a nuclear power, and its role as one of the four powers with responsibility for Berlin and for Germany as a whole. Aside from this last, which involved relations with East Germany, these priorities demanded that Eastern Europe not be the focus of British foreign policy.

SUMMITRY

Having secured the sort of alliance necessary to contain the Soviet advance, successive British governments devoted their best efforts to keeping open the lines of communication between the superpowers, bearing in mind the perils of the nuclear age. This "honest broker" approach to issues of war, peace, and influence occasionally irritated such allies as West Germany's Konrad Adenauer and France's Charles de Gaulle, caused occasional mistrust in Washington, and even led to Soviet attempts to open up divisions in the Western ranks. Nonetheless, the approach was pursued doggedly. Harold Macmillan's summiteering in the late 1950s and early 1960s has been described as coming both too late (because Britain no longer had the influence it enjoyed in the war) and too early (because the cold war was to continue until the 1970s).[9] However, it did pave some of the way to the first Soviet-American summits of the 1960s. Harold Wilson tried something similar during Aleksei Kosygin's visit to London in 1967.[10]

9. Richard Davy, "Überlegungen zur britischen Ostpolitik," *Europäische Rundschau* (Spring 1979), p. 118.
10. Gerald Segal, *The Great Power Triangle* (St. Martin's Press, 1982), pp. 110–13.

The trouble with encouraging superpower summitry, as successive British governments discovered, is that once the Americans and Soviets meet face-to-face, summitry becomes an exclusively American and Soviet affair. For Britain the negotiations that eventually led first to a partial test ban in 1963 and then to the Nuclear Non-Proliferation Treaty in 1968 exemplified its declining influence. Although it was a leading cosponsor of the treaty, Britain's real effect was to put the onus on the two superpowers to find ways of reducing the quantity of their nuclear arms. In the negotiations that followed, the Strategic Arms Limitation Talks (SALT I and SALT II), Britain, like the other members of the nuclear little league, stayed on the sidelines. However, when France began increasingly to reject participation in the nuclear discussions that continued within the Western alliance, Britain's role in all kinds of disarmament talks was enhanced, enabling it to play a larger part for longer as a minor nuclear power.

When it came to matters German, including the division of Germany and the handling of Berlin, Britain was at least the theoretical equal of both the United States and the Soviet Union. It was, after all, one of the Four Powers with continuing responsibilities for East as well as West Germany, since no peace treaty had been concluded with Germany after the war. Wartime musings on the dismemberment and pastoralization of Germany were soon overtaken by postwar realities. There had even been talk until the mid-1950s, in both West and East, of the possible reunification of Germany. Following Stalin's death in 1953, Churchill tried to convene a summit to discuss the possibilities.[11] His initiative, however, merely reflected the primacy of the Soviet Union in Churchill's thinking, which seemed to see policy toward Germany as a means to better relations with the new Soviet leadership. In any event, he overestimated both the extent of British influence on the issue and the degree of change that had occurred in the Soviet Union.

Otherwise, its formal legal duties aside, Britain saw no need in the 1950s and 1960s to take the initiative, either in resolving the German Problem as a whole or in promoting relations with East Germany.

Wilson tried and failed (in part because of American reluctance to go along) to organize a cease-fire between North Vietnam and the United States so that some progress might be made toward ending the Vietnam War.

11. Anthony Glees, "Churchill's Last Gambit," *Encounter*, vol. 64 (April 1985), pp. 27–35.

The real change in that branch of East-West relations was not to come until West Germany itself picked up the gauntlet of *Ostpolitik*, gingerly at first in the early 1960s, then with a flourish and a radical change of approach in 1969 when the government of Willy Brandt decided to recognize the separate existence of an East German state. Britain had anyway been less engaged directly in the outcome of the various East-West initiatives emanating from Europe, unlike Germany or especially France, which would have had a central role in the Gaullist vision of a "Europe from the Atlantic to the Urals." While others were pursuing their grand designs, Britain had its mind on the loss of empire, the loss of influence, and the on-again off-again relationship with the European Community. Yet it watched the developing West German *Ostpolitik* closely and with some sympathy.

EASTERN EUROPE: SIDESHOW

Aside from military and security concerns, Britain was, in principle, possibly less unhappy than most with the Soviet Union's creation of a sphere of influence in Eastern Europe. This idea was less inimical to the British traditions of balance-of-power diplomacy than to the American legalistic tradition. But there was a residual feeling that the East Europeans, and especially the Poles and Czechs, ought to be freer to choose their own systems of government and their own friends. Hence Britain's concern was less with promoting the dissolution of the Soviet empire in Eastern Europe than with maintaining the correct balance between practical accommodation to its existence and a desire to transform it into something more politically and morally acceptable. But these were long-term goals. In the short term it seemed little could be done—nor indeed should be done—if the price of change in Eastern Europe were to be a weakening of the Western alliance.

And so Britain did little. It had been hostile to the governments in Eastern Europe, which it regarded as Soviet puppets, since the 1940s. The creation of the Warsaw Pact in 1955 and the subsequent military integration of the Pact armies, for all practical purposes under overall Soviet command, merely reinforced the logic of this attitude. This hostility was combined with relative powerlessness. Britain had not found it possible to do much about Poland in 1944–45 or East Germany during the uprising in 1953 despite its supposed

Four Power rights. It was even less likely to want to do anything about the Hungarian uprising in 1956, however sympathetic it was and despite criticism that was leveled at some Western radio stations (but mainly Radio Free Europe) for encouraging false hopes of Western assistance. In any case, Britain would have found its hands embarrassingly tied at the time by its own attempt to regain the Suez Canal by force.

The 1960s saw something of a new tactical approach to Eastern Europe, however, even if objectives in the region remained limited and very long term. Following in the steps of France and West Germany, Britain signed a series of cultural, trade, and technical agreements with Czechoslovakia, Poland, and Romania. The British foreign secretary even engaged in some desultory discussion in Warsaw about the Rapacki plan for a new European security framework.[12] The argument for this change in tactics—one to be used later, too— was that increased trade and other contacts would bring benefits to the peoples of Eastern Europe, however unlikable their regimes.

With the advent of the Labour government in 1964, the policy was effectively hijacked by Harold Wilson for his own attempt at summit-mongering with the Soviet Union to resolve the Vietnam War. Wilson visited Moscow twice in 1966 and once in 1967 and welcomed Kosygin to London in between. Yet for all the to-ing and fro-ing, by the end of the 1960s Britain's trade with the Soviet Union and Eastern Europe remained a small fraction of its total trade. Political relations took a hard knock over the Soviet invasion of Czechoslovakia. Despite the new energy that went into Britain's *Ostpolitik,* little of commercial or political interest came out.

In principle, Britain's policy toward Eastern Europe, like that of the rest of the Western alliance, had been predicated on two often contradictory desires: for stability and security in all of Europe and for whatever political change for the better was possible in Eastern Europe. In practice, for at least the first two decades after the war, the desire for security overrode the desire for change. Britain's concern with the Soviet threat and its close relationship with the other superpower, the United States, even at times to the exclusion of its West European allies, left little room for active diplomacy in Eastern Europe.

12. Elisabeth Barker, *Britain in a Divided Europe, 1945–1970* (London: Weidenfeld and Nicolson, 1971), pp. 265–66.

What is more, Britain had neither the traditional trade links of countries such as West Germany, nor a strong local communist party such as those of France and Italy, nor the human interest of Germany's division to influence and drive its foreign policy. The unsinkable aircraft carrier sailed on regardless until the generalized détente of the 1970s put the issue of relations with Eastern Europe back on the alliance map.

The Era of Détente

Britain's *Ostpolitik* was low-key as it moved with the rest of Europe and the two superpowers into the decade of détente in the 1970s. Britain did have some supporting role to play in détente, which by bringing some degree of stability and calculability to East-West relations was welcomed as very much in the tradition of postwar British diplomacy. But as West Germany, at the local level, and the United States, at the level of arms control talks, took the lead in forcing the pace of East-West relations, Britain's part inevitably became smaller. Technically, of course, Britain had to be directly involved, as one of the four occupying powers, in the negotiations leading to the Berlin Agreement of 1972. On a wider stage it had an active role in the Conference on Security and Cooperation in Europe (CSCE) that led to the Helsinki Final Act in 1975, and it participated in the marathon Mutual and Balanced Force Reduction (MBFR) discussions at Vienna.

Bilateral policy also continued but was very much swamped by the multilateral negotiations under way. And although Britain continued its official contacts with individual East European countries, they were conducted at levels well below those of the headline-catching West Germans. Perhaps drawing on the experience of contacts made during the two-year negotiation that produced the Helsinki accords, both Conservative and Labour governments began to differentiate more between the East Europeans and the Soviet Union and among the East Europeans themselves. Yet there were few dramatic gestures. Although Nicolae Ceauşescu of Romania paid a state visit to London in 1978, this was if anything a pay-off for past services rendered, not an impetus to better relations in the future.

Putting the best face on it, Britain's policy toward Eastern Europe had to be measured realistically against its political priorities. While West Germany was preoccupied with reordering its relations with the East, Britain was adjusting slowly and painfully to its neighbors in Western Europe and its new membership in the Common Market. Besides, relations with the Soviet Union still took precedence over policy toward the rest of the Warsaw Pact, and these relations had suffered a series of setbacks. In the early 1970s, after the government expelled more than one hundred Soviet diplomats for spying, academic and cultural exchanges between the two countries were blighted for some time. Some of the momentum toward détente was recovered with Harold Wilson's visit to Moscow in February 1975, during which Britain announced a £950 million credit on favorable terms in an effort to stimulate trade. But by the end of the 1970s trade with the Soviet Union still amounted to only 2.9 percent of all Britain's exports and 2.4 percent of its imports. When the credit expired in 1980 the Soviet Union had used only £550 million of the amount available.

Despite the trips to Moscow, in a decade of considerable activity in East-West relations Britain was intrinsically less interesting to the Soviet Union than either the United States or West Germany. And because Moscow had established flourishing direct links with both Washington and Bonn, London was not even needed as an intermediary.[13] (However, Britain did have occasional useful contributions to make to the American negotiating position: the British Foreign Office helped considerably, for example, in working out acceptable wording for the agreement on preventing nuclear war that protected the interests of America's allies, including the United Kingdom.) Finally, once the multilateral bandwagon of détente started rolling, there was also less distinction (and probably few votes) to be gained from being photographed Macmillan-style with Russian leaders in Moscow—everyone was doing it.

Underlying all this, both Labour and Conservative governments in the 1970s maintained their earlier healthy suspicion of Soviet motives and, unlike partners on both sides of the Atlantic, their skepticism about any enduring political fruits of détente. Britain stood to gain relatively little directly from better relations with Moscow and even less from relations with Eastern Europe. Nor was there in the late 1970s alarm simply at the prospect that relations might once again

---

13. Davy, "Überlegungen zur britischen Ostpolitik," p. 120.

deteriorate. Good relations were preferable to bad, but Britain did not feel it had to pay a high price to keep them sweet.

As an interested but not heavily engaged observer, London could contribute experience and judgment to the process of détente. A member of both the European Communities and NATO, but without any particular axe to grind in relations with Eastern Europe, Britain tended to see détente very much in terms of alliance security and the management of basically hostile East-West relations, not as a means to the settlement of East-West conflict. Inevitably, therefore, Britain was inclined to devote relatively more of its Foreign Office energies to the multilateral frameworks of détente—CSCE and MBFR—than to its own bilateral bit parts. Britain was again at the negotiating table but was happy enough to play the role of good NATO partner, involving itself in the back room staff work and leaving command in the field to others.

With modest expectations of what the multilateral détente negotiations might achieve, Britain initially approached the CSCE with some diffidence. The conference started, after all, as the Western payoff to the Soviets for their agreement to negotiate on Berlin and on force reductions; for the Soviet Union it was a way of putting a respectable international cachet on the postwar boundaries in divided Europe. Nor did the negotiations attract intense public attention in Britain, in contrast to West Germany where the opposition Christian Democrats had tried to fling the constitutional book at Willy Brandt's *Ostpolitik*. Britain had little to gain, either, from any of the three "baskets" at Helsinki (dealing respectively with political, economic, and societal relations). However, like its NATO partners it was determined not to allow the statement of political principles to be turned into a formal, legal recognition of Soviet domination in Eastern Europe, although by the time the Final Act was signed, the Soviet Union had already implicitly achieved much of what it wanted through West Germany's "Eastern treaties." Otherwise Britain felt that more concrete security issues, such as arms control, were better dealt with elsewhere. Since the second basket concerned trade, and Britain did little of that with Eastern Europe anyway, that left the third, human rights, as the one of current interest. That issue gave NATO countries a new interest in the Helsinki negotiations, by turning what had at first seemed a piece of diplomatic confetti into a human rights document with substantial political meaning. For Britain the affirmation of human rights turned the Helsinki Act into a convenient document with which to nag the Soviet Union about conditions in Eastern Europe.[14] This was not calculated to endear London to Moscow, but it probably did help discharge some of that sense of moral obligation left on Britain's conscience since 1944–45.

More important to the Foreign Office and government than the meager gains and moral victories at Helsinki was that the preparations for the negotiations and the follow-up review conferences in Belgrade and Madrid led to a deepening of political cooperation with Britain's partners in the European Communities.[15] During their first decade the CSCE negotiations spanned four British governments, three prime ministers, and five foreign secretaries without any discernible change in London's policy toward the process. If anything, the CSCE came to be seen as a barometer of East-West relations and a useful measure for the observance of human rights in Eastern Europe and the Soviet Union. It therefore had diplomatic and moral value but little real political importance for Britain. Because of London's overriding concern for stability and security in Europe, its approach to the parallel MBFR talks in Vienna was as cautious as that to the CSCE, if not more so.

British Objectives in the 1970s

Because the primary concerns of successive governments since World War II have been with the Soviet Union on the one hand and the Western alliance and the special relationship with the United States on the other, Britain's interests and therefore its policy objectives in Eastern Europe have been modest. There was traditionally little interest in Eastern Europe and little expectation of diplomatic returns, so British governments, both Conservative and Labour, faced little disappointment. This attitude simply reinforced relative official indifference, which considerably irritated the East Europeans.[16] Because

14. Michael Clarke, "The Implementation of Britain's CSCE Policy, 1975–84," in Steve Smith and Michael Clarke, eds., *Foreign Policy Implementation* (London: George Allen & Unwin, 1985), pp. 144–45.

15. Ibid., p. 144.

16. The Poles were apparently particularly angry that Harold Wilson sought an invitation to visit only after he was out of office. They told him they would be happy to invite him when he next became prime minister.

of Britain's limited interests and limited aims in the region, no great gap could be discerned from the 1950s through the 1970s between declaratory policy and practical diplomacy. The rhetoric of rollback, bridge-building, and later of détente itself was largely left to others. For all these reasons, it is easier to sum up what Britain's *Ostpolitik* was not and did not achieve.

Britain never developed a grand design for Europe. Although it was very conscious of being on the edge of a Eurasian land mass dominated by the Soviet Union, that consciousness led to a focus on Western Europe and the Western alliance as a counter to the Soviet threat, not with Eastern Europe as a main target of policy. For this reason Britain remained thoroughly skeptical of such proposals as the Rapacki plan or de Gaulle's idea of a Europe "from the Atlantic to the Urals." From Whitehall's point of view these plans necessitated tinkering with the security of divided Europe (and in de Gaulle's case, ending the Anglo-Saxon domination of NATO), whether the aim was supposedly simply to lessen tension or more ambitiously to overcome Europe's division. Because of this skepticism, Britain was less prepared than almost any of its major NATO partners to work actively to promote change in Eastern Europe if such change might incur a risk of starting the unravelling of Western security ties.

Britain was also politically and emotionally less uncomfortable with the possibility of a permanently divided Europe than either France or West Germany. Given the reality of Soviet power, how normal could Europe be? Britain did not appear unduly bothered when the answer came to "not very." The conflicting pulls of stability in Europe, on one hand, and change in Eastern Europe, on the other, thus left successive British governments far less torn than some of their West European neighbors. Britain's foreign policy instead displayed a deep and steady skepticism about the possibilities for real change in either Eastern Europe or the Soviet Union. Taking the broad view, in the 1950s, 1960s, and much of the 1970s Britain was inclined to accommodate itself to a divided Europe if that were the price of stability and security for the members of Western alliance.

By the end of the 1970s, however, several factors brought the British government to realize that it should not and could not neglect Eastern Europe entirely, and the moral or transformational threads of policy began to show more clearly in the pattern of its diplomacy. First, the history of upheaval in Eastern Europe, to be highlighted dramatically in 1980 by the Polish crisis, suggested that it would be at least prudent to keep an eye on developments there for security reasons. Second, like several other Western governments, the British government was keen to make sure that those East-West agreements to which the Soviet Union and the East European regimes had also put their name were honored—or at least highlighted in the breach. Third, London believed that once West Germany's *Ostpolitik* had been supported by the Western alliance, the policy's legitimate aims, whether with respect to East Germany, the rest of Eastern Europe, or the Soviet Union, were best accommodated within an overall alliance framework. This put the onus on all NATO members to contribute something to keeping that framework intact.

Britain had approached the decade of détente—as it was to be seen in retrospect—as a loyal ally, not totally disinterested in the outcome but pragmatic and skeptical of how far things could go and especially of Soviet intentions. There was no great intellectual or political investment in the process, but there was an investment of time and, where the occasion arose, of diplomatic skill in making sure the multilateral components of détente functioned properly and according to Western and British interests. Where that fitted the aim of seeing some evolution in Eastern Europe too, all the better.

Since Britain's stake in détente was limited, so was the damage done to British interests from its demise. The Soviet invasion of Afghanistan nonetheless came as a shock, even if it also justified the earlier skepticism toward Moscow's intentions. Followed hard by the Polish crisis, it marked a dramatic chilling of East-West relations and focused attention sharply on the need to respond more actively in the short term to a developing crisis in Eastern Europe. This brought about several changes of style, if again not of great substance, in Britain's policy toward the region.

Britain's *Ostpolitik* in the 1980s

Partly because of the joint impact on East-West relations of events in Afghanistan and Poland and partly because of the timing that brought to power avowedly conservative administrations in Britain in 1979 and the United States in 1981, Britain's apparent shift in policy toward Eastern Europe and the Soviet Union seemed like a caricature of Ernest Bevin's supposed anti-Sovietism of the early postwar years. In practice, as far as *Ostpolitik* was concerned, the basic values that governed British foreign policy had not changed greatly in the intervening decades. The generalized détente of the 1970s had brought about more a change of style than substance, with only the Wilson government in the mid-1970s trying to push Anglo-Soviet relations faster in the direction that Britain's European allies had already gone—toward improved trade, cultural, and political relations.

However, the coincidence in 1981 of a stridently anticommunist President Ronald Reagan and a more explicitly anti-Soviet Prime Minister Margaret Thatcher did for a time appear to disguise an underlying prior evolution in British government and Foreign Office thinking about the individual countries of Eastern Europe, with greater emphasis on encouraging change instead of passively accommodating Soviet domination of the area. For a while at least under the influence of the Polish crisis, Reagan's sometimes violent anti-Soviet rhetoric found a natural if muted echo in the Thatcher government. But away from the megaphone, Britain responded to the combined impact of events in Afghanistan and Poland as it had to the multilateralization of détente in the 1970s—as a good ally, whose main aim was to uphold Western security interests. The government answered President Jimmy Carter's call for sanctions against the Soviet Union by urging its athletes not to take part in the Moscow Olympics in 1980 and by curtailing political and cultural contacts with the Soviet Union. London was clearly concerned about the lack of agreement within the alliance on sanctions, but mainly because it felt that sanctions themselves, even if applied across the board, could not turn a single Soviet tank in its tracks.

However, a new element had come into British thinking about alliance solidarity: its membership in the European Communities. For some of Britain's allies in Europe, especially West Germany, the rapid cooling of East-West relations after the invasion of Afghanistan posed greater dilemmas than it did for Britain (though West Germany, unlike France, Italy, and the Benelux countries, did boycott the Moscow Olympics). When remaining a good ally both to the United States and its main EC partners became difficult, Britain tried to keep communications open between Europe and America. But when conciliation proved impossible—later over American attempts to block European trade with the Soviet Union and prevent European equipment from going to help build the Urengoi gas pipeline—the Thatcher government took all the steps it could to make sure Britain's companies did not lose out in the competition for contracts with its European neighbors.[17]

Britain may also have revived past irritations by occasionally seeming to revert to its 1950s and 1960s role as honest broker. The trip by Foreign Secretary Lord Carrington to Moscow in July 1981, in an unsuccessful attempt to break the deadlock over Afghanistan and find a compromise that might lead to a Soviet pullback, was also greeted with suspicion in some quarters. Lord Carrington was in fact acting in his capacity as president of the EC Council of Ministers, although as friction between the United States and several West European governments increased in the early 1980s, that may not have recommended his efforts to Washington.

THE POLISH CRISIS AND BRITISH FOREIGN POLICY

Although in the late 1970s the British government had shown a little more direct interest in Eastern Europe than earlier, it was Eastern Europe that imposed itself on the British political agenda in the early 1980s. The crisis in Poland that began with a wave of strikes during July and August 1980 was immediately recognized as being qualitatively different from the more limited upheavals in 1970 and 1976. The events in Poland required no special response from Britain (the warmth in Polish-French and, under the influence of *Ostpolitik,* Polish–West German relations had not spread as far as Britain), but for a variety of reasons almost all sections of British public opinion welcomed the agreement on reforms reflected in the Gdansk accords of August 31 and the replacement a few days later of discredited party leader Edward Gierek by Stanislaw Kania.

Throughout the months of crisis, all parties in the House of Commons sympathized with what Solidarity was trying to achieve. Indeed, from far left to far right the different political groupings

17. Britain's "perfidy" on the pipeline issue is still a source of some rancor among certain members of President Reagan's staff. They have a tendency to attribute such impudence to creeping Finlandization, rather than to the folly of a policy whose result, whatever its political intention, was to differentiate to America's commercial advantage between trade in European manufactured goods, especially the pipeline equipment, and the continued sale of American grain to the Soviet Union—also a strategic resource, given the Soviet Union's inability to feed itself.

now battled to be the "friend of the Polish working class." Britain may have had little direct influence on the course of events in Poland, but the crisis produced some remarkable, if temporary, alliances in British politics as journals and spokesmen, from the Communist party's newspaper *Morning Star* to groups with stridently anticommunist views, welcomed the emergence of the new independent trade unions.

The only group to be caught out by the crisis was the British Trades Union Congress, whose leaders found themselves caught red-handed in possession of an invitation to visit Poland in September 1980 issued by the discredited and now almost nonexistent government-backed unions. The row over whether the delegation should go caused a very public and embarrassing rift at the TUC conference in early September, and the organization was put out of its misery only when the Polish ambassador delivered a letter disinviting the TUC delegation, pleading that the moment for a visit was not opportune. The best gloss that can be put on the episode is that those TUC leaders who were determined to press on with the visit at such a momentous time were carried along by their own bureaucratic procedures. But the incident actually reflected the ambivalence of some British trade unionists to the upstart Solidarity, which threatened to disrupt the long history of contact with the official unions of Eastern Europe and the Soviet Union (despite Britain's equally long dissociation from the Soviet-controlled trade union federation in Eastern Europe).

With no particular stake in Poland, London found it relatively easy to coordinate its reactions with those of its major allies in NATO and the EC. The main Western concern was to prevent Soviet intervention, both to protect the reforms Solidarity had won (the best hope for a long time that genuine transformation could occur in Eastern Europe) and especially to avoid conflict and instability close to the Iron Curtain in what was Europe's most destabilizing crisis since the Berlin blockade in 1948. Like other Western officials during the months of Solidarity's battles with the Polish government over reform, Mrs. Thatcher and Lord Carrington helped keep up the barrage of warnings to Moscow not to intervene in Poland's affairs. Beyond this attempt to prevent the explosion of the crisis and its potential spillover to the West, Britain, like its allies, tried to support the emergence of genuinely independent trade unions and to aid Poland in a difficult economic passage. However, it was quickly realized all around that the best way to help Solidarity politically was to do nothing that the Soviet Union or the Polish government could claim was Western interference in the crisis. Because the British government was conscious that threats of political and economic sanctions against the Soviet Union would be less credible in view of the NATO confusion that had followed the invasion of Afghanistan, it was more determined than ever to consult closely with its partners in NATO and the EC to ensure there was no repetition of the previous poor performance.

In the meantime, however, within the constraints of other commitments and priorities Britain worked for a peaceful settlement of the crisis. Early on it hinted that as long as the reforms continued, Whitehall would look sympathetically on Polish requests for aid.[18] British banks participated in a number of international loans to Poland during 1980 and 1981 despite being heavily exposed as it became clear that Warsaw would be forced to reschedule existing debts owed to both private and government institutions in the West. The banks came high on the list of creditors, after West Germany, France, and the United States. Similarly, the government's Export Credit Guarantee Department (ECGD) continued to look favorably on credits for trade until the Polish government imposed martial law in December 1981. Even the TUC redeemed itself somewhat by threatening to cut contacts with Soviet trade unions in the event of a Soviet intervention. After a slow start, the TUC provided financial aid for equipment purchases by the fledgling unions and offered to train their officials.

The events in Poland offered Britain's Polish community its one real chance to influence government policy, at least on the fringes. In August 1980 emigré organizations appealed for funds to support the Polish workers, and during the crisis they organized shipments of food and medical aid. However, the Polish government in exile, an anachronism left over from the 1940s, gave only a cautious welcome to the Gdansk accords, preferring to see how the communist government responded to the political challenge posed by Solidarity. When the Polish government stepped up pressure on Britain in the spring of 1981 to return the ashes of General Wladyslaw Sikorski, Poland's World War I hero who became premier of the Polish government in exile in London during World War II, Britain's Polish community,

18. *Times* (London), November 29, 1980.

still suspicious of Warsaw's commitment to real change, opposed the move vociferously. No doubt partly because of their strong feelings, London turned down the request despite a visit from the Polish foreign minister in June.

Aside from such historical footnotes, Britain played no special role in the crisis. Indeed, as Poland's party and people wrestled over the future during 1981, the West in general had to acknowledge that it could do little to help Solidarity aside from warning off Soviet intervention and providing material assistance to stave off economic collapse.

When martial law was imposed, the Western nations once again joined together to condemn the action. Once again Britain mustered support from all shades of the political spectrum. But the question of how to react to the crisis exposed cracks in the Western alliance. Close coordination of responses had seemed entirely possible only if the Soviets intervened. Martial law imposed by the Polish army and riot police left the West divided over who should be punished— Poland alone, as most Europeans seemed to feel, or the Soviet Union too, as President Reagan insisted.

Following the failure of its efforts to secure a coordinated response, Washington announced unilateral sanctions against Poland followed by sanctions against the Soviet Union that included the suspension of export licenses for equipment, much of it supplied by West European firms, to build the Urengoi gas pipeline.[19] Unlike the United States the EC did not immediately suspend food shipments to Poland, although it did block new government-backed credits and eventually imposed a moratorium on rescheduling Poland's debts. Britain stuck by its EC partners on sanctions policy, although it was sympathetic to the American arguments in principle (but not to the embargo on pipeline equipment). While the debate on sanctions continued, Britain took the additional step of expanding BBC broadcasts to Poland, increasing the air time of the Polish service from twenty-one to twenty-six hours a week. Eventually, when it became clear that martial law was not going to be lifted quickly, NATO managed to define a set of conditions to be fulfilled before sanctions would be lifted, including the ending of martial law, the release of

19. *International Herald Tribune* (Paris), December 26–27, 1981, and December 30, 1981.

detainees, and the resumption of a dialogue among the government, Solidarity, and the Roman Catholic church.

Although the British government was not in full harmony with U.S. policy on sanctions, it was the first EC government to announce its own in February 1982, prodded hard by the Labour opposition in Parliament. Britain also tried to press some of its EC partners into moving more swiftly to impose sanctions. And although British banks took part in a private-sector rescheduling agreement with the Poles, the British government kept to its boycott on rescheduling repayments of government loans and maintained its suspension of ECGD credits until after martial law was lifted and a general amnesty for political prisoners declared in the summer of 1984. (Even when the political block was lifted, the traditional caution of the Treasury meant that Poland found new credit backing hard to obtain.) Like its European partners but unlike the United States, Britain was keen to see Poland made a member of the IMF as a way of keeping up the pressure for domestic economic reform.

Although Britain never fully shared the tough attitude toward the Jaruzelski regime adopted by President Reagan, Foreign Minister Sir Geoffrey Howe made it clear to the Poles during his fence-mending visit in 1985 that no new government money would be available until after a rescheduling accord was signed that summer. In Poland itself, Britain was considered one of the least sympathetic of the Western governments when it came to issuing visas for travel. It was, however, generally sympathetic, at least in the early months of martial law, to extending the permits of Poles who found themselves stranded in Britain by the crisis.

IMPETUS FOR A NEW *OSTPOLITIK*

Mrs. Thatcher's appreciation for President Reagan's tough-talking style following the Afghan and Polish crises and the chilling effect of both crises on East-West relations successfully masked for a time the underlying continuity in foreign policy toward the Soviet Union and Eastern Europe: the Conservative governments in the early 1980s carried on much of the policy of their Labour predecessors. As the decade of détente had worn on and worn out, differentiation in the albeit faint hope of encouraging some limited degree of transformation in Eastern Europe had become the usual practice of British governments, although nobody bothered to use the term much in public or provide a theoretical or practical political case to support it.

If the lesson still had to sink home, the Polish crisis reemphasized how different individual East European governments and peoples could be and how important it was to recognize new developments in Eastern Europe early so as to be able to react to them coherently. The crisis also brought up once more the old Western dilemma: whether to work to promote change in Eastern Europe or to worry more about the stability of the relationship between East and West, and how to balance the two to avoid provoking a Soviet-inspired clampdown. Nor could the dilemma be avoided; like its Western allies, Britain had learned that upheaval in Eastern Europe could not be ignored, even though neither the Soviet Union nor Polish party hard-liners could claim that the Solidarity movement was Western-inspired. Above all, the crisis in Poland showed the complexity of politics in the region and the difficulty of formulating policies to deal with that complexity.

Britain was now prepared to create an active policy toward Eastern Europe. The desire to promote "progress" in the region and encourage those regimes that seemed prepared to adapt in a timely manner to national pressures for change, rather than simply echo Soviet ideological platitudes, encouraged the government in 1982 to help provide financing for Hungary, which was crippled by the general drying up of credits after the Polish collapse. Hence, perhaps, the Hungarians' later willingness to play host to Mrs. Thatcher once she had decided to change the style of her policy toward Eastern Europe and temper her rhetoric toward the Soviet Union.

All the same the new drive in Britain's *Ostpolitik* in 1984 and 1985 deserves some better explanation. With a policy that was less a grand strategy and more a return toward establishing East-West dialogue, Britain nonetheless found itself in the unusual position of being pacesetter among its European allies when, in 1984–85, Sir Geoffrey Howe became the first British foreign secretary ever to visit all the Warsaw Pact countries (and the first to visit Bulgaria in a hundred years). Partly this initiative was simply an attempt to make the best of a unique opportunity. Since the government of Helmut Kohl had come to power, West German–Soviet relations had cooled considerably. NATO's deployment of new intermediate-range missiles in 1984 deepened the chill. As a result, West Germany's wider *Ostpolitik* had stalled even if West German–East German relations seemed barely affected. Similarly, France's relations with the Soviet Union had suffered under President François Mitterrand, who took a hard line toward events in Poland and proved a firm supporter of the intermediate-range nuclear force (INF). That left a gap that Britain, with less to lose than the rest and for its own reasons, was happy temporarily to fill.

When Howe was brought in as foreign secretary in 1983, part of his brief was to review the ways in which Britain's handling of East-West relations might be improved.[20] The prime minister took a personal interest in the subject, convening a conference in which academic specialists in Soviet and East European studies confronted her own specialists in an attempt to reexamine the issues and challenge existing government policy. (The government's comfortable majority in Parliament after the 1983 election left the prime minister with greater freedom to annoy her right-wing supporters with impunity on foreign policy issues.)

Despite the recent crises, several factors combined to reawaken interest in better relations with both Eastern Europe and the Soviet Union. One was clearly concern about what Lord Carrington, Sir Geoffrey's predecessor, called megaphone diplomacy, the replacement of dialogue by belligerent rhetoric. Some observers worried that relations between the superpowers had deteriorated too far and too fast, especially in the confrontation over INF. The government may also have wanted to spike the opposition to placing new NATO missiles in Britain itself by showing that talks with the Russians could continue despite the NATO deployments. For these reasons Britain appears to have become more active in keeping East-West diplomatic channels open. Although Whitehall remained concerned with the Soviet threat, it felt that what was increasingly seen as an American obsession with that threat could be undermining alliance cohesion and also causing concern in the British public.

A more long-term consideration leading to renewed interest in Eastern Europe has been Britain's increasing political involvement in Western Europe and consequent greater exposure to the worries of its EC partners, especially West Germany. Like the rest of Western Europe, though perhaps less intensely, the British government has

20. Simon Jenkins and Anne Sloman, *With Respect Ambassador: An Inquiry into the Foreign Office* (London: British Broadcasting Corp., 1985), p. 102.

become conscious of a potential political problem for Europe whether the superpowers, like the proverbial elephants, make love or war.

Again, stimulated by the Polish crisis, Whitehall has also shown renewed concern for crisis management. It evinced a greater recognition that crisis and change in Eastern Europe would inevitably affect the security of all Europe and directly influence Soviet attitudes. This flowed from and reemphasized interest in the East European regimes in their own right, not simply as mere adjuncts to Soviet policy. Such interest is bound to grow when the junior allies show signs of particular interests that do not necessarily coincide with those of any particular Soviet leadership.

Yet, having now launched itself into motion on the Eastern front, the British government may not have the necessary political steam to go very far. Mikhail Gorbachev's visit to London in late 1984 was a sign that Britain still counted for something in the big league of international politics and gave the Thatcher government a chance to emphasize its chief political concerns to the man who was to become the next Soviet leader. Yet since then all eyes, including Britain's, have focused on Gorbachev's meetings with President Reagan. The West Europeans have a value to the Soviet Union mainly for the influence they can bring to bear in Washington—and above all on President Reagan's support for the Strategic Defense Initiative. Britain is no exception.

Means of Policy and Influences on It

In the British political system the responsibility for determining foreign policy rests with the government of the day. The responsibility for shaping that policy by influencing government decisions rests with institutions and pressure groups, formal and informal, that have an interest in the policy and work either directly on the government and the Foreign Office or through Parliament and the media. Although Mrs. Thatcher has put her strong personal stamp on foreign policy, she is as susceptible to such pressures as any other British prime minister. Indeed she may have had wider pressures to contend with than most.

FOREIGN POLICY INSTITUTIONS

Mrs. Thatcher's chief source of advice on foreign policy, including Eastern Europe, is the Foreign Office and a staff of professional public employees rather than political appointees (even at the highest ranks), but in recent years there have been important changes in the relatively closed policymaking process. Most important, in the early 1980s the system of parliamentary committees was reorganized and strengthened. In particular, the House of Commons Foreign Affairs Committee has paid close attention to the Soviet Union and Eastern Europe, and the relationship between the two. Once again, the crises in Afghanistan and Poland helped bring the issues into sharper focus in Parliament. The considerable media attention to them, together with the morbid fascination of the Western press with the procession of funerals in Moscow between 1982 and 1985, has made *Ostpolitik* an obvious topic for investigation (although, again, the Soviet Union has been the main target). Because they take evidence from a wide range of experts, the new committees on foreign affairs and defense have themselves helped widen public debate on these issues.

The Polish crisis, along with the debate over the role of nuclear weapons that preceded the deployment of American cruise missiles, has spurred other groups to take a keener interest in government policy toward the Soviet Union and Eastern Europe. For various reasons the business community has stepped up its lobbying of the government and Foreign Office over *Ostpolitik*. The recent drying up of government-backed credits for trade with Eastern Europe, combined with recession in the West, has forced the few companies that do want to trade with the East to lobby hard in Whitehall for support.

The impression from both outside and inside the government is that the foreign policy process has opened up considerably. Issues involving Eastern Europe drifted into focus just at a time when they could attract far greater attention than they might have in the relatively untroubled 1970s.

All the same, because Britain has limited national interests in Eastern Europe, British diplomatic activity has never been decisive in shaping Western relations with the Warsaw Pact nations. Indeed, the contrast between the activity of the 1970s and 1980s and the passivity of the 1950s and 1960s has been largely one of style rather than the pursuit of radically different interests in the region. The stridency marking Mrs. Thatcher's first term of office appears to have reflected personal preference rather than advice from the Foreign Office. Where the British response to the Polish crisis differed from that of its allies, this reflected a concern with the unity of the Western alliance. It was an attempt to play honest broker between France and Germany on the one hand and the United States on the other rather than any distinctive approach to Eastern Europe.

The two pillars of British foreign policy remain NATO and the EC. Especially in its recent phase of more active diplomacy, the British government has kept its allies informed of its intentions and their results. With such care taken to coordinate policy toward Eastern Europe through these institutions there is little room or purpose for independent initiative. Although the Labour party, the largest opposition party in Parliament, has attempted to achieve a higher profile by proving that it can do a better job of talking to the East than the "iron lady," it suffers from the problem that afflicts all opposition parties—that the real business is done by the government of the day. In any case, the Soviet Union knows that in the past a Labour government has done little to alter the basic framework of East-West relations.

To the extent that Britain has used trade and finance as instruments of policy in Eastern Europe, it has pulled these levers less vigorously than in Western Europe. Britain's trade record in the region has been undistinguished. Even the attempt by the Wilson government to oil the mechanism with government credit failed. Because that failure to expand trade cannot be attributed either to the lack of political will or the lack of money, the cause must lie elsewhere, perhaps in the private sector. British companies, with some significant exceptions, have a reputation of being uninterested in Eastern Europe by comparison with their West European competitors. However, complaints are often heard that the British government does not offer the same sort of political and financial support at the opportune moment as its Continental counterparts.

Yet while British business with Eastern Europe cannot be described as brisk, even the hands-off Thatcher government has protected commercial interests when it felt justified. It made no attempt to discourage British banks from renegotiating outstanding debts with Poland, despite the block on government debt rescheduling. And it moved quickly in 1982 and 1983 to protect British companies threatened by the Reagan administration's effort to stop sales of equipment using American technology to Eastern Europe and the Soviet Union.

Although successive British governments have seemed skeptical about any political benefit to be gained by applying sanctions to East-West trade, they have been applied selectively for demonstrative effect. As a member of CoCom, Britain automatically restricts strategic trade with both Eastern Europe and the Soviet Union. But like its European allies, it does not share the most extreme views within the Reagan administration on "economic warfare" with the Soviet bloc. Similarly, trade has been viewed neither as the great lever to pry Eastern Europe away from the Soviet Union nor as the great harmonizer in East-West relations. Instead trade and credit policy seem to follow the political approach of differentiation. Where trade can be carried on to mutual benefit at no great cost to the Treasury, it is officially encouraged. Government backing for trade credits is a political instrument; it was withdrawn from trade with Poland between 1982 and 1984 and yet during the same years deliberately used to aid Hungary. But this political instrument is not wielded with any great energy.

Britain's cultural diplomacy was energized when the Foreign Office set aside money to promote the contacts called for in the Helsinki Final Act. However, the funding has never been overly generous. The two chief pillars of British cultural diplomacy in Eastern Europe are the British Council (the equivalent of the U.S. Information Agency in its cultural activities) and the BBC external services. But both often seem more appreciated by their target audiences than by their government paymasters in Whitehall. The semi-independence of the institutions allows the Foreign Office, where expedient, to disregard them as adjuncts to its diplomacy. Thus it can downplay their significance and, in times of economic stringency, their budgets. Cultural links have also suffered as political relations have cooled. In the wake of the Soviet invasion of Afghanistan, the British government withdrew its backing for major cultural exchanges with Eastern Europe and the Soviet Union, thereby restricting the British Council's activity to its libraries and language classes (the policy was changed back only in mid-1985).

Of the two institutions, the BBC, by virtue of being able to reach a larger audience, has the greater potential for influencing attitudes in Eastern Europe—but only if its relative independence and unbiased reporting survives. During the Polish crisis the extra funding for Polish broadcasts signified government recognition of this role; persistent Soviet jamming of BBC broadcasts to Poland was further proof. Yet the BBC's need to preserve editorial independence to maintain its reputation for impartiality limits its ability to lobby effectively for extra funds, especially when the Foreign Office budget, like that of other government departments, is being cut.

Although the BBC's charter obliges it to "broadcast in the national interest,"[21] independence seems to have been preserved. Mrs. Thatcher's call in May 1980, in the wake of the Afghanistan crisis, for a "massive propaganda campaign of the kind we have never mounted" toward the Soviet Union and its allies provoked a swift and damning rebuke from the BBC's external services.[22] Internal concern has nonetheless surfaced from time to time that the impartiality of the service, especially to the Soviet Union and Eastern Europe, is being eroded by the appointment of increasing numbers of emigrés to write, edit, and broadcast. There is also disagreement over whether news bulletins should continue to be issued by a central bureau, and therefore remain more detached, or be left in the hands of regional services. Officially, the BBC has so far stuck to its view "as seen from London" and resisted the temptation to broadcast to individual countries more of the views of political emigrés, a temptation other Western radios have given in to.

The chief exception to this pattern of none-too-vigorous diplomacy has been Britain's attitude toward arms control and its involvement in the related multilateral and bilateral discussions. Partly because it is one of the few nuclear powers, it has special interests and responsibilities in arms control negotiations. But these issues also go to the heart of successive governments' preoccupation since the war with East-West security and stability.

At the government level at least, Britain has pursued arms control as a component of its defense and security policy and not, as some on the far left of the European political spectrum have implied, as a way of redrawing the political map of Europe. This has meant a generally skeptical response to the occasional attempt to establish

21. Peter Fraenkel, "The BBC: Broadcasting to Eastern Europe," paper delivered before the Conference on Broadcasting over the Iron Curtain, Valley Forge, Pennsylvania, September 23–28, 1984, p. 3.

22. *Guardian* (Manchester), May 13, 1985.

special zones in Europe, whether nuclear free, chemical weapons free, or battlefield nuclear weapons free. The general approach of the British government to the various talks suspended or under way— including the comprehensive test ban talks (CTB), the Conference on Confidence- and Security-Building Measures and Disarmament in Europe (CDE) in Stockholm, the UN disarmament conference in Geneva, and MBFR—has been cautious. Caution has not, however, prevented Britain from making specific proposals, for example, the one at Geneva to ban chemical weapons, that do not necessarily agree with American positions. Britain was also clearly disappointed when the CTB negotiations were suspended by the incoming Reagan administration.

British governments have generally favored American-Soviet arms negotiations. Mrs. Thatcher made a point of urging both sides to resume superpower talks during the year-long suspension of the Geneva arms control discussions following the Soviet walkout in November 1983. But that did not stop her from pursuing the policy— originated but then later disavowed by the Labour party—of accepting deployment in Britain of American cruise missiles when the INF talks failed to produce the necessary reductions in Soviet deployment of SS-20s.

While Mrs. Thatcher's support for superpower dialogue won backing from all parties in the House of Commons, defense policy has been the one issue on which the original postwar bipartisanship in East-West relations has all but collapsed. This could have serious implications for Britain's defense policy and its relations with both the Soviet Union and Eastern Europe, should a Labour government be returned to power. Following its defeat in 1979 and under strong pressure from its hard left, the Labour party has moved increasingly toward support for unilateral disarmament. Should the party win the next election, it is by no means clear that the old compromise— unilateralist in opposition, multilateralist in government—would be revived.

INDEPENDENT PRESSURE GROUPS

Although policy is made by the government of the day, other political parties, labor unions, churches, and opposing currents of public opinion all exert some influence on it. There are and always have been clear distinctions between right and left in Britain in their views toward the Soviet Union. But the political appeal of East European communism for the left was weakened by disillusionment with Stalinism and the Soviet Union's demonstrably poor record on human rights at home and abroad. The hopes for a degree of working-class solidarity raised by the wartime alliance were soon dashed by Stalin's brutal treatment of the Poles and the Czechs and his clash with Tito. Partly as a result, the British Communist party was never very strong and now has fewer than 30,000 members, although its newspaper, the *Morning Star,* probably has a readership of twice that. The fascination with nationalization and with Soviet-style central planning has persisted among some sections of the left in Britain, but the Soviet Union itself has seldom operated as a vote-catcher for left-of-center political groups.

To the extent that Labour governments, such as Harold Wilson's, have tried to force a faster pace in attempts to improve relations with the Soviet Union, it has been out of a conviction of being better able than Conservatives to explain Western interests rather than a feeling of common cause with the East. The left's relations with Eastern Europe have generally taken their cue from relations with the Soviet Union. The recent exceptions have been Czechoslovakia in 1968 and Poland in 1980–82. In both cases, even left-wing opinion was behind the changes the Soviet Union sought to suppress. During the Polish crisis, the *Morning Star* was one of the first to the barricades in support of the "genuine" aspirations of the Polish working class. The Communist party has since made the headlines only because it has been in process of tearing itself apart in a battle between Stalinists and Eurocommunists. It is not an important political factor among the electorate, although it has considerably more influence within the trade union movement.

Two events, the Polish crisis and the British miners' strike of 1984, illustrate the connections that have long existed between trade unions in Britain and official trade unions in Eastern Europe; they also illustrate the division within the British trade union movement that makes attempts to translate such ties into influence on foreign policy particularly difficult. Despite the East-West division in the international labor movement since the 1950s between the Soviet-controlled World Federation of Trade Unions and the Western International Confederation of Free Trade Unions, formal ties have long existed between British unions affiliated with the ICFTU and their East European counterparts. Official delegations have been exchanged on a reasonably regular basis. When news is slow over the summer, papers publish stories on individual officials from different unions holidaying or taking trade union courses of study in Eastern Europe (Bulgaria seems to be a popular venue). A number of key trade unionists in Britain are members of the Communist party, and most make no bones about their politics.

As we have seen, such on-going contacts caused the British TUC considerable embarrassment as the Polish crisis developed in the summer of 1980. And although it recovered, the movement's dithering and internal divisions did little to enhance its voice in Whitehall. Especially under Mrs. Thatcher's Conservative governments, but also to some extent in the eyes of right-wingers in the Labour party, such trade union contacts with the East have been considered at best empty formalities, at worst potentially subversive. The British miners' union was portrayed very much as subversive for its contacts with and support from Soviet, East European, and Libyan sources during the year-long miners' strike in 1984–85. Striking miners and their families received food aid from East European and Soviet labor unions as well as those in the West. Some miners spent holidays as guests of Soviet trade unions.

Even before the strike, Arthur Scargill, president of the miners' union, had broken with the ICFTU's miners' group. Since the strike was settled, plans have apparently been drawn up to form a new international organization for miners that would include unions in communist countries for the first time since 1949.[23] Yet despite material aid received from Soviet and East European unions during the strike, it is by no means clear that their public political support did the British miners' cause much good. It may even have done harm by highlighting the political aims and sympathies of some miners' leaders at the expense of trade union issues such as jobs and pit closures. If reaction to the miners is anything to go by, even under a future Labour government such ties to communist trade unions abroad are likely to be seen as a political embarrassment—and hence discouraged—rather than as a useful backup to Labour government policy.

23. *Sunday Times* (London), March 31, 1985.

The ties certainly would not be popular with the British public. A recent attempt to comb through evidence on how the British public feels about East-West relations, defense, and the NATO alliance was forced to conclude that the feelings, such as they are, are "faint and fragmentary."[24] Foreign policy issues have seldom grabbed attention. From the mid-1960s to the early 1980s, domestic economic issues dominated national politics and debate.

There are several good reasons for the low saliency (to use the pollsters' jargon) of foreign policy issues. They have not until recently (the EC referendum excepted) been a major point of conflict between the principal political parties. Parliament has held few debates on foreign policy and even fewer on defense. Although different views have existed, they have been as likely to show up within political parties as among them. And, lunatic fringes of left and right aside, Atlanticists have dominated and held the center ground.

This picture has changed somewhat in the early 1980s with the Labour party's adoption of a unilateralist policy on nuclear disarmament and the election of two party leaders in succession with firmly held unilateralist beliefs. Denuclearization has also risen to prominence with the considerable publicity generated by antinuclear groups (mainly the Campaign for Nuclear Disarmament or CND, European Nuclear Disarmament or END, and the Greenham Common women's peace camp) in their opposition to the arrival in Britain of new American cruise missiles. Changes in public opinion on East-West issues are interesting to watch because under the Thatcher government, partly by design and partly as a result of the flow of events after the invasion of Afghanistan and the imposition of martial law in Poland, Britons have probably been given a greater dose of anti-Soviet argument than at any time since the 1950s.

The evidence suggests that Mrs. Thatcher has been preaching to the converted. The bedrock of British political attitudes toward East-West relations is an enduring hostility to the Soviet Union.[25] The

24. Ivor Crewe, "Britain: Two and a Half Cheers for the Atlantic Alliance," in Gregory Flynn and Hans Rattinger, eds., *The Public and Atlantic Defense* (Totowa, N.J. and London: Rowman & Allanheld, and Croom Helm, 1985), p. 11. Crewe's chapter is the basis for most of the following discussion of public opinion.

25. Ibid., p. 15. See also Edwina Moreton, "Images of the Soviet Union: A More Typical Adversary," in Gregory Flynn, Edwina Moreton, and Gregory Treverton, *Public Images of Western Security*, Atlantic Papers 54155 (Paris: Atlantic Institute for International Affairs, 1985), pp. 16–35.

Soviet Union is seen as a militarily strong, if not dominant, power and a potential threat to the security both of Europe and of Britain (though a largish minority would say similar things about the United States). There is also detectable an undercurrent of concern about East-West conflict and war that occasionally breaks to the surface but does not translate into support for unilateral renunciation of Britain's deterrent. Indeed, by European standards Britons are a pugilistic lot, prepared to see nuclear weapons used in their defense rather than surrender to an aggressor.

Yet within Britain there has clearly been increasing sympathy and support for antinuclear groups such as CND, which increased its membership from about 3,000 in 1979 to some 100,000 by 1985. Much of the peace movement tends to be antinuclear; parts are anti-NATO too. It has attracted a lot of media attention, but has not yet had much impact on the nation's basic attitudes as reflected in the polls, although recent poll data show an increasing dislike of reliance on American nuclear weapons for Britain's defense and a mistrust of the Reagan administration's wisdom in handling the larger East-West issues.

Within the antinuclear movement, ranks divide between those who want to concentrate on the national campaign against nuclear weapons based in Britain and those who espouse broader political aims. Though British-based, END is a loose organization of European peace groups that originated the idea of European disarmament "from Poland to Portugal." Yet relations with unofficial peace movements in Eastern Europe have sometimes been controversial, partly because antinuclear campaigners in Western Europe have at times been assiduously courted by official Soviet and East European peaceniks. For example, END and affiliated groups have been criticized by Charter 77, the human rights opposition group in Czechoslovakia, for failing to understand the link between the aims of the peace movement in Europe and human rights. Recently, similar criticism has come from Solidarity supporters in Poland, who argue that peace must go hand in hand with freedom if it is to mean anything. The dream of disarmament from Poland to Portugal took a nasty knock with the crushing of Solidarity, which pointed to the pressures for change in Eastern Europe but also to the greater pressures, backed by armed force, in support of the status quo.

Unlike West Germany, for example, Britain has no political party that uncritically accepts all the aims of the antinuclear movement. And unlike the churches in Holland and some other countries, in February 1985 the General Synod of the Church of England backed away from further discussion of the cruise missile issue after two years of being unable to decide upon its position. Although Eastern Europe as such did not figure much in all this public debate, the issue of defense in Europe has wider aspects than the purely military. But there is no sign yet in Britain of public pressure to give revision of the European status quo any higher priority in the making of government policy.

Options for the Future

The first obvious conclusion from this discussion of British foreign policy in Eastern Europe and the pressures upon it is that Britain remains the least involved of the Western countries reviewed here. Although some interest has been kindled with the change of leadership in the Soviet Union, Britain has never had a clear, unambiguous, and separate set of aims to pursue in Eastern Europe. Nor has the region been high on Britain's list of foreign policy priorities, except as a potential trouble zone to be watched. There is little reason to expect that view to change. Eastern Europe may force itself onto Britain's agenda, as in the case of the Polish crisis, but events in the region do not flow from British diplomatic action. That is not to say that the British government will not continue to maintain a supporting role for its allies, and it may again find itself trying to mediate where the allies disagree on tactics in the region. Yet for Britain the Soviet Union remains the chief object of interest east of the Elbe.

The one potential change in Britain's foreign policy that would have some bearing on these issues would be the coming to power of a unilateralist Labour government. Yet even such a major change as this in British foreign and defense policy would initially have its greatest impact on relations among Western nations and on NATO. Such a blow to the security policy of the NATO alliance could, however, speed other developments. These could conceivably change the political balance within the Western alliance in a way that might be exploited by the Soviet Union, which could use the offer of some sort of regional pact as bait to bring about a major political realignment in central Europe.

Left to its own devices, however, although Britain is an island geographically speaking, politically it is not likely to become a separate island of détente in East-West relations. Previous governments, whether Labour or Conservative, have been clear about the different political interests that maintain the division of Europe. Nor has there been any public pressure to overcome Europe's division. The suggestion of Zbigniew Brzezinski that Europe should be allowed to reconstitute itself because that is what it wants has no relevance to Britain; the issue is not dead there, it simply has never arisen.

Britain's strategic objectives in Eastern Europe since the war have been remarkably consistent. Foreign policy practitioners like to call this consistency "realism." In practice, successive British governments have, for want of great interest, great incentive, or grand design, eschewed the extremes of political debate about Eastern Europe. They have rejected the school of thought, particularly in its American form, that has argued that the West should use economic and military competition in an attempt to push the Soviet Union into collapse. For one thing, there seems to be a consensus that the Soviet political system, if not the regimes of Eastern Europe, is more stable than proponents of such ideas recognize. For another, a collapsing empire might make for dangerous neighbors.

British governments have also consistently rejected the map-redrawing exercises promoted by a few prominent individuals on the left of the political spectrum, especially in West Germany. Such excercises ignore the fundamental fact that Europe's division is dictated by competing political interests and prefer to regard that division as simply a function of military deployments by the two superpowers. That leaves successive British governments, including most probably future ones, with the realistic but uninspiring conclusion that what can be hoped for in Eastern Europe is at best a very, very slow change for the better for the peoples there. At worst, what will have to be coped with and managed are crises endemic to the region because of its subordination to Soviet economic, political, and military control.

Out of this framework there has evolved a policy of limited differentiation that is likely to remain the hallmark of future British policy in the region—albeit with occasional interruptions during crises.

The policy contains an acknowledged paradox: encouraging the regimes in Eastern Europe to make adjustments in response to economic and political pressures that would make them more palatable will also, up to a point, enhance their stability and prolong their lives. The more stable a regime, the more successful it will appear in the eyes of its own people. Only instability could bring rapid and dramatic change. Similarly, maintaining only government-to-government contacts to the exclusion of contacts with unofficial, sometimes dissident groups in East European societies might greatly ease official diplomacy, but it would ignore the moral content of Britain's postwar diplomacy in the region.

Yet, while there are obvious tensions of this kind within the policy of differentiation, and at some times Britain's policy in the region may seem more aggressive and active than at others, overall policy will be tempered with extreme caution. The strong underlying principle of British postwar diplomacy toward Eastern Europe is that little moral force, or indeed realism, lies in being prepared to fight to the last Pole or Czech for the end of the Soviet empire there.

Despite all the recent diplomatic activity, therefore, as far as the British government is concerned, Eastern Europe is likely to remain a sideshow. To the extent that British diplomacy treats the East European regimes, from time to time, as mere stepping stones to greater influence in Moscow, the East Europeans themselves will no doubt remain skeptical of the value of British interest. To the extent that they are objects of British policy in their own right, relations stand a chance of improving. However, as Poland after martial law has amply demonstrated, in a region where the regimes in power often lack popularity at home, balancing improvements in state-to-state relations with support for local aspirations for change is sometimes impossible. The complexity of the political choices to be made, combined with the still limited interest of Britain in the region as anything other than a potential challenge to stability in Europe as a whole, suggests that for the foreseeable future Britain is unlikely to develop strong ties or special interests that would mark a radical shift in the basic character of its postwar *Ostpolitik*.

EIGHT

The Views from Vienna and Rome

J. F. BROWN

IN TRADITIONAL DIPLOMACY the major West European powers, notably the Federal Republic of Germany, have had the most impact on Eastern Europe. But it would be unwise to ignore the impact, especially on East European societies, of some West European states or institutions that may have less power but still remain influential psychologically, culturally, and spiritually. In this context two European capitals, Vienna and Rome, exert unmistakable influence in certain parts of Eastern Europe.

Vienna

As the former capital of an empire that included all or parts of what are now Hungary, Czechoslovakia, Romania, Poland, and Yugoslavia, and as the contemporary capital of a neutral, independent, democratic, and successful Austria, Vienna has closely intertwined functions that give it a peculiarly important role in Eastern Europe. There is little need to dwell on Austria's historical relevance or its geographical proximity to Eastern Europe. While the various nationalities over which the Habsburg monarchy so uneasily ruled and the nationalistic feelings they spawned were the basic cause of the eventual downfall of the Austro-Hungarian Empire, some links forged during that time were not easily broken. And now that most parts of the empire except Austria itself and the former Habsburg possessions in Italy are under communist rule, and all of these except the Yugoslav parts are under Soviet domination, the attractions of Austria have perceptibly increased. What is at work here is something more than nostalgia; it is a historical affinity magnified by the present situation of Eastern Europe and relevant to East European aspirations. It is not quantifiable but few would doubt its impact.

Vienna's contemporary importance stems from the example it sets. The sheer fact of its existence and its achievements, rather than any conscious *Ostpolitik* on its part, have had a decisive role. So accessible geographically, Vienna has become a magnet for most Hungarians, many Czechoslovaks, and some Poles. Austrian television and radio, designed exclusively for domestic consumption, have large followings in those areas of Hungary and Czechoslovakia where they can be received. Television, with its more decisive impact, has the more dedicated audience. Austrian media generally have become a feature of life in communist Eastern Europe. The historical interaction between Austria and its neighbors is illustrated by the extensive coverage the Austrian media give to East European developments. Television coverage of that region from Vienna is generally the best in the Western world.

Austria appeals to the spiritual, political, cultural, and economic aspirations of East Europeans. Austrians, they often ruefully feel, might have been what they are. Austria could have become part of the Soviet empire—a very small part at that, since its population of 7.5 million is smaller than any East European country's except Albania's. Or the country could have been partitioned as Germany was. But by a political miracle the Soviets allowed Austria to go free in 1955, the only restriction being a neutrality that to any East European would be no unbearable deprivation. Austria may be the object of envy, but that envy is tinged with hope rather than dislike. Such hope may seem unrealistic, but to many East Europeans even unrealistic hope has a sustaining quality that makes their present situation more endurable. The gravitation toward Austria is somehow also a sublimation of or compensation for their being tied to the Soviet Union. In this sense its independent existence represents an escape from the reality that overcame them forty years ago.

For at least two countries, Hungary and Czechoslovakia, and also for some Poles, Austria is also an economic yardstick. Most Hungarians and Czechs, for example, measure their present material condition not against what it was before World War II, and certainly not against what it is elsewhere in Eastern Europe, but against the level of prosperity in Austria (similarly, East Germans measure theirs against the Federal Republic's). And when comparing economic progress, most older Czechs ruefully recall that before the war many parts of Bohemia and Moravia were more advanced than most parts of Austria.

More recently Austria's reputation in the West has become somewhat tarnished. The election of former UN Secretary-General Kurt Waldheim as Austria's president, in the face of evidence that he had concealed his role as a German army officer in World War II, seemed to show a lack of sensitivity. In addition, the recrudescence of right-wing nationalism, declining economic prosperity, and the cracks that have developed in the social welfare system indicate deep-seated weaknesses that Austrians themselves must tackle. But they are unlikely to cause Austria much damage in the East unless they go unrecognized or unchecked for a long time.

No population is affected more by the pull of Austria than the Hungarians. The Habsburg connection, with its comprehensive impact on the Hungarian habit of mind and way of life, is an obvious factor. First, in spite of all the bitterness that existed between Vienna and Budapest, Hungary itself, especially after 1867, was also a considerable imperial power, with the Hungarian nation not just a *Staatsvolk* but a *Herrenvolk* in a large part of Eastern Europe and the Balkans. Second, all Hungarians had been united in the same state, a state dismembered by the Treaty of Trianon in 1920. In the discreditable and nightmarish interlude between 1918 and 1938, Hungary and Austria shared the status of pariah. Many Hungarians, susceptible to the growing notion that theirs had become a historically rejected nation, were almost pathetically grateful to Austria for not ganging up on them as Czechoslovakia, Romania, and Yugoslavia did in the Little Entente, the loose alliance formed in 1920–21 to contain Hungary and prevent the restoration of the Habsburgs.

Nor was the connection broken after 1945. Many would agree with former Chancellor Bruno Kreisky's view that the granting of Austrian independence in 1955 was important in hastening the restlessness that led to the Hungarian Revolution a year later.[1] After order had

1. See "Free Austria, Europe's Symbol of Peace," *Observer* (London), May 11, 1980, on the twenty-fifth anniversary of Austria's independence.

been restored in Hungary, the Kádár leadership not only sought to improve relations with Austria at the state level but also, wisely realizing that popular contacts made a most effective safety valve, gradually lifted the iron curtain separating the two countries.

The interaction of peoples that has developed from these modest and hesitant beginnings is extraordinary. It is more intense, friendly, and many-sided than at any time in history—much more so than during the Dual Monarchy, perhaps more so than between any two Western countries. Although many more Austrians visit Budapest than Hungarians visit Vienna, largely because they have more money and because Hungary's regime imposes residual travel restrictions on its citizens, still nearly 300,000 Hungarians came in 1984 (the reverse flow was close to 2 million).[2]

One of the most exhilarating examples of this intermingling is that between Burgenland in Austria and Sopron county in Hungary. Here the border hardly exists. The number of Austrian-owned shops, even hairdressing salons, on the Hungarian side is considerable, as is the number of similar Hungarian establishments on the Austrian side. The situation is probably unique in the whole of Europe.

In such an atmosphere many must find it difficult to keep in mind that Hungary is a communist state and that Budapest and Vienna (despite Austrian neutrality) officially represent different and adversarial political systems and sets of values.[3] Edward von Taaffe and Kálmán Tisza, the Austrian and Hungarian premiers in the late nineteenth century, would be incredulous about what is happening today on the Sopron-Burgenland border. So are those citizens who can remember the trigger-happy Hungarian border guards and minefields of barely a generation ago.

ECONOMICS: A DELIBERATE ASPECT OF POLICY

Simply by being where it is, what it is, and what it once was, Austria is a powerful attraction for many East Europeans. But is there more than that? Is Austria just a passive attraction or does it exercise a more active policy, an *Ostpolitik,* in Eastern Europe?

2. See Alfred Reisch, "Prime Minister Lazar Visits Vienna," *Radio Free Europe Research,* vol. 10, pt. 1 (April 19, 1985), situation report 4/85.

3. Various Western press articles have illustrated the extraordinary range of Austrian-Hungarian societal relations. See, for example, Heiko Flotrau, "Politische und andere Signale entlang der Donau," *Süddeutsche Zeitung,* May 18, 1985.

Austria clearly takes an active economic interest in Eastern Europe, the importance and scope of which is sometimes overlooked in Western Europe and the United States. Generally, East-West trade as a proportion of total trade is most important to those countries geographically contiguous to the Comecon area—Finland, the Federal Republic of Germany, Austria, Yugoslavia, Greece, and Turkey. Of these, Finland is the most deeply involved, most of its trade being with the Soviet Union. Austria has generally taken second place in this respect. In 1975 more than 10 percent, the largest share so far, of its total trade was with Eastern Europe. By 1985 the share was just under 7 percent; with the Soviet Union added it came to 10.9 percent.[4] Imports from the USSR are dominated by oil and natural gas.

The Soviet Union has been Austria's biggest Eastern trade partner since 1955, but trade with the East European countries proper has been considerable. Austrian trade with Eastern Europe is based on geographical and historical factors. Exports and imports travel relatively short distances, with the Danube providing a basic artery of communication. The historical factors are today less obvious and more difficult to gauge, but as two Austrian economists have aptly put it, "previous common history may facilitate mutual understanding, and some knowledge of each others' languages often plays a decisive role. . . ."[5] Traditionally, Czechoslovakia and Hungary have been Austria's closest East European trade partners. Hungary has always been an important outlet for Austrian exports, although these decreased in the early 1980s, mainly because of the Hungarian government's policy of domestic austerity. For a while in the 1970s Poland became Austria's biggest East European trading partner, thanks to the expansionist economic policies of the Gierek regime, but by the 1980s the Polish economic crisis had sharply limited imports. In the meantime, trade with the German Democratic Republic began to flourish, and in 1983 the GDR took Poland's place as Austria's most important export market in Eastern Europe. But the GDR's jump to the top largely resulted from the completion of several deals to deliver

4. See appendix tables A-3 and A-9. See also Friedrich Levcik and Jan Stankovsky, *A Profile of Austria's East-West Trade in the 1970s and 1980s,* prepared for ECE/UN (Vienna Institute for Comparative Economic Studies, May 1985), p. 3.

5. Levcik and Stankovsky, *Profile of Austria's East-West Trade,* p. 5. For details on Austria's trade with Eastern Europe, the USSR, and the world as a whole, see appendix table A-9.

factories, and by 1985 Austrian exports to Hungary were once again double those to the GDR. The GDR had, however, established itself as an important trading partner, a relationship that Austrian Chancellor Fred Sinowatz's visit to East Berlin in November 1984 was designed to strengthen.[6] Trade with Bulgaria, especially imports, has never been really important, and trade with Romania, after an Austrian export peak in 1980, dropped considerably by the mid-1980s.

This situation obviously needs to be kept in perspective. In 1985 Eastern Europe accounted for only 7.3 percent of Austria's world exports; its imports from Eastern Europe were only 6.2 percent of its world total. In the 1980s two-thirds of its exports went to Western Europe, with the Federal Republic dominating its commercial relations generally. Still, Austria's role in Eastern Europe cannot be ignored; it is the second largest Western supplier to both Hungary and Czechoslovakia and makes a strong showing with the GDR and Poland. Its key exports are steel, chemicals, dyes, paints, plastics, and food-stuffs. In the 1960s Eastern Europe was a big market for Austrian machines and vehicles, but its demand for these commodities declined considerably.[7]

Finally, a word about cooperation in Austria's economic relations with Eastern Europe. This term includes both governmental cooperation through trade promotion agreements and cooperation at the level of individual enterprises. It is relevant because these types of contracts usually have more national and political influence than other forms of economic relations.

Austria was a pioneer in long-term agreements with Comecon countries, usually involving trade, industrial cooperation, and scientific-cultural cooperation. By 1983 twenty-one such agreements were in operation. In industrial cooperation at the enterprise level, Austria was also a pioneer. In 1975 about 12 percent of all the East-West agreements involved Austrian companies; relations with Hungary were very close in this respect. More recently, however, the Austrian share has declined as American, Italian, and especially West German companies have moved in on a considerable scale.[8]

6. "Wien und Ost-Berlin fordern den Dialog," *Frankfurter Allgemeine Zeitung,* November 7, 1984.

7. Levcik and Stankovsky, *Profile of Austria's East-West Trade,* pp. 7–8, 12, 32, and table 10.

8. Ibid., pp. 21–22, 67.

Thus Austria's economic relations with Eastern Europe, though not vital to either side, are not without importance to both. Certainly the well-being—although hardly the existence—of a number of Austrian industries is affected by these relations. On the East European side, some Austrian commodities and products have acquired a good reputation and, if only in a minor way, the Austrian economic presence is an attractive alternative to the sheer massiveness of the Western presence represented by the Federal Republic. But even if trade were to expand greatly—which does not seem likely—Austria could never depend on its economic weight alone for its influence in Eastern Europe.

AUSTRIAN NEUTRALITY

A unique obstacle to any Austrian *Ostpolitik* is the country's neutral status, which Moscow insisted on before agreeing to allow independence in 1955. The Soviets not only closely monitor Vienna's international behavior but also tend to put a restrictive interpretation on what neutrality should mean.

In practice, however, neutrality cannot be rigidly defined. There is no fixed set of rules by which a neutral country should abide. Even if there were, the spirit of the law is always as important as the letter. The Soviet Union, for its part, has never been noted for its attempts to be objective in its definition of neutrality. Its interpretations vary according to other foreign policy considerations. Its only consistency appears to be in favoring a neutrality that hews closely to Soviet policy.

Of the four major European neutral countries—Finland, Austria, Switzerland, and Sweden—the Soviet Union sees itself as having a proprietary interest first in Finland and then in Austria. As historical neutrals, Switzerland and Sweden are free from this embrace, although Sweden is continually being threatened, mainly for strategic reasons. As a former part of the Russian Empire and, for the most part, an enemy country after it achieved independence, Finland is severely restricted by Moscow in its foreign policy while thoroughly democratic domestically (though its institutions are often inhibited). The Soviet Union sets the parameters for a considerable part of Finnish public life. Austria is much freer. Its domestic policy suffers no inhibitions, and though neutrality precludes its joining any Western alliances or groupings, the tenor of its foreign policy—despite occasional growls from Washington—is clearly pro-Western.[9] The USSR may chafe at this posture, but there is little it can do beyond invoking the 1955 peace treaty, for which Moscow seems to claim the major rights of interpretation because it conceded most by the treaty's terms. With their neutrality and independence guaranteed de facto also by the Western powers, the Austrians are considerably more secure than the Finns. But they are wise enough—and on this there seems to be bipartisan agreement in Vienna—to realize that an activist policy in Eastern Europe, even if it were viable, would not be tolerated by Moscow.

A LINK BETWEEN EAST AND WEST

That there is no evidence to suggest Austria would seek an activist policy toward Eastern Europe does not mean it has no role at all, although Austrian officials are reluctant to define what the role is. Even the Austrian media have seemed unwilling to commit themselves to any clear statement on this subject.

But gleanings and observations suggest that Austria sees itself as a link between East and West. "Link" in this context does not mean intermediary or mediator in any diplomatic or political sense, but rather an all-European *Schalterhalle,* a communications center and booking office for relations between East and West, facilitating movement, commercial connections, and cultural and social contacts of all kinds. This is not the same as the role President Eduard Beneš naively saw for Czechoslovakia after World War II. Beneš thought in political terms, with Prague as the bridge between two adversarial power blocs. He thought, too, in terms of relations between states. The Austrian concept, though recognizing that the two cannot be clearly separated, concerns societal relations.

There is little doubt that Chancellor Kreisky saw the Austrian role in these terms. Indeed, his vision was broader and higher, conceiving of Vienna as an international capital, a third center for the United Nations alongside New York and Geneva. Many educated Austrians

9. The loudest of Washington's complaints concerned alleged Austrian laxness in allowing the passing of technically sensitive goods, originating in the United States, to the Soviet Union. In early February 1983, however, Chancellor Kreisky visited Washington and the differences were apparently resolved.

thought similarly. They saw Austria as uniquely fitted for this role—and not simply because of history and geographic location. They realized that since 1955 Austria had acquired a separate identity for the first time in its history.[10] Not only had it shed the connection with *Deutschtum*, the concept of Germanness that had plagued its history for centuries, but it had also rid itself of all but the sentimental residuals of the Habsburg heritage. Austria had become a distinctive nation, few in numbers, occupying a territory drastically cut down, almost miraculously lucky to be independent. In such circumstances neutrality is probably the best status, but within that constraint Austria must find a positive role. The role of international *Schalterhalle* is consistent with everything Vienna is at present and much of what it has been in the past. It is consonant with the dignity of a small, historic nation, and by no means without its economic rewards.

That Austria has made deep inroads into Eastern Europe in its own peculiar, idiosyncratic way, is beyond question. The *Schalterhalle* approach has been effective. Among the more concrete signs of that effectiveness are the proliferation of institutes dedicated to the promotion of East-West relations. It is easy to be cynical about such establishments, and no one is more so than the Austrians themselves, for whom cynicism has always been a protective cloak against the realities of the world they have faced. But the institutes do symbolize the effort toward being a link between Eastern and Western societies, an effort that may be somewhat theatrical, but one that also shows sincerity, imagination, and even a touch of creative fantasy.

One such institution, small but worthy of note for what it symbolizes, has been the Forschungsinstitut für den Donauraum, established in 1955 and dedicated to the study of problems concerning the Danube and the states along its banks. Its creation was a scholarly, perhaps simplistic, effort to stimulate attempts to find what the Danubian states had in common in the present as well as the past. Conferences were organized, and a journal, *Donauraum*, was published.[11] In the second half of the 1960s the institute aroused considerable interest. It was dismissed by some as yet another symptom of nostalgic romanticism, by others (less credibly) as a symptom of resurgent

10. The classic work on this subject is by Friedrich Heer, *Der Kampf um die Österreichische Identität* (Vienna: Bohlav, 1981).

11. It began publication in 1955 and developed a close association with the University of Regensburg in the Federal Republic.

Habsburg sentiment. Obviously, elements of both were present. But more important was the spirit that pervaded this and similar institutions: that Austria accepted its new status and was anxious to find constructive ways of collaborating on an even footing with the states it had formerly ruled and that the Danube linked in a common destiny.

While the concept of Danubian cooperation attracted some attention in Austria itself, interest was perceptibly greater among the cultural elites of the communist Danubian countries that had formerly been under Habsburg sway. The leaders of the Prague Spring obviously had more important things on their minds than schemes for Danubian cooperation. Still, in the freedom that pervaded those few months in 1968, Czechoslovak scholars and publicists, ebulliently searching for new vistas and solutions, enthusiastically embraced this vague idea of Danubian cooperation. Officially, Yugoslavia was cool to the idea, as was Romania, but a semiofficial interest could hardly be disguised. Hungary showed the most interest, and some loosely reined Budapest publicists gave considerable support.[12]

Too much should not, however, be made of the concept. Although the vision of Danubian cooperation persisted into the early 1970s, the Soviet-led invasion of Czechoslovakia dispersed the atmosphere in which it had been born and nurtured. The concept is now dormant. But it is not dead; if the atmosphere were ever to become propitious again, the chances are that the concept would reawaken, its champions perhaps wiser but hardly less enthusiastic.

Danubian cooperation has not been the only Austrian attempt at becoming a *Schalterhalle*. The many Western scholars, journalists, and businessmen who have visited Vienna and experienced the range of opportunities for an Eastward orientation are aware that Danubian cooperation was but one of the many avenues in the Austrian capital leading to the historic Habsburg hinterland.

How long might the Soviet Union be prepared to tolerate this Austrian intrusion? Though it is hardly an immediate threat, some in Moscow must consider it a creeping danger. Certainly the Austro-Hungarian connection has been noticed by Soviet observers. And while there may be some who see it as potentially advantageous in that it might draw Austria more toward the East, most would emphasize

12. Charles Andras, "Neighbors on the Danube," *Radio Free Europe Research* (December 1967), background report.

the dangers of Hungary's being drawn toward the West, for the growing links with Austria are but one aspect of the general movement toward reform that has characterized Hungary these past twenty years. And just as Hungarian officials have skillfully sought to persuade the Western powers that their country should be excluded from the cold war calculations that have recently dominated East-West relations, so have the same Hungarians assured their Austrian neighbors that relations must intensify and deepen.

Hungary's room for maneuver has, like that of other East European states, been enlarged in recent years by the disarray in the Soviet leadership. Now it appears that the disarray may be over and the Soviet Union moving into a period of stable leadership. How Gorbachev will eventually react to the Austro-Hungarian association is still difficult to tell. His reaction will largely depend on the overall concept of Soviet–East European relations he eventually conceives and formulates. But in spite of the shadow cast over its reputation by the scandals associated with President Kurt Waldheim, the new Austria is again significant in Eastern Europe, even if in a different guise and a different way. Precisely because of this, Austria can be a greater threat to Russian power in Eastern Europe than it ever was under the Habsburgs.

Rome

Rome is a unique city in many respects, none more so in that today it contains three institutions—the Italian Foreign Office, the Italian Communist party (PCI), and the Vatican—each conducting a separate foreign policy with its own motivations and impact. These institutions are obviously independent of each other. The PCI, especially, is often in an adversarial relationship with both the Foreign Office and the Holy See. But although it would be too much to speak of occasional collusion among the three organizations, a tacit understanding does sometimes govern the conduct of two or all of them. No one openly admits to this, of course, and if questioned, some will indignantly deny it. But private hints are occasionally given. In policy toward Yugoslavia, for example, the PCI has given unofficial support and advice to the Foreign Office, as it has in relations with the GDR. Between the Vatican and the Foreign Office there is constant contact.

Most intriguing of all is the possibility of contact between the PCI and the Vatican. While there has been no direct interaction between Pope John Paul II and either party leader Enrico Berlinguer or his successor, Alessandro Natta, some knowledgeable Italian journalists suspect that informal contacts between Vatican officials and PCI experts on relations with Eastern Europe have occurred at a lower level. It would be self-defeating and against the proud tradition of Italian diplomatic practice if there were not.

ITALY'S STATE RELATIONS

Italy's relations with Eastern Europe are long established, going back far beyond the creation of the united Italian state in 1870. The history of Venice, to mention only the most obvious example, has always been closely tied to developments in the Balkans. Under Benito Mussolini, the natural Italian strategic interest in the Adriatic degenerated into outright imperialism. Fascist Italy supported both Hungarian and Bulgarian irredentism, financed Croatian and Macedonian terrorism, and openly sought the breakup of Yugoslavia. Albania became a client state in the 1920s and in 1939 was occupied by Italian troops. With the collapse of royal Yugoslavia, Italy occupied most of the Dalmatian Coast and became the patron and protector of the puppet kingdom of Croatia.

After World War II a defeated and chastened Italy hesitated to pursue any policy in a region where it had so recently shattered its reputation. Indeed, the whole course of Italian foreign policy changed. From being an imperialist power in the Mediterranean, the Balkans, and Africa, Italy became a member of the American-led Western alliance. Its geographic location made it of great strategic importance. The question was whether Italy would persist in playing a passive role as a NATO member or, sooner or later, begin a nonaggressive active role, with a profile of its own in a region that it still regarded as important. And if it did, would its intentions be taken seriously by the East European states concerned, particularly those of southeastern Europe?

These are questions to which a qualified yes can be given. Concerned first with postwar domestic reconstruction and then with anchoring its place firmly in the Western alliance, until the 1960s Italy had little time or interest for Eastern Europe. But having achieved its most important postwar goals with remarkable success, it did join, albeit on a lesser scale, its European allies, France and the Federal Republic, in the moves eastward. In the late 1960s it mounted a considerable economic offensive toward Eastern Europe, which resulted in general increases in trade with the Soviet Union and in the volume and level of economic cooperation that produced the famous Fiat automobile and truck deals. A similar deal with Poland produced the Fiat Polski. Italian credits were made readily available in the 1970s, although they constituted only a small part of the overall credit flow eastward during that decade. The volume of trade with Eastern Europe grew considerably. But as in the case of Austria, some perspective must be maintained. In 1985 Eastern Europe was the source of more than 2 percent of Italy's imports, and Italy was very active in cooperative projects in the region, yet Eastern Europe accounted for only 1.4 percent of Italy's exports.[13]

Economic relations, then, assumed a significant role in Italy's new policy in Eastern Europe, but with quite different aims and motives than had inspired them before World War II. Culture had a strong supporting role. Perhaps wishing to compensate for its former aggressiveness, successive Italian governments, in collaboration with universities and other institutions of culture and learning, have concluded a number of agreements with East European capitals providing for exchanges of scholars and students, exhibitions of Italian art, and an intense cultural role for the Italian embassies.

It is impossible to measure the impact or even the extent of Italy's political role in Eastern Europe. But there seems little doubt that recent Italian governments, notably that of Bettino Craxi, have conducted a more vigorous *politique de présence* in the region. Craxi has been an assiduous traveler, visiting all the East European countries between 1983 and 1985 except Bulgaria (where relations have been clouded by allegations of Bulgarian involvement in the attempted assassination of the pope in 1981) and Albania. This increased openness toward Eastern Europe was part of a more generally activist foreign policy favored by Craxi and his Christian Democratic foreign minister, Giulio Andreotti. One of the more controversial aspects of the policy was the development of closer relations with Arab forces, including Libya and the Palestine Liberation Organization.

Italian relations with the GDR in the early part of the 1980s were marked by considerable cordiality, with President Erich Honecker

13. See appendix table A-10 for trade percentages. For cooperative projects see Levcik and Stankovsky, *Profile of Austria's East-West Trade,* p. 67.

visiting Rome in 1985, returning the visit paid by Craxi the previous year. Earlier, Andreotti had delighted East Berlin, and annoyed Bonn, by criticizing the notion of German reunification.[14] But Italy has shown more particular interest in Hungary, Albania, and Yugoslavia. Hungary is of no strategic interest to Italy, and the warmth of the relationship, at least on the Italian side, stems partly from an appreciation of both the domestic and foreign policies of the Kádár regime. Italy has also been anxious to reciprocate the readiness of Hungary for improved relations with the West. With Albania and Yugoslavia, the interests are obviously strategic.

While Rome was not sympathetic with the Hoxha regime, it was increasingly responsive to feelers put out by Tirana for an improvement in political and economic relations. These feelers became more evident after Albania's final break with Peking in 1978. A symbol of this rapprochement was the inauguration in 1984 of a thrice-monthly ferry between Durres and Trieste, commercially disastrous but politically expedient. Since Hoxha's death in April 1985, relations have continued to improve. His successor, Ramiz Alia, has favorably mentioned Italy in a major foreign policy speech, and Italian industrial aid to Albania has increased.[15]

Yugoslavia's worsening political and economic situation has caused substantial concern in Rome that the country is in real danger of disintegration and that the Soviet Union could take political or even military advantage from it. Although Italian-Yugoslav relations after World War II were originally strained over lingering territorial issues (notably Trieste) and bad memories, both subsequently felt that the international situation required an accommodation of views and close cooperation. Certainly in terms of East-West confrontation, Italy, along with most Western powers, regards Yugoslavia as part of Western Europe.

The crucial question, though, is whether any Italian government would be prepared to pursue the logic and accept the consequences of this view by joining in economic or military guarantees for the security and integrity of Yugoslavia. Italy has neither the economic nor military capacity to make such commitments alone. But it could

14. James M. Markham, "For Both East and West Two Germanys Is Better," *New York Times*, September 23, 1984.

15. *Zeri i Popullit* (Tirana, Albania), August 27, 1985. See also Louis Zanga, "Ramiz Alia's Foreign Policy Statement," *Radio Free Europe Research*, vol. 10, pt. 1 (September 9, 1985), background report 98/85.

certainly take the initiative, for example, in organizing concerted European financial help and reiterating, in common with its Western allies, its commitment to the integrity of Yugoslavia. It would thus show a more active concern over the danger directly facing it.

Among well-informed observers, opinion appears divided as to how far Italy has gone in reassuring the Yugoslavs. Some believe that its support has been considerable and that Belgrade asks for no more out of concern over upsetting Soviet sensibilities. Others would aver that the Craxi government has preferred posturing in the Eastern Mediterranean to confronting the danger just a few miles across the Adriatic. Some Italian governments are said to have been content to leave Yugoslav contacts mainly to the Italian Communist party. But the excellent relations that have existed for more than twenty years between the PCI and the League of Communists of Yugoslavia would seem to be no substitute for vigorous activity by the Italian government.

THE ITALIAN COMMUNIST PARTY

Ever since party leader Palmiro Togliatti expounded his doctrine of polycentrism in 1956, arguing that national communist parties should not be controlled from a single center in Moscow, the PCI has been a challenge to the Soviet Union's influence in both the world communist movement and in Eastern Europe. Indeed, Moscow may have perceived the PCI's threat in Eastern Europe to be the greater, perhaps even endangering, although indirectly, its very hold on a region vital to its interests.

After 1956 the PCI—sometimes alone, sometimes as the spearhead of the short-lived Eurocommunist movement—came to stand for a philosophy threatening the two foundations on which East European communism originally rested: Soviet domination and domestic total-itarianism. Its impact on the East European parties was considerable if uneven. Its contacts with Czechoslovak reformers had some influence, dramatized by the visit of PCI leader Luigi Longo to Prague in April 1968, although the meaningful discussions had taken place earlier at a lower level. Similarly, aspects of the great Yugoslav political and economic reform of 1965 may have been inspired by contacts with the PCI—contacts reaching right up to summit level in January 1964 when Togliatti visited Belgrade.[16] The PCI also influenced the

16. See Kevin Devlin, "Tito and Togliatti," *Radio Free Europe Research,* January 25, 1964, background report.

dissident Polish intellectuals who later advised Solidarity, and it
established close contacts with a broad spectrum of Hungarian
intellectuals in the 1970s.

This is not to say that the changes in Eastern Europe were not
largely self-initiated. Romanian semi-independence, the Prague Spring,
the zig-zag course of Yugoslav reform, the Hungarian reforms,
Solidarity—all began in the countries concerned, and the PCI then
supported them with courage and energy. But its role as a fount and
articulator of ideas should not be overlooked. It is this spontaneous
originality that has probably worried Moscow the most.

The PCI has also served reform initiatives in Eastern Europe by
publicizing them. Beginning in the early 1960s some of the best
reports and analyses of Eastern Europe anywhere in the West were
to be found in the PCI daily, *Unità,* and its periodical, *Rinascità.* Such
correspondents as Giuseppe Boffa, Adriano Guerra, and Romolo
Caccavalli have contributed to recent East European history simply
by their incisive understanding of it and their skill in narrating it.

But in the last analysis the PCI's influence on the ruling elites has
necessarily been limited. The party operates within a democratic
framework in Italy that is entirely different from those in Eastern
Europe and that forces its policy on international communist and
domestic affairs in a liberal direction. Still, within this basic limitation
its role has not been insignificant. It has certainly owed something to
the personalities and prestige of two leaders, Togliatti and Berlinguer.
The latter's death in 1984 removed a powerful and beneficial influence,
not only in world communist affairs but also in domestic politics.
Whether his successors can exert a similar influence is doubtful.
Indeed, the PCI's main activities abroad may now be devoted to
achieving mutual understanding and joint action with a broad section
of the European left. The Euroleft is replacing Eurocommunism as
a concept, and in the process the PCI's impact on Eastern Europe
may diminish.

THE VATICAN

The Vatican's East European policy has shown a steady evolution
over the past thirty years. Sometimes it has appeared contradictory,
although many of the apparent contradictions could be explained by
the very complexity of the Holy See's diplomatic process.

Just as many analysts failed to note that West German *Ostpolitik* began slowly with a reluctant Chancellor Adenauer in his last years, so they overlooked that Pope Pius XII (1939-58), perhaps even more reluctantly, also recognized in his last years that events were forcing the Vatican into some kind of relations with the East European communist regimes. The precarious hold of the Catholics and their church in Eastern Europe demanded it. With Pius's successor, John XXIII (1958-63), the need for action was not just understood but energetically acted upon. Contacts with Poland, Hungary, Czechoslovakia, and Yugoslavia—the main Catholic countries in Eastern Europe—were quickly established, and the Vatican-communist dialogue began. This was followed by a fifteen-year period of Pauline diplomacy in Eastern Europe, a diplomacy which, despite the death of its founder Paul VI in 1978 and the almost immediate accession of Pope John Paul II, still dominates Vatican policy.[17]

Briefly, Pauline diplomacy derived from the principle that the organizational basis of the church was its bishops. Without bishops the Roman Catholic church in Eastern Europe or anywhere else would disintegrate. And since disintegration was to be avoided at all costs, agreements—however limited—with the communist authorities to allow empty dioceses to be filled were essential. From this it followed that negotiation and compromise were necessary, and that a policy of small steps was unavoidable. Under Paul VI a group of able diplomats emerged who became experts both on the overall situation in Eastern Europe and in dealing with the communist authorities there. Three of the most prominent of this group were Archbishop Agostino Casaroli (now cardinal), Archbishop Giovanni Cheli, and Monsignor Luigi Poggi, for many years the Vatican's main negotiator in Eastern Europe. Such senior diplomats were backed by a staff of formidable intellect and knowledge.

The policy that emerged toward Eastern Europe, inspired by Paul VI but directed and implemented by these men, has often been criticized as naive, ingenuously allowing the church to be manipulated, even humiliated, by the East European regimes. Alternatively, the policy has been dismissed as realistic to the point of cynicism, disregarding the ultimately spiritual aspects of the church and ignoring

17. The best history of the Vatican's policy in Eastern Europe is Hansjakob Stehle, *Eastern Politics of the Vatican, 1917–1979* (University of Ohio Press, 1981).

the ideological incompatibility between Christianity and communism. The results of the Pauline policy have also been called into question.

These criticisms have not been totally baseless. The Vatican did sometimes appear overly solicitous in seeking accommodation—most notably over the agreement to exile the Hungarian primate, Jozsef Cardinal Mindszenty, to Vienna after his nineteen-year residence in the American Embassy in Budapest following the 1956 revolution. The concessions made by the regimes were tardy and meager, certainly in Czechoslovakia in the 1970s and even in Hungary, where church-state relations were probably at their most cordial. But against this the Pauline diplomats could point to the undeniable fact that papal policy, though not exactly to be seen *sub specie aeternitatis,* is set against the aspirations of the long term, not the hopes of the short term. They could also argue that the overall situation of the church in Eastern Europe—in Hungary, Poland, and Yugoslavia (though not Czechoslovakia)—has improved and that no basic church position has ever been surrendered. In general the Pauline philosophy was summed up in the privately expressed opinion of one of its ablest practitioners: that to get only 50 percent of what is hoped for is still better than 40 percent. These are formidable arguments, but when Pope Paul VI died in 1978 and was succeeded, after the brief interval of John Paul I, by John Paul II, who had served his whole priesthood in the embattled Polish church, there was much doubt whether the previous diplomacy would be continued.

Pope John Paul II brought to the Vatican from his native Poland an intimate knowledge of communism in action and of all layers of communist bureaucracy, together with charisma, spiritual enthusiasm, and a strong sense of political and social justice. He was quite different from Paul VI and his Italian advisers in style, temperament, and outlook. Instinctively, he was impatient with the niceties of diplomacy. He was a man of mass, almost messianic, appeal, seeking to breathe new life and spirit into the church and what many considered its bureaucratic ways of government. He was also a pastor and man of action.

Since his accession in 1978, therefore, there has been not one Vatican *Ostpolitik* but two—the pope's and that of the diplomacy inspired by Paul VI. John Paul II has, however, tried hard to bridge the two, to make them complementary. With the notable exception of Archbishop Cheli, who became the Vatican's chief observer at the

United Nations, he kept the old Pauline group intact and actually appointed Casaroli head of the Congregation of State, which makes him the Vatican's unofficial prime minister. And, in general, the two approaches have worked well together. The combination has not impeded the Vatican's policy toward the East, the continuity of which has been largely preserved, although there have been differences of emphasis and probably some differences of policy.

Some Vatican diplomats, for example, appear to have considered the pope's attitude toward church-state relations in Czechoslovakia too direct and lacking in subtlety. The persecution of organized religion there since 1968 has been of a viciousness unknown in Eastern Europe since Stalin's day. This persecution has been accompanied, again in the Stalinist manner, by the setting up of a priests' organization, Pacem in Terris, that supports the regime. Probably 15 percent of all Czechoslovak priests joined Pacem in Terris, which was led by Bishop Josef Vrana of Olomouc. In 1982 the Vatican issued a decree forbidding the clergy to engage in political activity. This was at first thought to be directed mainly, if not exclusively, toward Latin America, but a papal spokesman made it clear that it also applied to Pacem in Terris.[18] Obviously, the Vatican considered the organization disreputable, but some members of the church hierarchy felt that such a direct assault on it only aggravated a delicate situation and reduced the chances of improving church-state relations, especially in appointing bishops. Only three of Czechoslovakia's thirteen dioceses had fully consecrated bishops, a state of affairs that had existed for more than ten years because the Czechoslovak government and the Vatican could not agree on suitable candidates. (In all the East European states, including Poland, the government has at least the right of veto in these appointments.)

Opponents of the pope's directness might seek vindication in the fact that, even at the end of 1986, the situation regarding bishops in Czechoslovakia was still the same, and other aspects of church-state relations, despite an occasional flicker of hope, still showed no progress. The Czechoslovak government did allow celebrations in 1985 marking the eleven hundreth anniversary of the death of St. Methodius at Velehrad in Moravia (it hoped—mistakenly as it turned out—to

18. For a good discussion of this issue see [Vladimir V. Kusin] "Proregime Priests Contest Vatican Decree," *Radio Free Europe Research* (July 27, 1982), situation report 14/82.

secularize and politicize the festivities to its advantage), but it refused permission for the pope to come and denied entry to both Franz Cardinal König of Vienna and the Polish primate, Josef Cardinal Glemp.[19] As the pope's representative, Cardinal Casaroli did attend, and he had talks with Czechoslovak representatives, including President and party leader Gustav Husák himself. These talks could eventually bear fruit. If they do, they could be seen as a proof of the efficacy of patient diplomacy rather than the direct action manifested in the attack on Pacem in Terris.

Pauline diplomacy could point to its biggest success in Hungary, where its most solid achievement has been the agreement with the regime on the appointment of bishops, the first breakthrough being as early as 1964. Today all Hungarian dioceses are filled, and a limited number of Catholic orders are allowed to operate. Anxious for domestic calm and Western approval, the Hungarian authorities have followed a skillful policy that has brought considerable dividends and little danger. Budapest has been the Vatican's favorite communist capital for more than twenty years. But many Hungarians feel that the price the church has had to pay for its tranquility and concessions has been too high. In practice, they argue, the Hungarian authorities have been considerably less than tolerant on vital matters like religious instruction and priests who speak up on public and social issues. They blame all except a few Hungarian bishops for being too pliant. Their chief target of criticism was the Hungarian primate himself, Laszlo Cardinal Lékai, who died in 1986 and was known to be anxious not to disturb relations with the regime, even to the point of publicly endorsing some of its foreign policy and domestic initiatives. Pope John Paul II himself at first seemed to share these reservations about Lékai. He wrote the Hungarian bishops a letter at the beginning of 1979 implicitly criticizing the degree of their cooperation with the authorities.[20] But during Lékai's visit to Rome the following April, he demonstratively praised the Hungarian primate.[21] Some construed this as a sign that the pope had altered his view and had come to

19. See "Heitere Demonstration des Glaubens in Mahren," *Neue Zürcher Zeitung,* July 11, 1985.

20. See "Der Papst mahnt den ungarischen Episkopat," *Frankfurter Allgemeine Zeitung,* January 6, 1979.

21. See Josef Schmitz van Vorst, "Ungarn hat den Vatikan überspielt," *Frankfurter Allgemeine Zeitung,* April 4, 1979.

realize the solid achievements made by Lékai's approach. More probably he had not changed his mind but, aware of the speculation caused by his letter, wished to reassure Lékai personally by praising his career and publicly acknowledging the difficulties the Hungarian church had survived.

The Vatican's relations with Poland are in a category of their own, partly because Polish Catholicism is unique, partly because John Paul is Polish. From the death of Pius XII in 1958 to the accession of John Paul II in 1978 these relations were characterized by a high degree of independence from Rome enjoyed by the Polish church under its great primate, Stefan Cardinal Wyszyński. For two decades, then, church-state relations in Poland were almost entirely an internal matter. This independence was enhanced by the stature, growing experience, ability, and success of Wyszyński. In the light of his later dominance, it is worth recalling that during the reign of Pius XII his reputation had not been so high. He was remembered by senior Vatican officials as having signed in 1950 an agreement between the Polish church and the communist state that many thought contained too many concessions. But Vatican hostility subsequently diminished as the courage and wisdom of Wyszyński's action became evident. Under Pope John XXIII all doubts about the Vatican's total support disappeared. Even after the accession of John Paul II in 1978, with his natural concern for Poland, and even with Wyszyński's own obviously weakening health, the cardinal's authority did not diminish. Only after Wyszyński's death in 1981 did the pope himself need to become so directly concerned with Poland. His first visit as pope in 1979 had had a tremendous impact on internal developments and had perhaps laid the essential psychological groundwork for the emergence of Solidarity. But as long as Wyszyński lived, John Paul did not need to be as preoccupied with his native land as he was evidently later to become.

The new pope's involvement in Poland was deepened by the crisis caused by the rise and fall of Solidarity and, simultaneously, by questions concerning the ability of Wyszyński's successor, Cardinal Glemp, to cope with the task of leading the church and guiding the nation during such a trying period. The pope's attitude toward and relations with Glemp at first attracted much speculation. The almost lurid gossip about John Paul's outspoken disapproval of the cardinal can be discounted, but so can the counterclaims of implicit trust and mutual understanding that the two men were supposed to have shown right from the beginning. The pope clearly saw the need to demonstrate his trust and faith in Glemp's leadership. Yet there seems little doubt that he was more enthusiastic than the cardinal about the national spontaneity exemplified by Solidarity and less distrustful of some of Solidarity's intellectual guides. John Paul II could also not have been anything but dismayed at Glemp's early maladroitness. On the critical issue of policy toward the regime and resistance in Poland, however, there may have been little basic disagreement. There was certainly no disagreement on the overriding need to show unity between pope and primate, between primate and the Polish episcopate, and within the episcopate itself.[22]

Great efforts were made to demonstrate this unity; and the realization of its need tended to reinforce it. Church unity, therefore, especially between pope and primate, became an important political factor in Poland. But also important was the persistent popular suspicion that the unity was contrived rather than genuine, that the pope's instinct was for a stronger assertion of national rights than was Glemp's. This suspicion was shared by many Polish priests, and it sustained them in their resistance to Jaruzelski's military dictatorship.

In a way, the reported differences between the pope and the cardinal mirrored those between the pope and the Pauline diplomats in the Vatican itself. They are primarily negotiators; he is primarily the pastor with his appeal to the masses. His overall appraisal of a given situation might be similar to or identical with that of the Vatican diplomats. But his policy is imbued with an approach they do not share.

Obviously both approaches have their place. Pope John Paul II has tried to make them complementary and has generally been successful. There need be nothing contradictory in seeking to strengthen the church organization and its hierarchy while appealing to the masses at the same time. In Poland, Slovakia in Czechoslovakia, and Croatia in Yugoslavia, the two aims can be self-reinforcing because of the intimate links among church, people, and national feeling. The church is also seen now as the most powerful obstacle to communist totalitarian goals. As long as it remains so, there is no danger of

22. For an excellent (and sympathetic) view of Glemp's strategy, see Jörg Bremer, "Weder Unbesonnenheit noch Feigheit," *Frankfurter Allgemeine Zeitung*, October 24, 1985.

contradiction. But the restlessness of many Polish clergy in the period after December 1981 against a hierarchy they regard as not militant enough could have established a dangerous precedent for the church in Poland. In the Czech Lands (Bohemia and Moravia) and in Hungary, the dangers to the hierarchical order are perhaps more serious, but they stem from the same cause. The Catholic church there, especially in the Czech Lands, was historically a symbol of foreign Habsburg domination. In Hungary, only two-thirds of the population are Roman Catholic in any case. In the Czech Lands, though almost 90 percent are believing, nominal, or lapsed Catholics, whatever nationalism exists is associated with the traditional Hussitism that was virtually wiped out by the Czech defeat at the Battle of the White Mountain in 1620.

Recently there has been a revival of religiousness, especially on the part of the young, in both Hungary and the Czech Lands (in Slovakia it never needed much reviving). This movement has taken several forms, one of which is a renewed interest in Catholicism itself. In the Czech Lands, the loyalty and affection of many was sparked by the strengthening resolve of the aging primate, Frantisek Cardinal Tomasek. Among the reasons for the revival, disillusionment with communism as an ideology is probably the biggest. But the Catholicism that is emerging has been of an individualistic, spontaneous kind, often tending to reject organization and formal structures. It has little affinity for the traditional Catholic hierarchical system. In Hungary it has already caused some consternation among senior church officials. In the Czech Lands, too, there are signs of this spontaneity, often with ecumenical leanings. Although it is on a far smaller scale, it has similarities with the restless movements of the church in other parts of the world. Thus, the Roman Catholic church, which has been remarkably successful in surviving and repelling communism, could be faced by a growing problem with the younger generation among its own ranks. That problem could be more difficult to manage than the direct persecution the church has endured under communism. It could make Vatican policy all the more difficult to formulate, articulate, and implement.

NINE

Convergence and Conflict: Lessons for the West

LINCOLN GORDON

WHAT CONCLUSIONS can be drawn from this review of Western attitudes, interests, and policies toward Eastern Europe? Does the region receive the attention it warrants? Have Western relations had any appreciable influence on developments in Eastern Europe? To what extent do the aims, strategies, and tactics of the principal Western nations converge or conflict? Is there a basis for greater convergence among the nations of Western Europe or those of the Atlantic alliance? How much policy coordination or harmonization should be actively sought? Is the West adequately prepared to cope with new crises in Eastern Europe? What are the possibilities and prospects for constructive change?

The Importance of Eastern Europe

In recent years we have observed a spate of anniversaries that remind us of the importance of Eastern Europe to the West: the fortieth anniversary of war's ending and the conferences at Yalta and Potsdam, the thirtieth of near rebellion in Poland and outright rebellion in Hungary, the tenth of the Helsinki Final Act, and the fifth of Poland's Solidarity movement. As it was forty years ago, Eastern Europe remains the East's front line in the largest standoff of organized military power in history. Almost 600,000 Soviet ground troops are deployed there, along with large air forces and tactical and intermediate-range nuclear weaponry. In Eastern Europe itself the Soviet forces are outnumbered, except in the GDR, by the local national contingents, which account for more than one-third of the total Warsaw Pact ground and tactical air forces deployed in the entire region, including European Russia.[1] Eastern Europe's collaboration, therefore, would be indispensable to any Soviet armed aggression against the West. Scenarios can be imagined, moreover, in which instability there would provoke East-West hostilities by accident or misunderstanding.

Military contingencies apart, Eastern Europe's unsettled condition makes it a variable weight in the geopolitical balance, not merely between the superpowers but between East and West as a whole. In J. F. Brown's terms, the Soviet Union has not found and is not likely to find a stable balance in Eastern Europe between viability and cohesion. The governing regimes have no assured legitimacy. Eastern societies deeply mistrust the workability of their economic systems. Smooth transitions in leadership cannot be taken for granted. And the elementary freedoms and human rights promised in national constitutions, United Nations declarations, and the Helsinki Final Act—freedoms and rights that East Europeans can observe at first hand in the neighboring neutral and Western nations—are still denied. These basic instabilities create a presumption of ongoing change, gradual or sporadic, punctuated by recurrent crises—all with a significant potential for altering the global prospects for liberal institutions and humane values.

At the same time, and partly as a means of seeking greater legitimacy, East European governments have shown increasingly frequent manifestations of particularist nationalism or "domesticism," the pursuit of individual interests separate from those of the Soviet Union or the so-called socialist community. That trend is to be welcomed by the West not only for its weakening of bloc cohesion but also because it presses the Soviet Union toward accommodations that improve the prospects for renewed détente in Europe. Such pressures played a significant role in the Helsinki negotiations in the early 1970s and have been visible more recently in the MBFR and CDE discussions in Vienna and Stockholm.

1. For details, see International Institute for Strategic Studies, *The Military Balance 1985–1986* (London: IISS, 1985), especially pp. 25–36, 186–87.

Other indications of efforts to dilute Soviet hegemony by diversifying external relationships include resistance to excessive economic integration and Moscow-dictated country specialization or "division of labor." These tendencies reduce the Soviet capacity to use the combined weight of Comecon in bargaining for unilateral advantage. In economic terms, although its output is small by comparison with Western Europe's Common Market, Eastern Europe produces more than $500 billion in goods and services, has enjoyed vigorous rates of growth until the late 1970s, and carries on a significant volume of trade with the West, especially West Germany, Austria, and France.[2] As pointed out in this book's country-by-country discussions, East European markets are much more important for certain West European industrial sectors and individual firms than would be suggested by the small proportions those markets represent in the West's total foreign trade. It should also be kept in mind that East-West economic relations are generally much more important to the East Europeans than to their Western counterparts. In addition to trade, those relations have included substantial quasi-investments in the form of industrial cooperation agreements and much larger volumes of bank credits— some guaranteed by Western governments—especially during the era of high détente in the 1970s. All these economic relations were curtailed by the East European balance-of-payments and debt-servicing crises of the early 1980s. They are gradually being rebuilt in the mid-1980s, again with West European banks showing greater readiness than American ones to provide export financing and general lines of credit, but they show no early prospect of returning to the scale of the previous decade.

The East European countries display significant variations in systemic arrangements for managing socialist economies, with a broad trend toward greater variety.[3] Their small size makes economic experimentation much easier than in the Soviet Union. At least at the sectoral level, they may point the way toward workable reforms without threatening the Kremlin by appearing, like China, to be

2. For quantitative data on the relative size of the East European economies, rates of growth, and trade with the West, see the tables in the appendix.

3. One is reminded of Justice Oliver Wendell Holmes's well-known description of early twentieth century actions by American state legislatures: "the making of social experiments . . . in the insulated chambers afforded by the several states." See *Truax v. Corrigan,* 257 U.S. 312 (1921).

centers of doctrinal rivalry. Their potential for influencing the USSR's own system should not be overstated, but it is not entirely negligible.

Other, less tangible, elements contribute to Eastern Europe's importance to the West. They include the historic relationships of France, Austria, Italy, and Germany with the East and the blood ties of tens of millions of Americans. On both sides of the political-military dividing line there is a widely held feeling that Eastern Europe shares in the European cultural heritage and that "Europe," however ill-defined as an operational conception, is somehow incomplete without the full participation of its Eastern peoples.

Notwithstanding these formidable claims to attention, it must be recognized that Eastern Europe has ranked high among Western policy concerns only in times of crisis, and even then not for very long. The great exception is West Germany. There the GDR and *Ostpolitik* are always matters of the highest priority. For others, Eastern Europe is overshadowed by preoccupations with bilateral relationships with the Soviet Union, or with intra–West European or intra–NATO concerns, or with global economic issues, or with the special regional interests of individual Western countries.

There is a simple explanation for this apparent paradox: the deceptive appearance of stability in Eastern Europe. In terms of basic status and orientation, it can be argued, nothing has changed since the Austrian State Treaty of 1955 (aside from Albania's defection from the Warsaw Pact in 1961). The German treaties pursuant to *Ostpolitik*, the Berlin Agreement of 1971, and the Helsinki Final Act simply consolidated an already durable status quo. The six East European countries remain within the Soviet empire, the Warsaw Pact, and Comecon; their regimes continue to be single-party communist dictatorships; and every attempt at basic change, whether initiated by societies or regimes, has been repressed by Soviet force, either directly (1953, 1956, and 1968) or by proxy (1981). Therefore, that line of argument concludes, it is futile for the West to waste high-level time and attention on this region.

The fault in the argument, however, lies in the implicit assumption that the only meaningful kinds of change are alterations in formal international status or in the basic character of governing regimes. That is simply too narrow a concept. History elsewhere, and in Eastern Europe itself, shows that conditions can be transformed by incremental and evolutionary change as well as by revolutions, and often with more durable results. One reason that the West (and perhaps the East as well) has been repeatedly taken by surprise in Eastern Europe is that it has paid insufficient attention to the more subtle types of change that modify social structures and economic systems, to shifting attitudes of successive generations, and to new formative influences, both domestic and external, on the opinions and aspirations of the leaderships. Apart from moments of crisis, such matters cannot compete effectively for the time and attention of top policymakers in the West. Given the basic importance of the region, however, they certainly warrant more ample scholarly examination and continuous governmental analysis and assessment at high professional levels.

The Influence of the West

To suggest greater policy attention to Eastern Europe implies that Western countries are not mere observers of events but a group of actors with significant influence, actual or potential. Western influence is clearly less important than domestic developments within each East European country. It is also clearly less important than the Soviet Union's. Its third-place ranking tends to make Western policy reactive rather than initiating. Nevertheless, the record over four decades, and especially since the evolution of West German *Ostpolitik* and American differentiation policy in the mid-1960s, shows that Western influence can be very substantial.

Chapter 3 describes the high importance placed on the Western connection by both East European peoples and their governments. That in itself is eloquent testimony to the strength of Western influence. There are also visible linkages between Western actions and the broad movement in Eastern Europe away from Stalinist conformity and toward various forms of more nationalist individuation.

It is sometimes said that the greatest source of influence for the West lies in simply being itself. Its political, economic, and social success provides Eastern Europe with models of free, prosperous, just, and peaceful societies they might wish to emulate. But this effect depends on Eastern Europe's access to knowledge about the West, an access not to be taken for granted where communist regimes monopolize public information. Radio and television broadcasting, tourism and travel in both directions, educational and cultural exchanges, the dissemination of high and pop culture, business contacts for trade and investment, and relations between churches, trade unions, and professional organizations all contribute to this access. Austria's visa-free admission of Hungarian tourists and West Germany's television transmissions and millions of personal visits each year to East Berlin and the GDR are only the most spectacular examples. Public opinion polling and much other evidence shows that Eastern Europe's peoples in general and educated elites in particular have a relatively accurate understanding of Western conditions and attitudes in spite of propagandistic distortions in their official media. This situation contrasts sharply with that in the Soviet Union.

Western influence depends in part on the condition of overall East-West relations, which alternate between periods of tension and of relative détente. With respect to state-to-state relations, there was a classic debate in West Germany during the 1950s and 1960s—described by Josef Joffe in chapter 5—about whether the road to the East can be direct or must go via Moscow. The answer appears to be some of each. It would be naive to suppose that relations can be developed behind Moscow's back or in the face of clear-cut Soviet opposition. Yet there is substantial scope for national initiative, as exemplified by the Germanys themselves following Bonn's decision to permit the deployment of U.S. intermediate-range missiles in the early 1980s. Contrary to expectations of a more reluctant *Ostpolitik* from a right-of-center government in Bonn and predictions in East Berlin of a deep freeze in inter-German relations, and notwithstanding the heightened tension between the superpowers, West and East Germany mounted a vigorous effort to maintain at least an inter-German détente. And, for the first time, that effort was pressed overtly by the GDR, even in the face of Soviet criticism.[4] Nevertheless, in the broader field of European East-West relations there are clearly fewer constraints on Western access and influence when the Soviet Union and the United States are engaged in active and more cordial dialogue.

The economic dimension of potential Western influence is especially

4. These events are documented in detail in A. James McAdams, *East Germany and Détente: Building Authority after the Wall* (Cambridge, England: Cambridge University Press, 1985), especially chap. 6.

interesting because of Eastern Europe's intense interest in Western trade, finance, and technology. East Germany's unimpeded access to West German markets and partial access to the rest of the European Common Market, together with substantial West German subsidies, have contributed greatly to the GDR's strong economic performance by Comecon standards. But Germany is a special case. A question of broader interest is whether extensive Western economic relations promote or retard the reform of Eastern economic systems toward greater rationality and wider reliance on market forces. On the evidence thus far, the answer must be that such relations are a necessary but not sufficient condition.

Except when subsidized, East-West trade must offer benefits to both sides or it will not take place. But for would-be economic reformers in the East, trade with the West has the added advantages of setting quality standards, providing market-determined price relationships, and bringing to bear competitive pressures completely lacking in centrally planned systems. These have been indispensable assets for the considerable economic reforms initiated in Hungary in 1968 and given a major new forward thrust in the 1980s. Credits from Western governments and Western-dominated international institutions—the Bank for International Settlements, the International Monetary Fund, and the World Bank—enabled Hungary to overcome its balance-of-payments liquidity crisis of 1981–82 without a formal rescheduling of debt or the kind of drastic austerity measures imposed in Poland and Romania.

In contrast, the very liberal private and official credits from the West to Poland's Gierek regime during the 1970s did not lead to meaningful systemic reforms. Those credits have often been termed substitutes for reform, implying that in their absence the public's unsatisfied aspirations for economic improvement would have forced the government to adopt genuine and effective reforms. There is no way of testing this hypothesis. But the Polish experience, like that in many developing countries, makes clear that Western trade and finance do not automatically engender reform and that leadership for effective reform must come from within. The subtle issues arise when national leadership is divided or uncertain. In those circumstances the outcome may be subject to Western influence exercised in the form of conditions on liberalizing market access or providing financial credits.

With hindsight, Western bankers came to regret their unconditional credits to Poland during the 1970s, credits that neglected even the normal "sound banking" requirements for economic data and project assessment. Commercial bankers, however, are not well equipped to judge the broader issues of systemic reform, a task more appropriate to the International Monetary Fund. Even though the IMF must by its charter avoid political issues and its spokesmen take the public position that reform of economic systems is not its proper business, it may be better placed than any single Western government to exert constructive influence in the direction of reform. Since Hungary's admission to the IMF in 1982, the Fund has been able to work with a cooperative and like-minded government. With Romania it has been frustrated in recent years to the point that relations are almost suspended. The acid test in Poland is only beginning.

When particular economic favors are strongly desired by an East European government, they can be offered in exchange for specific political concessions. As chapter 5 shows, such trade-offs are frequent in relations between East and West Germany. Romania's easing of emigration restrictions in order to maintain most-favored-nation trade treatment by the United States is another example. This kind of Western influence, however, can operate only within the general limitations on the effectiveness of sanctions, an issue reviewed later in this chapter.

Other kinds of influence on political decisions are hard to evaluate. Romania's deviations from Soviet foreign policy orthodoxy and Warsaw Pact military doctrine during the past two decades have been supported by China and Yugoslavia as well as the West, but Western encouragement has almost certainly provided important reassurance and some degree of security against economic (although not military) pressures from the USSR. The multiplicity of recent high-level Western political visits may prompt East European leaders to think in terms of national interest and sovereignty, even if their autonomy is limited. The remarkable East German peace movement of the early 1980s was directly inspired by its Western counterpart, and Western arms control initiatives have encouraged East European questioning of new Soviet missile deployments. In the Helsinki follow-up conferences, East European participants are said to have been responsive to both Western and neutral representatives, leading to positions more moderate than the initial Soviet ones. Eastern regimes have welcomed the opportunity for briefings on Western arms control positions, indicating that they are beginning to think for themselves about their own interests in this area. And special regional or historic relationships, notably the inter-German but also including those between Poland and Sweden, Poland and France, Hungary and Austria, Slovakia and Austria, Romania and France, and Balkan connections with Italy and Greece, all help to soften the rigors of ideological conformity.

Taking the past two decades as a whole, how should the West assess the trends in its overall influence in Eastern Europe? Compared with the far-reaching aspirations of the early 1960s—whether de Gaulle's "Europe from the Atlantic to the Urals," Egon Bahr's *Wandel durch Annäherung* (change through rapprochement), or Zbigniew Brzezinski's forecasts of early Finlandization—the reality of the mid-1980s is very disappointing. Compared with the actual earlier situation, however, the balance sheet has more gains than losses. The country-by-country reviews by J. F. Brown in chapters 2 and 3 show Eastern Europe's clear movement away from being a monolithic bloc and toward a growing interest in diversified connections with the West. The Hungarian trend in that direction is unmistakable. Bloc conformity by Poland is of course greater than in the heady months of 1980–81 but still less than in the 1960s. Internal repression in Romania has worsened, but the elements of nationalist autonomy have been largely preserved. Bulgaria and East Germany, by tradition the most satellitic countries, have been asserting their national personalities, sometimes in ways disagreeable to the West but no longer as puppets controlled from Moscow. Moreover, if German reunification (hoped by some and feared by others) must in any event be relegated to a very remote future, then it can be argued that the West benefits from the existence in East Berlin of an *interlocuteur valable*. The sole exception in the region is the apparent stagnation in Czechoslovakia.

In short, if Western policymakers can forego expectations of imminent formal revision and settle in for a long haul of evolutionary change, punctuated by periodic crises that may speed change or reverse it for a while, there is no reason to denigrate Western influence. The game is very large and worth many candles.

Convergence and Conflict in Western Aims and Aspirations

To compare the attitudes, interests, and policies of the principal Western countries toward Eastern Europe, it is helpful to distinguish among the three time frames outlined in chapter 4: long-term aspirations or ultimate objectives, medium-term operational objectives, and short-term specific measures. They correspond to the classic military distinctions among war aims, strategy, and tactics.

The analysis of convergence and conflict, however, must also take into account profound differences in the intensity and character of attitudes and interests among the various countries. West Germany's are unique because Germany is Europe's only divided nation and has been forcibly expelled from the East, a historic reversal of the ancient *Drang nach Osten.* For the Federal Republic, relations with the GDR (but not with the rest of Eastern Europe) are always among the central issues of foreign policy, comparable in importance to relations with the United States, the Soviet Union, NATO, and the European Community. For reasons of history, geography, and the terms of the 1955 State Treaty, the intensity of Austria's interests is similar, although on a much smaller scale.

But for other Western countries, Eastern Europe is of secondary or tertiary concern. It ranks highest in the United States, somewhat lower in France and Italy, and even lower in Britain, where it is the "sideshow" described by Edwina Moreton in chapter 7. (One recalls Neville Chamberlain's unfortunate words in 1938 about the Sudetenland: "a quarrel in a far-away country between people of whom we know nothing.")[5] Economic interests in Eastern Europe are substantially greater in Western Europe than in the United States but nowhere are they of controlling importance. France's ancient ties to Poland and its prewar promotion of the Little Entente help to shape its current attitudes toward Eastern Europe. So also Italy's long-term ties with the Balkan states. The American political system's greater openness to pressure groups results in higher salience for East European matters in domestic politics there than in Western Europe except for West Germany. And there are the subtle differences in ways of conducting foreign policy suggested in chapter 6 by Pierre Hassner's quips: "the French talk like the Americans but act like the Germans"; "the Americans believe in sticks, the Germans in carrots, and the French in words."

At the level of long-term aims and aspirations, the policies of all

5. In his broadcast to the British nation on September 27, 1938, as quoted in Winston S. Churchill, *The Second World War: The Gathering Storm* (Houghton Mifflin, 1948), p. 315.

Western countries generally converge upon the objective of lightening the Soviet yoke in Eastern Europe, securing for the peoples more freedoms and better conditions of living. Full implementation of the Helsinki Final Act would mark a good beginning. Ultimately, but very remotely, movement in that direction would seem to imply some kind of Finlandization or Austrianization—in effect a peaceful detachment of Eastern Europe from Soviet political control. The earlier yearnings, especially in the United States, for more dramatic ruptures like those of Yugoslavia or Albania have been abandoned. Outside of Germany there is no significant interest in territorial revision, and within Germany irredentism is fading with time. Nor do even the more hopeful visionaries seek to assign a time horizon to their goals. But speculation about eventual formal changes in the status of Eastern Europe does raise the specter of the potentially divisive German Question.

THE GERMAN QUESTION

The official doctrine of the Federal Republic, enshrined in the Basic Law, looks to ultimate reunification in freedom by peaceful means. Berlin would then once again serve as the capital of a single German state. Josef Joffe and other qualified German commentators, backed by the results of extensive public opinion polling, contend that this goal has been largely abandoned, even as an ultimate aspiration. As Joffe puts it in chapter 5, it has been replaced by an operative policy of "reassociation," that "would eventually dispatch the goal of national unity by making its absence tolerable." On this kind of inherently emotional subject, however, attitudes are not confidently predictable if circumstances were to change. Nor is it clear how East Germans would react if they had a genuine choice. The GDR's rulers have gone far toward their goal of securing full international recognition as the third Germanic state (counting Austria as the second), except from West Germany itself. But in adopting Frederick the Great and Bismarck as national heroes, may they not be inadvertently sensitizing their own people to a renewed search for the German unification (excluding Austria) advanced by Frederick and consummated by Bismarck? And what of Berlin? It is easier to imagine a long-term separation of East and West Germany than a permanent status for Berlin as an enclave "occupied" by four non-

German powers. If East Germany is to endure as a separate state with its capital in East Berlin, logic would suggest that West Berlin at some point become a *Land* fully incorporated into the Federal Republic. But would East Germany voluntarily accept such an arrangement? Would West Berliners feel confident unless their status continued to be internationally guaranteed and backed by the presence of substantial Western garrisons? When and how would normalization permit the removal of the Berlin Wall or the barriers along the rest of the inter-German frontier?

In contrast to these uncertainties in the two Germanys, traditional attitudes in France and the smaller West European countries have been unambiguously opposed to German reunification. In France, Germany's continued division and the special restrictions against German nuclear weaponry have been thought necessary to maintain a parity of scale and influence between the two countries and to keep West Germany anchored in the European and Atlantic communities. While that position may be weakening as French confidence grows in West Germany's ties with the new Europe, reunification would raise a new key question of how it could be reconciled with continued German participation in the EC. In the United Kingdom there is less visceral concern, other than a general resistance to destabilizing changes in Europe, but there would be adamant opposition to German neutralization as a price for reunification. By now the Soviet Union, not Germany or France, has become the potential Continental hegemon to be controlled by such weight as Britain can bring to bear in the balance of power.

The United States might be confronted with a fearsome dilemma: a conflict between the basic principle of respect for democratic self-determination and the survival of the Atlantic alliance. NATO is the core instrument of American foreign policy, and the Federal Republic has become the keystone of its European structure. The critical issue would be the terms of reunification and their effect on the overall East-West balance. Absorption of the GDR into the existing Federal Republic and NATO would be perfectly acceptable to the United States but totally unacceptable to the USSR. Nor is there any prospect for a Germany reunified as a communized state along lines once contemplated by Josef Stalin. The best that is even faintly conceivable would be a demilitarized and neutralized East Germany in a loose confederal relationship to a West Germany remaining in NATO. But the obvious nightmare for American policy, and for the rest of Western Europe as well, would be a genuine Soviet offer of German reunification under conditions like those applied to Austria, in which all of Germany would be disarmed and neutralized under international guarantee while Soviet troops remained nearby in Poland and Czechoslovakia. Most German authorities are confident that such an offer would be refused by the Federal Republic, but it has not been put to the test. In the unlikely event that it were offered and accepted, American strategists would consider the rest of continental Western Europe virtually indefensible, easily subject to Soviet military intimidation even if no actual invasions were likely. Austrianization applied to the whole of Eastern Europe as well as Germany would be a different and possibly more interesting idea, but is even harder to visualize as a realistic prospect.

Thus there seems no likelihood for decades to come of Soviet agreement to reunification on terms even remotely acceptable to West Germany. It is ruled out by the relative success of the GDR, which has become the strongest and most prosperous member of the Eastern alliance. If that judgment is correct, the potential differences within the West on the German Question become of only academic interest. Yet they may be worth ventilating from time to time as a kind of precaution, even though the contingency be remote.

THE EUROPEAN QUESTION

The European Question is harder to analyze because it is not nearly as well defined as the issue of German reunification. It envisages a pan-European solution to the division of Europe, in which some form of community, federative or otherwise, would unite both sides in a new Continental-scale system free from military alliance with either of the present superpowers. In some versions, notably de Gaulle's vision of "Europe from the Atlantic to the Urals," it includes European Russia; in others, the USSR is wholly excluded. There is also a version including the United States and Canada as cultural and ethnic extensions of Europe, following the precedents of the United Nations Economic Commission for Europe and the Conference on Security and Cooperation in Europe, which generated the Helsinki Final Act.

In its broadest variant, pan-Europe almost merges into the West as a whole—a very large grouping of like-minded societies that now

encompasses Japan and Oceania as well as North America and Europe
and may come to absorb the more advanced developing countries as
they emerge into first world status. Its shared values include self-
determination and pluralist political systems, individual liberties and
human rights, and far-reaching economic decentralization ranging
from pure capitalism to mixed economies with elements of social
democratic planning. Those values originated in European intellectual
and political movements of the seventeenth to nineteenth centuries
and are part of the Western orientation that appeals to East European
elites. (The political-economic philosophy of Marxism also originated
in Western Europe, but many scholars would argue that the Leninist
version implanted in the Soviet Union was in basic conflict with the
European cultural heritage.) If a wider Europe is to be institutionalized, however, its scope would surely be narrower than the almost
globe-encircling West.

In one model of the pan-European concept, both Russia and the
United States must be excluded. That model is based on two assumptions: that the East European peoples and increasing numbers of
their elites feel themselves part of a "greater Europe" and would be
drawn to such an entity more than to the broader and looser West;
and that with Western Europe severed from the United States, the
Soviet Union would no longer fear aggression on its western flank
and would then be prepared to relinquish the military, security, and
political controls now exercised in Eastern Europe.[6] There is reason
to be deeply skeptical on both counts.

Those who make the first assumption are mainly interested in
differentiating Europe from North America. In their view the Europe
that gave birth to the Renaissance, the Reformation, and the great

6. These elements can be found in the widely read book, *The End of the Age of
Ideology: the Europeanization of Europe*, by the German author, Peter Bender, which is
unfortunately not available in English. See Peter Bender, *Das Ende des ideologischen
Zeitalters: Die Europäisierung Europas* (Berlin: Severin und Siedler, 1981). A more
summary presentation of similar ideas by a former official in the Federal Republic's
Press and Information Office is Klaus Bloemer, "Freedom for Europe: East and West,"
Foreign Policy, vol. 50 (Spring 1983), pp. 23–38. The title "The Europeanization of
Europe" was also adopted by Ralf Dahrendorf for an essay on domestic social and
political changes tending to separate Western Europe from the United States, although
his prescriptions favor retention of the essentials of the NATO alliance and are far
less radical than those of Bender. See Andrew Pierre, ed., Ralf Dahrendorf, and
Theodore C. Sorensen, *A Widening Atlantic? Domestic Change & Foreign Policy* (New
York: Council on Foreign Relations, 1986), pp. 5–56.

liberal movements of the past three centuries still possesses a unique set of cultural values. Intellectuals in Germany and elsewhere are prone to repeat Thomas Mann's characterization of America as "civilization without culture," and a considerable French literature decries the fate of poor, civilized Europe, squeezed between American and Russian barbarisms. For Americans familiar with their own country's intellectual and social history, those views are not persuasive. They consider the United States a full participant in the European cultural tradition. They acknowledge that the absence of an inherited aristocracy and the tasks of conquering an almost empty continent have created institutions and attitudes different from those of Europe, but consider the differences scarcely greater than those within Europe itself—say between Sweden and Spain or Britain and Italy.

What counts in the context of this study, however, is not the opinions of Americans but those of East Europeans. For obvious geographic reasons their opportunities for travel and direct contact and their economic relationships are far more intense with Western Europe than the United States. As appendix table A-12 shows, Eastern Europe's trade with Western Europe outweighs its American trade by more than eleven to one (with West Germany accounting for over 40 percent of the West European total). But in cultural and political terms, Eastern Europe is oriented not merely toward Europe in the narrow sense but toward the wider West, most explicitly including the United States. As J. F. Brown's discussion in chapter 3 points out, this orientation has long been the case for ordinary people and in the postwar decades increasingly so for cultural and political elites as well. It is borne out by their interest in all aspects of American culture, their pursuit of English language study, and their recognition of American economic and intellectual predominance within the Western community of nations. Family relationships are no doubt still one major influence, but the attitudes go much further, seeing in America, correctly or not, the kinds of freedoms and opportunities they would most like to see at home.

The second assumption behind the geographically limited idea of pan-Europe has historical antecedents in a variety of proposals in the mid-1950s for disengagement between the Soviet Union and the United States. As noted by Pierre Hassner in chapter 6, the postulate of Gaullist policy in the mid-1960s was that "to encourage the independence of Eastern Europe from the Soviet Union, one had to begin by making Western Europe independent from the United States." In that formulation American disengagement was to come first rather than be simultaneous with the Soviet, which raises the suspicion that it was de Gaulle's principal objective. There have been many other advocates of American troop withdrawal from Europe, including Senator Mike Mansfield in the 1970s and a substantial number of successors today, but only a few have seen American withdrawal as an effective means for ending the Soviet imperium in Eastern Europe.

Somewhat surprisingly, a modified version of disengagement calling for a unilateral withdrawal of American ground combat forces (although not air or strategic forces) and their gradual replacement by Europeans was advocated by Zbigniew Brzezinski in late 1984, when he wrote, "A Europe that can defend itself more on its own is a Europe that is also politically more vital, while less challenging to the Soviet Union from a purely military point of view, than a Europe with a large American military presence in its very center. Such a Europe would then be better able to satisfy the East European yearning for closer association without such association being tantamount to an American defeat of Russia."[7] These views are surprising because twenty years earlier Brzezinski was the most articulate and persuasive opponent of the Gaullist position. He stated then—in this author's opinion correctly both then and now—"that American inaction may eventually prompt isolated West European ventures, . . . that West Europe cannot by itself promote the climate of change, stimulate the pressures for unity, and finally provide the sense of security which will be necessary to attract East Europe and Russia."[8]

Although it is true that the past two decades have disappointed the hopes for rapid liberalization in Eastern Europe, they have been almost equally disappointing to the hopes for political unification in Western Europe. Even the consolidation of a genuine common market has encountered serious obstacles. So there is hardly the basis for a vigorous West European movement to incorporate its Eastern neigh-

7. "The Future of Yalta," *Foreign Affairs*, vol. 63 (Winter 1984–85), p. 299. He goes on to define this "closer association" as including "demilitarized or nuclear-free zones or extension of the Austrian-type neutrality to other areas, including later even to a loosely confederated Germany" (p. 300). A critical comment by Lincoln Gordon appeared in the letters column of the *New York Times,* January 17, 1985.

8. Zbigniew Brzezinski, *Alternative to Partition: For a Broader Conception of America's Role in Europe* (McGraw-Hill for the Council on Foreign Relations, 1965), p. ix.

bors. The disengagement proposal is similarly unpersuasive with respect to Soviet reactions, as witness the dramatic crises of 1968 and 1980–81. It is not credible that the absence of American troops from West Germany would have made the USSR more tolerant of the Prague Spring or more ready to see a genuine social compact in Poland among party, church, and Solidarity. The analysis of Soviet motivations in chapter 2 points to quite different conclusions. Forty years ago Stalin may have dreamed of a pan-European outcome with communist parties dominating the entire continent. That aspiration is surely no longer harbored by Stalin's successors, but for today and tomorrow any pan-European arrangement acceptable to the Soviet Union would still require much more drastic changes in Western Europe than the mere withdrawal of American military force, changes that would curtail Europe's own autonomy far beyond the limits of acceptability.

It is also difficult to envisage practicable institutional methods for gradual movement toward implementing the pan-European concept. Enlargement of the existing European Communities seems ruled out by their own internal dynamic. If they were purely economic institutions, expansion to include the East might be conceivable, but their political-economic character has excluded even the West European neutrals other than Ireland. And the thrust of movement, in addition to the recent inclusion of Spain and Portugal, is focused not only on "perfecting" the Common Market but also on strengthening and formalizing the harmonization of foreign policies through the European political consultations. As a much looser consultative body, the Council of Europe could expand more easily, but by the same token its influence on events is almost negligible.

All these obstacles notwithstanding, there is undoubted psychological appeal in the idea of a "greater Europe," especially if it can be freed from anti-American bias. That appeal is probably stronger in Eastern than in Western Europe precisely because it implies the relaxation or abandonment of Soviet imperial control. As a long-term aspiration, therefore, it should continue to be encouraged by the West but in forms eschewing intra-Western divisiveness and unrealistic expectations for early solutions. Meanwhile, a faint trace of pan-Europeanism can be seen in such institutions as the CSCE follow-up bodies and the UN Economic Commission for Europe, whose membership also includes the Soviet Union, the United States, and Canada.

Any real headway in further negotiations on confidence-building and the thinning out of conventional military forces would help to increase the relative weight of the small and medium-sized European states, both Western and Eastern, in forums of this type.

For the medium term, if very gradual transformation of East European conditions toward greater internal and external freedom is a realistic objective, the types of influence the Western nations can muster will need to be all pointed in the same direction, and not work at cross-purposes. That is surely the case with respect to the members of NATO, both European and North American. And the process would be greatly reinforced by the cooperation of European neutrals, the other industrialized democracies, and like-minded associates from the misnamed third world.

Convergence and Conflict in Strategy and Tactics

Turning from long-term aspirations to medium-term operational objectives—the aims of government policies that political leaders can think about seriously—we find substantially less consensus within the West. There are corresponding divergences in tactics, the day-to-day application of policy instruments. These differences can best be analyzed in terms of the spectrum of approaches to bringing about desired changes in Eastern Europe set forth in chapter 4, running from *accommodation* to Soviet control through *transformation* of Soviet control to *dissolution* of Soviet control. It should be emphasized again that these are not mutually exclusive policy options, but points along a spectrum that also permits intermediate positions.[9]

9. Several American scholars have tried their hands at taxonomies of policy options toward Eastern Europe. Francis Miko presents four basic approaches, two focused on superpower relationships and two more directly on Eastern Europe: (a) "strategic accommodation," (b) "strategic confrontation," (c) "local constructive engagement," and (d) "local confrontation." See "U.S. Interests, Issues, and Policies in Eastern Europe," in *East European Economies: Slow Growth in the 1980's*, vol. 1: *Economic Performance and Policy,* Hearings before the Joint Economic Committee, 99 Cong. 1 sess. (GPO, 1985), pp. 554–55.

Sarah Meiklejohn Terry arrays five hypothetical policy options, ranging from "hard" to "soft." In abbreviated form, they are: (a) active support of internal opposition efforts so as to destabilize existing regimes; (b) applying sanctions to Eastern Europe in order to influence Soviet behavior; (c) a selective policy of balanced leverage or conditionality; (d) reversion to liberal trade and credit policies—carrots without sticks; and (e)

The extreme end points of the spectrum are not occupied by significant groups anywhere in the West and certainly not by governments or major opposition parties. Full accommodation, in the sense of accepting Soviet imperial control as permanently desirable, is supported only by the dwindling minorities in Western communist parties that are still totally loyal to Moscow. But there is a widely held position, a kind of *faute de mieux* accommodationism, that the West is unable to bring about significant change in conditions in Eastern Europe, that efforts to do so may be dangerously destabilizing, and that hopes for ultimate liberalization must await spontaneous changes within the Soviet Union itself. Therefore, these accommodationists conclude, the West should relax, accept the status quo as normal, and develop such relationships as Eastern Europe permits, with no intention or expectation of altering conditions there.[10]

At the other end of the spectrum, dissolution by force, whether through direct military attack on the Soviet Union or through aid to armed rebellion by East Europeans, has no supporters whatever in the West. Proponents of dissolution instead look upon Eastern Europe as an arena for economic and political warfare against the Soviet Union, notably through policies of economic denial and encouragement to dissidence. In their view a certain minimum living standard is needed in each East European country to maintain internal order. If Western actions can worsen conditions, the Soviets will have to compensate by providing additional economic aid. More active political dissidence will tend to raise the economic threshold and make the USSR's task that much harder. Because the Soviets themselves suffer domestic constraints on resources and shortages of hard currency,

acceptance of Soviet hegemony as legitimate or in any case unchangeable. See "The Soviet Union and Eastern Europe: Implications for U.S. Policy," in Dan Caldwell, ed., *Soviet International Behavior and U.S. Policy Options* (D. C. Heath for the Center for Foreign Policy Development, 1985), p. 34.

F. Stephen Larrabee writes of four options: (a) destabilization, (b) benign neglect, (c) differentiation favoring domestic and external liberalization, and (d) full détente without regard to country-by-country differences. See "Conflict, Convergence, and Coordination," presentation to the review conference, The Future of Western Policies Toward Eastern Europe, at the Brookings Institution, September 24, 1985.

All these taxonomies suffer from mixing objectives and instruments. Depending on the objectives, the tactical means can often be drawn from a number of options, which are therefore not mutually exclusive. But there is obviously a large overlap between them and the analysis presented in this study.

10. This description fits fairly well the attitudes of British governments until the mid-1970s, but not in more recent years; see chapter 7.

the argument continues, at some point the costs of empire may become so high that they will prefer to abandon imperial control. By the same token, any economic transactions with the West that improve conditions in Eastern Europe will only serve to strengthen and prolong Soviet control. Hence the sobriquet describing the dissolutionists as favoring a policy of "the worse the better."

Supporters of transformation as the medium-term objective reject both the thesis that constructive change in Eastern Europe can occur only at the pace of change in the Soviet Union itself and the idea that change can be forced on the imperial system through political-economic pressures. They rather seek an evolutionary process of small steps (*kleine Schritte* in the German phrase) that do not challenge the existence of empire but look to a progressive change in its character. They see "eroding empire" as a process well under way that the West can and should encourage. They would not dispute the existence of a deep Soviet security interest in avoiding aggression from or through Eastern Europe and would not seek a shift of allegiance to the Western alliance. Thus they would recognize that Eastern Europe falls within a legitimate Soviet sphere of influence but reject categorically the idea that it should be an exclusive sphere of influence. Nor would they expect that erosion would go unnoticed by Moscow. It would suffice that at each stage of the evolutionary process the changes would not warrant the costly countermeasure of suppression by Soviet force. To the extent that liberalizing changes help to legitimize regimes, moreover, even as their character is being altered, the Soviets themselves might ultimately recognize those changes as contributing to security.

As set forth in chapter 4, the consistent main line of U.S. policy since 1956 has been in the middle of the spectrum, that is, transformationist. Most of the dissenters in Washington have leaned toward some aspects of dissolution, so the American position might be described as transformationist-plus. In Western Europe, however, although prevailing policies have also aimed broadly at transformation, there is far greater support for substantial accommodation, leading to an overall posture of transformationist-minus.

West Germany and the United States, each for reasons of its own, have more activist policies than others, so that convergence or conflict between them is especially important for the West as a whole. That a version of transformationism-minus is at the core of West German

Ostpolitik is implied by Josef Joffe's heading in chapter 5, "The Problems of Policy: How to Change the Status Quo through Its Acceptance." The cardinal aim of the policy is transformation in East Germany, decisively in inter-German relations and substantially in internal conditions as well. But that objective has made for a more accommodationist attitude toward the rest of Eastern Europe, for fear that instability there might impel the Soviets to force a reversal of progress in *Deutschlandpolitik*. That fear accounts for Bonn's re-strained sympathy for Solidarity in 1980–81 and Helmut Schmidt's seeming nonchalance when martial law was declared in Poland while he was on a visit to East Germany. The accommodationist element in West German policy is reinforced by the relatively high economic stakes in trade and investment in Eastern Europe, especially for specific firms and industrial sectors, even though the overall economic involvement remains small. In addition, although it is hard to know how the party would act if restored to power, the general foreign policy attitude of the opposition Social Democrats is more accom-modationist than the Christian Democratic–Free Democratic coalition.

As chapter 6 shows, French objectives in Eastern Europe are harder to define. The framework has included a consistent long-term aspi-ration for transformation; during the years of de Gaulle there was also a seeming strategy—at least in words—for a general European settlement. More recently, however, and despite strong historical and cultural ties to the region, France's low foreign policy priority for Eastern Europe has inhibited any systematic approach. In that situ-ation, policy becomes heavily influenced by particularist economic interests and therefore tilted in an accommodationist direction. Italy's position is similar.

In the United Kingdom in recent years, transformationist objectives and a policy of limited differentiation have been not unlike those of the United States, with special emphasis under the New *Ostpolitik* since 1983. But they are at a far lower level of intensity, justifying the term "sideshow" for London's general attitude. At the same time, as chapter 7 shows, Britain's strong interest in avoiding conflict between its American and continental European ties makes it a natural promoter of convergence among the Western allies. As in Germany, the opposition (Labour) party, even if tempered by a return to power, would certainly tend to be more accommodationist than the presently governing Conservatives or the Liberal–Social Democratic Party Alliance if that group should figure in a future government.

There are a few residues of classic European balance-of-power thinking among dwindling numbers of French advocates of renewed entente with Russia against the specter of German "revanchism." There are also Germans nostalgic for the spirit of Rapallo who advocate a new deal with the USSR at the expense of Eastern Europe. But these are fringe opinions, carrying as little weight as the sporadic contentions of some Americans that Western sanctions could readily bring about the early collapse of the Soviet economy.

Somewhat surprisingly, differences in attitudes toward Eastern Europe do not completely correlate with attitudes toward the USSR. There is of course substantial correlation: a stronger continuing West European desire for détente, at least in Europe, matched by a somewhat more accommodating attitude toward East European regimes and a lesser interest in differentiation than shown by the United States. But the renewed American hostility toward the USSR after 1979 did not apply to Eastern Europe except for Poland (after December 1981), an exception for reasons peculiar to Poland. This study also refutes the common observation that Western Europe is interested in Eastern Europe for its own sake, whereas U.S. interest is essentially derived from relations with the Soviets. While that observation is clearly true for West Germany's relationship with East Germany and for the special case of Austria, and may have been true for France under de Gaulle, for the rest of Western Europe and for France today, the direct interest in Eastern Europe appears less intense than the American.

In one respect attitudes all over Western Europe show almost complete convergence: the desirability of renewed détente between the superpowers, at least regionally in Europe and preferably more widely. This convergence does not imply endorsement of all aspects of the Nixon era détente or a readiness to make unilateral concessions to the USSR, as the French and British insistence on their own strategic nuclear forces demonstrates. But regional détente, as chapter 5 emphasizes, is a sine qua non for West German *Ostpolitik*. And for all West Europeans there is the lurking fear that a superpower confrontation might inadvertently make their homelands a battleground. Hence the united support for an unremitting East-West search for common ground and mutually beneficial negotiations. And hence the fears inspired by the rhetoric of American "megaphone diplomacy" in the early 1980s and the hopes inspired by the revival of Soviet-American summitry in 1985.

POLICY INSTRUMENTS AND TACTICS

Differences in operational objectives among Western governments are naturally reflected in tactical applications of policy instruments and are reinforced by straightforward differences in degrees of economic interest. Since the main potential for Western influence is through economic relations, economic policy instruments are a large component of day-to-day Western actions vis-à-vis Eastern Europe and present the most frequent occasions for tension and disputes within the West. Appendix table A-3 compares Eastern Europe's share of the total trade of the Western countries reviewed in this study. While it is not very large for any, the range in 1985 is striking: 0.4 percent for the United States, 0.9 for Britain, 1.1 for France, 1.8 for Italy, 3.6 for West Germany, and 6.7 for Austria. With the USSR added to Eastern Europe, the figures for Western Europe, except in the case of Britain, rise dramatically. As noted in earlier chapters, moreover, particular regions and industries are more dependent on Eastern export markets than these overall national figures suggest. So it is not surprising that disagreements have flared within the West on export controls, technology transfer, export subsidies, investment guarantees, conditionality for economic favors (carrots for what?) and sanctions for objectionable behavior (sticks for what?).

Political and diplomatic relationships also show tactical differences. Even in the area of government-to-peoples policies, notwithstanding the broad consensus on helping to maintain the general Western orientation of Eastern Europe, there have been occasional serious conflicts, such as when Willy Brandt and Helmut Schmidt in turn urged closing down Radio Free Europe to the consternation of Washington.

More broadly, there are at least two significant differences of foreign policy principle between the German Federal Republic and the United States, the two main actors on the Western side. With the transcendent exception of the GDR, West Germany has favored synchronization rather than differentiation in its approach to individual East European countries and has been more solicitous than the United States of Soviet sensibilities in the region. The priorities are naturally different: the Federal Republic is overwhelmingly preoccupied with East Germany, while ethnic group interests generate special American concern for events in Poland, Czechoslovakia, and

Hungary. Yet the identity of strategic interests in the security of Western Europe and the substantial overlap in medium-term objectives for Eastern Europe itself should make it possible, although not easy or automatic, for skillful policy managers to prevent these differences from generating major friction between West Germany and the United States.

THE DANGERS FOR WESTERN COHESION

There is no inherent reason for seeking identity or even convergence of Western policies toward Eastern Europe for its own sake. Conflicts are significant only in three kinds of cases: when they become so severe as to threaten Western cohesion more broadly; when the actions of one Western country frustrate the aims of another; and when convergent actions might bring about results desired by all but fail to do so because of inadequate consultative or coordinating arrangements—in effect, cases of missed opportunities. With respect to conflicts that threaten Western cohesion, what is at stake is not only the North Atlantic alliance, the West's principal security instrument, but also other forms of closer or wider Western association such as the European Communities and the Organization for Economic Cooperation and Development.

Eastern Europe has been involved in two alliance-threatening episodes: the Berlin crisis of 1958–61 and the Urengoi natural gas pipeline dispute of 1982. The former was resolved in the short run by the building of the Berlin Wall and more lastingly by West Germany's changed *Ostpolitik* and the Four Power agreement of 1971. The latter was not truly caused by differences over Eastern Europe. Poland was the pretext, but the real issue was the merits of economic pressures against the Soviet Union. There were adventitious factors arising from different interpretations of the nominal understandings "agreed" upon at the Versailles summit in June 1982. And there was intense resentment in Europe against the retroactive and extraterritorial application of American sanctions against exporters of pipeline equipment, as there had been in previous decades concerning West European exporters to China and Cuba. When it became clear that the dispute was doing more damage to Western unity than to the Soviet Union and that the pipeline construction would in any event not be greatly delayed, the United States wisely withdrew the most stringent sanctions against West European exporters in return for joint exploration of Western interests in related energy issues. Whether any lasting damage was done is hard to assess, but many observers view the affair as contributing to a progressive erosion of NATO cohesion. It was certainly sufficiently serious to warrant precautions against a repetition.

Lesser economic policy differences on such matters as the coverage of strategic export controls or limits on export credit subsidies are probably inescapable and not life-threatening to Western cohesion. The main target of export controls is the USSR, and no one disputes that weapons secured by East European governments automatically and instantaneously become available to the Soviet Union. This is also the case for most dual-purpose high-technology items, with occasional marginal exceptions involving fixed installations in Eastern Europe. The more important differences concern U.S. unilateral export restrictions on items other than those agreed upon in CoCom and then applied to European licensees of U.S. technology. In an ideal world the continuous multilateral updating of CoCom lists, dropping obsolescent items and adding the most sensitive new developments, would solve this problem by making unilateral restrictions unnecessary. That ideal is not presently in sight. Yet there is increasing recognition that enforcement of agreed restraints, including control over re-exports, and avoidance of industrial espionage and other illicit technology transfers may be more important than enlarging the formal coverage of the lists.[11]

In any event, agreement on two straightforward basic principles could greatly reduce the intensity of intra-Western differences on this issue: that CoCom restraints should be imposed only for strategic reasons and not on foreign policy grounds, and that nonstrategic exports to Eastern Europe should be treated like normal exports to other countries in similar income classes—neither more favorably nor less. Export subsidies would then be reserved for low-income developing countries. Disputes as to what constitutes a subsidy would be assimilated into the general discussions of trade policy rather than focused on Eastern Europe. Most other intra-Western disputes over trade with Eastern Europe simply reflect competition for markets.

11. For a comprehensive review of these issues, see Bruce Parrott, ed., *Trade, Technology, and Soviet-American Relations* (Indiana University Press in association with the Center for Strategic and International Studies, 1985).

They are natural to open and competitive economic systems and need not be construed as harbingers of new Rapallos or of creeping Finlandization.

The issues of mutually frustrating actions and missed opportunities are subtle and not easy to evaluate. They involve two closely related policy instruments: conditionality for favorable treatment and sanctions against objectionable behavior. Conditionality is a natural instrument of a transformationist strategy, since in most cases the conditions are designed to promote internal liberalization. If one Western country is seeking a particular set of conditions while others are offering similar favors unconditionally, the strategy can easily be frustrated, although sometimes a single country (usually either West Germany or the United States) has sufficient leverage by itself to secure the results it desires. An accommodationist strategy would not trouble itself with such issues, since it is premised on the absence of Western influence.

Sanctions are the reverse side of the coin of conditionality. On this topic opinions conflict on both sides of the Atlantic. Some hold that sanctions never succeed, others that positive ones (carrots) do but not negative sticks. Still others advocate sanctions every time any foreign government does anything objectionable, as much to gain domestic political support as in the hope of influencing foreign behavior. Disputes over sanctions against South Africa, Libya, and Syria exemplify the dilemmas as much as Eastern Europe. Several recent scholarly studies offer some possibility of common ground: recognition that sanctions can be effective when the stakes for the sanctioner are less than for the sanctionee and the desired change of behavior is not considered by the latter an issue of high national prestige or vital interest.[12] Collectively applied sanctions have often failed, but they are obviously more likely to succeed than unilateral ones. And the notion that carrots can succeed but not sticks is inherently illogical, since the withdrawal of one automatically becomes the other. Carrots

12. See Robin Renwick, *Economic Sanctions,* Harvard Studies in International Affairs 45 (Harvard Center for International Affairs, 1981); Gary Clyde Hufbauer and Jeffrey J. Schott, assisted by Kimberly Ann Elliot, "Economic Sanctions in Support of Foreign Policy Goals," *Policy in International Economics* (Washington, D.C.: Institute for International Economics, October 1983); and David Buchan, *Western Security and Economic Strategy Towards the East,* Adelphi Papers 192 (London: International Institute for Strategic Studies, 1984).

cease to be a reward for good behavior if their supply continues after the good behavior ceases.

When the negative sanctions of one Western country are deliberately frustrated by another, there is an evident potential for serious interallied controversy. In an extreme case such as the Urengoi pipeline dispute, which arose from unconcealed differences of policy, the only remedy is a change of policy by one of the parties. Nevertheless, more adequate consultative machinery to air complaints of mutual frustration might not only ward off such situations at an early stage but also make inadvertent conflicts less likely.

Missed opportunities are by definition speculative. The discussions in this study of the Polish crisis of 1980–81 show a variety of opinions within each Western country on what might have been done to what effect. But the issue of convergence or conflict is especially acute in relation to future crises in Eastern Europe. The likelihood of crisis is high, even in the coming few years, given the absence of normalization in Poland, the acute economic difficulties of Romania, the tendency toward economic stagnation in Czechoslovakia, Bulgaria, and Hungary, the certainty of successions in leadership in most of the countries of the region, and the ongoing tensions within both Comecon and the Warsaw Pact. In the Polish case, extensive Western consultation in 1980–81, bilaterally and in NATO, led to consensus on how to react to an outright Soviet invasion. But there was not adequate discussion of other contingencies or adequate effort for consensus on how to react to them, a weakness made apparent after the declaration of martial law in December 1981.

Conflicts in policies toward Eastern Europe cannot be isolated from other problems facing the Atlantic alliance. Since the early 1970s the alliance has been under strain from a variety of forces. Without pretending to be exhaustive, any listing would include dissension concerning policies in Southeast Asia, the Middle East, southern Africa, and Central America; a growing American conviction that Europe is not carrying its fair share of the burdens of common defense; a growing European concern that America takes risky unilateral actions without adequate consultation with its allies; a European priority for achieving détente and arms control that contrasts with an American priority for ensuring superpower parity; a series of disputes over economic policies; and the weakening or disappearance of internal consensus on Atlantic policies among major political parties in Germany, Britain, and other member countries.[13]

Eastern Europe does not figure in that listing. Precisely because that region is at the very core of the alliance, however, dissension on policies toward it may be more dangerous than toward remote areas where either American or European interests are marginal. The pipeline dispute of 1982, originating in an issue of secondary importance, threatened at one time to become a major breach. Thus erosion of the Soviet system of imperial control may be paralleled by erosion of Western cohesion. In that competition the West holds the superior cards of shared basic values and voluntary collaboration, but also suffers the vulnerabilities of volatile public opinions and the general democratic priority (in noncrisis times) accorded domestic social and economic issues. Mishandling of policies toward Eastern Europe could be costly indeed, but a well-managed and deliberate effort at agreement on medium-term objectives would help to contain Atlantic erosion while promoting that of the Soviet empire.

Coordination of Objectives and Strategy

The interests of the West, therefore, would be well served by systematic consultations aimed at joint assessment of the conditions and prospects in Eastern Europe and at convergence on objectives and strategy, while seeking no more than flexible harmonization (as outlined below) in policy instruments and tactics.

The starting point would be periodic reviews in each Western capital, perhaps quarterly, at cabinet-committee levels or their equivalent (in the United States at the National Security Council) of what is going on in Eastern Europe, country by country, whether or not there is an active crisis. In Washington the goal would also be advanced

13. These issues are discussed in a steady spate of articles in both U.S. and European journals concerned with foreign policy. Several of the issues are reviewed jointly by American and European authors in the EuropeAmerica publications commissioned by the Council on Foreign Relations in its project on European-American relations, edited by Andrew J. Pierre, four of which had been published by March 1986. For a more extensive bibliography through early 1984, see Michael Smith, *Western Europe and the United States: The Uncertain Alliance* (London: Allen & Unwin, 1984), pp. 122–41.

by annual congressional hearings.[14] Internationally, semiannual joint assessments are now held in NATO by official experts sent from the capitals to Brussels for this purpose. They are, however, essentially exchanges of intelligence information and evaluations. For policy reviews the experts should be joined by high-level officials and report, perhaps once a year, directly to NATO foreign ministers. Similar arrangements could be institutionalized as part of the European Community's political consultations. The objective is not to create an artificial atmosphere of continuous crisis but to maintain a watchful eye on developments within and among East European countries and to foster modifications of ongoing national policies as conditions warrant.

Beyond periodic joint assessments, it would be highly desirable to seek broad agreement on medium-term policy objectives. Even if not fully successful, the attempt could help clarify thinking in all Western capitals. It might be initiated through discussions among foreign policy planning staffs with their conclusions reviewed at higher levels, possibly resulting in a formal paper along the lines of NATO's celebrated Harmel report of 1967 that delineated the basic political strategy of the alliance. The first stage of discussions would be informal and bilateral between West Germany and the United States. From there they would move to the "Quad" (United States, West Germany, France, and Britain), and then be expanded to include Italy and Canada and finally NATO as a whole. As for economic issues, assessments and reviews of policy on Eastern Europe should become a regular responsibility of the OECD. Both political and economic reviews should be carried on at least at the assistant-secretary level and then placed on the agenda for undersecretaries and ultimately cabinet ministers. The process might reveal greater agreement than anticipated, or it could identify and define areas of serious disagreement and explore ways of containing their effects.

Policies toward Eastern Europe, of course, are not quasi-academic exercises conducted by planning staffs in isolation from political

14. It is remarkable that a presentation along these lines by Deputy Assistant Secretary of State for European Affairs William H. Luers in 1978 was described as the first of its kind. See *U.S. Policy Toward Eastern Europe,* Hearings before the Subcommittee on Europe and the Middle East of the House Committee on International Relations, 95 Cong. 2 sess. (GPO, 1979), p. 2. A somewhat similar review was made by Assistant Secretary of State Rozanne Ridgway in the autumn of 1985. See *Developments in Europe, November 1985,* Hearings before the Subcommittee on Europe and the Middle East of the House Foreign Affairs Committee, 99 Cong. 1 sess. (GPO, 1986).

pressures and bureaucratic tensions. The reviews of policymaking processes in chapters 4 through 8 show how these forces differ among the principal Western capitals. Nowhere does the foreign ministry have sole responsibility and, especially at moments of crisis, heads of government are likely to take over. In the Federal Republic, *Ostpolitik* is of such central political interest that the chancellor and party leaders are bound to be deeply involved. In France there is a tradition of foreign policy surprises hurled like thunderbolts from the Elysée Palace, a practice that may become further complicated in the period of "cohabitation" between opposing political forces in the presidency and the Chamber of Deputies. Policymaking influence in Washington is even more diffuse. And in all the Western nations, knowledge of Eastern Europe does not have sufficient priority in the defense ministries and war colleges. Coordination between the defense and foreign affairs ministries also leaves a great deal to be desired. These circumstances make a formal international effort at policy agreement even more important, since, as the annual economic summits among the Western Big Seven demonstrate, a major merit of such meetings is to induce policy consolidation within each participating government.

In terms of the accommodation-transformation-dissolution spectrum, the only possibility of securing broad agreement in the West would be in the transformationist middle. That would mean less bias toward dissolution in Washington and less bias toward accommodation in the various West European governments, especially the West German. The search for agreement would require open-mindedness on all sides because the Atlantic alliance has long since left the era, if it ever really existed, of automatic acceptance of U.S. or any other single-nation leadership. The search would have to include a common approach to two of the central dilemmas of policy toward Eastern Europe: stability versus peaceful change, and regimes versus societies or peoples.

On military stability Western governments are already in full agreement. No Western country will give assistance to armed rebellions: their occurrence would risk possible escalation into European hostilities across the East-West divide and perhaps into global warfare, whose avoidance is the highest priority for all. The West certainly objects to Soviet military interventions, and the collective warnings in 1980–81 may have had some weight in warding one off in Poland. But it is in no position to advise East European governments or security forces whether they should offer military resistance. The West need not, however, go out of its way to discourage resistance, as some historians believe was done in Czechoslovakia in 1968.

Policies toward political or economic stability are necessarily more complex. Peaceful change in authoritarian societies is rarely initiated from the top, since rulers normally have the greatest stake in the status quo. There are some exceptions; occasionally leaders of vision promote reforms because they find the status quo profoundly unsatisfactory for their nations, even though they are its personal beneficiaries. Deng Xiaoping and János Kádár appear to fit this mold, as did Alexander Dubček in his brief moment of glory. So does Mikhail Gorbachev, although the results remain to be seen. Most regimes, however, are unlikely to break the inertia of the status quo unless confronted by visible domestic discontent or feeling other kinds of pressure from outside. Hence it is logical for the West to deal with governments on a state-to-state basis and at the same time to reinforce popular dissatisfaction through broadcasting and other government-to-people and people-to-people relationships. Such activities do not constitute efforts to destabilize in the sense of overthrowing regimes; they are calculated to help shake regimes out of their lethargy and add a constructive push to the internal forces for change.

A two-handed strategy of that type clearly requires positive engagement with the East European governments—not indiscriminate but purposive engagement. Concern about legitimizing unpopular and objectionable regimes is understandable, but if they are not going to be dislodged by external force or internal revolution, that concern is not a sound basis for policy. Transformation rather than dissolution must be sought in domestic terms as well as in the character of Soviet imperial control. So there is no inconsistency in recognizing that change—whether initiated from above or in response to popular pressure—necessarily involves action by governments, while at the same time adding pressure for change through direct contacts with societies. The impression of excessive legitimation can be avoided by firmly rebuffing East European protests against government-to-people contacts and activities.

FLEXIBLE HARMONIZATION

In music, harmony not only does not require unison but depends on different pitches played at the same time. So in the tactical application of policy instruments, uniformity of policies would be undesirable even if feasible. The best means for pursuing agreed or closely similar objectives vary greatly among Western countries for reasons of geography, history, cultural tradition, economics, and politics. And sometimes a division of labor within the West, whether planned or spontaneous, can be more effective than concerted action. That has been demonstrated in the Helsinki follow-up negotiations, in which West European nations have on occasion succeeded in promoting positions with the East Europeans that would be resisted if sponsored by the United States. In political relations, history and geography have created special ties between particular countries in East and West that should be fully utilized in pursuit of the broad common objectives. In economic relations a division of labor is inescapable.

For some instruments of policy, there is no merit in seeking even the loosest form of coordination, which is the simple exchange of information. Examples include cultural exchanges, travel and tourism, family visits, and the general run of normal diplomatic relationships. At the other extreme there is a very limited category in which identical rules are essential to achieving the objectives. The clearest case is export controls on truly strategic military products and militarily applicable high technologies. For most other relationships, exchanges of information would generally be useful to all participants. A few would function more effectively with coordinating arrangements; they include broad agreement on policies for East-West trade and credits and guidelines for broadcasting. It would be going too far to try to coordinate high-level political visits, although exchanges of impressions following such visits are natural raw material for joint assessments.

The key desiderata for harmony are convergence on medium-term objectives and regularized policy discussions in which reciprocal grievances can be aired and suspicions laid to rest. In the economic field, transformationist purposes are more likely to be promoted through a broadening of relations with Eastern Europe than a narrowing. Within the suggested general guideline of treating non-strategic trade and finance in Eastern Europe on normal terms, neither subsidized nor specially restricted, there is ample room for argument about what constitutes normality or subsidy. By the nature of centrally planned and state-run trading economies, transactions cannot take place on exactly the same terms as interchange among private firms using convertible currencies and competing both as buyers and sellers in open international markets. Nor can rules of the General Agreement on Tariffs and Trade concerning most-favored-nation treatment and nondiscrimination be fully applied where the state has a monopoly of foreign trade. The West may therefore need to develop special guidelines to approximate normal economic relationships as closely as possible, especially for participation in large investment projects.

Such guidelines will tend to work in the direction of economic liberalization within Eastern Europe. Had the Western banks required standard economic data at both project and national levels as a condition for their loans in the 1970s, some of the excesses that supposedly substituted for reform would have been avoided. By the same token it was entirely appropriate for both private and official lenders to act more liberally toward Hungary during the 1981–82 liquidity crisis than toward Poland or Romania. Western countries are often engaged in sharp commercial rivalry for Eastern markets, so it would be unrealistic to hope for identical Western policies in these matters. But regular consultations among their economic authorities could help advance the basic objective. East European participation in the International Monetary Fund, the World Bank, and GATT provides further opportunities for the West to encourage liberalizing reforms without the complicating factors of bilateral political relationships. Western objectives would be well served, therefore, by the widest possible East European membership in these institutions.

Imposing political conditions on the East in return for favorable economic treatment is more controversial but cannot be ruled out in principle. In some cases, such as Bonn's bargaining with East Berlin on terms of family visits, unilateral conditions are appropriate. In others the adoption of parallel or identical conditions by a number of important Western economic partners could clearly be more effective. At a minimum there should be sufficient intra-Western coordination to keep one country's efforts from being inadvertently frustrated by the others.

It would not be easy for the West to implement these proposals for seeking convergence on medium-term objectives and flexible harmonization in operational tactics. Beyond the complexity and variety of policymaking processes already mentioned lie differences in public attitudes and perceptions that reflect back into domestic politics. Democracies tend to prefer dramatic interventions to the kind of steady, long-haul policies advocated here. There is also some inescapable tension between the historical fatalism of European cultures and America's traditional optimism. A successful effort could not be limited to discussions among chancelleries; it would also require serious attention to the education of Western publics on these aspects of East-West relationships. Yet the obstacles should not be insuperable, given the degree of broad consensus on ultimate goals and the importance of the stakes at issue.

CRISIS MANAGEMENT

Periods of crisis in Eastern Europe pose additional challenges for harmonizing Western policies. The West's record is poor: it has generally failed to anticipate crises, failed to concert maximum potential leverage on the outcome, and wasted considerable breath on recriminations in the aftermath. Although some crises are inherently unforeseeable, the best possible efforts should go toward improving intelligence and improving analysis of available intelligence. Standard arrangements for exchanging information and assessments should be reinforced when warning signals of instability go up in an East European country. As to concerting leverage, the West's collective warnings against Soviet military intervention in Poland were a major improvement over the experiences during the Hungarian Revolution in 1956 and the Czechoslovak crisis in 1968. But Western coordination was greatly facilitated by the long-drawn-out timing of the Polish crisis, something that cannot be depended on in the future. Nor did coordination extend to the contingency of repression by internal Polish forces actually encountered in 1981, not because policymakers failed to consider that possibility but because they did not press sufficiently for explicit agreement or disagreement on the appropriate reaction. Efforts to coordinate economic policies toward Poland during the crisis also left a lot to be desired, partly because of the disarray in Washington described in chapter 4. The postcrisis recriminations were partly efforts to find scapegoats for politically unappetizing events, but they also reflected the absence of agreed objectives of policy.

The precise shape of East European crises has always been unpredictable, even by well-informed citizens and officials of the countries directly involved. Nevertheless, since some kind of crisis somewhere in the region is highly likely within the next few years, the time to improve arrangements for coordinated Western crisis management is now. To use an old New England saying, that would be "fixing the roof while the sun is shining."

INSTITUTIONS FOR COORDINATION

There is no dearth of formal machinery for coordinating Western policies toward Eastern Europe. Within Western Europe, the political consultations developed by the European Community are likely to be strengthened by recent decisions of the member governments. The United States has worked out practical arrangements for informal liaison with these consultations. For matters affecting Berlin and inter-German relations, there are special consultations among the Federal Republic and the three Western "occupying" powers that could readily be extended to include regular discussions of Eastern Europe. Periodic exchanges of information among NATO member countries' ambassadors in Eastern Europe and semiannual assessments at NATO meetings of experts are now directed more at exchanges of information than at policy harmonization, but they could be converted to policy reviews along the lines suggested here. The OECD deals with credit policies of all the advanced Western countries, including Japan and the countries of Oceania as well as those of Europe and North America. And there are opportunities for coordination, whether or not they are used, through Western caucuses in the larger multilateral institutions—CSCE conferences, the IMF, World Bank, and GATT, and the relevant United Nations agencies.

All of this machinery, however, can be spinning its gears unless the Western nations make a serious effort to agree on operational objectives and to define policy areas for harmonization. The concluding years of the 1980s seem an especially propitious time for such an effort. There is new leadership in the Kremlin, the prospect of new leadership in most of Eastern Europe, a widely felt need in the region to adapt to new technologies and a changing global economic environment, and an ongoing redefinition of superpower relationships. In short, powerful forces move toward fluidity beneath the misleading surface of apparent stability.

The Stakes

Although the pace of change in Eastern Europe is slow, its potential significance is huge. Assuming that nuclear catastrophe will be avoided, change in Eastern Europe can be a critical factor in the evolution, and ultimately in the resolution, of the great East-West strategic and ideological competition of our era. In its present form the Soviet imperial system in Eastern Europe is a failing system whose regimes enlist neither wholehearted domestic support nor voluntary loyalty to the imperial center. Its former attraction for considerable numbers in Western Europe has virtually disappeared, marked by the apostasy of the Italian Communist party, Western Europe's largest. The security apparatuses, ultimately backed by Soviet troops, will prevent outright breakaways or revolutions, but the system as it stands does not and cannot satisfy all the material, political, or spiritual desires of the peoples. The appearance of stasis is illusory and continued erosion is more than likely.

Change that directly threatens the physical security of the Soviet Union is surely to be ruled out. The West has no interest in promoting that kind of change and should leave no doubt on that score. But change that adds to domestic legitimacy in Eastern Europe, even if it initially raises Soviet fears, might in due course come to be understood as advantageous for the genuine security interests of the USSR. The signals from Moscow during Gorbachev's early period as general secretary, including the Twenty-Seventh Party Congress, confirm the dilemma of cohesion versus viability and suggest an ongoing debate on how to cope with it, since it cannot be fully resolved.

Moscow is clearly trying to increase Eastern Europe's contribution to Soviet economic growth, both by improving the quality of goods traded for Soviet raw materials and by securing greater participation in joint projects planned through Comecon. The latter is an old story. It is hard to see why it should enlist more East European enthusiasm now than with similar Soviet efforts in the past. Nor are the conditions of lowered world oil prices and strains on its own oil production likely to enhance Soviet leverage. The Soviets are making no visible effort to limit East European economic dealings with the West or to constrain such systemic experimentation—including Hungary's—as the individual countries may choose to pursue. Given the widening gap in civilian technology between the West and the entire Comecon bloc, the announced goals of higher productivity and intensive growth should encourage continuing or even enlarged trade and investment relations with the West. Reversion to Stalinist conformity or a closed Eastern economic bloc would be grossly counterproductive for the USSR itself, as well as for Eastern Europe. So erosion and transformation are likely to continue. And there should be broad scope for continued Western influence on the direction of change, however slow the pace.

Where it may ultimately lead, and when, is for the future to reveal. For Western policy purposes the essential goal is movement in the right direction. Imagination need not be limited to previous models, just as the internal conditions and external relations of today's Hungary, East Germany, and Poland were not foreseen even a decade ago. If the pressures for systemic economic liberalization become irresistible, as many Western analysts believe will happen sooner in Eastern Europe but also inescapably in the USSR itself, some degree of political liberalization is likely to follow. This might take place within the structure of the ruling communist parties rather than through formal pluralism. Parallel changes could strengthen the tendencies toward greater national autonomy within Comecon and the Warsaw Pact. Coupled with new East-West confidence-building measures, they could enhance the sense of security on both sides that military confrontation is unlikely, easing the path toward more general arms limitation understandings.

In this order of speculation, formal revision—either of domestic institutions or of international relationships—comes late rather than early. If one aspect is to be the thinning out of Soviet troop dispositions in Eastern Europe, it would probably require a counterpart on the Western side, a genuinely "mutual and balanced" force reduction. One can imagine the Austrian or Finnish models eventually extended to parts of Eastern Europe, but in the nearer term new forms of partly autonomous association with the USSR in a nominally socialist commonwealth seem more likely. Formal revisionism is for the remote future; it must be preceded by de facto changes in attitudes and institutions. The challenge for the West is to use its collective influence wisely to accelerate such changes.

Appendix Tables

Table A-1. *Eastern Europe and the West: Relative Economic Standing, Based on Purchasing Power Parities, by Country, 1980*

Country	Population (millions)	GNP (billions of U.S. dollars)	GNP per capita (U.S. dollars)
East Germany	16.7	98.7	5,910
Czechoslovakia	15.3	72.5	4,740
Hungary	10.7	47.0	4,390
Poland	35.6	132.8	3,730
Bulgaria	8.9	31.6	3,550
Romania	22.2	59.5	2,680
Eastern Europe total	109.4	442.1	4,040
Soviet Union	265.5	1,112.4	4,190
Warsaw Pact total	374.9	1,554.5	4,150
West Germany	61.6	622.2	10,100
France	53.7	518.7	9,660
United Kingdom	55.9	395.8	7,080
Italy	57.1	370.6	6,490
Other NATO Europe[a]	137.9	663.3	4,810
NATO Europe total	366.2	2,570.6	7,020
United States	227.7	2,623.1	11,520
Canada	24.0	243.4	10,140
NATO total	617.9	5,437.1	8,800
Austria	7.5	63.7	8,490
Finland	4.8	38.9	8,100
Sweden	8.3	90.1	10,860
Japan	116.8	991.6	8,490

Sources: Population from United Nations Department of International and Social Affairs, Statistical Office, *Demographic Yearbook, 1981* (New York: UN, 1981), pp. 177–80. GNPs per capita for Eastern Europe and the USSR are the "adjusted purchasing power" estimates for 1980 from Paul Marer, *Dollar GNPs of the U.S.S.R. and Eastern Europe* (Johns Hopkins University Press for the World Bank, 1985), p. 7 (for Bulgaria, the commercial exchange rate was used rather than an adjusted purchasing power parity proxy exchange rate). Data for the principal NATO member countries and for Austria and Japan are based on the 1975 estimates in "international dollars" of the Kravis study—Irving B. Kravis, Alan Heston, and Robert Summers, *World Product and Income: International Comparisons of Real Gross Product* (Johns Hopkins University Press for the World Bank, 1982), p. 12. The 1975 estimates are adjusted to 1980 in proportion to real growth data reported by the Organization for Economic Cooperation and Development and the International Monetary Fund—(see IMF, *International Financial Statistics: Supplement on Output Statistics* (Washington: IMF, 1984), pp. 18–21—and converted to 1980 prices in proportion to the U.S. GNP price deflators as found in *Economic Report of the President*, February 1984. For other countries, official data on GNP per capita, converted to dollars at market exchange rates, are adjusted in proportion to Kravis study estimates for countries in similar income groups. All figures on GNP per capita have been rounded to the nearest ten.

a. Includes Spain, which became a member in 1982.

Table A-2. *Eastern Europe Comparative Economic Growth Rates, by Country, Selected Periods, 1960–85*
Compound annual rates of growth of total GNP

Country	1960–65	1965–70	1970–75	1976	1977	1978	1979	1980	1981	1982	1983	1984	1985
East Germany	2.9	3.1	3.5	2.0	3.0	1.7	2.8	2.1	2.1	−0.4	1.8	3.2	2.4
Czechoslovakia	2.0	3.4	3.4	1.8	4.3	1.6	0.8	2.3	−0.5	−2.0	1.5	2.7	1.7
Hungary	4.2	3.0	3.3	0.3	6.3	2.4	0.3	1.0	0.7	3.7	−1.0	2.7	−0.9
Poland	4.1	4.0	6.5	2.5	1.9	3.5	−1.8	−2.4	−5.3	−1.0	4.9	3.4	1.6
Bulgaria	6.3	5.1	4.7	3.0	−1.0	2.2	3.8	−2.9	2.7	3.2	−1.8	2.9	−0.8
Romania	5.0	4.9	6.7	10.8	2.5	4.7	3.6	−1.5	0.2	2.6	0.0	4.6	1.8
Eastern Europe total	3.7	3.7	4.9	3.2	2.8	2.8	1.0	−0.3	−1.0	0.9	1.8	3.3	1.4
Eastern Europe except for Poland	3.6	3.6	4.1	3.6	3.3	2.5	2.2	0.7	0.9	1.8	0.5	3.3	1.3

Sources: For 1970–75 and all subsequent years, see Thad P. Alton and others, *Research Project on National Income in East Central Europe*, occasional papers 90–94 (New York: L. W. International Financial Research, 1986), p. 22. For 1965–70, see Thad P. Alton and others, *Research Project on National Income in East Central Europe*, occasional papers 75–79 (New York: L. W. International Financial Research, 1983), p. 21. For 1960–65, see Thad P. Alton, "Economic Growth and Resource Allocation in Eastern Europe," *Reorientation and Commercial Relations of the Economies of Eastern Europe* Joint Economic Committee, 93 Cong. 2 sess. (GPO, 1974), pp. 268, 274.

Table A-3. *Western Trade with Eastern Europe, by Western Country, Selected Years, 1965–85*
Millions of U.S. dollars unless otherwise specified (exports f.a.s., imports c.i.f.)

Country	1965	1970	1975	1980	1981	1982	1983	1984	1985	Eastern Europe + USSR 1985
Western exports to Eastern Europe										
United States	94	235	950	2,343	1,901	1,000	884	894	781	3,204
West Germany	743	1,535	5,237	7,983	6,664	6,278	6,027	5,554	6,414	10,017
(Inter-German)	(302)	(660)	(1,594)	(2,908)	(2,467)	(2,626)	(2,724)	(2,247)	(2,684)	
France	229	375	1,456	2,170	2,058	1,272	1,102	1,006	1,022	2,904
United Kingdom	195	376	830	1,568	1,219	883	758	758	842	1,529
Austria	186	287	1,064	1,630	1,327	1,184	1,259	1,199	1,251	1,904
Italy	225	394	1,150	1,457	1,190	936	836	883	1,100	2,643
Japan	43	106	574	810	749	574	743	483	569	3,341
All industrial countries	2,229	4,111	14,834	22,938	19,264	15,441	14,659	13,974	15,308	35,958

Western imports from Eastern Europe

United States	96	163	519	1,070	1,315	912	1,096	1,749	1,666	2,109
West Germany	693	1,306	3,272	7,542	6,295	5,972	5,822	5,932	5,992	10,682
(Inter-German)	(315)	(546)	(1,359)	(3,065)	(2,677)	(2,732)	(2,697)	(2,713)	(2,594)	
France	126	249	923	1,689	1,569	1,446	1,242	1,265	1,289	3,783
United Kingdom	284	347	624	1,147	802	846	866	1,195	1,098	2,034
Austria	174	253	637	1,346	1,188	1,175	1,198	1,296	1,302	2,244
Italy	255	542	1,044	2,258	1,628	1,659	1,677	2,037	1,960	4,971
Japan	35	111	206	259	227	197	289	417	306	1,744
All industrial countries	2,173	3,733	10,216	20,312	17,309	16,252	16,152	17,992	17,824	40,269

Eastern Europe's percentage share of total Western trade (exports plus imports)

United States	0.4	0.5	0.7	0.7	0.6	0.4	0.4	0.5	0.4	0.9
West Germany	4.0	4.3	5.1	4.0	3.8	3.6	3.6	3.5	3.6	6.0
(Inter-German)	(1.7)	(1.8)	(1.8)	(1.5)	(1.5)	(1.6)	(1.7)	(1.5)	(1.5)	⋯
France	1.7	1.7	2.2	1.5	1.6	1.3	1.2	1.1	1.1	3.2
United Kingdom	1.6	1.8	1.5	1.2	1.0	0.9	0.8	1.0	0.9	1.7
Austria	9.7	8.4	10.1	7.1	6.8	6.7	7.1	7.1	6.7	10.9
Italy	3.3	3.3	3.0	2.1	1.7	1.6	1.6	1.9	1.8	4.5
Japan	0.5	0.6	0.7	0.4	0.3	0.3	0.4	0.3	0.3	1.7
All industrial countries	1.8	1.9	2.2	1.7	1.5	1.3	1.3	1.3	1.3	2.9

Source: Calculated from data in tables A-4 through A-12.

Table A-4. *Industrial Countries' Trade with Eastern Europe,*
by East European Country, Selected Years, 1965–85[a]
Millions of U.S. dollars unless otherwise specified (exports f.a.s., imports c.i.f.)

Country	1965	1970	1975	1980	1981	1982	1983	1984	1985
Exports to									
East Germany	571	1,043	2,695	5,331	4,891	4,299	4,675	4,030	4,123
Czechoslovakia	421	725	1,848	2,828	2,296	2,086	1,917	1,866	2,144
Hungary	273	574	1,819	3,178	3,162	2,836	2,539	2,475	2,799
Poland	451	803	5,461	6,335	4,231	3,188	2,858	2,932	3,084
Bulgaria	206	298	1,058	1,532	1,765	1,482	1,496	1,384	1,817
Romania	307	668	1,953	3,734	2,919	1,550	1,174	1,287	1,341
Eastern Europe total	2,229	4,111	14,834	22,938	19,264	15,441	14,659	13,974	15,308
Soviet Union	1,065	2,387	12,395	21,526	21,988	22,752	22,444	21,647	20,650
World (billions of dollars)	118.4	208.8	568.8	1,242	1,221	1,158	1,143	1,217	1,261
Eastern Europe as percent of world	1.9	2.0	2.6	1.8	1.6	1.3	1.3	1.1	1.2
Imports from									
East Germany	544	911	2,346	5,062	4,785	5,035	5,033	4,935	4,819
Czechoslovakia	392	664	1,595	3,076	2,641	2,602	2,518	2,536	2,562
Hungary	258	497	1,222	2,698	2,415	2,247	2,269	2,480	2,549
Poland	591	946	3,122	5,535	3,535	3,257	3,181	3,861	3,889
Bulgaria	128	210	346	762	731	652	568	571	587
Romania	260	505	1,585	3,179	3,202	2,459	2,583	3,609	3,418
Eastern Europe total	2,173	3,733	10,216	20,312	17,309	16,252	16,152	17,992	17,824
Soviet Union	1,531	2,219	8,675	23,616	23,679	25,265	24,399	25,167	22,445
World (billions of dollars)	120.2	212.8	590.7	1,372	1,300	1,222	1,203	1,312	1,363
Eastern Europe as percent of world	1.8	1.8	1.7	1.5	1.3	1.3	1.3	1.4	1.3
Balance with									
East Germany	+27	+132	+349	+269	+106	−736	−358	−905	−696
Czechoslovakia	+29	+61	+253	−248	−345	−516	−601	−670	−418
Hungary	+15	+77	+597	+480	+747	+589	+270	−5	+250
Poland	−140	−143	+2,339	+800	+696	−69	−323	−929	−805
Bulgaria	+78	+88	+712	+770	+1,034	+830	+928	+813	+1,230
Romania	+47	+163	+368	+555	−283	−909	−1,409	−2,322	−2,077
Eastern Europe total	+56	+378	+4,618	+2,626	+1,955	−811	−1,493	−4,018	−2,516
Soviet Union	−466	−168	+3,720	−2,090	−1,691	−2,510	−1,955	−3,520	−1,795
World (billions of dollars)	−1.8	−4.0	−21.9	−130	+79	−64	−60	−95	−102

Sources: Except for trade between West and East Germany, data for 1980–85 are from International Monetary Fund, *Direction of Trade Statistics Yearbook 1986* (Washington, D.C.: IMF, 1986). Data for 1975 are from *Direction of Trade Statistics Yearbook 1982* (Washington, D.C.: IMF, 1982). Data for 1970 are from *Direction of Trade: Annual 1970–76* (Washington, D.C.: IMF, 1977). Data for inter-German trade have been added in, drawn from Statistisches Bundesamt, *Statistisches Jahrbuch für die Bundesrepublik Deutschland, 1986* (Wiesbaden, West Germany: SB, 1986), p. 247, and corresponding tables in earlier annuals, with deutschmarks converted to dollars at the average annual exchange rates published in International Monetary Fund, *International Financial Statistics Yearbook 1986* (Washington, D.C.: IMF, 1986).

a. Industrial countries include the United States, Canada, Japan, Australia, New Zealand, and all of Western Europe except Portugal, Greece, and Turkey.

Table A-5. *U.S. Trade with Eastern Europe, by Country,*
Selected Years, 1965–85

Millions of U.S. dollars unless otherwise specified (exports f.a.s., imports c.i.f.)

Country	1965	1970	1975	1980	1981	1982	1983	1984	1985
Exports to									
East Germany	12	33	17	478	296	223	139	137	73
Czechoslovakia	28	23	53	185	83	84	59	58	63
Hungary	9	28	76	80	78	68	110	88	95
Poland	35	70	583	716	682	295	324	318	238
Bulgaria	4	15	30	162	258	106	66	44	104
Romania	6	66	191	722	504	224	186	249	208
Eastern Europe total	94	235	950	2,343	1,901	1,000	884	894	781
Soviet Union	45	118	1,849	1,515	2,432	2,593	2,003	3,284	2,423
World (billions of dollars)	27.5	43.2	108.1	220.8	233.7	212.3	200.5	217.9	213.2
Eastern Europe as percent of world	0.3	0.5	0.9	1.1	0.8	0.5	0.4	0.4	0.4
Imports from									
East Germany	7	10	12	49	52	59	64	167	102
Czechoslovakia	17	25	38	75	73	68	68	96	85
Hungary	2	7	38	118	140	145	172	242	241
Poland	66	104	263	460	401	229	209	244	248
Bulgaria	2	3	21	27	37	31	30	31	39
Romania	2	14	147	341	612	380	553	969	951
Eastern Europe total	96	163	519	1,070	1,315	912	1,096	1,749	1,666
Soviet Union	43	77	280	486	377	247	375	600	443
World (billions of dollars)	21.4	42.5	105.9	257.0	273.4	254.9	269.9	341.2	361.6
Eastern Europe as percent of world	0.4	0.4	0.5	0.4	0.5	0.4	0.4	0.5	0.5
Balance with									
East Germany	+5	+23	+5	+429	+244	+164	+75	−30	−29
Czechoslovakia	+11	−2	+15	+110	+10	+16	−9	−38	−22
Hungary	+7	+21	+38	−38	−62	−77	−62	−154	−146
Poland	−31	−34	+320	+256	+281	+66	+115	+74	−10
Bulgaria	+2	+12	+9	+135	+221	+75	+36	+13	+65
Romania	+4	+52	+44	+381	−108	−156	−367	−720	−743
Eastern Europe total	−2	+72	+431	+1,273	+586	+88	−212	−855	−885
Soviet Union	+2	+41	+1,569	+1,029	+2,055	+2,346	+1,628	+2,684	+1,980
World (billions of dollars)	+6.1	+3.7	+2.2	−36.2	−39.7	−42.6	−69.4	−123.3	−148.4

Sources: See table A-4.

Table A-6. *West German Trade with Eastern Europe, by Country, Selected Years, 1965–85*

Millions of U.S. dollars unless otherwise specified (exports f.a.s., imports c.i.f.)

Country	1965	1970	1975	1980	1981	1982	1983	1984	1985
Exports to									
East Germany	302	660	1,594	2,908	2,467	2,626	2,724	2,247	2,684
Czechoslovakia	101	289	679	1,036	891	803	758	734	820
Hungary	77	143	582	1,207	1,176	1,086	950	961	1,053
Poland	92	180	1,301	1,459	960	884	833	828	972
Bulgaria	55	66	418	478	501	501	488	470	568
Romania	116	197	663	895	669	378	274	314	317
Eastern Europe total	743	1,535	5,237	7,983	6,664	6,278	6,027	5,554	6,414
Soviet Union	146	422	2,824	4,373	3,394	3,870	4,418	3,800	3,603
World (billions of dollars)	18.2	34.9	91.7	195.8	178.6	179.1	172.2	174.0	186.6
Eastern Europe as percent of world	4.1	4.4	5.7	4.1	3.7	3.5	3.5	3.2	3.4
Imports from									
East Germany	315	546	1,359	3,065	2,677	2,732	2,697	2,713	2,594
Czechoslovakia	84	199	469	1,045	921	845	866	840	859
Hungary	72	134	365	999	886	761	733	722	772
Poland	109	203	582	1,376	943	879	854	971	1,060
Bulgaria	41	65	94	179	206	194	176	151	162
Romania	72	159	403	878	662	561	496	535	545
Eastern Europe total	693	1,306	3,272	7,542	6,295	5,972	5,822	5,932	5,992
Soviet Union	275	342	1,313	4,076	4,072	4,690	4,631	5,031	4,690
World (billions of dollars)	17.9	30.5	76.3	191.1	166.6	158.1	155.6	155.7	161.1
Eastern Europe as percent of world	3.9	4.3	4.3	3.9	3.8	3.8	3.7	3.8	3.7
Balance with									
East Germany	−13	+114	+235	−157	−210	−106	+27	−466	+90
Czechoslovakia	+17	+90	+210	−9	−30	−42	−108	−106	−39
Hungary	+5	+9	+217	+208	+290	+325	+217	+239	+281
Poland	−17	−23	+719	+83	+17	+5	−21	−143	−88
Bulgaria	+14	+1	+324	+299	+295	+307	+312	+319	+406
Romania	+44	+38	+260	+17	+7	−183	−222	−221	−228
Eastern Europe total	+50	+229	+1,965	+441	+369	+306	+205	−378	+422
Soviet Union	−129	+80	+1,511	+297	−678	−820	−213	−1,231	−1,087
World (billions of dollars)	+0.3	+4.4	+15.4	+4.7	+12.0	+21.0	+16.6	+18.3	+25.5

Sources: See table A-4.

Table A-7. *French Trade with Eastern Europe, by Country,*
Selected Years, 1965–85

Millions of U.S. dollars unless otherwise specified (exports f.a.s., imports c.i.f.)

Country	1965	1970	1975	1980	1981	1982	1983	1984	1985
Exports to									
East Germany	69	60	179	316	465	258	258	212	209
Czechoslovakia	35	57	161	160	123	108	115	114	133
Hungary	21	47	166	234	236	198	165	146	169
Poland	36	81	624	825	664	443	318	275	203
Bulgaria	24	48	123	169	157	106	111	104	166
Romania	44	82	203	466	413	159	135	155	142
Eastern Europe total	229	375	1,456	2,170	2,058	1,272	1,102	1,006	1,022
Soviet Union	72	273	1,143	2,465	1,866	1,559	2,240	1,950	1,882
World (billions of dollars)	10.1	18.1	53.1	116.0	106.4	96.7	94.9	97.6	101.7
Eastern Europe as percent of world	2.3	2.1	2.7	1.9	1.9	1.3	1.2	1.0	1.0
Imports from									
East Germany	16	42	164	274	261	284	276	260	293
Czechoslovakia	27	40	104	179	161	172	157	158	160
Hungary	16	27	92	195	177	173	163	163	157
Poland	31	68	352	587	363	330	316	340	302
Bulgaria	7	19	36	47	87	101	68	55	58
Romania	29	53	175	407	520	386	262	289	319
Eastern Europe total	126	249	923	1,689	1,569	1,446	1,242	1,265	1,289
Soviet Union	146	203	770	3,556	3,360	2,884	2,801	2,550	2,494
World (billions of dollars)	10.3	19.1	54.0	134.9	121.0	115.7	105.4	103.7	107.8
Eastern Europe as percent of world	1.2	1.3	1.7	1.3	1.3	1.2	1.2	1.2	1.2
Balance with									
East Germany	+53	+18	+15	+42	+204	−26	−18	−48	−84
Czechoslovakia	+8	+17	+57	−19	−38	−64	−42	−44	−27
Hungary	+5	+20	+74	+39	+59	+25	+2	−17	+12
Poland	+5	+13	+272	+238	+301	+113	+2	−65	−99
Bulgaria	+17	+29	+87	+122	+70	+5	+43	+49	+108
Romania	+15	+29	+28	+59	−107	−227	−127	−134	−177
Eastern Europe total	+103	+126	+533	+481	+489	−174	−140	−259	−267
Soviet Union	−74	+70	+373	−1,091	−1,494	−1,325	−561	−600	−612
World (billions of dollars)	−0.2	−1.0	−0.9	−18.9	−14.6	−19.0	−10.5	−6.1	−6.1

Sources: See table A-4.

Table A-8. *British Trade with Eastern Europe, by Country,*
Selected Years, 1965–85
Millions of U.S. dollars unless otherwise specified (exports f.a.s., imports c.i.f.)

Country	1965	1970	1975	1980	1981	1982	1983	1984	1985
Exports to									
East Germany	23	41	72	219	171	111	92	125	83
Czechoslovakia	41	49	113	188	142	122	104	104	132
Hungary	22	46	99	160	169	136	140	133	141
Poland	71	143	403	689	363	230	230	227	236
Bulgaria	11	27	53	82	69	80	67	74	147
Romania	27	70	90	230	305	204	125	95	103
Eastern Europe total	195	376	830	1,568	1,219	883	758	758	842
Soviet Union	129	245	464	1,058	832	620	676	976	687
World (billions of dollars)	13.7	19.4	44.5	110.1	102.3	96.9	91.6	93.9	101.2
Eastern Europe as percent of world	1.4	1.9	1.9	1.4	1.2	0.9	0.8	0.8	0.8
Imports from									
East Germany	34	39	86	205	186	233	255	264	262
Czechoslovakia	49	55	131	204	142	145	152	154	153
Hungary	19	26	58	101	82	77	82	100	113
Poland	136	151	254	452	270	265	269	360	412
Bulgaria	15	20	16	34	27	36	19	23	29
Romania	31	56	79	151	95	90	89	294	129
Eastern Europe total	284	347	624	1,147	802	846	866	1,195	1,098
Soviet Union	333	528	900	977	846	1,101	1,101	1,123	936
World (billions of dollars)	16.1	21.7	54.2	115.7	102.6	99.6	100.0	104.7	109.0
Eastern Europe as percent of world	1.8	1.6	1.2	1.0	0.8	0.8	0.9	1.1	1.0
Balance with									
East Germany	−11	+2	−14	+14	−15	−122	−163	−139	−179
Czechoslovakia	−8	−6	−18	−16	—	−23	−48	−50	−21
Hungary	+3	+20	+41	+59	+87	+59	+58	+33	+28
Poland	−65	−8	+149	+237	+93	−35	−39	−133	−176
Bulgaria	−4	+7	+37	+48	+42	+44	+48	+51	+118
Romania	−4	+14	+11	+79	+210	+114	+36	−199	−26
Eastern Europe total	−89	+29	+206	+421	+417	+37	−108	−437	−256
Soviet Union	−204	−283	−436	+81	−14	−481	−425	−147	−249
World (billions of dollars)	−2.4	−2.3	−9.7	−5.6	−0.3	−2.7	−8.4	−10.8	−7.8

Sources: See table A-4.

Table A-9. *Austrian Trade with Eastern Europe, by Country, Selected Years, 1965–85*
Millions of U.S. dollars unless otherwise specified (exports f.a.s., imports c.i.f.)

Country	1965	1970	1975	1980	1981	1982	1983	1984	1985
Exports to									
East Germany	28	26	116	229	212	209	351	344	214
Czechoslovakia	37	62	190	237	206	244	199	173	194
Hungary	42	80	270	381	420	378	338	345	444
Poland	32	45	332	468	225	133	170	167	209
Bulgaria	25	27	67	118	119	122	144	114	134
Romania	22	47	89	197	145	98	57	56	56
Eastern Europe total	186	287	1,064	1,630	1,327	1,184	1,259	1,199	1,251
Soviet Union	57	82	217	477	484	551	599	707	653
World (billions of dollars)	1.6	2.9	7.5	17.5	15.8	15.6	15.4	15.7	17.2
Eastern Europe as percent of world	11.6	10.0	14.1	9.3	8.4	7.6	8.2	7.6	7.3
Imports from									
East Germany	26	28	70	165	161	173	152	127	130
Czechoslovakia	38	67	192	452	396	427	410	395	405
Hungary	31	60	138	337	317	278	327	403	416
Poland	46	58	147	240	164	187	196	252	235
Bulgaria	12	11	25	46	45	34	26	33	37
Romania	21	29	65	106	105	76	87	86	79
Eastern Europe total	174	253	637	1,346	1,188	1,175	1,198	1,296	1,302
Soviet Union	53	80	318	1,027	1,301	990	826	979	942
World (billions of dollars)	2.1	3.5	9.4	24.5	21.0	19.5	19.4	19.7	21.0
Eastern Europe as percent of world	8.3	7.1	6.8	5.5	5.6	6.0	6.2	6.6	6.2
Balance with									
East Germany	+2	−2	+46	+64	+51	+36	+199	+217	+84
Czechoslovakia	−1	−5	−2	−215	−190	−183	−211	−222	−211
Hungary	+11	+20	+132	+44	+103	+100	+11	−58	+28
Poland	−14	−13	+185	+228	+61	−54	−26	−85	−26
Bulgaria	+13	+16	+42	+72	+74	+88	+118	+81	+97
Romania	+1	+18	+24	+91	+40	+22	−30	−30	−23
Eastern Europe total	+12	+34	+427	+284	+139	+9	+61	−97	−51
Soviet Union	+4	+2	−101	−550	−817	−439	−227	−272	−289
World (billions of dollars)	−0.5	−0.6	−1.9	−7.0	−5.2	−3.9	−4.0	−4.0	−3.8

Sources: See table A-4.

Table A-10. *Italian Trade with Eastern Europe, by Country, Selected Years, 1965–85*

Millions of U.S. dollars unless otherwise specified (exports f.a.s., imports c.i.f.)

Country	1965	1970	1975	1980	1981	1982	1983	1984	1985
Exports to									
East Germany	16	26	87	140	163	126	85	131	104
Czechoslovakia	42	75	122	177	146	115	119	119	179
Hungary	37	92	190	267	266	230	209	203	238
Poland	50	72	405	382	233	172	191	200	248
Bulgaria	33	50	131	164	151	161	117	137	168
Romania	47	79	215	327	231	132	115	93	163
Eastern Europe total	225	394	1,150	1,457	1,190	936	836	883	1,100
Soviet Union	98	308	1,023	1,267	1,285	1,499	1,884	1,581	1,543
World (billions of dollars)	7.2	13.2	34.8	77.7	75.3	73.5	72.7	73.3	79.0
Eastern Europe as percent of world	3.1	3.0	3.3	1.9	1.6	1.3	1.1	1.2	1.4
Imports from									
East Germany	14	35	87	186	203	163	119	114	127
Czechoslovakia	36	75	126	262	223	250	224	216	219
Hungary	52	122	214	380	277	306	305	302	309
Poland	61	121	307	575	338	287	303	350	307
Bulgaria	31	54	65	255	124	118	101	80	84
Romania	61	135	245	600	463	535	625	975	914
Eastern Europe total	255	542	1,044	2,258	1,628	1,659	1,677	2,037	1,960
Soviet Union	181	282	877	3,063	3,073	3,529	3,582	4,019	3,011
World (billions of dollars)	7.3	14.9	38.4	99.5	91.1	86.2	80.4	84.2	91.0
Eastern Europe as percent of world	3.5	3.6	2.7	2.3	1.8	1.9	2.1	2.4	2.2
Balance with									
East Germany	+2	−9	—	−46	−40	−37	−34	+17	−23
Czechoslovakia	+6	—	−4	−85	−77	−135	−105	−97	−40
Hungary	−15	−30	−24	−113	−11	−76	−96	−99	−71
Poland	−11	−49	+98	−193	−105	−115	−112	−150	−59
Bulgaria	+2	−4	+66	−91	+27	+43	+16	+57	+84
Romania	−14	−56	−30	−273	−232	−403	−510	−882	−751
Eastern Europe total	−30	−148	+106	−801	−438	−723	−841	−1154	−860
Soviet Union	−83	+26	+146	−1,796	−1,788	−2,030	−1,698	−2,438	−1,468
World (billions of dollars)	−0.1	−1.7	−3.6	−21.8	−15.8	−12.7	−7.7	−10.9	−12.0

Sources: See table A-4.

Table A-11. *Japanese Trade with Eastern Europe, by Country, Selected Years, 1965–85*

Millions of U.S. dollars unless otherwise specified (exports f.a.s., imports c.i.f.)

Country	1965	1970	1975	1980	1981	1982	1983	1984	1985
Exports to									
East Germany	1	15	49	139	148	194	326	153	138
Czechoslovakia	9	10	45	64	109	69	62	63	58
Hungary	2	12	33	108	96	73	66	51	84
Poland	5	22	257	230	99	61	79	63	74
Bulgaria	11	21	54	66	111	86	141	83	125
Romania	15	26	136	203	186	91	69	70	90
Eastern Europe total	43	106	574	810	749	574	743	483	569
Soviet Union	168	341	1,626	2,796	3,253	3,893	2,822	2,515	2,772
World (billions of dollars)	8.5	19.3	55.7	130.4	151.5	138.4	147.0	169.7	177.2
Eastern Europe as percent of world	0.5	0.5	1.0	0.6	0.5	0.4	0.5	0.3	0.3
Imports from									
East Germany	1	39	29	40	44	37	30	42	44
Czechoslovakia	7	15	26	50	46	45	51	60	53
Hungary	0	4	11	18	25	22	34	48	52
Poland	2	40	80	62	36	39	57	71	68
Bulgaria	6	9	14	22	18	20	20	66	23
Romania	19	4	46	67	58	34	97	130	66
Eastern Europe total	35	111	206	259	227	197	289	417	306
Soviet Union	240	481	1,169	1,873	2,020	1,668	1,458	1,388	1,438
World (billions of dollars)	8.2	18.9	57.8	141.3	142.9	131.6	126.5	136.1	130.5
Eastern Europe as percent of world	0.4	0.6	0.4	0.2	0.2	0.1	0.2	0.3	0.2
Balance with									
East Germany	...	−24	+20	+99	+104	+157	+296	+111	+94
Czechoslovakia	+2	−5	+19	+14	+63	+24	+11	+3	+5
Hungary	+2	+8	+22	+90	+71	+51	+32	+3	+32
Poland	+3	−18	+177	+168	+63	+22	+22	−8	+6
Bulgaria	+5	+12	+40	+44	+93	+66	+121	+17	+102
Romania	−4	+22	+90	+136	+128	+57	−28	−60	+24
Eastern Europe total	+8	−5	+368	+551	+522	+377	+454	+66	+263
Soviet Union	−72	−140	+457	+923	+1,233	+2,225	+1,364	+1,127	+1,334
World (billions of dollars)	+0.3	+0.4	−2.1	−10.9	+8.6	+6.8	+20.5	+33.6	+46.7

Sources: See table A-4.

Table A-12. *East European Trade with Industrial Countries, by Country, 1985*
Millions of U.S. dollars unless otherwise specified (exports f.a.s., imports c.i.f.)

East European country	United States	West Germany	France	United Kingdom	Italy	Austria	Other Western Europe	Total Western Europe	Other industrial countries	Total industrial countries
East Germany										
Exports	93	2,594	266	238	115	118	1,136	4,467	56	4,616
Imports	80	2,684	230	91	115	235	593	3,948	239	4,267
Total trade	173	5,278	496	329	230	353	1,729	8,415	295	8,883
Share (percent)	1.9	59.4	5.6	3.7	2.6	4.0	19.5	94.7	3.3	100.0
Czechoslovakia										
Exports	78	781	145	139	199	368	496	2,128	123	2,329
Imports	69	902	146	145	197	213	561	2,164	125	2,358
Total trade	147	1,683	291	284	396	581	1,057	4,292	248	4,687
Share (percent)	3.1	35.9	6.2	6.1	8.4	12.4	22.6	91.6	5.3	100.0
Hungary										
Exports	197	680	115	124	251	460	445	2,075	65	2,337
Imports	245	944	152	158	230	527	585	2,596	195	3,036
Total trade	442	1,624	267	282	481	987	1,030	4,671	260	5,373
Share (percent)	8.2	30.2	5.0	5.2	9.0	18.4	19.2	86.9	4.8	100.0

Poland										
Exports	226	963	274	375	279	214	1,085	3,190	119	3,535
Imports	262	1,070	223	260	272	230	843	2,898	232	3,392
Total trade	488	2,033	497	635	551	444	1,928	6,088	351	6,927
Share (percent)	7.0	29.3	7.2	9.2	8.0	6.4	27.8	87.9	5.1	100.0
Bulgaria										
Exports	36	147	53	26	76	34	126	462	35	533
Imports	114	624	183	162	185	147	421	1,722	162	1,998
Total trade	150	771	236	188	261	181	547	2,184	197	2,531
Share (percent)	5.9	30.5	9.3	7.4	10.3	7.2	21.6	86.3	7.8	100.0
Romania										
Exports[a]	865	496	290	118	831	72	330	2,137	106	3,108
Imports	208	317	141	103	163	56	194	974	158	1,340
Total trade	1,073	813	431	221	994	128	524	3,111	264	4,448
Share (percent)	24.1	18.3	9.7	5.0	22.3	2.9	11.8	70.0	5.9	100.0
Eastern Europe totals (imports plus exports)										
Total trade	2,473	12,202	2,218	1,939	2,913	2,674	6,815	28,761	1,615	32,849
Share (percent)	7.5	37.1	6.8	5.9	8.9	8.1	20.8	87.6	4.9	100.0

Sources: See table A-4. "Other industrial countries" comprises Canada, Japan, Australia, and New Zealand. Differences from the corresponding figures for 1985 in tables A-4 through A-11 result mainly from the inclusion of insurance and freight here on the East European import side, whereas in tables A-4 through A-11 insurance and freight are on the side of East European exports (or Western imports).

a. Romania's exports are f.o.b.

A Note on the Authors

Lincoln Gordon

Born in 1913, Lincoln Gordon was educated in political science and economics at Harvard and Oxford Universities. From 1936 to 1961 he taught at Harvard in the field of international economics and subsequently became president of the Johns Hopkins University (1967–71), fellow of the Woodrow Wilson International Center for Scholars, and senior fellow at Resources for the Future (1975–80). He has been a guest scholar at the Brookings Institution since 1984. In government service, he was program vice-chairman of the U.S. War Production Board, member of the U.S. delegation to the UN Atomic Energy Commission, consultant to the Department of State on the Marshall Plan and NATO, economic advisor to the Honorable W. A. Harriman in the White House, chief of the Marshall Plan mission and minister for economic affairs in London (1952–55), chief of staff for the NATO Committee of Three on Non-Military Cooperation, U.S. ambassador to Brazil (1961–66), assistant secretary of state for inter-American affairs (1966–67), and member of the Senior Review Panel at the Central Intelligence Agency (1980–83). His publications include *Government and the American Economy* (1940, 1959), *A New Deal for Latin America* (1963), *From Marshall Plan to Global Interdependence* (1979), *Growth Policies and the International Order* (1979), and *Energy Strategies for Developing Nations* (1981), as well as many articles and conference papers.

J. F. Brown

J. F. (Jim) Brown, born in 1928, was educated in history at Manchester University (England) and the University of Michigan. Most of his professional experience has been at Radio Free Europe (RFE) in Munich, first as an analyst for Albania, Bulgaria, and Romania, subsequently as director of the Research and Analysis Department (1969–76), deputy director of RFE (1976–78), and director of RFE (1978–83). In 1968–69 he was a senior research fellow at Columbia University's Research Institute on Communist Affairs. In 1983 he returned to the United Kingdom to pursue scholarly research and writing on Eastern Europe and is affiliated with St. Antony's College, Oxford. He has also served as a consultant on East European affairs to the Rand Corporation and the Stiftung Wissenschaft und Politik. His major publications include *The New Eastern Europe: The Khrushchev Era and After* (1966), *Bulgaria under Communist Rule* (1970), *Relations between the Soviet Union and Its Eastern European Allies* (1975), and *Eastern Europe's Uncertain Future* (1977). He is now working on a history of Eastern Europe since 1968 and a study of superpower rivalries in the Balkans.

Pierre Hassner

Professor Hassner was born in Romania in 1933. A naturalized French citizen, he was educated in political science in Paris at the Ecole Normale Superieure. Since 1957 he has been associated with the Fondation Nationale des Sciences Politiques as both researcher and professor. He is also visiting professor at the Bologna (Italy) Center of the Johns Hopkins University and has held research appointments at the University of Chicago, the International Institute for Strategic Studies (London), Columbia University, and the Woodrow Wilson International Center for Scholars. His major publications include *Les Alliances Sont-Elles Dépassées?* (1966), *Les Diplomates Occidentales* (1966), *Change and Security in Europe* (1968), *Europe in the Age of Negotiation* (1973), *The Left in Europe* (1979), and *Totalitarismes* (1984). In addition, he is the author of numerous articles and chapters in symposia on East-West relations.

Josef Joffe

Born in 1944, Josef Joffe was educated in political science at Swarthmore College, the Johns Hopkins University, and Harvard

University, where he received his Ph.D. His professional career has been divided between scholarly research, teaching, and journalism. He has been a fellow at the Woodrow Wilson International Center for Scholars, a research associate at the Harvard Center for International Affairs, and a senior associate of the Carnegie Endowment for International Peace. He has also held teaching appointments in Munich, at the Johns Hopkins School of Advanced International Studies, and in Salzburg. On the journalism side, he was for several years a senior editor of *Die Zeit* (Hamburg) and since 1985 has been a foreign editor and columnist of the *Süddeutsche Zeitung* (Munich). His articles in major journals of foreign policy and strategic affairs include, "European-American Relations: The Enduring Crisis" (*Foreign Affairs* (Spring 1981), "Europe and America: The Politics of Resentment," *Foreign Affairs: America and the World 1982* (1983), "Europe's American Pacifier" *Foreign Policy* (Spring 1984), and "The Cost of Abandoning Europe," *The National Interest* (Spring 1986). He is currently at work on two books dealing with German foreign policy.

Edwina Moreton

Born in England in 1950, Edwina Moreton was educated in German and Russian at the University of Bradford, political science at the University of Strathclyde, and Soviet and East European Studies at the University of Glasgow. She was then appointed a Harkness fellow of the Commonwealth Fund of New York for postdoctoral studies at the Massachusetts Institute of Technology. From 1978 to 1980 she was a lecturer in political science at the University College of Wales, Aberystwyth. Since 1980 she has been a member of the editorial staff of *The Economist* (London), with responsibilities covering Soviet and East European affairs, East-West relations, and China. Her major publications include *East Germany and the Warsaw Alliance: The Politics of Détente* (1978), *Soviet Strategy Toward Western Europe* (1984), *Nuclear War and Nuclear Peace* (1983), and *Germany Between East and West* (forthcoming, 1987).

Index

349